With the Indians in France

WITH THE INDIANS IN FRANCE

WITH THE INDIANS IN FRANCE

BY

GENERAL SIR JAMES WILLCOCKS

G C.M.G., K.C.B , K C.S I , D.S.O., LL.D.

LONDON

CONSTABLE AND COMPANY LTD.

1920

TO MY BRAVE COMRADES
OF ALL RANKS OF THE INDIAN ARMY
I DEDICATE THIS BOOK WHICH IS AN
EARNEST ENDEAVOUR TO RECORD THEIR
LOYALTY AND UNPERISHABLE VALOUR
ON THE BATTLEFIELDS OF
FRANCE AND BELGIUM

IV

The village yokels round him flocked to hearken to his tales,
　　How he had crossed the Kala [1] sea,
　　From India's strand past Araby,
　　Thro' Egypt's sands to Europe's shores,
　　Where the wild stormy mistral roars,
　　　　And anchor'd in Marseilles.

V

" Is it the truth," said one more bold than village yokels be,
　　" That men with wings ascend on high
　　And fight with Gods in yonder sky ?
　　That iron monsters belching wrath,
　　Beneath their wheels of Juggernaut,
　　　　Claim victims for Kali ? "

VI

" Now list all ye," said Hurnām-Singh, " the aged and the youth,
　　The tales they told in bygone days,
　　Of Gods and Ghouls in ancient lays,
　　Are true, not false ; mine eyes descried,
　　Mine ears have heard as heroes died,
　　　　The Mahabharut's [2] truth.

VII

" The land of France is wide and fair, the people brave and free,
　　I fain would tell, but orders came,
　　' Push on, the foe awaits the game '—
　　The game of death ; the Khalsa cry,
　　The warriors' slogan, rent the sky,
　　　　Fateh Wah Guru Ji ! [3]

[1] Black ; a term applied to the sea
[2] Mahabharut or " Great War " ; the great epic poem of India
[3] The Sikh war-cry.

VIII

" The Sahibs' faces told their tale ; no craven thought or sloth
    In those brave hearts, as we had learned
      When Gujerat the tide had turned,
      And left the names of Aliwal
      And Chillianwala as a pall
        Of glory to us both.

IX

" And thus the sons of Hindustan, from Himalaya to Scinde,
    From Hindu Kush to Deccan plains,
      Rent in a day the ancient chains
      Which isolated class from clan,
      And joined in battle as one man,
        To die for Mata Hind.[1]

X

" Hur Mahadeo ! Guru Ji ! and Allah's sacred name,
    Shri Gunga Jai ![2] from brave Nepal,
      Re-echoed loud through wild Garhwal ;
      From Dogra vale, Afridi clan,
      To the proud homes of Rajistan,
        Was lit the martial flame.

XI

" As pitiless the bullets rained, 'mid angry storm and flood,
    Khudadad Khan ! immortal name,
      Stood by his gun, for India's fame
      Was in his hands ; the Huns advance,
      Recoil ; Retire ; the soil of France
        Is richer with his blood."

[1] Mother India.
[2] War-cries of Hindus, Sikhs, Mahomedans, and Gurkhas.

XII

And Hurnām paused as he recalled, one dark November morn,
  When twice thee thousand foes had rushed
  Our trenches, powdered into dust,
  And bayonet point and Kukry blade
  Avenging retribution made,
   Before the break of dawn.

XIII

" Garhwal will tell," he said, " with pride her children oft recite,
  How Durwan Negi, lion-heart !
  Was first and foremost from the start ;
  He led the charge which won the day,—
  Oh, brothers, 'twas a glorious fray,
   For victory came with light "

XIV

Shābāsh ! Shābāsh ! from every tongue, and mothers' hearts stood still,
  As sons stepped forth and made demand
  They too should join the glorious band,
  They too should hear the battle's din,
  Or purge the soul of every sin,
   If such were Ishwar's [1] will.

XV

Hurnām went on : " At Neuve Chapelle, at Festubert, we bled,
  On Wipers field, at Moulin Piètre,
  We heard the German hymn of hate ;
  Above our lines the war-ships soared,
  Our trenches rocked while cannon roared
   The requiem of the dead."

[1] God

XVI

The Jhelum's banks had witnessed oft her waters stained with
  gore,
> Had heard the tramp of countless feet,
> Had known both triumph and defeat,
> But never had her waters swirled
> A prouder message to the world
>> Than Hurnām's story bore.

XVII

For India's sons had sealed their oath, according to their laws;
> Sealed it with blood across the sea,
> From Flanders to Gallipoli,
> On Tigris' banks, on Egypt's sands,
> 'Mid Afric's swamps and hinterlands,
>> And died in England's cause

XVIII

For ages long the Mullah's cry, the temple bells shall wile,
> And call to prayer for those who died,
> The father, mother, son, and bride,
> Descendants of the loyal brave
> Who rest in warriors' simple grave,
>> And need no marble pile

CONTENTS

MAPS

xv

INTRODUCTION

I HAVE not attempted to write a Military History of the Indian Army Corps in France. I lay no claim to describing the course of events on the British Front, as a whole, during 1914–15, except in as far as they concern the Corps. The excellent account written by Lieut.-Colonel Merewether, C.I.E., Indian Army, and Sir Frederick Smith, Bart. (*The Indian Corps in France*, published by John Murray), both of whom served on my Staff as Recording Officers on behalf of the India and War Offices, and who have had at their disposal all the official records, furnishes ample details of the movements and the doings of the Corps as forming an integral part of the British Army in Flanders.

I have not had the advantages of papers of reference, nor have I seen all the diaries of the various Commanders and others, and have had the handicap of writing most of my story far removed from England; but it must be borne in mind that a great part of their information was naturally derived from my own reports and correspondence, and of nearly all such I kept copies, and have used them. If, therefore, in some cases our descriptions of military events appear somewhat similar the reason will be readily understood. Also I kept a very careful Diary from day to day which has enabled me to write with certainty of the events recorded.

My object has been to deal with the Corps alone, only bringing in outside movements sufficiently to describe the

operations it took part in.   I have tried to bring before
the public, and more especially my numerous friends in
India, the inside of the story as opposed to its general
aspect.   Books on the war are already numerous, and will
increase in large numbers, and to attempt to enter into
competition with many brilliant writers would be foolish.
I therefore only deal with the small portion of the war as
it appeared to me, and as few if any have a better knowledge
of the brave Indian soldiers and the deeds they performed
than I have, I hope I may succeed in bringing before my
readers a true statement of facts.

It must not be imagined that I have any illusions as
to the part played by the Indians, as will be made clear
throughout this book.   No one knows better than I do
how utterly impossible it would have been for them to do
what they did, without the help and example of their
illustrious comrades of the Scotch, Irish, and English
battalions which formed part of each Brigade, or of the
splendid Territorial units which later joined us, and the
superb British Artillery which paved the way for all our
efforts.

But of these History will assuredly furnish a brilliant
account.   It is not always so of Indian troops ;   their
raconteurs are few and far between ;   the chief actors in
the play, still living, will probably be counted by tens not
thousands.   The rank and file will furnish no writers to
thrill the generations to come ;   they will just pass with
the great masses of India, content that they have done
their duty and been faithful to their salt.

It has not been possible to record all, or even many,
of the deathless deeds performed by both British and
Indian officers and men, but I have added an Appendix
extracted from the official list of Promotions and Rewards
of Officers, N.C.O.'s, and Men of all Arms of the Indian
Army who served with the Army Corps or with other

Indian troops or with British Corps in France prior to 1916 ; and there will be found under the heading of Staff, Units of all Arms and Departments, etc., what I presume is a complete roll of rewards.

It will be observed that the early fighting prior to the battle of Neuve Chapelle is described in far greater detail than the operations which took place subsequently. For this there are two reasons. First, I was able to keep very full notes of all occurrences as they took place, and for the first three months indeed all ordinary papers went no farther than my own Army Corps. But on the formation of the First and Second Armies the Indian Corps passed under the orders of the First Army, and the same opportunities did not offer as previously ; hence it became much more difficult to retain copies of all correspondence. Secondly, I consider it far more interesting to record even the smallest fights, in which the Indians bore a share whilst they were still new to the game and had not become versed and seasoned in the intricacies of trench warfare.

I have considered it a sacred duty, and to the best of my ability I have endeavoured to place on record the loyalty, courage, and devotion of the King's soldiers from Hindustan.

It has been impossible to write a book of this kind without entering into personal matters, but so intimately connected is a Commander of Indian troops with the whole being of his officers and men, that the doings of the one cannot be separated from the other, if their combined efforts are to be intelligently described. But putting this aside, so erroneous are many of the opinions and so ill-natured have been some of the criticisms of the part taken by the Indian Corps in Flanders, that it has been impracticable to avoid writing strongly when I considered it necessary, and hence I have not hesitated to do so. Moreover, it is due to India to be told the facts. The day is past when that great portion of our Empire could be kept in comparative darkness ; the light is dawning, and the Great War has opened to her an opportunity which she never had before. Her sons have shared the glory of the Empire. From the boggy fields and trenches of Flanders and the desert sands of Egypt ; from the immortal heights of Gallipoli ; from the burning plains of Mesopotamia and the impenetrable jungles of East Africa, comes up with one voice, from the thousands who fought and bled for England :

India has taken a new birth ; the heavens above, the sea, the earth
Have changed for aye, the darkness dies, light has illumined all
    men's eyes,
Since Armageddon's day.

I am indebted to many officers of the Army Corps for short stories and some details regarding their units, but I have avoided asking any of them for information which might raise controversial matters, and for anything contained in this book I take full responsibility. My thanks are due to Professor John Wardell, late Professor Modern History and Lecturer Military History, Trinity College, Dublin, for having furnished me with some interesting diaries of deceased and other officers as well as extracts of letters written from France.

In a few instances I have taken the liberty of copying the numbers of casualties suffered by the Corps, as well as the names of certain officers and men rewarded, from the semi-official history quoted above—*The Indian Corps in France.* Unfortunately many very useful manuscripts, notes, and returns on the way to me in Bermuda were lost in the *Adana* when that ship was torpedoed in the Atlantic.

BERMUDA,
20th October 1919.

CHAPTER I

ON the 5th September 1914 I was quartered at Murree in the Punjab, and within a few days of finishing my four years' tenure of command of the Northern Army in India, when the good news reached me that I was to proceed to France in command of the Indian Army Corps, then already on its way to take part in the Great War. My luck was once more " In." I say " once more," for I had had the good fortune to serve in fourteen campaigns or expeditions, and in all but two of these had been associated with or in command of British and Indian troops combined.

From Sandhurst I had passed on to Afghanistan in 1879 and had served under that grand soldier Lord Roberts. The Indian Frontiers from the North-West to Burmah were all familiar to me. I had shared the bivouac and the camp for thirty-six years with my brave and loyal Indian troops, on Afghan hills and in the dense jungles of the Irriwaddy and Chindwin, in Munipoor in the far North-East of India, in Ashanti and blood-stained Kumassi in distant West Africa. I had sheltered with them in the living squares of man and beast in the deserts of the Soudan, and now I was about to participate in their trials on the plains of Flanders. It had been my good fortune to command brigades and divisions in peace, and twice to be in chief command of expeditions on the North-West Frontier in 1908; and finally the Northern Army of India for four years.

Dull indeed must be the man who with all this experience did not know the Indian soldier, did not appreciate his great worth, or recognise his limits. I never joined the Indian Army, but did all my regimental duty with an

1   B

Irish Corps, the 1st Battalion Leinster Regiment. To Irish soldiers I owe much ; from them I first imbibed that spirit of camaraderie which is worth more in war than all book discipline ; the spirit which recognises common sense to be one of the greatest of gifts, and which willingly renders loyal service, so long as no attempt is made to exact it by misplaced force.

The Irish soldier is unsurpassed in the field, but you must trust him as an Irishman. He has a right to a distinct nationality, and is justly proud of it. No man could serve with cheerier, better comrades than the 1st and 2nd Connaught Rangers, which belonged to my Army Corps in France ; but of them more anon.

A word more as to myself ; for in writing of Indian troops it is absolutely necessary that a man should thoroughly understand his subject, or his story would be worthless. I need only say that their religion, habits, castes, and language (Hindustani, the lingua franca of India) are as familiar to me as my own religion and language, and that from long and sometimes perhaps weary toil I had acquired a knowledge of many of the dialects of the Native Army. Thus equipped I found myself the fortunate commander of an Indian Army Corps, for the first time in history to be employed in Europe.

The Army of India was little understood in Great Britain. At the commencement of the war I read, not with any surprise but with considerable amusement, accounts of the composition of the Army Corps. A great part of the public appeared to think that Indian brigades and divisions were composed of Sikhs and Gurkhas alone, and did not trouble about any of the many other races of India ; nor were they aware that in each brigade was a British battalion. As for cavalry, of course the " Bengal Lancers " were the only specimens known to them ; a Sikh squadron being described by one correspondent as " fierce turbaned Moslems on fiery Arab steeds." The artillery, which was composed of the finest British batteries in the Army, superbly horsed, was reported by one paper as consisting of " mountain guns borne on Abyssinian mules " ; and a foreign paper, writing of the arrival of the

Corps at Marseilles, solemnly announced that " this Corps has been raised and equipped entirely at the expense of three great Indian Princes, who are now occupying the finest hotels in Marseilles. Their names are Prince Sikya (evidently a corruption of Sikh); Prince Gorok (Gurkhas); and Prince Balukin (meant for Baluchis)."

The Germans at any rate were to be rudely awakened. The shell-torn trenches and blood-stained fields of Neuve Chapelle were to prove to them that, given a fair chance and a sufficient artillery support, the men from the banks of the Ganges and Indus, from the plains lying to the south, and the Highlanders of Nepal and North-West Frontiers, could take as fierce a toll on the day of battle as their white comrades.

The Army of India in 1914 was trained for a Frontier war or minor oversea expeditions, and for these purposes was to a certain extent sufficiently well armed and equipped, but by no means fully so. The training had been improved out of all recognition since Lord Kitchener formed a General Staff and instituted his " Test "; at the time a much debated innovation, but one which, in my opinion and that of many of those best qualified to judge, was a turning point in the field training of the Army. It had at least set up emulation and given a chance to all classes of which that Army is composed, so that even Corps in outlying unknown stations were brought into the competition, and the spurt thus given to military training had far-reaching effects.

The Army had had no opportunities for the higher training which was required for European warfare. The parsimony of the Indian Government had put a heavy clog on the military wheel. Money could be had for everything except preparation for war. It was far easier to get thousands of pounds for some perfectly useless scheme which might possibly benefit some local cause, than to extract a hundred pounds for anything to which attached the aroma of the Army. Indeed, so extraordinary was the antipathy to spending a farthing on anything savouring of gunpowder that officers and men, British and Indian, had accepted it as a cardinal principle that expenditure on the Army, however necessary or urgent, was a matter of small concern to the Government, and that, sink or swim, nothing but unforeseen upheaval or disaster, would ever worm a rupee from the civilian rulers in whose hands rested the decision.

In England there was at least our Expeditionary Force (or a great part of it) ready for war ; its transport and equipment could be completed at the shortest notice, and its Reserves could be quickly called up. But in India, where, if anywhere in the Empire, it was essential that several divisions should be able to take the field at any moment, no such organisation existed. True it is that many thousands of men stood armed and ready to quell local disturbances or Frontier forays, but the mobilisation of a force consisting of even two divisions could not be completed in all its details for weeks. It is no answer to say that India was able to despatch two divisions to Europe at short notice. Two divisions certainly sailed from Karachi and Bombay, but their equipment had to be completed at Marseilles, at Orleans, and actually in the battle area itself, whilst the artillery was only made up by denuding other divisions of their guns. The rifles were of a pattern which did not suit the latest class of ammunition with which the Army at home was supplied, and both rifles and ammunition had actually to be handed into store at Marseilles and fresh arms issued. To any one acquainted with the science of musketry, and that in the days when our infantry had to depend on this arm alone ; when hand grenades and trench mortars were unknown ; it will readily be understood that the handicap of going into action with brand new arms was a very real one. Even the machine-guns, which in some cases were much worn, had to be refitted with new tripods as best it could be managed at Orleans. Further, there were no howitzers, no mechanical transport, a scant supply of medical equipment and signalling apparatus, and innumerable other shortages which were essential to a force suddenly dumped down from railhead into the trenches. All these were supplied in abundance in France as soon as it was possible ; indeed the excellence and rapidity with which this was done was astonishing to us who remembered the cheese-paring days in India, but it proved what a fool's paradise we had been bred in, and on what sandy foundations the structure of the Indian Army rested.

I have no desire unnecessarily to string out the manifest disadvantages the Indian Corps laboured under, but I have heard too much the criticisms of our Indian troops by soldiers and civilians, who are without the faintest knowledge of what they talk about, and it is only right that the truth should be known. There is a growing body of Indians who have every desire but no means of ascertaining the facts, and if this book can be of any use in helping to explain to my numberless friends and acquaintances in India the splendid deeds of their brethren who fought and bled on the sodden plains of Flanders under handicaps which must have been seen and felt to be understood, I shall be more than rewarded. Moreover, as commander of those troops during a year of the war I had opportunities of knowing many details unknown to others, and now that the war is over I am free to write the truth which for years has been of necessity suppressed.

Whatever may have been the shortcomings of the Indian Army it possessed one asset which never stood it in better stead than in France; its British officers, although far too small in number, were the salt of the earth. As leaders of men, comrades and friends of their Indian officers, sepoys, and sowars, as loyal and brave gentlemen, they could not be surpassed. I always believed in them, but in France my belief was heightened to profound admiration, and as death took its heavy toll day by day I knew that by no means could they be replaced ; for the great essential was that they should know their men and their language, and this became impossible as India sent more and more troops to the various theatres of war.

Next to the British were the Indian officers, most of them men who had earned their commissions by brave and loyal service, of fighting stock, with martial traditions, ready to give their lives for their King Emperor, proud of the profession of arms ; they formed the essential link between the British officers and men. In ordinary circumstances in the Field they were well fitted to fill temporarily the place of their lost British leaders, and many instances of this I shall relate.

I tread perhaps on thorny ground, but after a life spent with them in many lands, I do not consider they can replace the British officer in the field. I have discussed this with numerous Indian officers and soldiers of all classes, but I never met one who did not practically agree with me. There no doubt are in India some who will lay claim to this, but I firmly believe the British officers, who are the truest friends of the Indian soldier, will unanimously agree with me. If bravery and self-sacrifice were alone to be considered then by all means the Indian can take his place in any rank, but training and temperament at present stand in his way.

What is now being wisely done is to increase the pay of the Indian officers and men. The pay of Indian officers especially was almost an insult to a class so loyal and devoted, and it must be very largely increased ; they should be given rank corresponding to their British comrades, and precedence equal to, if not above, their civilian confrères.

This was one of the sorest points with Indian officers. To the ordinary observer like myself, at Durbars and public gatherings it was plain that they never received their proper share of *Izzat* (honour). No doubt I shall be told this was all thought out and arranged by the Government, but I speak from practical experience, not from the edicts of Simla and Delhi. The Indian officer was not treated with the respect which was his due and which he has earned in arduous service on many fields of war. It was a feeling very strongly held by them and must be set right. *Izzat* is a thing little understood by any but Indians, but it is a great driving force ; it raises men in the estimation of their fellows, whilst the loss of it debases them.

Public opinion as understood in this country was non-existent in India. It was a one-man country ; if the man was a strong personality he could do much ; if he was undecided his share became a small one, and good old

Indian *dustoor* (custom) settled the question in the pre-historic fashion.

Under the Indian officers are the N.C.O.'s and men. I have soldiered with Rajputs and Jats, Pathans, Sikhs, Gurkhas, Punjabi Mahomedans, Madras Sappers and Miners, Dogras, Garhwalis and other races. Each has its characteristics, and these must be recognised by any one entrusted with the command of Indian troops. You cannot place them in one mould ; you will not get from them their best, unless they recognise that they are understood.

One of my chief difficulties at the beginning of this war was to make it understood that the Indians cannot be treated as pure machines, and that they possess national characteristics as varied as those between Scandinavians and Italians. I own that Sir John French and his Staff generally made every allowance for these facts, but there were others who made none ; an Army Corps (no matter its fighting strength in numbers) was an Army Corps and nothing else. An Army Corps was supposed to be able to occupy so many thousand yards of trenches, and the orders were issued by this routine rule.

It might be said the Indian Corps was sent as a Corps and times were too pressing to go into such details ; this is perhaps true, and we all recognised it at the beginning of the Flanders fighting ; but as time went on and the German attack was beaten off, I saw plainly that you cannot expect a ship to keep up full steam when the engineers and stokers are lying shattered in the hold. And yet those brave men not only filled a big gap in our battered line, but, helped and encouraged by their comrades of the British battalions of the Indian Corps, held it against incessant attack. Minenwerfers, hand grenades, and high explosives tore through them and flattened out their trenches ; blood flowed freely ; but as often as they were driven back from their front defences they managed to return to them again. India has reason to be proud of her sons, and their children may well tell with pride of the deeds of their fathers.

I can look back to the time when the Indian Army

was commanded by Lord Roberts, and he paid two visits to Delhi whilst I was Staff Officer there. Whoever may follow him as Commander-in-Chief, one thing is sure ; no individual will ever be as closely connected in the minds of Indian soldiers with the name of Chief as he was. It was truly surprising how he was beloved by all ranks. It is no uncommon thing to hear of Viceroys or Commanders-in-Chief who were well known to and liked by Indians, but no sooner do they vanish from the scene than they are practically forgotten for all time. Perhaps it is human nature, perhaps it is common to all countries, but one thing is sure, viz. that Lord Roberts' name has, and will have, an abiding place in many an Indian home for years to come. He had the nature which earns confidence, the open mind which breeds loyalty, the fearless character that binds men to their leaders with hoops of steel. An Indian Army led by Lord Roberts was doubled in its fighting capacity by his presence, which to them was the sure presage of victory. Without that affection which he had established, neither to-day nor in the times to come, will the soldiers of India give of their best on the field of battle. May be it is a fault, and in the eyes of some reduces their value as fighting units, but if the Empire calls on all its sons to fight in one field, it must not forget that human nature is stronger than Service Regulations, and that blood is thicker than water.

Lord Roberts left an indelible mark on the Indian Army and one which has proved invaluable to all who have since served in India.

Another great soldier who left his mark, but in a different way, was Lord Kitchener. His reforms were sweeping. The training of the Army received at his hands an impetus which will stamp his rule as remarkable so long as we remain in India. His re-grouping of brigades and divisions, the creation of a General Staff, the erection of new barracks and cantonments, quite upset the slow calculations of those who looked on and wondered. And yet if analysed his work was only a putting into force of principles which had long been recognised as necessary but which others had not had the power to carry out.

Lord Kitchener with a master eye saw what was needed and did it; he rode rough shod over *dustoor* or custom; he was a mighty organiser and the civilians were afraid of him. He never bothered himself over minor details in India; he left them to his subordinates. He chose them himself and trusted them. The inside life of Indians was unknown to him, he went to India too late in life to learn; he was too busy with big tasks to attend to what he did not consider an essential for a Commander-in-Chief.

Among his many reforms were some which I venture to say have not been beneficial. The terms of service which passed men to the Reserve after a short period in the ranks proved a veritable stumbling-block, and created a Reserve which proved not only useless but a danger in war time. The Reservists sent to the Indian Corps in France were of this type, largely worn out, hating the very idea of war, many physically unfit and incapable of a single day's work.

Even Lord Kitchener had found it hard to get sanction for sufficient British officers for Indian regiments and battalions. The numbers eventually sanctioned were sufficient for frontier work, but altogether inadequate to meet the requirements of European warfare, and this very soon made itself manifest.

The reduction of ambulance *kahars* (trained bearers) was another very serious drawback, but in this case it reacted worse on the Frontiers than in Europe, for in France, of course, a totally different system prevailed. In 1908, during the Zakka Khel and Mohmand Expeditions, in order to equip even one division and an extra brigade, bearers had to be collected from all the divisions in India as far as Madras; an impossible system in an Army supposed to stand ready for Frontier wars.

During Lord Kitchener's rule, manœuvres or large gatherings of troops were few and far between; all the money available was spent on reorganisation; nevertheless the battalion training reached a far higher scale of efficiency than had ever previously been the case. In order to increase the numbers of brigades and divisions, to meet the requirements of his scheme for mobilisation,

Lord Kitchener reduced the number of British battalions in a brigade from two to one. This for European warfare proved a great mistake, as I shall endeavour to show.

Lord Kitchener's name will, in India for all time, stand as a landmark of great changes long needed. He has been described as a hard man ; this he may in a sense have been, but underlying his hardness, to those who were privileged to know him well, was the very kindest heart that ever beat in a soldier. He set himself a definite task and allowed nothing to stand in his way, and yet I never knew a man who was more ready to listen to reasonable suggestions, more ready to acknowledge that there were two sides to all arguments, and when you had convinced him on any point he was always prepared to give your views a chance. As I shall show later he had an intense wish to do justice to the Indian Army and was the best friend of the Indian Corps from the day we landed at Marseilles to the day the Corps left France. The first telegram I received in Europe was from him.

I am glad to hear that the Indian troops are *razi* (happy), give them my salaams and tell them I feel sure they will maintain their records of the past when they meet the Germans.

If there had been a few more in authority who knew how to deal with Indian soldiers, and who understood that a word spoken at the right moment is worth a volume on paper, it would have been of inestimable advantage to the Corps in France.

The first Viceroy with whom I had any direct dealings was Lord Minto. A soldier by instinct, a gentleman by nature, and the kindest of friends : he was very much liked by the Indian officers. He always made a point of having them all introduced to him after any parade at which he was present.

During the Frontier expeditions of 1908, from the inception of the operations to the last day when we recrossed the Frontiers, Lord Minto never failed to bear the troops, British and Indian, in mind ; and his advice on the political questions involved and his desire to spare the enemy once he had been well beaten and submitted, at once showed his nature. During his Viceroyalty the Indian soldiers learned that the representative of the King Emperor had a heart of gold, and having been a soldier himself was anxious, as far as his high position would allow, to meet them as comrades.

Such men leave behind them traditions which in India far outlive those established during their comparatively short periods of high office by some others who place Western attainments on a higher plane than human nature. In the East this never pays ; India is very susceptible of influence but it must be based on common sense.

On the Frontiers amid the wild hillmen, Lord Minto at once established himself as a soldier by appearing on his first parade in uniform, with the badges of a brigadier general (which in military life he was), and I well remember the surprise and pleasure of the Indian soldiers who told me (then a Brigadier myself), that now they understood that Brigadier was in reality a very high rank, and that in the next expedition they hoped the Viceroy would himself command troops.

On this his first visit to the Frontiers he was accompanied by Lady Minto, who attended the parade and later went over the Malakand Pass. She spoke to all the Indian officers and many of the wild transborder chiefs, and years afterwards the memory of her visit was still a theme of conversation amongst the Maliks beyond Chakdara and *en route* to distant Chitral. You can do much in the East by personal example, you can do little without it.

Lord Kitchener was followed as Commander-in-Chief by Sir O'Moore Creagh. As a very young subaltern I had first met him after the Afghan War in 1880, when he was a Captain and had just won the V.C. at Kam Dakka in the Khyber. His cheery character had impressed me, and I instinctively felt I had met a soldier I might meet again in a higher sphere. His intimate knowledge of India, its people and languages, and his early promise marked him for distinction, and in 1910 he left the India Office, where he was Military Secretary, and assumed command of the Indian Army.

Sir O'Moore Creagh had to follow a difficult man. Lord Kitchener had dragged out of the Government what in India is spoken of as a colossal sum of money. In truth it was nothing of the kind, but it has in the past pleased that country to call anything a waste of money which is required for military purposes.

The military are the very root of our rule in the East, and if you refuse sustenance to that root the tree will wither. Time has proved the truth of this, and in 1914, when the trumpet of Death resounded all over the world, the Government of India awoke to the fact that there are other things than education and law on which to spend the revenues of an Empire.

During Sir O'Moore Creagh's tenure of command, the Northern Army, which I commanded, was given many opportunities of holding manœuvres on a much bigger scale than usual. Comparatively large concentrations took place in the Peshawar Division and near Soneput in the Punjab, which offered scope for working entire war divisions against one another and also allowed many Corps of Imperial Service troops to share in the work. The Chief was present at some of these operations, which he thoroughly enjoyed.

The Indian Staff College at Quetta, which has proved so beneficial to the Army at large, was founded during his regime, and the General Staff was permanently established on a modern basis. He, however, like his predecessors found himself handicapped by the difficulty of getting sufficient funds to keep the Army efficient for war. The shortage of ammunition; the deficiency of a reserve of rifles; the totally inadequate numbers of Field Artillery; the absence of howitzer batteries properly armed; the inadequate pay of all ranks of the Indian Army, and a hundred other most important items had to remain in abeyance, and very soon after he left the Great War came to test the machine.

The test has proved the fine fighting spirit of officers and men and the dire need that existed for modern equipment. The aeroplanes, the howitzers, the reserve materials were *non est,* and although I do not know whether the

Indian or Home Governments found the cash, whoever it is has had to pay pretty heavily for the failure to provide it in time.

During my tenure of command of the Northern Army nothing struck me more than the hopelessness of the system adopted both by the War Office and the Government of India in fixing the age for the higher Commands, such as divisions and brigades, and in the Indian Army of regimental and battalion commanders. The Indian rules were hopeless; promotion was given by length of service and selection had to take a back seat. Money was saved by keeping on officers, long after many of them had ceased to be fitted for command, as it kept down the pension lists, and when money could be saved on anything connected with the Army, there was no doubt it would be done readily. The consequence was that in a country like India, where youth and vigour should rank first in apportioning work, exactly the contrary was the case. Merit had to subordinate itself to rules and customs, and far too old a race of officers were frequently placed in positions for which they were unfitted. In themselves mostly good and gallant soldiers in their day, it was no fault of theirs but of the pernicious system under which they served.

But if this was the case in the Indian Army, encrusted in obsolete traditions, what excuse can be offered for the methods adopted by the War Office in selecting officers of the Home service for higher commands in India? Here at least was an opportunity for sending out young brigadiers and generals, but nothing of the kind was done. On the contrary, although good soldiers with good records were frequently selected, they were generally long past the age for brigade commands and would not have been given them in England. In fact the War Office used India as the dumping ground for senior officers whom they wished to reward, but for whom they did not mean to find a place in this country.

No one can deny these facts; they are to be found in the Army lists of the period. It was very hard on the many gallant officers themselves, but still harder on the Army of India. Any one anxious to examine the matter need only consult the comparative ages of Brigade commanders at the beginning of the war in France. In the Indian Corps drastic changes had to be carried out in the field in the first months, as, to quote one instance only, it was at once discovered that in combined operations the Indian Brigade and Divisional commanders became senior to Divisional and Corps commanders of the other Army Corps. Such a state of affairs could not long continue, and if for no other reasons, for this alone, the changes became imperative. How unfair on the Army of India was such a state of things! How unjust to those brave and loyal officers themselves, who after long years spent in gallant service for their country were pushed out of their places in presence of the enemy—the great goal they had lived for. And yet it was looked on as quite the usual thing, and no one at the War Office ever seemed to have troubled themselves where India was concerned. Such remarks may be called vindictive, but call them what you will the Army Council of those days is to blame, and secure as that body may feel itself when confronted with one whose experience has not been acquired in Whitehall, the Army of India of 1914 will support me in what I say.

The most important event in Sir O'Moore's Chiefship was the great Delhi Durbar, when His Majesty the King was present. No need to write of this, except to say that knowing India, its Army and people, as I do, whatever may have been the impression left on the millions of the King's subjects, speaking of the Army I can say that his presence among them has left an impression which no other occasion in the history of that wondrous land could ever have equalled. Men who had never dreamed of seeing their Emperor in person, saw him with their own eyes, knew him to be a living entity, and went away feeling themselves sharers in an unequalled Empire. It is not too much to say that the King's visit did more to bind to the Throne in loyal bonds the Indian Army than any triumphs won by the greatest of India's former Emperors. Only those who know India and its people, and know them well, can understand the magnitude of the event.

The last of the Viceroys in my day in India was Lord Hardinge. I had the honour of knowing him sufficiently well to appreciate thoroughly the very great interest he took in the Army.   In fact I go so far as to say that none of the high officials I ever knew in India felt a keener sense of his duty towards the Indian soldier than he did. Grandson of a great soldier-Viceroy who had fought the Sikhs, his sympathies were equally with the men who had fought for and against us on many a fierce battle-field, and from the day I first met Lord Hardinge to the last day I commanded the Indian Army Corps in France, I never failed to enlist his unflagging interest in the men I commanded.   He attended the big Delhi manœuvres of 1912 and camped near the troops.   Up at dawn and till evening in the saddle, the Viceroy imparted his own enthusiasm to the men.   He rode over every part of the large manœuvre area, enquired into everything, and during the final phase on the last day was like a boy in spirits, thoroughly enjoying the spectacle, which turned out to be as realistic as mimic warfare can well be made.

It was Lord Hardinge who urged the employment of Indian troops in France.   He and Lord Kitchener were the two moving spirits in the scheme, and from the day I left India he never failed at once to answer all my long letters ; never failed to give me not only his advice on all matters connected with the semi-political aspect of affairs, as far as they concerned my Corps, but used his great powers to meet every request regarding the classes of troops, the terms of service, changes in the system of enlistment and Reserves, and in short nothing was more noticeable than the determination, throughout the first year of the war, which he evinced, to make the employment of Indians in Europe a success.

I write plainly, as the Indian Army should know the facts.   The work of Viceroys, although frequently performed in the glare of publicity, has two sides.   Much of what Lord Hardinge did for the Indians in France is the other, or unknown side, of the picture.   What was done in India no doubt was put down as the work of the Indian Government, but much of it was originated by him personally, because he took the pains to enquire and knew the facts, and more still because he sympathised with the difficulties which attended the steering of the ship in uncharted waters.

Of one more official I must write before I proceed with my story, for not only were we much thrown together in peace and on active service, but his name is so intimately connected with the North-West Frontiers of India and the personnel of an important part of our best fighting material, that for many years past one had naturally associated the name of Roos-Keppel with that of the Pathans and other border clans.

Fifty-three years of age, Roos-Keppel had lived on the Frontiers for over twenty years. In many political appointments, as Commandant of the Khyber Rifles, and since 1909 as Chief Commissioner of the North-West Frontier Province, he has learned all there is to learn of the tribesmen, and has taught them, if not all, then most of what is necessary for them to understand. His life has been a romance of the wild border land ; his success has been achieved by manly and just conduct in the face of semi-barbarism. His fearless nature, fine personal appearance, and intimate knowledge of the habits and language of the clans, stamp Roos-Keppel as a Paladin of the Frontiers. You must know the man and his task to understand what he has done for India. Governors and generals come and go, Maliks and Khans change or disappear, but for many long years Roos-Keppel has been the true Warden of the Marches.

The Afridis and Afghans know the white man came decades ago and planted himself firmly on his borders, and means to remain there ; but the white man to the present generation of these wild warriors is Colonel Sir George Roos-Keppel and no other. His influence has won their admiration, his stern justice tempered with mercy has won their fear, and his belief in himself has made them believe in him also.

Often in France, in the dark days of 1914, have I quoted to the Pathans things he had said, and it always acted with them like a trumpet call to duty. Still more often did I wish I had had him with me, but it was not to be. He happened to be on leave in England when war broke out and came to Orleans to meet the Corps, and although I tried to secure his services, he was wanted back at his post in India, and I lost the aid of a good soldier and a remarkable man, which I deeply regretted.

CHAPTER II

THE decision to send Indian troops to France was at first limited to sending two Divisions with their artillery and other arms, and it was not till these had actually begun to leave that orders were issued constituting them into an Army Corps with its full Staff. I was selected for the command, and most of my limited Northern Army Staff were attached. The remaining officers required to complete were appointed direct from Army Headquarters at Simla, but I was allowed to nominate the personal Staff. Of course it was a drawback not having a Staff with whom I had worked in peace time, but such an organisation had not been contemplated, and in any case I had nothing to complain of, as no General could have found a more loyal and devoted body of officers ; many with very high attainments and experience in the field, and all with a knowledge of British and Indian troops. I very soon found that notwithstanding the fact we were all new to the peculiar warfare and unversed in the details of Army Corps organisation, the common-sense training which India gives men enabled us to quickly gather up the threads of the work.

The following was the composition of the corps which left India :

LAHORE DIVISION

Lieut.-General H. B. WATKIS, C.B. (Indian Army)

FEROZEPORE BRIGADE.—Brig.-General R. M. Egerton, C.B. (Indian Army).
  1st Connaught Rangers.
  57th Rifles (Frontier Force).
  9th Bhopal Infantry.
  129th Baluchis.

JALANDAR BRIGADE.—Major-General P. M. Carnegy, C B. (Indian Army).
  1st Manchesters.
  15th Sikhs.
  47th Sikhs.
  59th Rifles (Frontier Force)

SIRHIND BRIGADE.—Major-General J. M. S. Biunker (late R.A.).
  1st Highland Light Infantry.
  1st Battalion 1st Gurkhas.
  1st Battalion 4th Gurkhas.
  125th Rifles.

DIVISIONAL TROOPS.
  15th Lancers.
  Headquarters Divisional Engineers.
  20th and 21st Companies Sappers and Miners.
  Signal Company.
  34th Sikh Pioneers.
  Headquarters Divisional Artillery.

ARTILLERY.
  5th, 11th and 18th Brigades R.F.A.
  Ammunition Columns.
  109th Heavy Battery.

MEERUT DIVISION

Lieut.-General C. A. ANDERSON, C.B. (late R A.)

DEHRA DUN BRIGADE.—Brig.-General C. E. Johnson (Indian Army).
  1st Seaforth Highlanders.
  1st Battalion 9th Gurkhas.
  2nd Battalion 2nd Gurkhas.
  6th Jat Light Infantry.

GARHWAL BRIGADE.—Major-General H. D'U Keary, C.B., D.S.O. (Indian Army).
  2nd Leicesters.
  2nd Battalion 3rd Gurkhas.
  1st Battalion 39th Garhwal Rifles.
  2nd Battalion 39th Garhwal Rifles.

BAREILLY BRIGADE.—Major-General F. Macbean, C.V.O., C.B. (late Gordon Highlanders).
  2nd Black Watch.
  41st Dogras.
  58th Rifles (Frontier Force).
  2nd Battalion 8th Gurkhas.

Divisional Troops.

    4th Cavalry.
    3rd and 4th Companies Sappers and Miners.
    107th Pioneers.
    Headquarters Divisional Engineers.
    Signal Company.

Artillery.

    Headquarters Divisional Artillery.
    4th, 9th and 13th Brigades R.F.A.
    Ammunition Columns.
    110th Heavy Battery.

By 26th September 1914, or a little over seven weeks after the declaration of war, two Brigades of the Lahore Division had arrived at Marseilles. The Sirhind Brigade had been detained in Egypt to reinforce the garrison and did not reach France till the end of November, its place in the Corps being filled, on and off, by a British Brigade from the Expeditionary Force.

I myself with the Corps Staff reached Marseilles by ordinary P. and O. mail on 30th September. I was met by the General in Command and an A.D.C. sent by General Joffre, and in a moment grasped the reality of our alliance. I was only an Army Corps Commander, but the honour thus conferred on us was a token of the unequalled tact and politeness of the French people. Every day I served in France I learned more, that with all our *esprit de corps* we are not in the same street with their army in *camaraderie*.

The Meerut Division was disembarking by 11th October. The Secunderabad Cavalry Brigade also arrived in Marseilles before I finally left for Orleans, and later was attached to the Indian Corps in Flanders, until the arrival of the remainder of the Indian Cavalry Corps. This fine Brigade was commanded by Brig.-General F. Wadeson, Indian Army, and consisted of

    7th Dragoon Guards,
    34th Poona Horse,
    20th Deccan Horse,
    " N " Battery R.H.A. ;

and with it came the Jodhpore Imperial Service Lancers, under command of that fine old veteran chief, Major-

General Sir Partab Singh.   His name is too familiar even in England to need any description here ; suffice it to say he has, by his glorious personal example throughout the war, earned a prominent niche in the temple of fame, and as long as India endures the Rathore and other Indians will treasure the name of Maharaja Sir Partab Singh, Bahadur.

Amongst Indian princes and chiefs who came to Europe, the following were attached on various duties to the Indian Army Corps, and by their loyalty and devotion well maintained the fame of their ancestors.   Indeed, as I look back on those stormy days and recall many rides over execrable roads and fields deep in mire, from one end of our line to the other, I conjure up these scions of noble and great houses, sodden and mud-stained, and cease to wonder why Great Britain had gained so firm a hold over the millions of Hindustan.

It is something which our race may well be proud of. On many a bitter field their powerful ancestors had fought against one another ; some had disputed with us our sovereignty over the peninsula now called India, and all were of different race, creed and religion to ourselves ; and yet here on the plains of Flanders they were intent on one thing alone, and that was to share our toils and our honours, and give if necessary their lives for their King-Emperor.

Lieut. His Highness the Maharaja of Jodhpore was serving with Sir Partab Singh in his own regiment of Lancers.

Colonel His Highness Sir Ganga Singh, Bahadur, Maharaja of Bikanir, was attached to the Meerut Division. I have long known this Indian prince ; his devotion to the British and his readiness to be always doing something were conspicuous in France.   His own Camel Corps was serving in Egypt, and later on he went and joined it for a time.

Major His Highness Sir Madan Singh, Bahadur, Maharaja Dhiraj of Kishengarh.

Captain the Hon. Malik Sir Umar Hayat Khan Tiwana was attached to the Ferozepore Brigade.   A lithe, active man, he was the chief Mahomedan representative with the corps.

Lieut. Raj-Kumar Hira Singh of Panna was with the Bareilly Brigade ; and Lieut. Maharaja Kumar Hitandra Narayan of Kuch Behar was attached to the Dehra Dun Brigade.

Lieut. Maharaja Kumar Gopal Saran Narain Singh of Tikari served with the Corps Signal Company and was a most versatile man, always ready to turn his hand to any job. Cheery and energetic, I had many opportunities of observing his work.

Lieut. Malik Mumtaz Mahomed Khan, Native Indian Land Forces, was with the Staff of the Secunderabad Cavalry Brigade ; and Captain Shah Mirza Beg, Jodhpore Lancers, was an A.D.C. in the same Brigade.

Last, but by no means least, was one of the best soldiers I ever met, Risaldar Khwaja Mahomed Khan, Sirdar Bahadur, I.D.S.M., of the Guides Cavalry, my Indian A.D.C. He had served as A.D.C. to Lord Kitchener when he was Commander-in-Chief, and twice with me on frontier expeditions in 1908. Brave, loyal to the core ; hard as nails ; always cheerful and very hard working, it was a pleasure to serve with such a real gentleman. He was invaluable in France, for although he knew but little English and very little French he was liked by all, British and Allies. He was the connecting link between me and all our Indian officers, and by his tact arranged many matters of considerable local importance to us. The Indian Government owes him a debt of gratitude ; I hope they will not forget it.

No one who knew *The Khwaja*, as he was familiarly known, could fail to see in him the best type of Indian officer ; and in his remote village of Hamza Kot in the Yousafzai plain beneath the shadow of the Buner hills, he will often recall the bleak but stirring days we worked together from Givenchy and Festubert to Neuve Chapelle.

At Marseilles the Indian troops were camped in various localities either in or within a few miles of the town. We had our field service tents, and except for the surroundings and the awful state of the ground from incessant rain, one might have been back in Northern India. But in those early days of the war everything was new to all ranks, and no matter what the discomforts it was a sudden drop into dreamland.

Take a look at the race-course by the sea. Leaning on the rails are twenty or thirty French, men, women, and children, watching our Indian soldiers cooking their evening meal ; these have doffed their khaki uniform and are now clothed in the scantiest of garments. They exchange words, French and Hindustani ; a French child offers one of them a sweet, the Indian gives a chapatty in return ; cigarettes are offered by a passer-by ; a Mahomedan pulls out from his haversack a bamboo flute and plays a ditty ; all laugh heartily. The West has already conquered the East ; the East has sown a seed which gradually grew until within a few months Indians in Flanders were entering shops, bargaining and buying as if they were to the manner born, and the vendors were even more civil to them than to Europeans, and that is saying much for those fine people the French.

What may eventually be the result of all the friendliness and *camaraderie* between the French and Indians is hard to say. It will have its advantages ; it will assuredly have its disadvantages. " East is East and West is West " : the Ganges and the Seine flow in different directions ; the artificial meeting of these waters may not be an unmixed blessing. The Hindu on his return to Kashi (Benares) or the Mahomedan at his prayers at the Jumma Musjid at Delhi may think differently of the white races across the sea to what he thought before the transports bore him across the *kala-pani*, the black water.

However, although everything may be changed after this war, personally I believe the East will return to its own ways, and very rightly so, and that the next generation of ordinary Indians will talk of France, Gallipoli, and Mesopotamia much as we do of the conquest of Mexico or of Peru.

Whilst the Corps was collecting and getting re-equipped with new rifles, etc., I was summoned to General Headquarters, on the Aisne, and travelled *via* Paris and thence by motor car. At General Headquarters I saw Sir John French, and learnt from him that our Army was very shortly to be transferred from the Aisne to Flanders, and that the Indian Corps was to hasten its departure and join them there ; he indicated the region of La Bassée, and although heavy fighting went on before we actually took our place in the trenches, it was immediately west of La Bassée that we eventually did so. He asked me many questions, and whether I had anything particular to point out. My only request was that I hoped my Corps would not be split up before we could be more or less concentrated, for I had a very shrewd idea we should find ourselves in trenches in Flanders and that the days of normal past European warfare were near their end on the Western front. I was not far wrong, but, as I shall show later, the situation was such when the Lahore Division arrived, that several battalions were at once taken from their brigades and thrown in anyhow with cavalry and infantry to help stem the German rush between Ypres and La Bassée.

The times were abnormal and the necessity was great, but it was very unfortunate for the Indian troops that before they had time to realise their position, or gather whether they were facing east or west, they were separated from their own British battalions and broken up into half battalions and even companies, and rushed into the whirl-wind of Ypres amidst those who were strangers to them.

Then came realistically home to them the shortage of British officers. Twelve was the total war complement per battalion — twelve marked white men ; nobly these and the gallant Indians did their duty, but the tempest was on them and the British officers were practically blotted out. The Indian officers and men fought fiercely, but notwithstanding that the other British troops of all classes around them were setting a deathless example of glory, the fact remained that the Indians were fast losing the officers who knew them and whom they trusted beyond all things ; and of the strangers there were none who could talk their language or understand them.

Those who take up the pen to criticise should first put

themselves in the place of these men, who had crossed the seas to fight for England, without any personal cause in the quarrel, and inspired alone by the duty they owed their King-Emperor because they had eaten his salt. It is a story of loyalty never surpassed in the annals of history, but the narration of these events will follow in the next chapter.

I returned to Marseilles, and was in Orleans a few days later; here the two Divisions and all their belongings were being concentrated and moved on, as equipped with mechanical and horse transport. The French General in Command of the District was greatly interested in the troops and witnessed a march past after an inspection parade.

The Indians were much impressed by the statue of Joan of Arc, which stands in a large square of the town; they had just heard the story of the Maid, and I saw them assembled in groups round the statue, and some companies which happened to be passing came to attention and turned their faces towards it. Could the Maid have ever dreamed that the Aryans from the far waters of the Indus and the slopes of the great Himalayas would one day learn to honour her as her own countrymen would do? But every day in France in 1914–15 was a lesson in psychology.

The mechanical transport handed over to us at Orleans was a revelation. The great retreat from Mons had taken its terrible toll, England was being called on to face difficulties of sea and land transport undreamed of but a few months previously; our armies were fighting for dear life, and these must needs of course be supplied first, and yet that great organiser Lord Kitchener had found it possible to send us motor transport sufficient for our immediate needs, and all up to time. Indeed it was we who had to hurry to keep pace with the urgent call from the trenches.

Had the mechanical transport been the sole difficulty, that had already been solved, but with the horse vehicles it was a totally different affair. No need to dilate on this; we knew they were doing their best for us and we meant to do our best with what was given us; but in truth the medley of carts of every description that met my eye the first morning at Orleans was enough to turn one's hair grey.

A vast plain, now converted into a bog, was literally strewn with vehicles and horses ; every species of conveyance found a place, and the fair at Nijni Novgorod could not have shown greater variety ; the char-a-banc and the baker's cart ; structures on prehistoric springs ; pole and draught harness ; horses in hundreds without collars, head or heel ropes—in fact, just loose. It might have appeared grave if it had not been so amusing. But the cart horses and harness were all as nothing to the drivers. Good fellows, who a month later had become useful soldiers, to-day they were indeed a sore trial. I went round to one diminutive man and said, " Do you know anything about horses ? " " I do not," was his reply. " How many days have you been a soldier ? " " Thirteen days." He was doing his best to find his horses, which in company with many others were taking a stroll along the banks of the Loire anywhere within five miles of the camp. I liked that man.

Such were some of our first trials, but what minute ones in comparison to the real ones we should soon be facing. The Indian soldiers could not understand all these things ! The motor lorries were new to them, and they simply took it for granted that in a European war everything was going to be new. But to see hundreds of magnificent horses wandering about because there was nothing to fasten them with, and drivers who were very much at sea, with a force going into the field, they did not understand. They have learned a good many things since.

Of all arms of the Indian Corps there was one not surpassed in any army—the Field Artillery. True, that to furnish the British equivalent of a corps in guns many other divisions in India had lost their brigades, but the artillery as it stood was near perfection. Superbly horsed ; with officers and men who had been trained on excellent and varied manœuvre grounds ; comparatively old, and in every respect highly disciplined soldiers ; the field artillery I had in France was a thing any General might well envy. And moreover, as it was put to no such test as the Mons retreat it went into action fully equipped, and remained throughout the year the Corps was in France a fine fighting machine. Officers and men disappeared as in other brigades of the Expeditionary Force, but the nucleus remained, and improved as time went on.

The Indian Divisions had each an entire regiment of cavalry attached as Divisional troops, and in addition a battalion of Pioneers, and in this respect were ahead of British troops in organisation. These Pioneer battalions proved of inestimable value, being trained in various kinds of technical work as well as all ordinary fighting duties. In addition each Division had two companies of Sappers and Miners ; acknowledged by all who have ever seen them in the field to be some of the finest engineer troops in our army.

The Indian *kahars* or stretcher - bearers attached to the field ambulances are a peculiarity of India. In France they did most excellent work ; purely non-fighting men, they are callously brave under fire, going about their duty with a calm air which appears to say, " I am not a fighting but a healing man, therefore they will never shoot me "—for this in fact is what one of them said to me. The *kahar* of course takes his chance, but I doubt if that man had ever heard of the Huns.

On the 18th October two Brigades of the Lahore Division left Orleans and were on the Flanders front by the 21st, and the Meerut Division following them reached St. Omer by the 29th of the month. These were followed by the Secunderabad Cavalry Brigade and Jodhpore Lancers, and thus the whole of the Corps that had so far arrived in France was at last facing the Germans.

A great surprise to me, once we found ourselves in Flanders, was the ease with which everything worked. The Indian troops, as is well known, have their own peculiar customs. Their religious scruples and their feeding have to be arranged for on lines entirely different to British soldiers. All these details might reasonably have been expected to cause considerable difficulties, but we had been preceded by Staff Officers conversant with all the require-

ments, and General Headquarters gave such a free hand
in these matters and so readily fell in with every suggestion
which they felt was necessary, that in a very few days
things were working more smoothly than in India itself,
where unfortunately red tape, Babus, and Returns clog
the wheels to such an extent as to render the machinery
frequently almost immovable.

India was now to be put to the test. Thirty, and
even twenty, years previously it had been looked upon as
the best training ground for the army. Indian campaigns
had produced many distinguished soldiers. Names like
those of Nicholson, Colin Campbell, Havelock, Roberts,
had immortalised its army; and only recently Lord
Kitchener had reorganised it, but the years of desert
warfare in Egypt and the war in South Africa had shorn
India of many of its attractions. It was no longer looked
on by many good soldiers as the best, or even as a good
school. I had known some who had refused high commands; others who felt European war was in the air and
had no intention of cutting themselves adrift from home,
where lay the best chance of being employed. For me
personally there was the ever-present knowledge that but
few of those directing the great military machine in France
knew anything about the Indians, and yet the very nature
and composition of the corps must be thoroughly recognised
if the fullest advantage was to be taken of it. We did
know, fortunately, that His Majesty the King not only
had his Indian soldiers' welfare at heart, but also that we
should always have his earnest support, and this was a
tower of strength to us. We knew also that Lord Kitchener
would watch our progress and back up our needs.

So far so good, but something more was needed. Did
our immediate commanders grasp the fact that our strength
in bare numbers as compared with a British Army Corps
was 5400 bayonets short? Did they realise that our
reinforcements were precarious, and had to come thousands
of miles across the seas? They could not know what I
did, viz. that a very large proportion of our reservists,
which must form a great part of such reinforcements,
were quite useless for European warfare, owing to the

pernicious reserve system then prevailing in India. Could
they tell that the drafts, before many months had gone by,
would begin to consist of recruits enlisted immediately
before or during the war ?

A former War Minister in England had once told me
that in four months Britishers could be turned into good
soldiers, fit to fight in Europe. Perhaps he was right ;
perhaps this great war has proved it ; but " East is East
and West is West," and notwithstanding my admiration
for the Indians and believing them to be first-class fighting
material, I can positively assert that it is impossible to
make good soldiers of them in four months or even in a
much longer period. Education, temperament, the difference between having and not having a cause in the quarrel,
must perforce be considered. From the day I left India
I had revolved all these matters in my mind, and now the
time had come when we must put our whole soul into the
battle.

The day of my arrival at St. Omer, the British Headquarters, was indeed one to be remembered. Asia had
dropped into Europe ; the descendants of Timour, of
Guru Govind, of the ancient Hindus, had come to fight
the Huns on the historic plains of Flanders. Seventy
miles in a direct line from us lay the immortal field of
Waterloo ; seventy-five miles away were the cliffs of
Dover. The man must have been carved out of wood
who would not have rejoiced at his good fortune ; the
heart atrophied that did not beat the faster at the thought
that he was given a chance, however humble, of taking
his share in the greatest conflict of all times.

As I motored to General Headquarters, methought
the temple bells on Ganges banks were ringing, and the
millions of devotees offering their prayers for their loved
ones so far away, in a land which none could conjure up
even in imagination. The voices of the muezzins were
ascending from thousands of mosques, from the Afridi
hills to the Deccan plains and away beyond, calling on
Allah to protect their kith and kin and give them victory.
The Golden Temple of Amritsar was sending up its call
to Ishwar, with *fatehs* for the soldiers of the Khalsa. On

the mighty Himalayas, the home of the Highlanders of Nepal, the sturdy little Gurkhas, I could see many thousands who knew nothing of Europe or any land beyond their own, but who did know that their kinsfolk could die like men, and they were calling in their simple faith on the Creator to watch those who from loyalty to their King-Emperor had crossed the great unknown sea.   And then the car stopped, and my vision faded, for I was at General Headquarters, and on a large table covered with small flags was the map of the British trenches, and standing beside it was the Field-Marshal Commander-in-Chief.

I had only met Sir John French three times in my life, but even had I never met him before I would have been glad to serve under his command, for he spoke so directly and with a manner that proved his sincerity and his confidence in himself and his army.   There was no bluster, but just a man in high authority speaking to another, who, he recognised, had a difficult task before him and meant to do his level best.   I went away happy.

I once asked one of my African soldiers, " Who is the greatest man in the world ? "   He promptly answered, " You are."   I asked him why, and he replied, " Because you are my Commander-in-Chief."   Simple fellow, but I felt rather like him for the moment.

CHAPTER III

FROM General Headquarters I proceeded to my billet at Merville for the night, and was met by the Frenchman, his wife and children, in whose house I was quartered. The room had only been vacated by another occupant an hour previously, and the hall and drawing-room bore the marks of hurry and scurry everywhere. I was often in the year to come to be the uninvited guest of other French people, but these were enough to show me the great heart of France; a heart so true and brave that it at first set one wondering what manner of people is this.

When I got to know them better I ceased to wonder; I ceased to doubt what might be the end of it all; this glorious race in its dire trial was indeed setting an example to the whole world. My hosts could not do enough to help me; tea was served: the children ran up and down stairs carrying something, anything, so long as they could show they were anxious to make me welcome. I thought perhaps they imagined the Indian General was some peculiar class of animal, but no! I soon discovered it was because I was an ordinary Englishman and they were typical French, that their kindness was lavished on me. And as months went on and we mixed more and more with them, we all discovered that high as had always been our opinion of our neighbours across the Channel, we had known but little of them after all. The unselfishness of their race is to my thinking unique; and from civilians, men and women alike, I never received anything but the greatest courtesy. For two months my corps held the trenches next to the French, and during that time I conceived a liking for their soldiers, and an admiration

31

for their brave and courteous Generals and Staffs that I had never thought possible to entertain towards any other than our own army.

There was never any kind of difficulty in working with a French General; one was only too glad to meet his wishes, for they were always expressed with courtesy, a natural gift with them, sometimes sadly lacking with us.

I had the honour of knowing and working with General de Maud'huy, Commanding the Xth Corps, and General Maistre, Commanding the XXIst Corps d'Armée, both splendid comrades in the field. Many others, too, I had dealings with; and amongst Staff Officers attached to the Indian Corps none could have been a greater favourite with British and Indians alike than Captain de la Ferronays. He joined us at Marseilles, and remained for some months until transferred to the French General Staff.

One of my saddest days in France was when we had to part from our French comrades for our first period of rest, and we did not serve next to them again except for short periods.

My great hope had been that the Indian Corps would not be split up as it arrived but be given a few days wherein to pull themselves together and form some idea of what was before them. This later on became the policy, and troops new to the country and form of warfare were not only kept behind the trenches but were instructed in all that was necessary, so that when their turn came they did not walk blindly into the hurricane.

It was, however, impossible in these days; every man as he arrived was wanted, and wanted badly, and hence some of the first arrivals were just pushed into the firing line and took their chance. The Indians had one disadvantage: their Generals and officers had no previous training in this novel form of fighting. The British forces, even though composed of men of all kinds, had most of them a nucleus of officers and soldiers who had already seen the backs of the Germans. The retreat from Mons was fresh in their memories, but the advance to the Aisne was a retort that no retreat could dim, and with these to their credit they felt that no matter how strong the foe, they were the same men who had turned to bay on the Marne and driven the Prussian Eagles away from their goal.

The orders however were given, and with that spirit which they had shown on many a field from Meance to Delhi and Lucknow the soldiers of India entered into battle.

The 1st Connaught Rangers, forming part of the Ferozepore Brigade, was the first battalion of the Army Corps engaged, and the 57th Rifles and 129th Baluchis were the first Indian regiments. As the Dorsets rightly carry on their colours the motto, " Primus in Indis," so surely should each of these two battalions be given " Primus in Europa," a fitting reward for their good fortune. On the 22nd October 1914 the Connaughts arrived at Wulverghem by motor buses, a new form of battle transport, and on the 23rd a portion of them took the place of the Essex regiment in the trenches in front of Messines. The remainder of the battalion next day relieved cavalry on the same front.

On the 26th October they were again relieved by cavalry, during which operation they suffered some casualties. Rendezvousing near Wytschaete they shortly afterwards received orders to attack the German trenches near Gapaard in conjunction with the 57th Rifles, both then being under the orders of the First Cavalry Division. The 129th Baluchis attached to the 3rd Brigade of the Second Cavalry Division operated on their left.

The Connaughts' attack was led by Lieut.-Colonel H. Ravenshaw, Major Murray being in command of the firing supports. Owing to darkness it was found impossible to keep touch with the 57th, but eventually Captain Payne's company, after passing through a fairly heavy fire, rushed three German trenches, taking an officer and some men prisoners, and skilfully withdrew. Ravenshaw specially commended Major Murray and Captain Payne on this the first occasion of an attack by the battalion. The total casualties were seventeen men.

On the 29th October the Connaught Rangers rejoined the Lahore Division. This fine battalion, which did excellent work on many occasions, was the only Irish corps then under my command ; six weeks later the 2nd

D

battalion, which had originally formed part of the 5th Infantry Brigade of the Second Division, was also sent to me to supplement its sister battalion ; it arrived in a very depleted state, and with only one of its original officers, but soon recovered its condition and rendered splendid service.

I have the greatest affection for Irishmen and have done all my regimental soldiering with them and was proud to have so distinguished a regiment under my command. To those who know how to treat them they are indeed impossible to beat in any Army, and I shall hope again some day to meet my comrades, such as may be left of them.

The 57th (Wilde's) Rifles on arrival at the advanced scene of operations found themselves in occupation of trenches near Oost Taverne and between Wytschaete and Messines. Sepoy Usman Khan of the 55th (Coke's) Rifles (commonly known as "Cookies" on the Frontier) on this occasion won the Indian Distinguished Service Medal. I believe he was the first Indian to gain a decoration in France.

As stated before, the 57th took part with the Connaught Rangers in the attack on Gapaard. Lieut.-Colonel Gray, the Commanding Officer, was unfortunately wounded early in the day by shrapnel. He had served with me on Frontier expeditions, and his wild fighting spirit and cheery manner made him a typical leader of Indian troops. It was not long after before he was back in France with his beloved regiment and later went on to the Eastern Mediterranean as a Brigadier-General.

The 57th was composed of exceptionally good officers and a fine class of Indian officers and men all round. In this affair they did not have a chance of doing much and their casualties were slight. The composition of this unit was two companies of each of the following classes, Sikhs, Dogras, Punjabi-Musalmans, and Pathans, and their last active service had been in China, 1900.

Meantime the 129th Baluchis who were attached to the 3rd Cavalry Brigade and were operating on the left of the Indian battalion had to advance over very bad ground and made but small progress. This battalion had taken over trenches already prepared by the cavalry on the 23rd October, and came under rifle and machine-gun fire for the first time, and as the Commanding Officer reported, " they stood it well."

In the attack on Gapaard a company of the Baluchis got to within 300 yards of the German trenches and were quite annoyed on receiving orders to retire, but it was necessary as the enemy machine-guns were skilfully posted. Captain Hampe-Vincent was killed, and besides there were forty-six other casualties. The battalion carried out various duties between this date and the 30th, losing another twelve men.

The movements and duties of the 57th Rifles and 129th Baluchis, during their detachment from their own Brigade, read strangely to any one who was not in the area at the time. Here were two Indian battalions, suddenly dumped down in a maelstrom, depending for guidance entirely on their few British officers, split up into half companies, attached to various British corps in turn, cavalry, infantry, guns ; hurried from one trench to another, from one front to another, hardly realising the meaning or object of it all ; and then comes the hardest trial ; their gallant leaders are everywhere, encouraging and guiding with a spirit of unselfish bravery that will live for all time, when the hand of death strikes them down ; others fall sorely wounded ; Indian officers share their fate ; the sepoys bewildered but faithful still fight on. They may be driven (they were driven) time after time from their trenches but such a retreat is glory, and they shared it to the full with their newly found British comrades in those few but stormy days of Ypres.

The difficulty of recording these events may be gathered from the Commanding Officer's report on the actions round Wytschaete and Messines, which he begins with the remark : " It is not possible to submit a detailed report or make special mention of individuals, owing to the fact that six out of seven British officers employed with my companies were killed or wounded." With the help of the Indian officers later on, all that could be discovered was noted, and as many rewards were given by the Commander-in-Chief as there was evidence to prove had been earned.

As a record of the kaleidoscopic movements of the 57th Rifles the following orders are interesting : On the evening of 28th October the Commanding Officer was directed to place one company at the disposal of the G.O.C. 4th Cavalry Brigade, and another at that of the G.O.C. 5th Cavalry Brigade ; these two companies relieved portions of their British comrades in the trenches. Later the same evening he was ordered to send his two remaining companies to report to 3rd Cavalry Brigade at Messines by 5 A.M. next morning. Headquarters of the battalion were ordered to remain at Wytschaete ; and to complete the break up, the machine-gun section was sent to the 4th Cavalry Brigade. Of course the situation was such as to render even such extraordinary orders necessary, but my object in quoting them is to show the immense difficulties the battalions had to face under most abnormal conditions, and the fact that notwithstanding the shortage of British officers, and hence the absence of any one who could speak their language, these gallant men of the 57th and 129th put up and sustained so good a fight as to earn the high encomium and thanks of leaders as distinguished as Generals Hugh Gough and Allenby, no mean judges of human nature.

During the 29th, the 57th Rifles suffered only a few casualties, but on the morning of 30th October the Germans plastered the trenches of the 4th and 5th Cavalry Brigades with shrapnel and high explosive and attacked with infantry. About 2 P.M. a portion of the troops north of the 5th Cavalry Brigade was compelled to fall back, thus exposing the trenches to the south to enfilade fire, and the Brigade commenced a retirement from its left flank.

Captain Forbes of the 57th, with No. 3 Company, by some mischance did not receive the orders to retire in time and became isolated. The enemy was soon on both his flanks, but Forbes is made of the stuff that never acknowledges danger. He was severely wounded a day or two after and invalided, but I was glad to have an opportunity on his rejoining, of placing him on the Corps Staff as Camp Commandant. As the company retired, a half of it with its leader, Lieut. I. H. Clarke, was mown down by machine-gun fire, only a few getting away. As the Commanding Officer put it tersely but with how much pathos —" They did not return." The survivors moved back to Wytschaete.

Major Willans, a sturdy soldier, with No. 1 Company farther to the right had fared slightly better and was able to withdraw with his machine-gun to the east of the Wytschaete—Messines Road. The bombardment of the trenches and Wytschaete continued during the 30th and 31st October, and on this latter night, between 3 and 4 A.M., the Germans made an infantry attack in overwhelming numbers. The supports were commanded by Major E. E. Barwell, and on hearing the burst of musketry he pushed forward but was killed as he advanced. A personal friend and a brave gentleman, he died as he once told me he hoped he might.

No. 4 Company of the 57th was bearing the weight of a strong attack at the same time, and Captain R. S. Gordon commanding No. 2 Company at once led them to its assistance. As the Highlander leaped from his trench he was killed; and thus passed away an ideal soldier. " Jock " Gordon was a very uncommon man, loved by all who knew him, of a nature that knew no guile, literally worshipped by his men, on that cold October morn he found his place in the Valhalla of his northern land.

Lieut. Malony, notwithstanding that he was opposed to vastly superior advancing numbers, kept up so heavy a fire that the enemy began to cry a halt and endeavour to dig themselves in. He held on as long as his ammunition lasted but was then himself severely wounded and incapacitated.

Meantime half of No. 4 Company was nearly surrounded, and the detachment was left without a single British officer; but the occasion generally discovers the man, and he was there in the person of Subadar Arsla Khan, one of those legendary heroes of the days of Timour. I had known him for years in peace and war; he had won his Order of Merit with me on the North-West Frontiers of India, and has since added the Military Cross to his numerous decorations. Leading a counter-attack with the bayonet he gained sufficient time to pull his men together, and then, although vastly outnumbered, skilfully withdrew both companies to Messines; here the men became separated in the streets and were eventually taken in charge by Lieut. Reardon, the British interpreter attached to the battalion. In the counter-attack Jemadar Kapur Singh, a Dogra, was killed after all his men had been placed *hors de combat*.

It is instructive to read in the reports that some of the men in Messines " had the good fortune " to come across an officer who spoke Hindustani, and was thus able to direct them to rejoin their Headquarters ; and the report concludes with, " and some of them did arrive at Kemmel."

Necessity may know no law, but you cannot expect a dweller of these islands to ask his way of a Chinaman of the Yangtse, especially should both have the misfortune of being under a heavy fire of high explosive shell at the time. You may perhaps expect it, but one often expects too much.

Captain Forbes, of whom I wrote above, was severely wounded whilst conducting his men back from the north of Wytschaete, where the Germans had gained a footing. A withdrawal also became necessary from other portions of our trenches, and Major Willans, finding his position untenable, had retired his Sikhs on to a battery near a windmill south-west of Wytschaete. Lieut. Fowler, who commanded the regimental machine-guns, was severely wounded. He had exercised his command with great coolness.

Major Swifte, who had succeeded to the command of the 57th when Lieut.-Colonel Gray was wounded, collected all the men he could and on the morning of 1st November was ordered to report to G.O.C. 4th Cavalry Brigade, who directed him to take up a position on the right of the 3rd Hussars. Here he was joined by Major Willans with his own company and what remained of the companies from Messines, and late that night was ordered to report himself to O.C. 129th Baluchis.

This battalion had, like the 57th Rifles, been doing its share in another place. After its first experience in the trenches it had a rest in billets on 27th October, and was at work again on the 29th entrenching a position. Whilst at this duty, at 11 A.M. on the 29th, two companies received orders to proceed to a bridge over the Canal north-west of Hollebeke to support the cavalry in the château there, but at 1.10 P.M. it was moved to Klein Hollebeke to form part of the reserve to the 1st Army Corps, and at 7 P.M. marched back to its billets. The casualties only amounted to twelve killed and wounded.

Orders for relief had been issued for 7 A.M. on 30th October, but at 6.30 A.M. the enemy opened a heavy fire which continued throughout the morning. Lieut.-Colonel W. M. Southey was in command of the 129th. His was one of the few battalions of the Indian Corps that I did not then know well, but I had seen them for a few days and made as thorough an inspection as was possible. It had in its ranks Mahsuds and some Mohmands, good fighters in their own Frontier hills; the Mohmands were now being for the first time tested in our regular Army. In consequence these were of necessity young soldiers, but under Southey all soldiers will fight, and notwithstanding their youth the new classes gradually acquired the discipline which is so essential for any military body. Southey soon after this got command of a brigade and at once justified his selection.

The 129th was originally raised in 1846 and has always been known as a " Baluchi " battalion. It consisted in 1914 of two companies of Punjabi Musalmans, three of Mahsuds, and three of other Pathans, and had seen service in Persia, Afghanistan, and Egypt, 1882. The Duke of Connaught is their Colonel-in-Chief.

A story is told of Southey during the heavy fighting near Givenchy and Festubert in December 1914. When commanding his battalion in the advanced trenches he received a message from some higher authority directing him to hold on at all costs to his somewhat precarious position—" Never mind about holding on, I will of course do that, but where are my rations ? "

In this battalion was an Indian officer of whom also I

must tell a story. Six years previously I was in command
of an expedition on the North-West Frontier of India,
when one day the tribesmen had gathered in force and
held a very strong Pass. All arrangements were completed
and our attack was just beginning when suddenly, 800
yards directly in front of my own position, a single man
carrying a large white flag appeared on a knoll and
deliberately began walking towards us. Had there been
no firing, or had the tribesmen ceased firing, the flag would
of course have been respected, but on the contrary as he
advanced the Martinis of the Mohmands began to crack
louder than ever, and presently casualties occurred here
and there in our ranks. Of course such conduct could not
be tolerated, and it appeared as if one fanatic had adopted
this ruse to put us off our guard. However on came the
flag, now at the double, and I do not think I exaggerate
when I say scores of shots were aimed at it. The man
kept tacking from side to side, appearing and disappearing
in the holes and hollows and behind rocks, but remaining
scatheless, until he was less than 400 yards from us, when
as if from a chivalry inborn every one ceased to fire at him,
and only stared at what they thought was a madman.
The firing went on steadily elsewhere. At last he arrived
where I was standing, and saluting delivered himself of
the following speech : " General, my name is Ahmed Din,
I am a native officer of the 129th Baluchis. I am on
leave from my regiment. This is my home and these
people on the hills are fools and do not know the power
of the British Government. I ask you to cease firing and
they will at once surrender. I have only one request and
that is that you spare the large village just the other side
of the Pass and we will pay any fine you impose." Whatever else he was he certainly did not fear death, for he had
faced it as coolly as man could do. I sounded the " Cease
fire," and in five minutes all firing had ceased and white
flags floated all along the ridges and peaks. We marched
over the Pass and occupied the village but every precaution
was of course taken and picquets posted. Ahmed Din
remained with me as a hostage and guest combined.
No sooner was it dark than from every side bullets

came raining into our camps, and for that form of warfare
we had quite a number of men, horses, and mules hit.   I
told my gallant friend that if I was killed (he winced)
the sepoys would certainly see that he followed suit.   He
took me aside and said, " Remember, General, this is not
my village, mine is farther on."   " All right," I answered,
" I will burn yours to-morrow," and he believed I would,
but of course I did not.

We left next morning but not before the rear-guard
had left the village in ashes, and Ahmed Din smiled as he
looked back on the smoke being borne towards his own
untouched belongings.   The climax was reached when
later he came to me in Peshawar and asked to be given
the medal for the expedition ; he got it, but thought it
rather hard luck that he was not given the field allowance
as well.   Poor fellow, I met him again in France and we
laughed over the incident.   He will see his native hills
no more.

Amid the sloughs of Festubert, where India's heroes sleep and share
With England's sons a common grave ; when Azrael's trump shall
        call the brave,
And ranks fall in and stand to arms, to answer God, not war's alarms,
A tomb with crescent marked in green shall yield the soul of Ahmed
    Din.

The 129th experienced varying fortunes during the
30th October ; after reinforcing the firing-line with all
available men, they were pushed back by a strong German
attack.   One company held on to a farm where it was
reinforced by Colonel Southey himself but eventually had
to retire.   The demoralising effect of continued retirement
was beginning to tell on the men, many of whom were
very young soldiers, and it was necessary to pull them
together.   Detaching a portion of them to hold a wood
to the right, the remainder were rallied in the vicinity of
a château which was held by Lieut. H. Lewis and Subadar
Adam Khan.   Evening saw them still holding the wood
and some trenches north of the château, and later
three companies moved to billets near the canal bank,
leaving one company to hold the trenches north of the
château.

On 31st October further moves took place, resulting in three companies taking over some cavalry trenches, with one company in support and forty men in reserve. Firing by the enemy continued till 11 P.M., when it increased, and news was received through some French officers that a farm held by the Baluchis had been captured by the Germans. Colonel Southey at once proceeded with Major Hannyngton and Lieut. Lewis to find out what was happening. The truth was soon ascertained, viz. that Major H. W. Potter, in local command, was still holding on round the farm which was in possession of the enemy. It is a strange fact that notwithstanding the difficulty of the Indians recognising the difference between French and Germans, in this case they had been right and insisted they were Boches, but it was the British officer who thought them French, and would not open fire until they had arrived at twenty paces; too late to stop them, but what a fine example of self-control; even though it was a matter of life and death, the Englishman refused to kill until he was sure it really was the enemy.

Fifteen or more were accounted for when the party fell back, and the Germans entered the farm. The last bit of work that fell to the Baluchis is best told in the brief official report of Colonel Southey himself: " We formed up about 3 A.M. and advanced on the left of the farm, Major Potter taking the right, and marched up to the farm. We killed about three and wounded three, and the remainder who had not bolted surrendered, fourteen in number." That is all.

Thirty-five Germans had been accounted for, and many of our own brave fellows, but the adventure on a dark night in rain-soaked fields carried out by aliens in a strange land is dismissed in three lines.

Lieut. Lewis during this advance was twice shot at, at a distance of not less than fifteen yards; both shots hit his field-glasses in front of his left hip and smashed them to bits, the second one glancing off and hitting his hand. A few days later he received a letter from a friend in Ceylon who wound up by saying, " Take my advice and always wear your field-glasses in front of your belt." Lewis had another narrow escape at Givenchy two months later. Whilst working his machine-gun in the front trench the Germans broke in on his right, unknown to him. One of his team suddenly saw them coming down the trench a few yards away, and Lewis saw one man covering him with his rifle from the parapet only three paces off. He gave the order to retire (these stories were told me by a brother-officer of his) and heard the click of the man's rifle but no shot followed. The rifle was not loaded.

And if any have ever doubted the splendid gallantry shown under the severest trials let them read this example of what Indian soldiers will do when called on by their leaders. Each battalion had in those days two Maxim machine-guns. With the team of one gun of the Baluchis were three men whose names deserve to be recorded: Naik Sar Mir, Lance-Naik Hobab Gul, and Sepoy Redi Gul. These men worked their gun until it was blown to bits by a shell and only retired under orders of their commander Captain R. F. Dill, who, displaying splendid coolness, continued the fight with his other gun. And what of this machine-gun? I believe the Victoria Cross is made from the metal of guns captured at the Alma. The second machine-gun of the 129th Baluchis might well be manufactured into the future Victoria Crosses of the Indian Army, for it has a famous story attached to it.

Dill had lost one gun but whilst the other remained he would remain with it. He was disabled by a splinter of shell in the head, his glorious team fell fast, but as each man fell another took his place. Engrave these names in letters of gold for all time: 2524 Colour-Havildar Ghulam Mahomed, 2813 Sepoy Lal Sher, 4182 Sepoy Said Ahmad, 103 Sepoy Kassib, 3600 Sepoy Afsar Khan; and only one remained, severely wounded. He worked the gun till strength failed him and he lay unconscious and hence untouched by the enemy—No. 4050 Sepoy Khudadad! and he has lived to wear the Victoria Cross, the first Indian soldier who ever won it. His home is in the village of Chakwal near Jhelum's river. There I can see him in imagination, telling the children of the deeds of his regiment, but like all brave men saying little of his own share in it.

A tale which holdeth children from play, and old men from the chimney corner.

The 129th on relief by French cavalry rejoined their own Brigade on the La Bassée front.

And so the first experience of the Army Corps in the war had been gained and the price paid. Not that any one of them grudged it, nor was the toll as heavy as the British units had to pay, and yet comparatively it was heavier, because it was taken from men who had had no opportunity of realising what it was all about. They had been trained to the understanding that when they entered into the battle it would, at any rate at first, be alongside the British comrades with whom they had served in Brigades in India; these at least they knew and understood; and even if this could not be, they had every reason to believe they would at least fight as battalions under their own Commanding Officers ; but here none of these things happened. They were split up in fragments, and that they stood the strain as well as they did is the best possible testimony to their discipline and efficiency. As an Indian officer said to me on the return of the two battalions to rejoin their Headquarters, talking about the separation from their own Brigades, " Sahib, they do not understand anything about us."

The short fighting round Ypres had cost the 57th Rifles the loss of two British officers killed, three wounded, and one missing out of a total of eleven present, three Indian officers killed or missing, and one wounded, whilst 290 other ranks made up the casualty list for those few days. An Indian battalion numbered only 750 all told— 450 remained. In the 129th Baluchis the losses were three British officers killed, three wounded, and of Indian officers three were killed and two wounded, and other ranks totalled 230.

Of Major G. G. P. Humphreys his C.O. wrote : " I most deeply deplore his loss." Captain W. F. Adair, though mortally wounded, refused to allow a havildar and two of the men of the 129th to remove him as it might entail their being killed themselves. Colonel Southey calls him " a most gallant and cool leader."

Subadar Zaman Khan of the 129th had the honour of being singled out as an officer of the " greatest coolness and courage," and Havildar Sobat Khan of the same battalion "showed bravery and coolness above the average," and on the 30th October set a splendid example to his men under a heavy shell and rifle fire by rushing out from the support to the firing-line trenches and thus getting them to follow him.

Individual deeds of the men are difficult to record, for as the Commanding Officer wrote at the time : " Owing to the casualties amongst the officers of Nos. 1 and 2 Companies I find it very hard to get any information regarding individuals."

After the fighting near Messines the English papers got hold of a story of how one " Ganga Singh " of the 129th had won and received the Victoria Cross. Pictures appeared showing him being carried ashore in a stretcher " somewhere in England, the first Indian to win the V.C." Lord Kitchener wired to ask for information, but I had heard nothing of it and it was not till long after that evidence could be gathered from men who had themselves been wounded and left the battalion. Then the true story came out, and it was this :

On 31st October, when the trench held by his party was overwhelmed by the enemy, Havildar Gagna (for that was his correct name), who had been a gymnastic instructor, commanded his section and fought with his bayonet, killing several Germans, and his weapon being bent or blunted, and the enemy being still in the trench, he seized a sword which he had picked up and continued to fight. In this mêlée he received five wounds which left him disabled, and it was nearly a year before he could be sent back to India. He was awarded the Indian Order of Merit, which carried with it a life pension, and the Russian Cross of St. George.

Sir John French was always anxious to bestow well-earned rewards on Indian officers and men, and it was very rarely in the early stages of the war that any exception was taken to my recommendations. This was a very great help to all Commanding Officers, who felt that they could count on being supported in their selections. Later on this generosity was considerably curtailed, although Divisional and Brigade Commanders were very careful in sending in names.

To those who understand Indians there can be no greater mistake than to be niggardly in the bestowal of war honours. The Indian Order of Merit carried with it a small life pension, and this was of very great importance to men who gave their services for a totally inadequate remuneration. It was the highest honour a soldier could earn until the Victoria Cross was opened to him by His Majesty the King at the great Delhi Durbar. To show how well Lord Roberts understood the value of immediate rewards to the Indian Army, after the defence of Thobal in Manipore by Major Grant in 1891, a feat which made India ring with praise of the gallant little band, Grant was especially promoted from Lieutenant to Brevet-Major and awarded the Victoria Cross, and every man of his party (I think about seventy) received the Indian Order of Merit. How much greater were the toils and dangers of Flanders !

Willans of the 57th Rifles received a D.S.O., and his brother-officers, Captain W. S. Trail and Lieut. E. K. Fowler, the Military Cross. Dill of the 129th Baluchis received the D.S.O. ; and besides Sepoy Khudadad, who, as already told, won the first V.C. given to the Indian Army, the five men of his Maxim detachment who were all killed were rewarded posthumously, the havildar receiving the Indian Order of Merit, and his comrades the I.D.S.M.

It was the fate of the Indian Corps to be allotted for nearly fourteen months almost exactly the same part of front, with only two small breaks in the monotony. One has already been described, and the other was when the Lahore Division was temporarily detached for a few days to take its share in the second battle of Ypres in April 1915. With these two exceptions the Indians were con-fined to the fronts from just north of Neuve Chapelle to

Givenchy, a distance in a direct line of about seven miles.

If any one had thought how best to dishearten good soldiers, they could not have chosen a better method. Often did I urge that we might be given a change from the same bogs and swamps to somewhere north or south, but it was not agreed to, and so for over thirteen months the men went up to the same old trenches and returned to the same monotonous billets, until many of them believed it was probably all or a greater part of the entire British line. We often wondered what could be the reason : I knew myself, but that is another story.

Those were the last of the days of the old Regular Army, the staunchest and most trenchant weapon that Britain ever possessed. Signs were even then appearing of the younger formations, which were within a year to submerge the old and create a new Army, in which the names of historic corps would alone form the link between them. But owing to those very associations how strong did that link become ; what a heritage did the old regiments and battalions bequeath to their younger brothers. When the Territorials and the New Army began to swamp the battle front they had the good fortune to build on foundations of granite, the builders of which had learned their trade not in months or years, but in the school of generations of soldiers who had created and maintained the Empire of Great Britain.

The New Armies found the bogs and the climate the same, but they also found to hand implements to dig with, guns with countless ammunition to help to defend or clear the way for them, howitzers, grenades, trench mortars, searchlights, heavy guns, machine-guns galore, aeroplanes, balloons, communication trenches, light railways, flares, etc., etc. If they wished then to understand the conditions of those early months of the war it was not difficult. Remove all, or nearly all, of the above accessories, divide the numbers per mile of trench by five, reduce the gun ammunition to an almost infinitesimal amount, double the enemy and allow him the high *morale* he originally undoubtedly possessed, and they could then form some idea of the war as it had to be carried out in the winter of 1914–15.

The part played by the Indian Corps in the first great battle of Ypres, in as far as it relates to the fighting in the immediate vicinity of the town itself, has been told as nearly as I can gather it from official reports and private letters in my possession, but although the most critical time was in the north, the country to the south as far as La Bassée was the scene of incessant hard fighting and contests for every inch of ground. Behind us lay the plains of Flanders, and behind them the ports of Calais and Boulogne and the shores of the Channel. The eyes of Germany's War Lord were fixed on these ; could he but succeed in pushing back far enough, or breaking through, that thin khaki line, what was the prize ? Had he succeeded history might have had to tell a different tale.

There was at one time little else between the Hun and the sea he sought than the war-worn and battered troops of England. How they held that line, with what fortitude and endurance they fought, with what incredible valour they died is already a matter of history, but the object of this book is only to tell of the part played (small in comparison though it may be) by the Army Corps from India, the British battalions and batteries and the soldiers of Hindustan, inhabitants of warm climes, fighting in a country so strange and so unlike anything they had ever heard of or imagined. The man must be totally devoid of generosity who does not read and wonder with what fidelity and loyalty they gave their lives, and in doing so left behind a legacy of which not only India but Great Britain itself may be proud.

It was their good fortune to arrive just at the moment when they were most needed ; just when our troops were using their very last reserves and fighting against terrible odds, in fact just when two extra divisions could still help to stem the tide, and even if they had never done another day's fighting their advent would more than have justified their having been sent, for they helped in some degree to save the Army in the hour of its great trial.

CHAPTER IV

BEFORE describing the events in which the Lahore Division, the first to arrive on the scene of action, took part, north of La Bassée, it is well to take a look at some of the Commanders and Staffs who left India for France, and to study the types of Indians which constituted the Army Corps.

The Chief Staff-Officer was Brigadier-General H. Hudson of the Indian Cavalry, son of General Sir John Hudson, who had commanded the Bombay Army years previously. An able soldier with much Staff experience, he later commanded a British Division, and then became Adjutant-General in India. He had served on my General Staff in India when I commanded the Northern Army, and was as good a friend as he was a Staff-Officer. He was promoted Major-General after Neuve Chapelle. Whatever his rank he was always known as " Huddy."

Major J. R. Charles of the Royal Engineers had served on the General Staff and previously soldiered with me on Frontier Expeditions.

Major J. A. Longridge of the Indian Army later became a G.S.O.1. A splendid character, brave and modest, loyal to the core, and a perfect type of English gentleman, he was killed in the trenches in 1916.

The Chief of our Artillery was Brigadier-General F. Mercer. I seldom call men by anything but their surnames, but with Mercer somehow it was natural not to do so. He was always cheery and happiest on horseback, and such men are a useful asset in war. He afterwards went as Chief of Artillery to the First Army.

My Engineer Chief was Colonel H. C. Nanton of the

Royal Engineers. As good an officer as you could find in that line, he was a worker whom nothing could tire, full of new ideas, never happier than when in a trench devising methods for saving the lives of our men, or arranging how best to destroy the Huns, and for choice in the trenches nearest to them. Day or night Nanton's one object in life was to be hard at work doing his duty.

Colonel Treherne, our P.M.O., lived to save lives ; he was one of the most conscientious men I know.

And so I could go on adding names of good comrades, men of the stamp of Colonel A. Peck, Major H. L. Tomkins, Assistant Military Secretary ; Major W. L. Twiss of the Indian Army, and Major Barclay Vincent, 6th Inniskilling Dragoons ; all since risen higher in rank and in the estimation of their Corps Commander of those days.

Some there were in high places "over there" who, when we first arrived, commiserated with me on the fact that we were a scratch lot on the Headquarters of the Corps ; but one advantage I did possess and that was, that they were all men who knew the Indian soldier inside out. Camberley may turn out Napoleons, but it cannot provide them with the knowledge which is an absolute essential in dealing with Indian troops.

The commanders of the two Divisions belonged, one to the Indian and the other to the British Service. Lieut.-General H. B. Watkis of the Indian Army commanded the Lahore Division and was the first to arrive in France. Always an earnest student of his profession, on him fell the brunt of the German attack on Givenchy in December 1914. Watkis had a difficult task in those days, and that Sir John French singled him out as the only General among us all in the Indian Corps to be mentioned by name, in the body of his early despatches, was a high tribute.

Brigadier-General Cobbe, V.C., of the Indian Army was Chief Staff-Officer to Watkis ; he had served with me in Ashanti in 1900, being severely wounded and earning a D.S.O., which he supplemented in later years with a Victoria Cross in Somaliland—a staunch friend, as modest as he is brave. He served later on the Corps Staff, and left us in 1915 to serve on the Staff of the 1st Corps, and later commanded an Army Corps in Mesopotamia as a Lieutenant-General.

Colonel G. Hodson was A.Q.M.G. of the Division. A hard-riding polo-player and one of the cheeriest of soldiers, he died of wounds received in Gallipoli; another name inscribed on the Roll of Honour of that famous corps, the Guides, in which he had passed most of his life. The name of Hodson is known throughout India, since the days when the leader of Hodson's Horse scoured the northern plains and leaving a landmark in Indian history before the walls of Humaya's Tomb near Delhi, fell in the final triumph of Lucknow.

The Ferozepore Brigade of the Lahore Division was commanded by Brigadier-General R. M. Egerton, another of the Guides, another scion of a name known wherever the British flag floats in Hindustan. He served with his Brigade until it left for Mesopotamia, and there joined in the heavy fighting, receiving a K.C.B. and K.C.I.E.

Major-General P. M. Carnegy of the Indian Army commanded the Jalandar Brigade; son of another Indian General, he brought with him the tradition of a British family which had made that historic land its temporary home. His Brigade Major was Major Hugh Hill of the Royal Welsh Fusiliers; I met him a week before he was killed in the trenches in 1916, and the last words he said to me were: "Your son will do all right." No one who knew him is likely to forget this gallant English gentleman.

The commander of the Sirhind Brigade was Major-General J. M. Brunker, Royal Artillery. He was detained in Egypt with his Brigade on the way to France, but joined in time to take part in the battle of Givenchy in December 1914.

The Divisional Artillery was commanded by Brigadier-General F. E. Johnson, one of those who act on the principle that "whatever thine hand findeth to do, do it with all thy might."

I am not writing a despatch, but just jotting down the names of comrades who come to mind; men who took part in our daily lives, whose watchword was duty, and who will, I am sure, forgive me for recording their names here, for they were as true as they were modest.

The Meerut Division was commanded by Lieut.-General C. A. Anderson, late Royal Artillery. A typical Irishman and a fearless soldier, he understood the Indian character well. No better man than " Paddy " Anderson could have been selected for a Division. His chief amusement was to visit the trenches, and if you wanted to find him you could not do better than make for the front line closest to the Germans. I do not believe there was a single General in the Expeditionary Force who so often visited his men in the trenches. On one occasion I was looking over a map with him at his advanced Headquarters; a few shells were going over or dropping within an uncomfortable range, when one planted itself close alongside us ; Anderson at that moment had his pencil on a particular spot on the map ; without moving it he just looked up and said with a strong Irish accent, " Pip-Squeak " (small German shell), and went on with his remarks. It was his way, nothing disturbed him. At Givenchy, Neuve Chapelle, Festubert, and on the day of Loos, " Paddy " Anderson did splendidly ; he succeeded me in command of the Indian Corps in September 1915, and shortly after orders were issued for the break up of the Corps and it moved to Egypt, Mesopotamia and East Africa. After the Indians left France, Anderson was given command of a British Army Corps on the Western Front.

To prove how little was known about us at G.H.Q. ; during an important action Anderson was placed under the orders of a junior General of a British Division, and informed that the officer concerned had been given the temporary rank of Lieut.-General. But Anderson was already a Lieut.-General, which Headquarters had evidently been quite unaware of, for the order directed that " Major-General Anderson, etc., etc." As four of the Army Corps were at this time commanded by Generals all junior to him, it was going a bit strong to reduce him still further. I think I am correct in saying that Anderson was the only Corps Commander of those days who was not given any French or foreign decoration, nor did he ever get one.

Anderson's Chief Staff-Officer was Colonel C. W. Jacob of the Indian Army. A very thorough officer, who later commanded the Dehra Dun Brigade and the Meerut Division, and on the departure of the Indians from France was given a British Army Corps with the rank of Lieut.-General.

Brigadier-General H. D'U. Keary of the Indian Army led the Garhwal Brigade. A bold horseman and good sportsman who had often first passed the post, ridden down the wiry black buck, landed record fish in the upper waters of the Irriwaddy, and shot every kind of game, Keary impressed one by his quiet manner. He assumed command of the Lahore Division in January 1915, and at the second battle of Ypres gained the unstinted praise of General Sir Horace Smith-Dorrien, then in command of the Second Army. Keary took his Division to Mesopotamia, earned his K.C.B. and K.C.I.E., and characteristically refused command of a Division in India, preferring to serve on in the field with the men he had led in action. Later he was given the Meerut Division in India and transferred to the Burmah command.

Brigadier-General C. E. Johnson, Indian Army, was in command of the Dehra Dun Brigade, and later commanded a Brigade in India; and the last of the Indian Brigades, the Bareilly, had for its Chief, Major-General Forbes Macbean, formerly of the Gordon Highlanders, who had served in Kabul, Tirah (where he was severely wounded), and South Africa.

The Artillery of the Division was in the competent hands of Brigadier-General A. B. Scott. He had served in South Africa, and later received his promotion to Major-General and command of a Division.

Lieut.-Colonels P. Twining and C. Coffin were the heads of the engineering branches of the two Divisions, and those who knew them felt safe in their hands.

The Field Brigades of Artillery were commanded by Colonels L. G. F. Gordon, Ouseley, and Maxwell in the Lahore, and L. A. Gordon, Potts, and Tyler in the Meerut Division.

Lieut.-General Sir Locke-Elliott, who had retired

from the Indian Army after holding the appointment of Inspector-General of Cavalry, was at first attached to the Army Corps as Technical Adviser, and later on for all Indian troops in France.   Locke-Elliott's name as a horseman was a household word in India.

Major the Right Hon. F. E. Smith, K.C., M.P., now Lord Birkenhead, joined us at Marseilles as Recording Officer to the Corps, and remained with us till after the battle of Neuve Chapelle.   He was a keen observer and a brilliant writer.   Had he been given a free hand, the story of our doings would have reached India from time to time, and whilst letting that country know something of the work of its soldiers, would at the same time have stimulated recruiting and cheered the populace ; but those were the days of reticence ; nothing could be told ; the cinematograph and the Press were kept on a leash, and " F. E.," as he is popularly known, was severely handicapped. All that could get past G.H.Q. was sent on, whilst he and I were continuously being goaded by all those who cared to send something more exciting than a bare statement of facts.   However, he kept an interesting record and one which has since been turned to good use in compiling the history of the Corps.   He had as assistant Major St. G. Steele of the Indian Army, and with him also Captain the Hon. Neil Primrose, a capital companion in the field. " F. E." is a keen soldier at heart.   He had no opportunities of doing anything but his own job, but to do that he never failed to accompany me on all kinds of missions.   On one of these occasions, when he accompanied me in the trenches, his stature was very nearly the cause of some other than he filling the place of Attorney-General in the Government ; and rather in the spirit of a schoolboy he was very often away in places where business did not carry him ; one day his horse was shot under him, but he turned up unhurt, and was always in the highest spirits.   He was held in high esteem by Lord Kitchener, who frequently consulted him on important questions.

And last, but not least, were my two A.D.C.'s, Captain A. P. Y. Langhorne, R.A., and my only son, Lieut. J. L. Willcocks, the Black Watch.   The boy has served through-

out the war, winning a D.S.O. and M.C.   Langhorne had
served with me for years on the Indian Frontier, earning
a D.S.O. in 1908.   A sterling soldier and a loyal friend, he
is now a Lieut.-Colonel, and has added a Military Cross
to his D.S.O.

On the departure of Sir Frederick Smith to become
Attorney-General, I was given Lieut.-Colonel J. W. B.
Merewether of the Indian Army as Record Officer, and he
remained with the Corps till it left France.   He was an
old regimental comrade and a man full of energy and
wit : a clever writer and a very entertaining companion ;
his presence at our Headquarters was much appreciated.
He was constantly with me when I visited billets, trenches,
etc., and he acquired a very detailed knowledge of all
that went on in the Corps.   He devoted his whole time to
visiting officers and men of every unit and collecting all
the information he could gain.   The results have been
embodied in the book, *The Indian Corps in France*, compiled
by him and Sir Frederick Smith, dedicated to His Majesty
the King-Emperor, and published under the authority of
His Majesty's Secretary of State for India in Council.
Particular care has been taken to bring to light the individual
actions of officers and men throughout the time the Army
Corps was in France.   He deserves well of the India
Office and the Indian Army in general.   After the Corps
left France Merewether was given the C.I.E.

It is interesting to analyse the different types of races
of which the Indian Army Corps was composed.   The
Christian, the Mahomedan, and the Hindu were ranged in
the service of the King who ruled the greatest Empire
known to history ; this in itself is a remarkable fact, but
far more remarkable was the reason ; it was this, that they
all felt in their hearts that the cause was just, and in feeling
it knew they were fighting for the right.   Had it been
otherwise it could never have been achieved.

England was represented by the 2nd Battalion of the
Leicesters and 1st Manchesters, both regiments which
could not be surpassed in the field.   Ireland furnished
the Connaught Rangers, like all Irish corps specially dear
to me.   Scotland sent us three battalions, the 1st Seaforths,

1st Highland Light Infantry, and 2nd Black Watch, fine specimens of that fighting race. It is sufficient testimony to them all to say, that they not only formed the backbone of the Army Corps, but their example in the dreary trenches, and in the battle, served as a beacon which guided their Indian comrades.

Of the Indians who served with me in France, the Gurkhas were the first in the permanent trenches to bear the shock of a German attack. They laboured under great disadvantages in taking over trenches too deep for their stature, and that at a time when rain and slush made it impossible to remedy the defect. They took time to accustom themselves to the uncanny conditions, but the soldier from Nepal has a big heart in a small body ; he has the dogged characteristic of the Britisher ; he will return if he can to a trench from which he has been driven, and it will not be so easy to turn him out a second time. After the first shocks they pulled themselves together. Taciturn by nature, brave and loyal to a degree, the Gurkhas ended, as I knew they would do, second to none.

The Dogras are quiet, steady, clean soldiers, of refined appearance. A Dogra battalion always turns out smartly, and this was noticeable even in the mud-laden swamps of Flanders. They felt the first bitter cold of November 1914 more than any other class, but they faced it bravely and rendered great service.

The Sikhs are a fighting race, the Khalsa or chosen people as they style themselves. Of all Indian soldiers I know the Sikh the best and have served with him in every imaginable condition. He does not so readily imbibe discipline as many of the other classes in the Army. He has grievances born of his own imagination, and can be troublesome when it is most inconvenient for him to be so, but he is a fine manly soldier, will share your trials with genuine good humour, and can always save something in cash out of nothing. In France some of the first fighting by Indians was done by Sikhs, as I shall relate. My own motto with Sikhs is to give them all they deserve, and we owe them much, but not to spoil and pamper them.

The Jats are strapping big men as a rule, slow in movement and decision, with some of the characteristics of the Sikhs (with whom they are closely connected). They always impressed me as stubborn fighters; not brilliant, but very reliable. They did good work in France.

The Pathans have quicker wits than the other races. They can see the light side of things. They do not always answer to a call as readily as some of their comrades, but are possessed of an innate chivalry which, although it makes them quickly resent whatever may be opposed to their own ideas of honour, does not prevent them from behaving like good soldiers when appealed to. Their *élan* is their chief asset.

The Punjabi Mahomedan did well all round during the war. He proved himself a reliable soldier. The mistake made in some cases in India was to enlist men who had no claim to join the Army. There is a line of demarcation which is well understood by those who enlist this class, but was frequently glossed over in order to get recruits. Careful selection is an essential if units are not to be handicapped in war.

The Garhwalis as a distinct type were being tested for the first time in Class Corps. The 1st and 2nd Battalions of the 39th Garhwal Rifles did splendidly on every occasion in which they were engaged. In fact they surprised us all; not that we did not expect them to do well, but they suddenly sprang into the very front rank of our best fighting men. At Festubert in 1914, and at Neuve Chapelle, nothing could have been better than their *élan* and discipline, and they at once established a reputation which will live in India.

After a long experience of the Indian Army, I do not think that what are called Class Regiments (*i.e.* composed of men all of one race) are the best, or in many cases even desirable. With the exception of Gurkhas, Mazbi Sikhs, and Garhwalis, I think the other races of Northern India are at their best in war when formed in half battalions or companies and mixed with other classes. In the case of Gurkhas I only know one example of their being mixed with other races, and that was a company of the Guides.

Their case, however, stands on a different footing, as it was a Corps which was stationary in ordinary times of peace, having its Headquarters at Mardan on the North-West Frontier, and besides the Guides were an exceedingly very fine corps.   I would advocate an exception to the above statement, and that is, in the case of some of the battalions, the Class system might, in recognition of their distinguished services during the war, be given a further trial.   The reasons for what I advocate are complex, but the truth is to my thinking undeniable.   Perhaps I shall be met with the statement that this has been disproved by the Class Regiment system in this war.   I do not agree, on the contrary in my opinion it has been proved, and I have seen much proof of it.

The different races have their own characteristics ; by mixing them you get a combination of *élan*, stubbornness, and endurance ; you make it easier to maintain one form of discipline for all classes; and while giving full play to each religion and its prejudices, you eliminate the narrow-mindedness that springs of clannishness in Eastern peoples. Moreover the mixed battalion system makes it easier to introduce gradually the *lingua franca* of India throughout a Corps, so that the loss of British officers will not mean an absence of Europeans who can talk the language of their men.   This is in any case a difficult matter under any system, but with Class Corps it is a quandary.

What then is the remedy with Gurkhas who speak a language absolutely their own ?   In this case we can do our best to make Hindustani understood as far as it can be, and for the rest, to encourage in every way a knowledge of their language amongst British officers of the Indian Army who can be persuaded to learn it.   The Indian Army without these fine fighters would be like a twin-screw steamer minus one screw.   Means can be found to keep the ship in trim.

I have endeavoured to give some general impressions, formed in a long life of soldiering and also during the year I commanded the Indian Corps in the war, of my associates of all ranks.   Many names, both British and Indian, will appear in this narrative, and some of them I hope may come across this loyal tribute from one who bears them in happy and honoured memory.

To the friends of those who have passed away no words of mine can adequately express the admiration I feel for the brave comrades I am writing of. They have left behind them imperishable memories, which are a precious inheritance.

> No need of marble pile to show
> Where sleep the illustrious slain, below ;
> No need of graver's art to trace
> In lettered brass their resting-place ;
> Their own right hands in death still feared
> Eternal monument have reared.

CHAPTER V

THE doings of the Ferozepore Brigade only have so far been narrated, and it is time to describe the actions of the Lahore Division farther south. At the time I write of General Sir Horace Smith-Dorrien was in command of the 2nd Corps, and was holding the Germans attacking from the general direction of Lille towards Bethune and La Bassée.

It is no part of this story to describe the gallant fights made by this Corps between the time of its arrival in the area and the date on which the Lahore Division joined it. Suffice it to say that on the 24th October 1914 the general line held by the British ran roughly from east of Givenchy, by Neuve Chapelle bending towards the Aubers Ridge and passing Mauquissart, which is south-east of Laventie.

The names of Givenchy, Festubert, Neuve Chapelle, and Fauquissart sum up the story of our existence. That short line holds more Indian dead than the whole of the rest of Europe combined. Who would ever have believed in the last days of that cold October that we had in fact taken up our permanent abode for a year to come ?

On the 24th October the Germans made a determined attack all along our line, but were repulsed, and it is at this stage that the Lahore Division was called on to replace some of the weary and war-worn units in the firing-line. Most accounts which describe the part taken by us in this particular fighting speak of the Lahore Division as if it had been a complete unit, but as a matter of fact at that time it consisted of less than one complete Brigade, with the Divisional Artillery and a regiment of Cavalry. As if determined to keep up the splitting process to the full, in this case also the 1st Manchesters of the Jalandar Brigade had been detached to help the French Cavalry, and then the 5th Division, and was away for over a week (47th Sikhs also detached and two companies Sappers and Miners), thus leaving a few Indian battalions to start the game by themselves. The Sirhind Brigade was still detained in Egypt and did not join till December, and the Ferozepore Brigade as already described had been split up and was fighting with the British Cavalry near Ypres.

On the 24th October the Sikhs, 59th Rifles, and 34th Pioneers moved up to the support of General Conneau's French Cavalry, and later relieved that body in the trenches. The wedge thus formed by these Indian battalions was between the 8th British Infantry Brigade on their right and the 19th Infantry Brigade on their left. This relief was the first conducted by any considerable body of the Corps, and to those who did not know the nature of the country or the difficulties of such movements under fire by night, perhaps the description of it given me by an Indian officer will be the simplest explanation. " I for the first time realised the difficulties and dangers run by Burmese dacoits approaching one of our own strongly held stockades fully manned, armed, and ready for them. I used to think Dacoits were a cowardly set of rascals; I changed my mind that night."

The enemy made frequent attacks during the night, one of which, on a British unit to the right of the 15th Sikhs, succeeded in pushing through, but another British battalion immediately regained the lost trench.

The attacks continued the next day, causing us severe casualties and thoroughly trying the temper of the men. The length of trenches held was far greater than the numbers available warranted, but necessity knows no law, and to those who know the British front only as it was in after days it appears incredible that the Germans did not now, and for eight long weeks to follow, break through our attenuated line on the Indian front. It was nothing but the dogged pluck of the men, with occasional bits of good luck thrown in, that prevented it. For it must always be borne in mind that the rifle and bayonet alone were in those days the arms of the infantry soldier, and as for guns, well! they did all that such guns as we then possessed could do, but the numbers of them were few and the ammunition altogether inadequate.

The Brigade Reserve on this date consisted of the ration parties alone (all others were up in the firing-line), until a company of the 47th Sikhs arrived to rejoice the heart of the Brigadier.

Talking of rations, it was extraordinary considering all things with what regularity the men were fed; during this and other particular times of course they had often enough to do without any of their accustomed food, as the Indian soldier does not indulge in tinned supplies; but by hook or crook the company cooks would manage to send up excellent viands, frequently preparing them under conditions anything but conducive to good cookery; and I do not think G.H.Q. ever had a complaint or any cause for doubt as to the ability of the Indians to feed themselves under all circumstances, at least none ever went through me as Corps Commander.

A *langri* (cook) of a Sikh regiment whom I was talking to one day not far behind the firing-line said to me, "We like cooking close up to the trenches, or otherwise the Government may refuse to give us a clasp to our medals," and being a bit of a wag, he added, "and then in India they will call us the Marseilles *walas* (fellows)." At that time many men landed at Marseilles and never got beyond.

The three battalions were put to a high test during those first days and went through the baptism of fire most creditably. On the early morning of the 27th October the Huns made a determined attack on the 59th Rifles, which was repulsed after a severe struggle. This battalion had served under me on the Frontiers and was composed of splendid material, and any commander could have put implicit trust in it. Colonel C. Fenner, the commandant, was a most conscientious, reliable soldier; he was killed near the trenches on 23rd November 1914.

The 59th Rifles began its career as the Scinde Camel Corps in 1843, and received its present title in 1903. It consisted before the war of three companies of Pathans, one of Punjabi-Musalmans, two of Sikhs, and two of Dogras. The regimental motto is " Ready, aye ready."

The 15th Sikhs had always been considered a crack corps in the Indian Army, and at the beginning of the war had as fine a lot of men as the Punjab could furnish. As time went on, like all other corps they had to take what they could get, but later in Egypt the General in command of the Brigade to which they were attached sent them a very satisfactory order, showing that a good battalion utilises its material to the best purpose. John Hill, then C.O., was a sturdy officer, whom I could always trust to place duty above personal considerations. Later he commanded a British Brigade. The 15th Sikhs were originally raised at "Ludhiana" in 1846, and had served in six campaigns from China to Tirah. It was a Class Corps of eight companies of Sikhs.

The 34th Pioneers consisted of Mazbi and Ramdasia Sikhs, and was commanded by Lieut.-Colonel E. H. Cullen. This battalion had served with me across the Indian Frontiers, and did very good work in France on all occasions when it was employed ; and as the work of a Pioneer Corps is never-ending, this means it well maintained its reputation. Like everything else in the early days of the war, it started with work which should if possible have been performed by another corps, but Pioneers were also trained for every kind of work in the field, in case of necessity. The battalion was raised in 1887, and had served in Chitral and China.

Sir John French sent his congratulations to the Jalandar Brigade for the manner in which they had done their share in the line.

For two more days the Indian battalions held on to their positions. I say advisedly " held on," for their numbers were very limited, and only the reinforcement by the 15th Indian Lancers enabled them to repulse two strong German attacks. On the 1st November the Manchesters and 47th Sikhs rejoined their own Brigade. The former had suffered some 100 casualties during its detachment, and the 47th had lost very heavily in its gallant fight at Neuve Chapelle (not to be confounded with the battle, which did not take place till March 1915), as I shall relate.

Between the 24th October and 1st November 1914 the Indian battalions engaged on this part of the line had suffered 705 casualties or practically the strength of a whole battalion, which numbered 750 at war strength.

The 15th Sikhs lost three British and three Indian officers wounded, including Lieut.-Colonel J. L. Gordon, then temporarily in command. The 34th Pioneers lost their interpreter, Captain G. H. Vaughan-Sawyer—killed, whilst two British and three Indian officers were wounded.

In the 59th Rifles Captain W. F. Scott was killed, and a fine specimen of an Indian leader, Captain K. D. Murray, was severely wounded, and in addition two Indian officers were wounded.

The 47th Sikhs (excluding their losses near Neuve Chapelle) had two more British officers and 118 men wounded, making a total for the first few days' experience of trench warfare of 294 casualties out of a strength of 750.

The names of many Indian officers were brought to notice, of which I particularly remember that of Subadar Natha Singh, 34th Pioneers, who took command of his portion of the defence after his British officers had been wounded.

It was during these events, to be accurate on the 27th October, that I reached my first Headquarters at Merville; it was also a year later to be my last, but that was still a long time ahead and unfortunately we cannot read the future. I took a sheet of paper to make a rough estimate of the whereabouts of my Army Corps, and I will quote what I find noted on it. It will give any one reading this an idea of what I felt, after my hopes that we might get a few days, or even hours, if possible to get into shape before actually entering the trenches.

General Watkis had had a rough experience of what breaking up a Division means, and he had with great loyalty accepted what was naturally a blow to a Divisional commander. It was a condition of things not only never contemplated, but opposed to all the principles on which the Brigades of the Army of India were constituted. If, then, here and there, things did not meet with the approval of the Higher Command, the cause did not lie at our doors. Orders must be obeyed.

As each battalion rejoined the Corps it brought its own story of the fighting ; a confused medley of combats fought heaven knows where, mixed up with British troops, none of whom the Indians had ever set eyes on before.

Sir John French's despatch of 20th November 1914 says, "The Lahore Division had concentrated on the 19th and 20th October," and on the 29th I find in my Diary :

Extract from Diary :

" Where is my Lahore Division ? "

Sirhind Brigade. Detained in Egypt.

Ferozepore Brigade. Somewhere in the north, split up into three or four lots.

Jalandar Brigade. Manchesters gone south to 5th Division (this disposes of the only British unit).

47th Sikhs. Half fighting with some British Division; half somewhere else !

59th and 15th Sikhs. In trenches. 34th Pioneers (Divisional troops) also in trenches.

15th Lancers. In trenches. Two Companies of Sappers and Miners fighting as Infantry with British Division.

Divisional Headquarters. Somewhere. ?

"Thank heaven the Meerut Division will get a better chance." Ends.

However, what did anything matter so long as we were actually to be allowed to collect and go into our very own trenches ?

Before beginning the story of the combined Corps it is necessary to tell the story of the first fight in the village of Neuve Chapelle, a village later to become famous in Indian history as the first in Europe in which, on a big scale, her soldiers attacked, dispersed, and drove from their positions the Germans in their own chosen and defended trenches.

Neuve Chapelle had already been the scene of severe fighting, portions of it being taken and retaken by the 7th and 9th British Brigades, until on the 27th October the enemy

F

bringing up considerable reinforcements gained possession of the whole village. Pushing his advantage vigorously, our gallant fellows were forced to retire, until a considerable salient was created in our defensive line, and one which it was imperative to straighten out if possible. The Wiltshires, Lancashires, and West Kents had been fighting all they knew, and there was a possibility of a wedge being driven between our Fifth and Third Divisions.

I have in my possession a very full description of the part played by a portion of the Indian troops, who were now called on to support the situation, and later to take part in the attack on the village. I can, however, make little use of this, as the orders received by different units were not only very vague, but one at least did not receive them until after the attack on the 28th had already begun. It was therefore impossible in this case to make any arrangements, and all that could be done was to join in as best they could.

What is clear is that half of the 47th Sikhs were on the 27th October ordered to counter-attack, with the 9th Bhopal Infantry in support, some trenches from which part of a British battalion had been forced to retire. The 9th Bhopals in the intricate country temporarily lost touch with the Sikhs and moved, as I shall tell further on. The 47th soon met the O.C. Lincolns, and the battalion was directed to advance and assist the companies of the Lincolns who were held up ; one company under Major H. E. Browne on the left, and another half company under Captain R. J. M'Cleverty on the right advanced, whilst half a company under Major S. R. Davidson was kept in hand.

Facing a heavy fire of machine-guns and howitzers, the 47th Sikhs receiving their baptism of fire, for the first time since raised in 1901, pushed forward, covering themselves with honour, and not halting a moment until they were into, and in the case of one platoon beyond, the farthest trenches occupied by the Lincolns. From this no farther advance was possible with the limited numbers at disposal.

During this advance Major Browne and two Indian officers were wounded, and seven men were killed and twenty-eight wounded. I have given details more fully than is perhaps necessary, but this as I said was the first experience the battalion had under fire, and it served to brace them up and spur them to the deeds which they so nobly wrought throughout their stay in France.

At 1 A.M. on the morning of the 28th October the 47th were ordered to move and take over the trenches of the Wiltshires, but on arrival learnt that they had already been relieved by the 20th and 21st Companies of Indian Sappers and Miners, and the 47th took up their position in a ditch 200 yards in rear, as daylight was appearing.

To those who know the Indian Army it will at once be evident that to employ such highly trained technical troops as Sappers as ordinary Infantry was to extract the very marrow from a Division engaged in this sort of siege warfare. As well employ a battle-ship to scout for destroyers ; but in those early days of the war the Lahore Division was turned topsy-turvy at every stage of its progress, and that it emerged fit to fight at all is its highest testimonial.

Early on the 28th October the half battalion of the 47th Sikhs was holding a line between the 20th and 21st Companies Sappers and Miners, with a frontage of some 800 yards, when orders were issued for the battalion to make a frontal attack in conjunction with their comrades of the Sappers. The plan of attack was laid down, and was to converge on a point in Neuve Chapelle which was indicated in the orders, and to be carried out without a stop.

Whilst these are waiting to carry out this duty, let us return to the 9th Bhopal Infantry, whom I left under orders to counter-attack with the 47th Sikhs on the 27th October. This battalion had arrived at Vieille Chapelle from near Ypres on that day, travelling by motor buses, then a novel means of locomotion for Indian troops. It brought no machine-guns (mark this) and very soon after received orders to move to Rouge Croix, and whilst *en route* further orders directed it to detach half a battalion to support the 47th Sikhs in their counter-attack, already described. This constant splitting up of battalions was one of the most senseless proceedings.

Touch was lost in the difficult country, but eventually this half battalion got into communication with the Royal Scots on their left, and after further varying fortunes reached the vicinity of another British unit, the West Kents.

The 9th then came into contact with the Germans to the south of Neuve Chapelle, killing several of them, and assisting in checking an enemy advance against the flank of a neighbouring unit.

Lieut.-Colonel H. L. Anderson, second in command, was mortally wounded, and Lieutenant J. C. Mullaly, son of a gallant General and old comrade of mine, was taken prisoner while endeavouring to stem an enemy rush, amid fighting which, owing to many causes, was becoming a confused medley, Germans firing from every direction. The situation now was that a big gap existed between the 9th and the 47th Sikhs, which was filled by No. 20 Company Sappers and Miners.

Before mid-day on the 28th we thus see that the two Indian half battalions and the two companies of Sappers and Miners were spread over a considerable frontage, and about to attack the village of Neuve Chapelle. It was at this stage purely an Indian fight, no British troops being engaged on this portion of the attack; why, I cannot say.

Major G. A. Jamieson of the 9th Bhopals has left it on record that the orders for his battalion only reached him at 11.15 A.M., *i.e.* after the attack had already commenced. Under such conditions all the battalion could do was to detach as many men as possible to help the Sappers and Miners who were on the move and advancing. Jamieson later on died of wounds received in Mesopotamia; I had known him for many years. Son of a soldier and descended from a long line of fighting men, he was one of the keenest of officers, always trying to do something to improve the efficiency of his men.

The moment had now come, and the Indians are advancing with the proud satisfaction that this is their own fight and that the eyes of their British comrades are on them.

The Artillery bombardment which preceded the attack

had hardly ceased, when the open country was already fast being crossed by our men ; of shelter there was little, but this only made the pace the faster, and 600 yards had soon been covered although with considerable losses.

The men, well led by their officers, were now thoroughly blooded, and raising the war-cry of " Shri wa guru ji ka khalsa," and the final yell of " Fateh," the Sikhs, and with them, every whit as keen, the two companies of Sappers, lowered their bayonets to the charge and were amongst the foe inside the village of Neuve Chapelle.

The Germans from houses all round kept up a heavy fire, but the Indian soldiers were not to be denied, and using the bayonet they cleared the streets, entering houses and killing freely, always fighting hand to hand. It was a glorious day for the Indian Army, and the story, although briefly told in despatches, is one of which the Sikhs as a race, and the Sappers and Miners as a Corps, may well be proud.

An officer of a British Corps, whose fighting zeal had led him into the fray, in describing it said : " I climbed up into a house and looked down the street, and the way those fellows fought was a sight to remember " ; and General Sir Horace Smith-Dorrien himself told me a few days later that from every side he heard nothing but the highest praise of the Indians.

Meantime the fight was raging in the centre of the village; Captain M'Cleverty, the bravest of the brave, leading his Sikhs, fell dead under a shot from a concealed German. This man was at once accounted for by a Punjabi Mahomedan of the Sappers. Through a hail of machine-gun fire both Corps continued the struggle, and had soon cleared the main street.

The Germans were meantime bringing heavy counter-attacks to bear on our scattered troops, but Davidson of the 47th was not the man to succumb to any foe, and was trying to form up for a final charge, when the Huns opened rapid fire from several machine-guns, literally sweeping the streets, and no reinforcements were at hand and there were no signs of them coming. Thus overwhelmed, the brave Sikhs were obliged to fall back. Once again they crossed the 600 yards of open ground, in retreat 'tis true, but covered with glory. They had left a mark behind them which must have impressed even their enemies, and as a German prisoner said months afterwards, they had taught his people a lesson which they remembered throughout the time they faced the Indian Corps. Davidson received the well-merited distinction of Brevet Lieut.-Colonel.

Had reinforcements been sent up the battle of Neuve Chapelle in March 1915 might never have been necessary ; but in war it is so often an " If." What is sure, and that is what concerns me here, is that the Indians fought in a manner which at once established their reputation as first-class fighting men.

The two companies of the 47th Sikhs went into action 289 of all ranks, and the muster-roll after the fight was 144, or a loss of exactly 50 per cent of their numbers. Amongst these were two Indian officers, of whom one was killed.

The 47th Sikhs was raised at Sialkote in 1901 as the 47th (Sikh) Regiment of Bengal Infantry, and received its present designation in 1903. It was composed of eight companies of Sikhs.

The 21st Company Sappers and Miners were all this time sharing to the full the brunt of the fighting. Captain J. S. Richardson was killed while leading a charge on the enemy's side of the village through which the men had swept ; and Almond and Rohde, his two Subalterns, shared his fate. Lieutenant Fitzmaurice was severely wounded, and nearly 60 other ranks out of 140 completed the casualties : A list which included every British officer borne on its rolls, and not one remained to direct the operations of a unit in which all skilled officers who knew their men were needed. The I.D.S.M. was conferred on Subadars Ismail Khan and Ganga Charn Dixit.

Their comrades of the 20th Company were likewise fighting hard ; when it was seen that reinforcements were not coming Lieutenant Nosworthy, rather than retire, hurriedly erected a barricade in a side street, and from this and two neighbouring houses kept the enemy at bay, until at last, seeing no further use in delay, he and his gallant band, now under twenty men, worked their way back over the open.

What a splendid record did this Sapper Company compile in a few brief hours of that October day. Lieutenant E. Hayes-Sadler was killed leading an attack on some German machine-guns which were playing havoc from a spot outside the village, he and his men being literally mown down. Lieutenant Rait-Kerr was severely wounded while voluntarily crossing the open to bring up reinforcements, but endeavoured nevertheless to try and rejoin his commanding officer. Captain Paris, who had boldly led the company from the start, was also severely wounded.

Like its sister company the 21st Sappers and Miners, the 20th also came out of action with the loss of all its British officers. Trained to the technical branches of their profession, they could still fight as Infantry with the best, even when they knew that " Some one had blundered."

Sapper Dalip Singh single-handed kept off numerous Germans, helped Lieutenant Rait-Kerr into safety, and gained the Indian Order of Merit for his bravery.

The Military Cross was the reward of Subadar Malla Singh, and the Order of British India that of Subadar Ganpat Mahadeo, both of whom earned their decorations by conspicuous coolness and skill.

The Indian Corps of Sappers and Miners is too well known to need description here ; as Sir John French said in his despatch of November 1914, they " have long enjoyed a high reputation for skill and resource," and " they have fully justified their reputation." I would only add, that ever after in the war they added greatly to it. I look forward with keen pleasure to visiting them again.

The 9th Bhopal Infantry, whom we left just when they had received their orders to join in the attack, found themselves in a dilemma, but Major Jamieson hastily told off as many men as were at his disposal to work along with the Sappers and Miners who were already advancing. The result was that while some parties got into Neuve Chapelle, and one under Jamieson passed through the village, they were compelled to retire and suffered considerable losses.   Lieut.-Colonel Anderson, second in command, died of wounds, and one Indian officer was killed ; Captain L. J. Jones and Lieutenant H. Wade were wounded and missing ; Lieutenant Mullaly, as already stated, was unfortunately captured, and Captain G. Irvine wounded ; the total casualties including missing were just under 300.

The 9th Bhopal Infantry was raised in 1859, and reconstituted and received its present title in 1903.   It served in Afghanistan 1878–79, and consisted of two companies of Sikhs, two of Rajputs, two of Brahmins, and two of Musalmans.   It was quartered in Fyzabad when war broke out, and I had inspected it early that year.   It was under orders for Secunderabad in the next reliefs, but so keen were all ranks to go to the north of India, and so eagerly did they do their field work, that I recommended to the Commander-in-Chief they should be given a chance on the Frontiers.   The battalion was not on the mobilisation list, but the Chief selected it to fill a gap, and hence it was sent to France.   Later it went to Mesopotamia and took part in the fighting there.

Sir John French, as he always did, acknowledged the good work done by all ranks, both before and on this day, in a telegram in which he said : " Please congratulate your Indian troops on their gallant conduct, and express my gratitude to them."

CHAPTER VI

I HAVE told the story of the Indian Corps up to the date of the arrival of the Meerut Division on the British Front. This Division began its experiences in the trenches on the 29th October, from which date the portion of the line allotted to the Corps came under my command. In place of the Sirhind Brigade detained in Egypt, and the Ferozepore Brigade still away in the north near Ypres, I was given two British Brigades of the Second Army Corps; in addition, two extra battalions were temporarily left with me. With the arrival of the Secunderabad Cavalry Brigade and Jodhpore Lancers, I was able to count on another 1000 men as long as this Brigade might be left at my disposal.

In nearly all the accounts of our doings at this time I find it stated that two and a half Brigades were left to strengthen the Indian Corps; giving the impression that these were in addition to our own full numbers. This is of course entirely erroneous. As a matter of fact, even with the two and a half Brigades lent to us, the Corps was far under the strength of British Army Corps; while in the matter of guns we had nothing but the bare complement of field guns and two heavy batteries of four guns each. In consequence the Second Corps left us, to start with, a proportion of its Corps Artillery.

Sir John French had said to me on the night of my arrival, " Are you prepared to take over the front of the Second Corps at once ? " and I replied, " Certainly." If it had been twice as long, and had we been half our strength, I should have made the same reply. We had arrived and were going to take on anything ordered, and I felt confident we were going to do it well; and looking back on it all, now that one can take an unbiassed retrospect, there is only one conclusion to which honest soldiers will come and that is that all ranks, British and Indians, did their duty nobly and deserve well of their King and our country.

Headquarters were established at Hinges (pronounced by us phonetically), a large château not far from Béthune. In a very few hours we had adapted ourselves to circumstances; electric lights, telephones, and telegraphs were all erected with surprising speed, the Indian Signalling Company under Captain Franklin working as if it had been accustomed to such luxuries, though here they were absolute necessities.

The Indian servants adapted themselves at once to kitchen ranges, and meals were served up as if in an Indian bungalow. In the hall, orderlies and messengers, French, British and Indian, fraternised and exchanged a jargon of words; outside stood a couple of German prisoners guarded by a mud-bespattered trooper, waiting to be interrogated. What must have been their feelings as they watched the medley, and heard the mother tongues of races as far apart as London and Peshawar.

As I leaned over the banisters, I felt a stern joy that it was my good fortune to be entrusted for the first time in war with so varied a task as the control of such divergent elements of humanity, in the heart of a great European country.

Before General Smith-Dorrien handed over the command and left the château, I had the advantage of a long conversation with him. For him I have a great admiration, and I felt his advice would be valuable, and in those two hours I learned much which stood me in good stead during the war. I discovered that in addition to his own war-seasoned Army Corps he had had an extra Brigade. This was news to me; and as I was taking over his front I knew I must hold my trenches very lightly. He knew India and its troops, and had been Adjutant-General as well as commander of a Division in that country, so could speak from personal experience. I received many useful hints from him, and as he drove away I felt we had with the Expeditionary Force a General who thoroughly under-

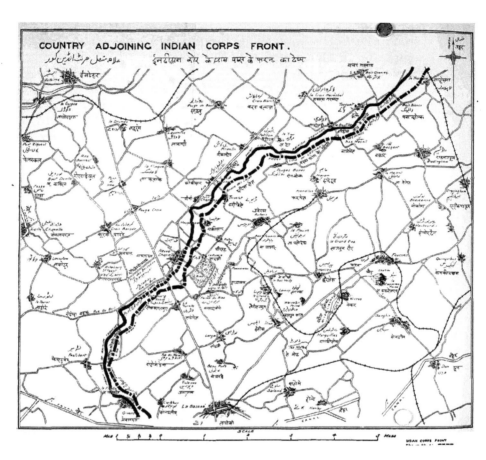

COUNTRY ADJOINING INDIAN CORPS FRONT.

stood the Corps, and when the day came, which it soon must, for the formation into Armies, I hoped might have us in his command.

With the exception of Sir John French and Smith-Dorrien I was at that time the senior officer in France, but I never for an instant suffered under the delusion that this 'meant anything to me. I had come with the Indians, and I knew that there I should remain and so long only as they chose to keep me. Commands of Armies were altitudes too dizzy to be reached by a soldier who had lived in khaki it is true, but had worn it in far-away portions of the Empire, and had seldom been seen on the Downs of Salisbury or in the purlieus of Pall Mall or Whitehall.

The front assigned to the Corps was about eight miles in length from north of Givenchy on our right, passing east of Festubert and Richebourg l'Avoue (only a name on the map), west of Neuve Chapelle, past Mauquissart, and taking a bend to Rouges Bancs on our left.

The Meerut Division held the southern portion of the trenches in the following order, commencing from Givenchy: Bareilly, Garhwal, and Dehra Dun Brigades; with the Jalandar Brigade of the Lahore Division on the left. This takes no account of the extra British Brigades which filled gaps as occasion required, until our own two absent Brigades rejoined us.

The night of the 29th October was ushered in by a storm of rain, and through the bogs, ditches, and darkness officers and men tramped to their first battle positions. It was difficult, but every one was keen to try it and learn for himself what manner of game it was that was being played in this novel war. And they soon enough learned it, for within a few hours of their arrival our Indian troops took the first shock. The 2nd battalion 8th Gurkhas was the unit which happened to be holding the portion of trenches chosen by the Hun to test our men in. Throughout the night the Gurkhas were subjected to a heavy fire—shells, rifles, and machine-guns all taking their toll; several Infantry attacks were also made but none were pushed home; and occupying trenches a foot too deep for them under a deluge of rain, the men from Nepal went through a severe ordeal. It was found impossible, under the circumstances, to do anything to improve the trenches, which in many places were merely the ordinary water channels or broad ditches, affording no shelter.

At dawn the Germans made a fresh attack, which however gave them no advantage, and about 8 o'clock concentrated a heavy shell-fire on the 8th Gurkhas and Devons, who with them formed the left of the line of the Bareilly Brigade. For four hours this inferno continued, and, as the Headquarters 5th Division reported, the trenches were seriously damaged.

From 11 A.M. onwards attacks followed one another in rapid succession, but these were splendidly repulsed. Before mid-day Colonel Morris, who was in command of the 8th, began to doubt if his ammunition would last out, and, whilst making the best arrangements possible, observed that the trenches held by Captain E. Hayes-Sadler and Wright were being heavily attacked. For an hour this attack continued. Major Wake also felt the full brunt of an attack against his trench, and on all sides the Gurkhas were being assailed, but held on. By 1.30 P.M. the whole battalion was in the firing-line.

Morris now sent word to General Macbean, his Brigadier, asking for reinforcements and saying his ammunition could not last much longer. He directed Major Wake to hold out at all hazards, which orders that gallant soldier carried on to the death. Captains Hayes-Sadler and H. Wright were killed whilst stemming the advancing tide. Captain E. Stack, although severely wounded, attempted to deliver a message and in this glorious act was again struck down, and killed. Major Barlow, already three times wounded, by strenuous exertions succeeded in driving back a German attack on the right, but here he found his men outflanked and the enemy in his rear, and whilst still endeavouring to do his duty he collapsed into a trench but fortunately after some time recovered his senses and survived to tell the tale.

Captain B. Hartwell was killed, and Colonel Morris, who from first to last had displayed every quality of an intrepid leader, was severely wounded, and lay in a trench till found by his men. He lived to command them once more, and died fighting on the day of Loos in September 1915.

Lieutenant MacLean carried on, although wounded, until unable to continue any longer ; and Captain Davidson was missing. Till half-past three o'clock the Gurkhas held on to their line, when a heavy attack succeeded in driving them from their fire trenches. Of Indian officers two were killed, one wounded, and two missing, and the casualties in other ranks totalled 207.

This serious set-back was caused chiefly by the right of the battalion being turned, thus exposing them to a flank attack ; but even this might have been averted under conditions less trying to new troops. The merciless shell-fire, the weather, and the trenches, useless to short men, all combined to severely shake them and afforded little opportunity of recovering the lost ground. They had to do what better troops have done over and over again in this war, viz. learn their lesson. It was a severe one and it takes time to obliterate the memory of such an ordeal, but that the battalion was soon again able to take its share in the heavy fighting in Flanders is the best tribute to its tenacity.

Whilst the companies which had suffered most made the best of their way back from the trenches, Major Cassels held his portion of the line, but was, like the remainder, eventually forced back, and Captain Buckland with a company rejoined his Headquarters that evening.

The shortage of British officers is well exemplified by this action, as owing to the number of casualties amongst them I was obliged to send Major Tomkins of the 28th Punjabis, my Assistant Military Secretary, to assume command of the battalion, no other officer in the Corps being available. An officer who had been present throughout the retreat from Mons told one of my Staff that he never experienced a heavier shelling than the Gurkhas were exposed to that day.

A pleasant reminiscence is the recollection of the ungrudging help given by the British Corps in the vicinity.

As soon as it was seen that the Gurkhas were being subjected to a very severe shelling and that the enemy was launching one attack after another at them, their comrades of the gallant English regiments whether in first line or in support at once came to their help.   Sir Horace Smith-Dorrien directed that the Bedfords and West Ridings, who were down for relief, were not to be withdrawn that night, and the Norfolks and Devons also remained on temporarily, until the situation could be cleared up and the line re-established.   An Indian officer who had been through the mill, in telling me about it said, " I do not know a word of English but I will remember the names *Napak* (Norfolk) and *Diban* (Devons), they are *burra bahadurs* (very brave men)."

And this gives me the opportunity of repeating with what real admiration the Indian soldiers looked on their British comrades, not only of the fine battalions which formed part of the Indian Corps, but Britishers of all Corps. It has been an example and a lesson that will never be forgotten, and under many a village tree as the sun goes down over Indian hills and plains the old soldiers of the days to come will recite to their listening brethren tales of the great days when the *Gora log* (white men) dashed themselves against heavy odds or hurled back the Kaiser's legions.

The enemy had gained a success, but he was not going to be allowed to retain his hold, and a counter-attack was led by the West Ridings and Bedfords, with the 58th Rifles and 107th Pioneers in support.   The attack succeeded in clearing the enemy out of his captured trenches nearly to the late support line of the Gurkhas ; and the 58th Rifles from this point were pushed through to the assault.   The Hun had had his fling and it was now his turn to run, with the result that the support trenches were captured with some farm-houses near them.   These were at once subjected to a severe shelling which caused many casualties, amongst them Colonel W. E. Venour commanding the 58th and Lieutenant J. M. Craig (attached to the battalion from the 57th Rifles) were both killed.

The 58th lost also a good soldier, Captain and Adjutant

W. Black, who was killed whilst closely reconnoitring the German trenches prior to the assault; but the regiment kept a firm hold of its gains at a cost of the lives of three British officers and five other ranks killed, and four Indian officers and eighty others wounded. The enemy still retained some of the Gurkha trenches he had captured earlier in the day.

I had known the 2nd battalion 8th Gurkha Rifles since 1886 when they were known as the 43rd Gurkha Light Infantry, and they had borne many different titles since, being reorganised as the 2/8th Gurkha Rifles in 1907. I had served beside them in Burmah 1885–87. They were composed of a fine sturdy lot of men, and had they not had the misfortune to start their very first day in France exposed to a prolonged shelling, followed by a series of heavy attacks, they would not have been so heavily handicapped during the entire campaign as they were by the loss of practically all their own officers at one sweep— the most severe trial an Indian battalion can possibly undergo.

The 58th Vaughans Rifles was an old Punjab Frontier Force battalion; and I soldiered alongside it in the days when it was known as the 5th Punjab Infantry. It was given its present title in 1903. The ranks were filled by Sikhs, Dogras, Pathans, and Punjabi-Musalmans. The battalion took part in nearly all the fighting of the Indian Corps in France, and was ably commanded by Lieut.-Colonel Davidson-Houston, who succeeded to it on the death of Colonel Venour; he later was awarded the D.S.O. and was killed in the attack on the German trenches opposite Mauquissart on the 25th September 1915, and thus the regiment lost two of its commanding officers. One of the last letters he ever wrote was to me (mostly about his beloved battalion) on the eve of his death.

No. 1811, Havildar Karam Singh of the 58th was awarded the Indian Order of Merit for gallantly remaining on in command of his section after being severely wounded.

The Army Corps being now established in its trenches, with different members of my Staff I began a regular round of various portions of the front and visits to the Divisional commanders and Brigadiers. During these tours, which I kept up regularly throughout my tenure of command, I saw over and over again every battalion, regiment and battery in the Corps and inspected every unit forming the Transport, Supply, Medical, etc., and of course every detail of the Hospitals, from the trenches to the railhead. I made a regular practice of doing as much of all this as it was possible to do on horseback, and I am convinced that no ordinary person on the Staff should ever have had a day's sickness who, wet or fine, mud or dust, took his exercise, and hard exercise too, without fail. Of course the regimental officers and men and all others connected with them had to live a life not only of daily labour, peril and discomfort, but had to do it on foot, and to them must always be awarded the palm of all toil. But I am now writing of the higher Staffs ; whatever their responsibilities, they lived in comfort, they slept in houses, and shared comparatively few of the dangers of the war, and yet there were some who were too fond of the motor car, and whose horses stood idle awaiting the great advance, which did not come till four years later.

Perpetual bodily exercise in war, as in peace, should be insisted on in all ranks ; it is the fulcrum of the health lever. In the early days of the war and in the bog which is an ever-present feature of the Flanders landscape I found it most difficult to get to the advanced trenches owing to the impossibility of dragging my steel-bound leg (a legacy of past campaigns) through the mud, and more than once in consequence I found myself riding past sentries who had been posted on roads leading to the vicinity of the trenches to stop all horses or vehicles proceeding any farther. I suppose it was wrong to disobey orders, but the gallant sentinels generally let me pass, only remarking, " All right, pass as the orders are your own." It was always an interesting experience.

After we had managed to dig communication trenches and improve the drainage, and as the wet decreased, visits to the firing-line were not only in themselves a very good form of exercise, but in truth the most interesting and exciting exercise one could take. I can see the reader, who perhaps spent most of his days in that unenviable region, smile, but I say again, for a General and his Staff the visits to the trenches form their most pleasant recollections.

When one talks of riding across country, it has to be borne in mind that during October and even into November there were days when this was quite feasible, later on it became absolutely necessary to stick to the roads, or what went by that name, as the fields were mere bogs ; and often have I been in deep sympathy with my brave chargers, who hammered along the stony tracks or *pavés*. It had to be done, however, if riding was to be a means of conveyance, and I had the satisfaction of feeling that in the case of my favourite arab, "Arabi Pasha," no one after his own master would ever mount the faithful horse, and I believe he knew it also. It was one of the farewells one does not wish to repeat.

What manner of country was it in which the Indian Corps now found itself ? A dismal dead plain, dotted with farm-houses and here and there clumps of trees. The uninteresting roads metalled only in the centre ; ditches and drains in every direction ; observation beyond a very limited distance impossible, and for months the morning mists enveloped everything in a thick haze well into mid-day ; canals, crossed here and there by bridges, added to the difficulties of communication. The fields soon became impassable ; ditto the paths except on foot ; rain fell almost daily ; snow fell heavily in November ; the trenches were first turned into water-channels and then frozen over. Above, the aeroplanes seemed the only moving things besides the clouds ; below was a water-logged soil, and on the surface lived and died men who will be handed down for all time as heroes. This monotonous land boasted no hills and valleys, not even a mound ; it was just a flat dreary expanse in winter, and studded with green leaves and some wild flowers in summer.

Only a few hundred yards beyond us lay the Aubers Ridge which we were never to reach, and a small wood east of Neuve Chapelle of which I shall have much to say, and which went by the name of the Bois du Biez. I have since been to Flanders to see that wood, for on it I longingly gazed for ten months, and my last day in France was spent in the trenches exactly opposite to it.

It was plain to see that with our weak battalions and the impossibility of receiving Indian reinforcements, it would be necessary to have in hand a small reserve. The only reserve I could count on was the Secunderabad Cavalry Brigade. Much as I hated doing it, I informed G.H.Q., and although the Commander-in-Chief was sorely pressed for troops I eventually got three battalions, and I forthwith wrote to say that I was now quite happy as to my position. I mention this as, although it may have been inconvenient or even dangerous to weaken the line elsewhere, the Indian Corps was the extreme right of the British line and joined hands with our French allies near Givenchy, and it would have been a blunder to allow any gap being created in that vicinity.

I also at once got into touch with the French Generals and commanders on my right, and we mutually arranged to support one another whenever it might become necessary. We became the best of friends, and many a time did I lend or borrow troops or guns for various operations.

The 2nd November was a day of trial for the Indian troops, as on that morning the 2nd Gurkhas, which held the trenches to the east of the road junction a mile N.E. of Pont Logy and N.W. of Neuve Chapelle, which formed an acute salient in our general outpost line, were furiously attacked. This salient was very much in the air; the trenches were badly sited and could hardly be called trenches at all; there was no plan; salients were open to enfilade fire and the position as a whole was practically untenable. In addition it was isolated from the rear by a spinney and orchard.

The Gurkhas were dumped into it on the night of the 29th and 30th October, and as the C.O. said at the time, there was no option but to hold and make the best of it. The Germans, who were only some forty to sixty yards distant, knew exactly the weakness of the position, and determined to take advantage of it, and with this object in view were fast sapping up to it.

The attack was opened with high explosive shell, and a trench mortar which was some 400 yards distant threw one shell after another in rapid succession, fired with a precision which showed they had the exact range and correct target; the trenches were soon practically obliterated and the occupants blown up, killed, or wounded, the position being rendered still more difficult by the fact that we were being enfiladed. Simultaneously with this the enemy commenced throwing hand-grenades from the saps they had run up close to our line, and No. 3 Company's trench was made the target for these, rendering its right half untenable. Aided by all these devices the Hun Infantry dashed into No. 1 and 2 Company's trenches, specially selecting any remaining British officers as their victims.

It is well to once remind those who may read this that all the story of those days must be read in the light of facts as they existed. With the accounts of fighting at a later date before them, they are apt to forget the dark days of 1914 when our men had to face mortars, hand-grenades, high explosive shell, and a hundred other engines or contrivances of war, with which they themselves were not provided. Here were these gallant fellows just arrived and exposed to every form of terror, and they could reply only with their valour and the rifles and two machine-guns per battalion with which they were armed, and yet they did it.

The left half of No. 3 Company's trench and that of No. 4 Company still remained; these were echeloned back to the left, towards the Connaught Rangers, and they were held till nightfall. The Irishmen, seeing the state of affairs and the tempest sweeping over the Gurkhas, first sent one platoon to their assistance, and followed it with two others.

At this juncture Lieut. J. Reid, the only surviving officer, ordered the occupants of No. 3 trench to fall back towards the left trenches; but the communication trench was full of dying and wounded, and as they crossed the open they suffered heavily. The survivors in the trenches who had managed to hold on were brought out late in the evening by Subadars Dalbahadur Rana and Fateh Singh Newar; this latter officer received the Order of British India for his conduct, and the commanding officer specially mentioned as fighting well and holding on to the last Jemadars Kharak Bahadur Gurung and Tirthe Gurung, who was wounded, as well as Bahadur Ghale and Suba Singh Gurung.

The 1st Battalion 9th Gurkhas were on the right of the 2nd, and well thrown back. Lieut.-Colonel C. E. Norie, commander of the 2nd Gurkhas, carries only one arm, having left the other in the mountains of Tirah; but with one arm he also has but one heart, and it is a brave one.

He was near the battalion reserve when the German attack began, and at once moved with it to the right of his forward trenches; having located the mortar which was doing all the execution, he silenced it by a concentrated fire; shortly after he again moved to his left as his ammunition was exhausted; having replenished this and meeting a squadron of the 34th Poona Horse coming up in support, Norie moved his reserve forward with the squadron to assist in the defence of his left trenches. Met by a furious machine-gun fire, this advance was held up as these trenches had meantime been captured by the enemy.

About 2 o'clock the Gurkhas were subjected to a concentrated fire of high explosive shell and had to move north. That evening reinforcements of Royal Scots Fusiliers and an Indian battalion arrived, and the 9th Gurkhas on the right were also reinforced by a portion of the 6th Jats and 7th Dragoon Guards. Norie himself advanced with the Royal Scots Fusiliers and his own men, and this party got within twenty yards of the Germans, but were then held up by machine-guns. One officer of the Fusiliers was killed and two officers of the Gurkhas were wounded; but although the push did not succeed in getting home, it was too much for the Huns, who forthwith left and returned to their own trenches, and ours were reoccupied.

At this stage Brig.-General Bowes commanding the 8th British Brigade, which was one of the two left with the Indian Corps, issued fresh orders and a new line was begun to be consolidated. During the time General Bowes was with me he invariably rendered good service, always being ready to take on any job.

Such is the story of the first experience of another fine unit being initiated in the form of fighting in Flanders, and brings to light the discipline and tenacity of the Gurkhas of Nepal. The odds were immense, but although hard hit they were ready to take part in a counter-attack, and their British and Indian officers performed many deeds of gallantry.

I have described the part taken by Colonel Norie, and his own Brigadier, C. E. Johnson, and General Anderson commanding the Meerut Division wrote in the highest terms of him and his battalion. Sir John French too wrote in his despatch: "The situation was prevented from becoming serious by the excellent leadership displayed by Colonel Norie of the 2nd Gurkhas." A very special compliment, as he was the only officer in the Indian Army Corps mentioned by name in this despatch. He was rewarded with a Brevet-Colonelcy.

Of the officers killed, Major H. S. Becher met his death in covering a portion of the retiring line. Lieutenants J. H. Walcott and I. Innes died leading a charge against the enemy as they were nearing our trenches.

Lieut. Reid, after hard fighting, fell whilst coolly conducting a relieving party of the Connaught Rangers to the Gurkha trenches. Lieut. Lucas was killed whilst collecting his men, and the same shell blew up several of them also.

Major Ross and Subadar Major Man Singh Bohra heroically led a charge which ended in a hand-to-hand fight, during which they and most of their men were killed.

Major N. Macpherson and Captain F. Barton fell at their posts.

Subadars Tekhbahadur Gurung and Gopal Singh Rawat were killed in the counter-attack with Innes and Walcott, and Subadar Chet Singh fell with them.

In the Connaught Rangers, Lieut. G. D. Abbott was killed while moving up with his company in the open to the help of the Gurkhas, and with him fell many of his brave Irish. Lieut. Hewitt of the same battalion was wounded, but the rest held on to their trench during the night. The Rangers suffered forty casualties.

In the 34th Poona Horse, the C.O., Lieut.-Colonel C. O. Swanston, a very keen and earnest soldier, was killed at the head of his men whilst crossing up to the support of the Gurkhas, and in this regiment Sowar Madhu was given the Indian Order of Merit for saving the life of a wounded Indian officer under a heavy fire. The Interpreter Lieut. Sturdee was also wounded and the casualties numbered thirty-eight. Major G. Molloy's name was brought to notice for good work.

The 2nd Gurkhas had seven out of their full complement of twelve British officers killed, but this did not complete the roll of casualties. Captain G. McCleverty was wounded while " showing great gallantry, always well to the front endeavouring to get to the trenches," and the same remark applied to Major F. H. Norie, attached as Interpreter, who owing to the heavy losses amongst the officers voluntarily took his place in the forefront of the fighting and was severely wounded, earning the grateful thanks of all ranks and a D.S.O.

No. 1618, Naik Padamdhoj Gurung received the Indian Order of Merit for conspicuous gallantry.

The total losses of the 2nd Gurkhas on this day were seven British and four Indian officers killed and two British and two Indian officers wounded; thirty-one other ranks killed and 100 wounded.

This action brings conspicuously to light the fact that even the best Indian troops in European warfare need the leading of British officers.

The 2nd Gurkhas was a regiment second to none in the Indian Army. The British officers were as good as those of any battalion in His Majesty's armies; the Indian officers, N.C.O.'s, and men were of the best stamp of fighting men in the East, and if I had been asked I could not have selected a better fighting battalion; and after this affair

my belief in them was confirmed.   They had been tried
in the fire and not found wanting.

I had known them since the days of the Afghan War
of 1878–80, and by common consent they were acknowledged to be a first-class fighting unit.   Bhurtpore, Aliwal,
Sobraon, Delhi, Kabul, Tirah are their battle honours,
and to these will now be added others well earned.

The 34th Poona Horse was originally raised in 1817,
and had under different names served from Ghazni (1839),
Meeanee, and Kushab to Afghanistan (1879–80).   The
Honorary Colonel was Lieut.-General H.H. the famous
Maharaja Sir Partab Singh, and the ranks were filled by
Rathore Rajputs, Kaimkhanis, and Punjab Musalmans.
It was the first Indian Cavalry regiment of the Cavalry
Brigades to be engaged in the war, and whilst it remained
with the Army Corps always gave a good account of itself.

CHAPTER VII

OCTOBER had ended with some exciting episodes in the Indian Corps; November had been ushered in with a fresh attack, and all classes of the troops, British and Indian, were destined to find plenty of work and fighting as the days went on.

On the 5th November a very gallant act was performed by Lieut. G. Brunskill of the 47th Sikhs in front of his trenches. Accompanied by one of his battalion scouts he traversed some 500 yards of " No Man's Land," until he found himself not thirty yards from the entrenched Germans. Making a detour he again crept forward, and finding the trench unoccupied, the two got over the parapet and inspected the interior; they then packed up various articles of equipment and papers, made a note of the dug-outs and snipers' posts, and began their return journey. They were suddenly fired on, but got back safely with their valuable information.

Brunskill made two similar journeys, on the last occasion reaching to within thirty yards of the enemy's second line, where he was fired on, and this firing brought on a wild fusillade from friend and foe, through which he and his brave companion, Sepoy Tawand Singh, also of the 47th Sikhs, managed to return unscathed. These reconnaissances discovered the line of advance of German supplies and gave other useful information, which enabled us to devote particular attention to the points noted. For his gallant work Brunskill was awarded the Military Cross. Two days later he was severely wounded whilst performing another daring deed during daylight.

One very important fact disclosed, and which stood

us in good stead thereafter, was that the enemy at that
time used few or no patrols and left his front line practically
unoccupied.   Thus the brave pay for their daring, and the
men behind reap the benefits.

The next troops to be engaged in a difficult operation
were the 1st Battalion Connaught Rangers (of the Ferozepore Brigade), commanded by Lieut.-Colonel H. L. S.
Ravenshaw.   To their front was a trench which had been
held by one of their companies and was now in German
hands, and it was decided to eject the enemy and fill it in.
At midnight on the 14th-15th November the Royal Scots
Fusiliers, of the 8th British Brigade, opened a heavy fire
under cover of which a company of the Rangers, commanded by Captain C. Hack, with Lieutenants F. George
and D. Tulloch, rushed and captured the trench in face of
a sharp fusillade.

Captain Payne, the same officer who had behaved so
well at Messines in October, at once sent forward the
digging party, and these set to work to fill in the trench.
But now the rifle-bolts of the attackers began to jam and
the men in the party had to take up the fire.   Filling in
soon became impossible and the casualties were heavy,
every officer having been killed, and a retirement was
ordered.

The trenches were deep in mud and very slippery, and
the enemy was superior in numbers.   Payne at once reoccupied his now half filled in trenches and advanced to
the attack, but was driven back with loss. A second attempt
was also repulsed.   The Germans redoubled their fire,
and as the Connaughts' rifles were fast becoming useless,
two platoons of the Middlesex of Bowes' British Brigade
came up to relieve them.   This caused the trench to become
overcrowded, and as some of the Connaughts were leaving,
in order to make room, they were caught under a heavy
machine-gun fire which caused many casualties, including
Lieut. J. Ovens, who was killed.   Lieut. George, the
adjutant, was severely wounded as he rushed forward,
but Lance-Corporal T. Kelly cleared the parapet, and in
face of a very heavy fire lifted his officer to carry him to
safety ; as he was doing so another bullet killed Lieut.

George in his arms. This was a splendid act, and from personal descriptions at the time a far finer one than I can describe it, and I should have liked to see him get the Victoria Cross; but as it was he was awarded the D.C.M. and it was never better earned. He died of wounds in January 1916.

Captain Hack was killed in the charge, and Lieut. Tulloch, although wounded early in the attack, bravely carried on till he also was killed. Payne received the D.S.O. for his share in the action.

The Irishmen suffered forty casualties in this affair, and had it not been for their rifles jamming, the trenches would have been rendered untenable for the enemy. At the same time they learned their lesson, not the least valuable part of it being that rifles are delicate weapons and must be looked after. There can be no doubt it was partly want of care that caused the bolts to jam, and the troops of all Corps very soon found that a little extra care, even if grease is not always available, will help to save lives.

Brigadier-General Bowes in his report stated that "everything possible was done by the Connaught Rangers to carry out the duty assigned to them." Within four days this battalion had lost five officers killed and two wounded.

On the 5th November the 8th British Brigade, attached to us, recaptured and filled in the trenches evacuated by the 2nd Gurkhas. On the same day Major E. H. Phillips commanding the 28th Battery, 9th Brigade R.F.A., was killed. He had climbed a haystack to get better observation, when a shell ended his career. He was one of my best friends and comrades in the days when we tramped and fought through the swamps and forests of Ashanti, and later we soldiered together in more peaceful times in India. A splendid gunner and a charming personality, he was a real loss to the service; but he left a perfect battery behind him. What more could a soldier do?

As the days went on both officers and men acquired a knowledge of the novel methods of warfare. The Indians were at last brigaded with their own British battalions;

they had behind them their own guns, transport, supplies and hospitals, and they were finding out that the wounded or strayed need only move in one direction to find friends who could understand their language. The chaotic state of affairs when they were mixed up anyhow with absolute strangers was passing away, and a sense of cheerfulness which was bred of this knowledge soon began to manifest itself. But even so it took time, and in some cases a very long time, to obliterate from their minds the memory of their first rough experiences, and in conversation with Indian officers and men I learnt many lessons on how things might have been done. They said plainly, " We were not given a chance ; and if we get ' bud nāāmed ' (a bad name) it is not our fault." Some of the tales the first arrivals in France brought back from Messines and near Neuve Chapelle were soon spread through the ranks of the new arrivals, and any one who knows India also knows what this means.

One incident at once proved the innate love of fair play inherent in the sepoy. In the German lines a document had been found, directing that mercy was not to be shown to the Indians, and a day later the 15th Sikhs brought back twelve prisoners from a raid. The only comment made by the havildar of the party was, that the Germans might do as they pleased, but he and his men were soldiers not dacoits.

The enemy early began to try the effect of using English when on the prowl near our lines, and one man, dressed exactly like a British officer of Gurkhas, came right up to the trenches, and in good English said the company was to move farther along the trench to make room for another company moving up in support. The British officer in command being suspicious of the accent asked, " Who are you ? " and the reply was the same as before. " Answer at once by what ship you came to France," was our officer's next query, and the disguised German started to run but was shot dead. Similar ruses were not uncommon, and notwithstanding the difficulty of our men being able to discriminate, the Hun generally got off second best.

Fortunately for us the perfectly idiotic accounts that used to appear in those early days of what the Indians were expected to do, or were doing, seldom reached or interested them. They simply did their duty and cared nothing for daily papers; but more than once Indian officers have told me how surprised they were that our newspapers could lie as they did. In any case such stories did much harm, for when instead of finding that the Indian soldiers were some mythical kind of beings, the British public discovered that they were only ordinary men trying to do their duty under inconceivable difficulties, they grew disappointed; but we did gain one advantage, and that was, we were left more alone, and pictures of charging Lancers and bearded Gurkhas ceased to appear.

The Seaforth Highlanders was the first British battalion of the Meerut Division to come up against the Germans, when on the 7th November they found their right flank assailed; but the Seaforths, the old 72nd, did not on service allow any man through their lines without a pass, and the enemy could not produce that document. One or two of the attacking Huns reached the trench and remained there for good, and the others were driven back faster than they came, leaving many dead and wounded behind them. The enemy on this occasion used a very large and long-range trench mortar, which did much damage, and to which of course we had no reply. Captain R. S. Wilson and sixteen men were killed and 2nd Lieut. I. Macandrew and sixty-three other ranks were wounded. It was a heavy toll for a short affair, but the battalion at once found that a Corps which had won battle honours from Mysore and Sebastopol to South Africa had nothing to fear from the Kaiser's legions.

During the short time the battalion had been in the trenches it had already, in addition to the above, suffered many casualties, losing four officers wounded, including their splendid Chaplain Rev. McNeill, and one missing, and other ranks suffered in proportion.

Part of the 2nd Gurkhas were again employed this day in support of the Seaforths, and during this operation Captain Beauchamp-Duff, son of the Commander-in-Chief in India, was killed.   He was a popular officer and a great loss to the regiment.

The description of the fighting by the Army Corps in France is of necessity nothing but a long record, practically of siege warfare, on the same front, relieved occasionally by an attack or defence against the enemy, and it therefore lacks the incidents which furnish the war correspondent with copy for stirring descriptions of battles. Nevertheless, even in this somewhat gloomy atmosphere will be found occasional bursts of flame helping to light up the otherwise sombre picture ; and after all what is being recorded is the long and patient sacrifice made of course by our own men who had everything at stake on the final decision, but still more by the loyal soldiers of India who were equally enduring.

From the day of arrival at G.H.Q. I had resolved in my mind how we were to meet the trench mortars and hand-grenades used by the enemy.   I had some years previously foreseen that these instruments would assuredly take a foremost place in the next war, and when on short leave home from India, whilst I was in command of the Peshawar Division, I had spent several days examining and seeing the "Hale's" hand- and rifle-grenades used. After learning their mechanism I had myself thrown and fired these grenades against roughly constructed wooden stockades, and been much impressed by their destructive effects.

It appeared to me that when once troops reached within a certain distance of a position held by an enemy who did not mean to quit it, it became a matter of hand-to-hand fighting, and the one who possessed some weapon other than the rifle alone would gain an immense advantage, which would carry him forward or stop his opponent. With this in view I was determined, to the best of my limited power, to introduce the "Hale's" grenades into the Indian Army ; but, as I shall show, I received little or no encouragement from our conservative administration.

At that time there were in England several officers of the Spanish Army who were testing these grenades with a view to their use in North Africa, and I was present when large numbers were being tried by them. On my return to India from leave I took out a certain number which Mr. Hale kindly placed at my disposal, and reported the fact to Army Headquarters. I instructed squads of Sappers and Miners in my Command in their use, and made a practical demonstration by myself firing several rounds from one of our service rifles. Later I had them tested by squads before the Chief of the General Staff in India, and it was obvious how useful they would prove.

But there the matter ended, and no further notice was taken of the experiment so far as I ever knew. Again, one of the officers who had served with me in Africa, Major A. L. McClintock, R.E., who was then in command of Sappers and Miners in Madras, invented and made grenades of his own pattern, and obtained permission to bring them up to Agra to be used before me and other officers quartered there, but there his experiment ended also.

And now arrived in France I found the Army still practically unprovided with them, except a few rifle-grenades, and I had no difficulty in obtaining the small supply available ; but of hand-grenades I could find none. In those days it was a case of " God helps those who help themselves," and I immediately set the Sappers and Miners to work to manufacture jam-tin hand-grenades, and gas and other pipe trench guns. Black powder was at first used for the latter, but the smoke emitted gave away their position, and later other devices were brought into play.

One of my R.E. officers was sent for by the War Office for consultation, and the Indian Corps was one of the first to capture a German trench mortar, which was at once sent home for examination. The Corps may well claim some credit for helping to initiate the use of these weapons ; a fact easily forgotten later on when grenades and trench mortars were perfected and supplied in abundance to all troops as they arrived in France.

Early in November we were able to start work with our primitive weapons, but it gave confidence to the men and made a beginning. The devices used by the Sapper officers were well worth seeing, and ranged from century-old mortars to jam-tins propelled by indiarubber tubing.

On the morning of the 9th November the 2nd Black Watch of the Bareilly Brigade, with the object of getting rid of an enemy machine-gun which was paying them particular attention, organised a small raid, and Captain R. E. Forrester with about twenty men made a surprise attack, killing ten Germans and returning with only two casualties, of which he himself was one, being wounded. This famous Corps was destined to take part in numerous fights, always emerging with honour, and finally strewing the sands of Mesopotamia with its gallant officers and men.

The 1st and 2nd Battalions of the 39th Garhwal Rifles of the Garhwal Brigade, a regiment which was doing its first service in the field, were the next to try their hand, this time not in defence, but in a small raid on the German trenches. On the night of the 9th November Major G. H. Taylor of the 2nd Battalion organised the affair and carried it through, and considering it was a first attempt it may be described as very useful, and certainly encouraged officers and men to further similar enterprises. A trench only fifty yards distant was occupied and partly filled in, with slight casualties, and then seeing he could not complete the work in time Taylor retired, his party bringing back with him six prisoners. The enemy kept up a hot fire, but our men had been into a German trench and seen them run for dear life, and this in itself was worth much on their first attempt. They had learned that if they kept low and used their own tactics they could outwit the Hun. Jemadar Khushal Singh Danu of the 2nd Battalion was specially commended by Taylor. Rifleman Ganesh Singh Sajwan had on the same morning won the Indian Order of Merit for a very gallant act whilst acting as scout.

The two battalions of the 39th were commanded respectively by Colonels Swiney and Drake-Brockman. Swiney, after being severely wounded at Neuve Chapelle in March 1915, was drowned in the P. & O. *Persia* when that passenger vessel was torpedoed by our "gallant" enemies in the Mediterranean.

The Garhwalis are best described as more or less related to the Gurkhas of Nepal; there were only these two battalions in the Army, and as a Corps they were an untried element.   From first to last they did splendid work, proving themselves to be really gallant soldiers, and their very heavy casualties attest to the fact that they bore a lion's share in Flanders.

Whilst I have described in detail some of the scraps which went on uninterruptedly, it must be borne in mind that the whole Corps was engaged all along our front, and the daily task was one which took heavy toll from all arms in proportion.   On referring to the rolls, for instance on the date up to which I have brought the narrative, the Indian Corps and the battalions still attached to it to fill the gap caused by the absence of the Sirhind Brigade in Egypt had suffered casualties amongst all ranks amounting to 3880 or on an average of 190 daily.   It does not need much imagination to discover that losses at this rate could hardly be replaced in the Indian ranks by reinforcements of ten per cent per month, which is what the Indian authorities had arranged to send to France.   Moreover, the time was not far distant when the numbers would jump up, first by 1200 casualties in a single night, and by many times more in two days' fighting a month later on.

And later still the day arrived when, at a parade of an Indian battalion in rest which attended to witness the promotion of a Naik to the rank of Jemadar for gallant conduct, the total muster that could be collected after detailing necessary billet duties was under 200 men.   Not for a long time did we receive any but small additions towards replacing officers and men of the British battalions, which in the Corps numbered at war strength only 850 of all ranks, though after November, in the case of these battalions, the deficiencies were better met.

At this stage it is of interest to explain briefly the methods of supply by which the Indian troops were fed and clothed, and the wonderful arrangements made for the care of sick and wounded ; arrangements in both cases so good as to astonish us all by the simplicity of their working and the celerity of execution.   Indeed in these, as in all branches of general Administrative Staff work, India was ages behind the Home Army. Staff work in India was only beginning to emerge from the bow and arrow days ; the Indian Staff College and improved status of Departmental officers had in recent years given a good start to the new organisations, but economy had kept them in leash, and there had not been time or the experience of active service or really big concentrations to put them to the test. Where ten motor lorries or fifty motor-cars had been available at English manœuvres, in India we had to put up with ten prehistoric bullock carts, and perhaps a few obsolete hired motors. It was thought extravagant to waste money on telephones, and luxurious even to mention wireless. It was not long, therefore, before we learned the difference between campaigns as conducted on economical Indian principles and the more up-to-date methods of the Home Army.

The Government of India had, however, been very wise in two things, and these were, in always insisting on the Indian troops being rationed strictly on Indian lines, and scrupulously observing every detail relating to their religious customs, especially in as far as their food was concerned. To some it may appear difficult to understand how it was possible in the heart of Europe to observe these matters to the letter, but we had with us officers who knew exactly what to do and how to do it, and the names of Colonels R. H. Ewart, Hennessy, Moore, Lindsay, Vaughan, to say nothing of many excellent junior officers, were a guarantee all would go well with the Supply and Transport ; whilst in the Indian Medical Services we had Colonels Grayfoot, Bowle-Evans, Wall, Hamilton, White, Moorhead, and Browse, who with their thorough knowledge of Indian troops were prepared to look after the interests of the men, and ably second the splendid work done by the Royal Army Medical Corps officers, to whom (though here we are now dealing with Indians alone) the Indian Corps owes a great debt of gratitude, and on whom fell the main responsibilities in this European War.

There were days when the ordinary chappati could not be kneaded or the meat cooked with the ingredients

H

dear to the sepoy's heart, and there were times when perhaps men were glad to eat their flour wetted and mixed with gur (Indian sugar), but this was seldom, and as time went on hardly ever; and after all when the enemy is only thirty, and never more than two or three hundred yards away, and a lively tune is singing overhead, the beginner at the game is not too squeamish whether his dinner is served hot or cold nor whether it is up to Savoy standard. These are the natural accompaniments of rough war, and the Indians are the easiest soldiers in the world to feed when they understand it is part of the game.

The rations consisted of meat for those who ate it, several days in the week according to the circumstances of the time; for non meat-eaters extra gur (sugar), dall (lentils), ghee (clarified butter), potatoes, tea, atta (flour), and five kinds of tasty ingredients; in addition dried fruits such as raisins, etc., and various kinds of vegetables as procurable. But this did not end their rations, for mixed sweetmeats were frequently supplied by friends and retired British officers; cigarettes in abundance for such classes as smoked them; European and Indian tobacco and chillums (native clay pipes) were sent by some of the Indian Princes. Rum was issued to those who were not prohibited from taking alcohol, and extra tea to those who could not indulge in the former. Goats were purchased from Southern Europe in large numbers; slaughtered at fixed stations on the line of communications by men of the various units; labelled with distinctive tapes and conveyed to destination by men of the different denominations. Nothing could have been more considerate than the details carried out to observe the customs of the sepoy; and Indian officers and men have said to me over and over again, "The British Government is wonderful; here in the midst of the Mahabharat (great war) they even label our meat. Truly the Badshah (King) is a Rustam and a Hatim (a hero and a just man)."

As for clothing and necessaries; beginning with somewhat scanty garments, the sepoys were gradually supplied with an outfit which it became an impossibility to move;

vests, balaclava caps, warm coats, goatskin overcoats, extra flannel shirts, socks, drawers, woollen mufflers, and gloves poured into their wardrobes or kit-bags until a man could neither put on nor even stagger under the burden, but the cry was, " Still they come." Kindly ladies in England and Regimental Committees continued to send gifts for the Indian soldiers, and I was obliged at last to cry a halt and find storage room for all that could not be moved forward from rest billets.

There were occasional complaints of shortage of warm clothing from units, chiefly Departmental ones; but though this may have been the case during the first month or so in France, the exact contrary was the case later on.

It is impossible in writing of the Supply and Transport to omit mention of the personnel. The British portion of the work was done with the thoroughness which characterises the A.S.C., but the Indian rank and file are a hardworking, patient body of men who do much and say little about it. In every campaign in which they have served the Transport driver is acknowledged as a very loyal servant of the State. Most of the Indian Transport was transferred to Gallipoli early in the war and did good work there.

The Medical establishments from India soon fell into the routine of trench warfare. The requirements of Frontier expeditions were of a nature so different from anything in France that it practically meant a fresh start as far as the transport and interior arrangements were concerned. There is no need to go into the details of removing the wounded from the firing line to the Regimental Aid Posts and thence on to the Field Ambulances, with their bearer and tent divisions, the dressing stations and finally the clearing hospitals from which they are conveyed by ambulance trains to the base. These things have become familiar to all during the past war years; but the friends and relations of the Indian soldier may rest assured that nothing was left undone by the authorities to make the removal of the sick and wounded as easy as it was possible to make it.

The Indians received in due course a complement of

the best ambulances, and at all times every attention that was their due. The buildings appropriated at St. Venant, Merville, etc., for their hospitals were fitted with every comfort that could be expected on service; the French authorities went out of their way to do all in their power to help " les Hindous " as they always called them, and the Medical officers of both Services worked with a devotion which can never be forgotten by the men. From France they were speedily removed to the special hospitals in England, and those for India left later for that country or Egypt, according to orders. At Marseilles also, which was the great Indian Base in France, the hospital arrangements were excellent, and when in July 1915 I visited that seaport I found a most perfect open-air hospital, with large tents, known as E.P. or European Privates in India, containing several hundred beds for patients, located on cliffs overlooking the Mediterranean. I asked an Indian officer recovering from a serious illness how he liked it and he said, " If there be a bhist (paradise) before death it is this."

The Red Cross Association too, with all its million activities, was blessed by none more than by the men who came from the far-off mountains and plains of India. Indeed nothing made a more lasting impression on them than the medical arrangements of the entire Army.

Their Majesties' gifts and thoughtfulness for their Eastern subjects were appreciated in a manner difficult for Britishers who know not the East to understand. One sepoy had wrapped up a small metal tobacco box given him by a British soldier and showed it to me with much pride. " General Sahib," he said, " this once belonged to the King, and I am going to carry it about as a charm; I shall get back safely enough to my home."

Another man, very severely wounded, whom I was seeing off in the ambulance, asked me for a " nishan " (souvenir) of the war, and I gave him a handkerchief with blue edges, a part of one of Her Majesty's gifts to the Staff; he asked me to tie it round his arm as it would be a passport at Bombay, and with a touch of humour he added, " When they see it the Customs officers will not dare to examine my baggage." This consisted of a German helmet which he had tied on to his haversack.

And whilst all these and other signs were not wanting to show the interest taken by our people at home in the Indian soldiers, there had started in England an association which has since rendered signal service to the Indian Army in many theatres of war. The "Indian Soldiers' Fund" was inaugurated in October 1914 under the Chairmanship of Sir John Hewett, late Lieutenant-Governor of the United Provinces of Agra and Oudh. Many ladies and gentlemen connected with India became members, and Lord Curzon of Kedleston very kindly lent his London residence as a Headquarters. Sir C. McLeod, with whom I had played many a game of polo when quartered with my battalion in Calcutta, was the Chairman of the City Committee. He paid me a visit in France and very generously gave some handsome prizes for competition amongst Indian soldiers of all corps.

Money and gifts of clothing, necessaries, and all kinds of comforts were liberally supplied. Lady Sydenham, assisted by many others, including my wife, helped to deal with the gifts, etc., and no one can appreciate or understand better than myself the immense benefits the Indians derived during the early days of the war from the gratuitous labours of all those who so ungrudgingly gave their services. It was then a different task from what it became afterwards when experience had perfected the machine.

It is not too much to say, that as far as the soldiers of India were concerned, for nothing that was done for them were they more grateful than the work of the "Indian Soldiers' Fund."

Through Mrs. Morant the hospital at Brockenhurst Park was started and named after the late Lady Hardinge of Penshurst.

The Fund also assisted with gifts towards other smaller but similar institutions and hospital ships, in England and abroad. Prisoners of war were not forgotten, and indeed little that could at that time be done was left undone. In the trenches, the billets, the hospitals, the India-bound hospital ships, and lastly the homes of the brave men who had come to share in the toils and glory of the Great War, there could be but one opinion, viz. that the Fund so generously contributed and so sympathetically administered would long be remembered with gratitude.

CHAPTER VIII

On the 9th November 1914 the right of the Indian Corps was still just north of Givenchy and in touch with the French. On this day our Allies projected some move, and I was asked if we could take over that village and its front, but anxious as I always was to help them in every way, I asked the Field-Marshal not to extend my front, as my strength was quite insufficient for such an extension. Sir John French, who had come over to see us, quite agreed and the matter was settled. I, however, sent one of my battalions to Givenchy as a support to them for a couple of days. Later on I was ordered to extend my front to include Givenchy and up to the La Bassée Road south of it. The order was of course carried out, but it was very unfortunate for us, as when, very shortly afterwards, we were heavily attacked on that front my numbers were altogether too small for the extended line, and, as I shall tell, the Indian Corps was very roughly handled and Givenchy was temporarily lost to us; it was retaken by the heroism of the 1st Manchesters of the Jalandar Brigade, and again lost, and finally only saved by the arrival of a Division of the First Army Corps which was in reserve behind the British positions.

On this date I withdrew the 9th Bhopals from the trenches at the request of their C.O. for a few days' rest, as the battalion had been subjected to a very severe shelling and had suffered losses which necessitated a short change.

In diary of November 10 I find, " Our fellows tried their hand on a mine of sorts to-day. Half a German fell into the Bareilly Brigade trenches." This was the

103

beginning of mining warfare for us ; though in this case the plant was only placed in a trench and fired by electricity.

Lord Roberts had been appointed Colonel-in-Chief of the Indian Corps, and we had the proud satisfaction of receiving the following telegram :

To Sir James Willcocks, Indian Expeditionary Force.— Allow me to welcome you and the Indian Expeditionary Force which has come to fight in Europe shoulder to shoulder in the cause of liberty and truth, and in upholding our great Empire. I am proud to be your Colonel-in-Chief.—ROBERTS.

I replied and said how rejoiced we all felt at such a message from the Chief under whose command the Indian Army had so often been led to victory.

In another telegram, to Sir John French, Lord Roberts also expressed his high appreciation of the " magnificent gallantry displayed by all ranks, British and Indian." Our great Hero, the victor of many fights, never forgot his Indian comrades.   God rest his soul !

On November 12, Lord Roberts paid us his memorable visit.   On the lawns, now deep in slush, in front of the Château of Hinges and whilst the roar of the guns shook the windows of the building, we drew up to receive the great Field-Marshal.   The Indian Corps was alone represented, and that only by the Headquarters Staff and such other officers and men as were not on duty in the trenches. Facing the entrance door was drawn up a Guard of Honour of all available men, British and Indian.   It was a mixed body, but it was all I could muster at short notice ; amongst them, however, were two Indian officers who knew Lord Roberts personally, and there was not a man in that small gathering who did not know the name and the fame of India's greatest " Jangi Lat " (War Lord).

There are times in life, fortunately rare, when one feels as if some sad moment was approaching and you cannot assign any reason for it.   This was one ; the solemnity of it was in any case visible, for it was a great occasion in itself for the Indian Army to have with it in the heart of France the aged soldier who had long been its Idol ; but there was some other indefinable feeling, and most of us felt it, that whatever might come this was to be the very last meeting in the Field of War of the Army of India and its beloved Chief.   We all knew that it was the lion heart of this great man which had determined him to come across the sea just once more, and by his presence encourage the troops of which he was the Chief in name and fact, and then, having done his Duty, which was his life's watchword, to return to England and have us in his keeping.

As the motor-car pulled up our Colonel-in-Chief stepped out, still with that brisk step so well remembered by all who had ever served with him, and we felt, as Tennyson has sung of another warrior :

> This is England's greatest son,
> He that gain'd a hundred fights,
> Nor ever lost an English gun.

It was a parade, but it was a duty every man present considered his greatest privilege and honour to have attended ; and who would have missed it ?

After shaking hands with every officer, Lord Roberts inspected the Guard, saying a word, with that charm he possessed, to each British and Indian officer and old soldier ; and finally giving a military salute entered his car, bidding me also in, and we moved off to Headquarters of the Meerut and Lahore Divisions.

During his short visit the sky was clear but a biting cold wind chilled us all, and no doubt this, combined with his insistence in pulling up and alighting at each spot where representatives of every Indian battalion and Cavalry regiment of the Corps (straight from the trenches) were collected along the route, helped to bring on the fatal illness which immediately followed.

During the motor journey I was able to give him an account of our doings and to answer numerous questions he put to me.   I also had the great benefit of his advice on some important disciplinary points, on which I would have consulted no man except him, and on which no one else could have formed so sound and just an opinion.

At Locon he stopped about half an hour, talking to General Anderson and his Staff and inspecting the few troops present. His pleasure was manifest when he met his old comrade Sir Partab Singh and also the Maharaja of Bikanir and the young Prince of Jodhpore and others from India. Here he addressed the troops in a few words, bidding us do our duty and saying he would keenly follow our fortunes. His last words were, " The fame of your doings will live for ever in India."

Passing on to the Headquarters of the Lahore Division, he saw General Watkis and his Staff drawn up in the Square at Estaires, and spoke for some time to an Indian officer who had served with him. He also saw General Wadeson and officers and men of the Secunderabad Cavalry Brigade.

Not the least touching part of his visit was the fact that he was followed by another car, in which travelled one of his daughters, the guardian angel of his last hours. The Indian officer to whom he had just spoken said after he had left, " Sahib, the English are a great race. Brave men, brave women. Peace or war they always hold fast together. The victory is already yours."

As I gave him my last salute and the hurrahs of the troops ceased, I felt the Indian Corps had a friend who was the lodestar which would guide us on our path of duty and that his visit had increased our strength. And only two days later the great Field-Marshal passed away. An honoured guard of Indian soldiers watched over the house where rested his body, and England had lost one of her most precious possessions and the Army of India its truest friend.

Most of the Indian Princes and Chiefs in France crossed to England and attended the funeral, and, to show how heartfelt was the sorrow of our Allies, I received letters the very next day from General de Maud'huy, commanding the Xth Army, and General Maistre, commanding the XXIst Corps d'Armée, who were on our right, deploring the great loss our country, and more especially the Indian Corps, had suffered.

He will not be forgotten " while memory holds a seat in this distracted globe."

I was informed at this time that it was now possible to shorten the line held by the Corps. I was naturally pleased when the change was carried out on the night of 15th–16th November. The 8th British Division relieved the two left brigades of the Corps, and our right then rested on Givenchy and our left on the La Bassée—Estaires Road. On the 11th November Captain H. Wicks, 1st Seaforth Highlanders, sent out a small party of his battalion under command of Lieut. D. MacKenzie to destroy three houses in his front. My chief recollection of this affair is, that one of the party in describing it said when they got within ten yards of the centre house the Germans shouted, " Allenmechty English," and bolted. It was told as if it was a huge joke, and somehow the story has always been one I laugh over. The party split up and entered all three houses, and were proceeding to set them on fire with the help of straw when the Huns attacked and drove them out, and from the upper story of one a machine-gun suddenly began to spit lead. The Germans had been surprised, but now it was the turn of our men. Covered by our own fire from the trenches the party got back without a scratch. Even such minor skirmishes had their lessons. In this case it was found that the Boches lived in cellars by day ; and instead of wasting lives the houses were demolished by shells shortly afterwards.

During the night of 11th–12th November the Germans sapped up and dug a short parallel within thirty-five yards of the left trenches of the Connaught Rangers, and the next night the Irishmen attacked this new trench ; but the enemy anticipated the attack, which failed, and at dawn, elated with his success, launched a counter-attack. This was carried out with determination and succeeded in penetrating our trenches and temporarily capturing a machine-gun.

But this triumph was short-lived as the Connaughts immediately rushed the lost position, recaptured the gun, bayoneting such Germans as were found, and turned the Maxim on to the remainder. A German officer showed great bravery on this occasion ; he remained to the last at one end of a trench and picked off three or four men with a rifle before he would retire, and then managed to escape. Twenty of the enemy lay dead on or near our parapet and two prisoners were taken. We suffered only eight casualties, amongst them three men killed and one officer wounded, Lieut. E. Morris.

The Irishmen did not mean to allow the enemy to hold on to his new parallel, and Colonel Ravenshaw arranged an assault for midnight, 14th November, when sixty men under Lieut. A. G. Moutray silently rushed the trench, supported by the cross-fire of two machine-guns. A few Germans were in occupation, of whom Moutray shot two himself. Our casualties numbered only five men. Sergt. Brown was commended for good work, and the parallel ceased to trouble us.

Daily small encounters were now the rule, with the more important of which alone I shall deal. On 13th November General Keary, commanding the Garhwal Brigade, ordered an attack on some German trenches which had previously been assaulted but had reverted to the enemy. Lieut.-Colonel W. R. Brakspear, 2/3rd Gurkhas, with six platoons of his own corps, and about sixty men of the 2/39th Garhwalis under Major Taylor, who had been in the previous attack on the same trench, carried out the assault.

The troops to fill in the trench when captured were drawn from No. 4 Company Sappers and Miners and 2/3rd Gurkhas. The assault was made at 9 p.m., but was at once shattered on its left and centre, and only a party on the right succeeded in reaching the enemy trenches, where Lieut. H. F. McSwiney and his Gurkhas quickly accounted for twenty-five Huns and made four prisoners. Brakspear, who had by this time himself come up, worked along the trench to his left until held up by a party of Germans behind a traverse. McSwiney tried to rush the enemy by climbing the parapet but was severely wounded in the gallant attempt.

Seeing that further help was necessary if the small party were to drive them from their comparatively safe position, Brakspear himself went back at considerable risk through a hot fire and, having organised a relief, together with Major E. G. Drummond advanced towards his goal; but the fire was very heavy and made doubly destructive by a searchlight which played incessantly on our men.

Drummond was killed as he left his own trench; the advance, however, continued until a number of high-explosive shells suddenly fell in succession all round the attackers, disjointing their efforts and scattering all but a mere handful who, with Brakspear, managed to regain their trench.

Meantime the position opposite to the traverse was being splendidly maintained by Subadar Dalkesar Gurung, but it was now past midnight and time to return, as that hour had been fixed for the covering Artillery fire to help our retirement, and this was already beginning. Finding that no further object was to be gained by remaining, McSwiney and his party moved back, but finding that Captain R. D. Alexander, who had been severely wounded near the traverse, had not been brought in, as he refused to be moved before the other wounded, McSwiney and his Subadar with a few men went back to search for him, but finding no traces had once more sorrowfully to retire, and on reaching our trenches, drenched in blood, McSwiney fell in a swoon.

Glorious fellows! Which was the braver, the gallant Captain who refused to be moved lest one of his men might be left in the hands of the enemy; or the equally gallant Subadar who, facing almost certain death, returned, severely wounded as he was, to try and rescue his comrade? Fine deeds, performed in company, by men of different birth, but as Thomas Moore sings:

> Shall I ask the brave soldier who fights by my side
> In the cause of mankind, if our creeds agree?

The object of this attack was to destroy the trenches; it was not achieved, as it did not come as a surprise to the enemy, and once launched our men were heavily handicapped by the German searchlight, an apparatus with which we were of course unprovided. Also the Huns had considerably improved and re-aligned their trench by throwing back a flank since our last assault on it and our scouts had not reported any changes. Another cause was that some men in their excitement started their rush with cheers contrary to orders. The prisoners also declared that our shells were not exploding. But the best lesson learned from this attack was, that it is easy enough to capture a small portion of a trench; it is a very different matter to hold on to it, unless ample provision has been made beforehand to ensure success. We were still learning in those early days of the war.

Colonel Brakspear behaved with great coolness, always being in the place of greatest danger. Drummond also of the 3rd Gurkhas only arrived that day, and I had wished him luck as he started for the trenches. McSwiney (son of a very old friend) received the Military Cross for his gallantry. Captain H. Bennett was missing.

The following were brought to notice by the Division : Subadar Dalkesar Gurung, Havildar Bahadur Thapa, Naik Rupdhan Dun, Lance-Naik Kabiram Thapa, Rifleman Ganpati Thapa, all of the 3rd Gurkhas; and Lance-Naik Jaman Singh Khatri, Rifleman Gajbir Bisht, and Ran Bahadur Saki, of the 1/9th Gurkhas.

The Gurkhas had fifty-seven other casualties, including two Indian officers.

Major Taylor, who had twice attempted the attack of this same trench, and Captain A. W. Robertson-Glasgow, both of the 2/39th Garhwalis, were missing, and the remaining losses of this battalion amounted to thirty-eight.

The 3rd Gurkhas were raised as far back as 1815, so the regiment was celebrating its 100th year of existence. Its name had undergone many changes, but in its ranks was the same breed as had originally taken service with the British Government after the fall of Malaun and Kumaon. In 1891 a second battalion was added, and in 1908 the present title of the 3rd Queen Alexandra's Own Gurkha Rifles was conferred on the regiment. They possess seven battle honours, from Delhi (1858) to Tirah and the Punjab Frontiers. At the outbreak of war, the 2nd battalion, with the Indian Corps, was commanded by Lieut.-Colonel V. A. Ormsby, who was later promoted to a Companionship of the Bath.

The Lahore Division had borne the first brunt of the fighting in France, and now almost daily it was the turn of the sister Division to be employed in some scrap or raid.

No one who reads the records of the Corps during its first two months in France can fail to be struck by the energy and initiative of the Divisional Commanders, Brigadiers, and C.O.'s of units ; if it was not in attack, it was in defence of our own trenches ; but, one or other, the Corps was as incessantly employed as any in Flanders. The numbers were being fast reduced and there were no daily ships bringing the sorely needed reinforcements; whilst that invaluable man, the British officer, was irreplaceable.

On the night of the 16th November the 6th Jat Light Infantry had their first experience of carrying out an attack on German trenches. Associated with them in this well-conceived scheme was half of No. 3 Company Sappers and Miners. The party consisted of 125 rifles of the Jats under command of Major P. H. Dundas and sixty Sappers under Captain E. H. Kelly, R.E., and I cannot do better than epitomise the report of these two officers, written with a modesty that makes them very readable.

The Jat report states that they were ordered by the C.O. to advance at 9 P.M. between two saps, made by the enemy towards the 107th Pioneers and 4th Cavalry, and to hold the portion of the German trench between these saps till 9.45 P.M., by which time the Pioneers would have reconstructed their trench (which had been partially destroyed by shell-fire), and the Sappers and Miners filled in the saps. Instructions were also given *re* the part to be played by our heavy and field guns. The Infantry were extended, and advanced with orders not to fire until the objective was reached. As they cleared the line of their own wire, the German saps on both flanks opened a heavy fire and some casualties resulted. At sixty yards they crossed a deep drain, and at 100 yards entered a trench loopholed to the front and rear. (Ominous !) This trench was unoccupied, but Germans were seen retiring. The mouth of one sap was closed and an advance with the bayonet began, so as to protect the Sappers who had begun work. Meantime the enemy who held the trench in prolongation of the portion captured by the Jats opened a heavy but ineffective fire on our men. The Jats replied vigorously, being rewarded by much groaning and yells proceeding from the Hun trench. The same success attended our men holding the right sap and a prisoner was captured. Lieut. Liptrott, who was on the left, also butted against the enemy. Before 10 P.M. our own guns and rifles in rear began to become troublesome, and the Jats, very well handled, began their prearranged return, a party moving along the top of the saps to finish off any enemy bottled up in them. Under a considerable fire from both flanks the retirement was coolly carried out, one of the Company officers being killed and another wounded, whilst in among the dead was a frightened German prisoner; he clung to Major Dundas rather than risk his skin in charge of what he deemed to be the terrible sepoys. The casualties were reported as two Indian officers and sixteen men wounded; and the only other Indian officer and ten men were missing and certainly killed. Then followed a list of booty taken.

The Sappers and Miners under Captain Kelly and Lieut. E. O. Wheeler advanced towards both saps. The left sap was full of Germans, who promptly ran. A large portion of the trench was filled in and Wheeler then retired, bringing with him some German grenades and other articles left behind by them. Kelly with the right party found Germans retiring, and a few of them were bayoneted. The traverses were then destroyed and booty collected before the time for retiring. The total losses of the Sappers consisted of only three killed and one wounded.

This ended a small enterprise which has been given in full as a sample of how things should be done, and the manner in which our Indian troops worked in those days, whilst the ranks still contained some of the fully trained men with which the Corps arrived in France.

Major Dundas received the D.S.O. and Kelly the Military Cross. Liptrott was unfortunately killed shortly afterwards. The following were brought to notice for good work: Jemadar Abdul Aziz and Colour-Havildar Chagatta, both of them Sappers. The latter was awarded the I.D.S.M., being already in possession of the Indian Order of Merit. I knew this fine Indian soldier well. The Jemadar received the same decoration.

In the 6th Jats Havildar Jailal received the I.O.M., and the following won honourable mention : Jemadar Incha Ram, who, although seriously wounded, continued with the attack ; Havildar Badlu, also seriously wounded ; Sepoy Risal, and lastly four gallant fellows who stayed till it was almost too late searching for the body of their Indian officer.

The 6th Jats were originally raised in 1803, and, like other regiments of the Bengal Army, had owned various names and numbers. In 1903 it received its present designation, and is composed of eight companies of Jats. Its colours bear, amongst others, such varied names as Ghazni and Kabul 1842, Maharajpore, Sobraon, Afghanistan, and China.

Lieut.-Colonel H. J. Roche was in command when the war began. He was later given the C.B., and his battalion have good reason to be proud of the part they played.

During the month of November the weather was such as to test severely the stamina of the Indians. Cold and wet accompanied frequently by biting winds is a plain definition of the climatic conditions during the first two weeks ; then snow began and by the 20th the whole country was clothed in a deep mantle. In the midst of the sea of mud, with scant bedding for so bitter a climate, lying in foul and insanitary trenches, often frozen hard, practically underground dwelt in thousands men, to most of whom ice and snow were unknown, their only knowledge of it being the distant views some had obtained of the mighty Himalayas, peopled with a myriad gods, towering like Titan sentinels over their plains and valleys. Imagine their feelings when now they found themselves in their embrace, faced by every devilish device of murderous science, and all from a sense of duty to an alien race. It is a subject for thought. It is a great triumph of fellowship for the British race. A Gurkha officer whom I asked one day what he thought of it all replied : " What can I say ? We live in a well and look up at God's sky by day, and at German flares by night, but we are going to win."

The subterfuges employed by the Indians were at times quite amusing, though not perhaps very much so for the

I

actors. A sepoy, native of Rustam, was out on patrol duty in " No Man's Land " when a German searchlight caught and exposed him in a semi-kneeling position, and the enemy only fifty yards distant. He had probably in his day taken part in uninvited nocturnal visits but not in quite similar circumstances; however, his native wit came to his rescue, and immediately rising up he stood still and saluted his foes. Surprised by the apparition, the Huns ceased firing and the Indian, now salaaming, moved on and entered their trench.

In the German lines facing the Indian Corps were one or two scoundrels from India, types of traitors which are common to all countries, who, finding Hindustan too hot for them, and preferring treachery to the noose which awaited them if they returned, had taken service with the Germans in pre-war days. What use was made of them it is difficult to say, but probably such leaflets as were dropped over our lines from aeroplanes were their production, as well as an occasional call from their trenches shouted in Hindustani advising our men to desert and join the generous Huns.

Be this as it may, our sepoy, seeing he must now feign hatred of us or go under, by signs and gestures soon assured his captors that his one object in life was to cut the throats of the English, and to give emphasis to his bloodthirsty proclivities he passed his hand across his throat, repeating with angry looks, " English, English." This was enough to at once bring him a liberal supply of rations and other trench luxuries. His next business was to discover some means of escape, and he managed by counting on his fingers and saying, " *Beimān* " (unfaithful) whilst pointing to our trenches, to impress his would-be friends that other scoundrels as black as he were willing to desert. Coffee followed this interesting bit of news, and after much palavering the sepoy was allowed to leave on his mission. Creeping carefully he rejoined his battalion and the Huns saw him no more.

All ranks felt the bitter cold and there were a large number of frost-bites and trench feet as they were called, but taken all round the Indian troops stood it far better than I had ever believed possible. A factor in their health was the extraordinarily good arrangements for giving the men baths and providing them with hot water. Once out of the trenches (such occasions were rare in those times) a man was certain to get a hot tub of sorts. All kinds of contrivances were gradually furnished by Government ; heaters, clothes driers, fumigators, travelling boilers were sent out by kind friends and by the " Indian Soldiers' Fund."

The Indian with water of any kind is like a child by the sea, he must at once dabble in it. Now the sea is pure, but our sepoy has a bad habit of entirely ignoring all sanitary laws where his *pani* (water) is concerned ; so long as it is water he will drink from any pool or wash in any gutter, and much as I admire and like him, I have in my time been obliged to inflict very severe punishments to lead and keep him in the path of sanitation. Hence when he found clean hot water was as easily procured as muddy cold water, he naturally chose the former.

Riding out one day I saw a shower of paper descending earthwards evidently dropped from an aeroplane. They were leaflets printed in Hindi calling on our Indian soldiers to rise against the British. Comically enough the call was headed, " True information " ! thereby proving the Germans can sometimes perpetrate a joke. Here is the text :

The Sheik Ul Islam has proclaimed a Jihad (Holy War) on the Id (a festival day) at Mecca against the British, Russians, and French. The Sultan of Turkey has started a war against the same oppressive people, and he has been joined by the King of Afghanistan.

But German humour is at best singular. Here was an incitement to Hindus and Mahomedans alike to revolt, and yet only Mahomedans are named, and to make it more ridiculous the language was Hindi, or the language of Hindus alone. I took a copy to the trenches of one regiment of each class and to one or two mixed Corps of both and read them out. The message was greeted with loud laughter, and one humorous Punjabi Musalman shouted out, "We now understand what 'Made in Germany' means ! "

On the 19th of November Prince Arthur of Connaught visited our Headquarters, and I took him round the billets of the Secunderabad Cavalry Brigade. He was much pleased with all he saw, and the Jodhpore Lancers drawn up near a farmhouse looked weird, coated with snow, a thing none of them had ever touched before.

On the 20th November I was the guest of General de Maud'huy commanding the Xth French Army at St. Pol. I always repeat that I have never served with finer soldiers than the French, nor known better Generals and Staffs than those of our great Allies. The Headquarters Staff were located in the most ordinary house in the main street, but the general order that prevailed all round showed the perfection to which a Command Headquarters can be brought. It was certainly far simpler than anything in our own Army. The General kindly furnished me with a very large scale map of the whole Western Front, giving all details of the German Corps from Nieuport to the Swiss Frontier. An ordinary Corps commander was not allowed such luxuries with us. I still hear from him, and shall certainly make a point of again going to see him wherever he may be.

The next day H.R.H. the Prince of Wales honoured the Corps by coming round and seeing all troops not in the trenches. The Indians were specially delighted and cheered lustily. Just after he left I was motoring to our Reserves to watch some newly manufactured trench mortars fired, when I saw a new German Taube come down ; it was the first in our lines and the excitement of the sepoys was worth watching. The two officers were taken prisoners and I saw them later at my Headquarters.

Regarding the trench mortars mentioned above, this first attempt was most successful. The Indian Sappers and Miners soon had the matter in hand and before long we were using them with good results. Fancy in this great war mortars made at first of wood and cast iron being employed and considered a great adjunct to our means of defence. The old British Army and the Indian

Corps had to learn many a lesson before the days of 15-inch guns and unlimited ammunition.

Every effort was made to alleviate the trials of the men in the trenches. Braziers and other roughly constructed devices were manufactured by our ubiquitous Sappers. Earthen vessels filled with charcoal, when procurable, were distributed along the trenches ; extra socks were issued and straw was rolled under the puttees. A percentage of gum boots were sent out by the " Indian Soldiers' Fund," and woollen gloves were freely supplied. General Head-quarters did all they could to help us, and the Medical Officers and unit commanders were indefatigable in their labours to keep the men fit during the severe ordeal of that ghastly winter.

In this war, when of necessity the Armies lay for so long opposite to one another in the same positions, the public naturally associated the Infantry soldier with the greatest hardships which had to be borne. He lived in the trenches, he held the front line when attacked, or led the assault when in advance, but behind him was the man with the big guns. This latter had some advantages over his Infantry comrade : he was farther from the rifle and machine-gun, and out of the range of the grenade and trench mortar, but without him no front line could have been held for an hour and no attack would ever have been possible.

Moreover, he was the target most sought by the enemy ; the prying aeroplane could easily trace the trenches, but its chief prey was the battery in rear, and once found it very soon received the concentrated attention of the hostile guns. The men in front knew all this well. They loved their field guns, their constant companions and always the nearest to them. The howitzers were their closest allies when the Hun trench had to be searched and knocked about ; the biggest pieces behind them were the loyal parents who closely supported them when necessity arose, and watching over all farthest back were the monsters in those days still in a state of manufacture, affectionately spoken of in later times as Grandmothers.

And so the gunners, like those farther forward, took

their full, and often more than full, share of the daily work. They lived in great discomfort, for you cannot be constantly moving guns in concealed positions; the labour is vast, and so long as you are undiscovered so much the better to remain there. Hence when the pits and dug-outs filled with water, they just made the best of it, and the confidence inspired by these splendid soldiers and their guns was something they could not help realising, however modest.

The Indians, even more than their British comrades, put implicit faith in the Artillery. So long as Jack Sepoy could hear the moan or the roar of the missiles from his beloved guns speeding overhead towards the enemy lines he rested assured that come what might all was well.

CHAPTER IX

THE Army Corps was now on the eve of its first considerable fight. Signs were not wanting that the Germans meant to break into, or through, a portion of our line, and the fighting that followed was confined to the Corps alone. It was in fact the only time during our stay in France that we conducted a combined operation entirely on our own, so to speak. At Givenchy in December, Neuve Chapelle in March, Ypres in April, Festubert in May, and Mauquissart in September, our battles, though on a far bigger scale, were fought in conjunction with and as part of combined forces; but on this solitary occasion we had it all to ourselves, and although it was a purely defensive action the results were highly satisfactory. We regained all our lost trenches and the heavy losses were more than repaid by the knowledge gained, viz. that the Indian Corps as a fighting unit could carry out its own rôle in the war without exterior assistance, so long as the ranks were not too far depleted to permit of our holding the front assigned, and we could employ our own guns as considered necessary.

It was not an unreasonable request we made, that we should not be expected to do more than our numbers warranted. Let us examine for a moment the fighting strength of the Indian Corps at this time. It amounted in rifles to 8500 British and 9500 Indian, and in Reserve about 1750 were available from the Secunderabad Cavalry Brigade, which might mean 1000 rifles. The combined strength therefore was little more than a British Division.

There was always the argument raised that this number was far under the "Ration strength," *i.e.* the number of men for whom rations were drawn. But without going into details which would not be understood by the ordinary reader, it may at once be said that the actual troops available for taking part in any fighting in or near the trenches was as stated above, and no more could be found.

The preliminary operations which preceded the German attack were directed against the Bareilly Brigade of the Meerut Division, which was commanded by Major-General Macbean. On the 21st November the Germans started a succession of bomb attacks from trench guns against the section held by the 6th Jats, causing many casualties and destroying the trenches. This was followed next day by a still heavier bombardment on the same trenches, and against those occupied by the 58th Vaughan's Rifles.

On this night, 22nd–23rd November, in accordance with orders, the Meerut Division was in process of relief by the Lahore Division, plus a portion of the Secunderabad Cavalry Brigade. By the morning of the 23rd November the relief had been partially completed, the result being that five units of the Lahore Division and two battalions of the Meerut were now in the line. The former from left to right were the 129th Baluchis and 57th Rifles composing the left section ; one company Connaught Rangers, 34th Pioneers, and 9th Bhopals formed the centre section ; and the 58th Rifles and a half of the 2nd Black Watch the right section. The other half of the Black Watch and the 41st Dogras were on their way to their billets, whilst the 8th Gurkhas and 107th Pioneers were at Gorre, and the 6th Jats at Festubert.

Pending the completion of the relief by Ferozepore Brigade the command remained under Major-General Macbean. In order to give a concise account of what followed, I will describe as a whole the action of the troops from the time of the first attack on the 23rd November until morning of 24th, when we had completely re-established our position, and then endeavour to explain in greater detail the part taken by the various Corps engaged.

At 7.45 A.M. the O.C. centre section reported that the Germans had broken his line, and a counter-attack was arranged. The 6th Jats were moved up and the Gurkhas and Pioneers ordered to stand fast. By 9 A.M. the enemy attack on this portion of the line appeared to be slackening, but grenade and rifle fire was vigorously kept up. Meanwhile a great part of the 34th Pioneers, who had been driven from their trenches, was ordered to make a counter-attack for their recovery ; but this attack never came to anything.

Half an hour later General Macbean was informed that part of the 58th Rifles had also been driven from their trenches, and this repeated retirement of our troops was rendering our hold precarious. The situation was not relieved by the fact that the right of the Connaught company was by this time being enfiladed owing to the 34th Pioneers' retirement.

About 10 A.M. the G.O.C.'s Meerut and Lahore Divisions mutually arranged that the latter's troops, who would in any case have taken over the front that night, should move up in support at once, and this was begun. The trench mortar of the Garhwal Brigade which was helping the Connaughts, after firing a few rounds, burst. Such were the engines of war in our possession in those days ! General Macbean by these moves would have ample means to resist any likely attacks, and there was no further report of the Germans increasing their effort.

A counter-attack was being arranged, when General Egerton commanding the Ferozepore Brigade arrived at Macbean's Headquarters. As he was the Brigadier to relieve him on this front, Macbean asked him to conduct the operations of this attack, and the 8th Gurkhas and 107th Pioneers were given him as a reinforcement.

By noon the situation appeared more serious than might be inferred from the above, as the 34th Pioneers and 9th Bhopals had been forced from all their trenches, and this, added to the gap caused by portions of the 58th Rifles retiring, left a long line of front trenches in possession of the enemy. A counter-attack by the 6th Jats was unsuccessful, being checked by machine-gun fire.

Our Artillery materially assisted in preventing any further enemy advance, and General Anderson ordered the 1/39th Garhwalis to Gorre, and the Leicesters and 3rd

Gurkhas to be prepared to move from La Couture. He also directed Macbean to recover the lost trenches and enemy sap-heads, and the Garhwal Brigade Reserve to move up to the rear of Macbean's left.

As the enemy increased in numbers and was plentifully supplied with bombs, General Joubert in command of the French on our immediate right was asked to co-operate if it became necessary, and the G.O.C. 8th British Division offered his Artillery support, but neither of these aids proved necessary. Whilst matters were thus shaping themselves, the company of the Rangers had been obliged by the exposure of its right flank to move to its left into the section held by the 57th Rifles and 129th Baluchis.

The position when General Egerton arrived to take over the direction of affairs was this. On our left the 57th Rifles and 129th Baluchis stood firm, whilst the company of the Rangers had moved into this section also and was defending itself with success. The section was commanded by Lieut.-Colonel Southey of the 129th Baluchis, and he had, by occupying some houses in rear of his exposed flank, completely held up the enemy, and saved any chance of their further advance in this direction.

The whole of the centre of our front trenches to the right, viz. those formerly held by the 34th Pioneers, 9th Bhopals, and the greater part of the 58th Rifles, were in German possession. The remainder of the 58th held on, and the Black Watch on the right had not moved. Seeing how matters stood I ordered the Secunderabad Cavalry Brigade up to close billets in Essars, to be available as a reinforcement.

Preceded by a heavy and most accurate Artillery fire directed by Lieut.-Colonel E. J. Duffus and ably supported by two French batteries which had been sent us by our ever-helpful allies, the Infantry attack was launched at 4.30 P.M. Portions of the following formed the attacking party, 8th Gurkhas, 6th Jats, Connaught Rangers, with 107th Pioneers in support. Notwithstanding that the guns had inflicted heavy losses, as evidenced by the numbers of dead Germans found in our trenches when we recaptured them next morning, this counter-stroke was only partially successful. The 107th Pioneers were now sent to support the right where the 8th Gurkhas had succeeded in re-occupying a portion of the lost trenches, whilst some of the 9th Bhopals had also recovered another portion and the 58th, very materially helped by the Black Watch on their right, had reoccupied part of their lost line. The Gurkhas assisted by a detachment of the 6th Jats in this operation captured a few prisoners.

Meantime part of the 107th Pioneers who, as previously stated, had moved to the right were temporarily held up by a furious fire of bombs, and were directed to hold on and gain touch with the 58th Rifles.

Egerton also directed the 1/39th Garhwalis to move to the left flank of the centre section, *i.e.* near where Colonel Southey was holding the Germans. The plan of the Garhwal attack was formed by Colonel Swiney after consultation with Colonel Southey and some other officers, and a suggestion for bombing down the German trenches was first made by Lieut. Robson, R.E.

On receiving definite news of the situation, and being quite determined that in this our first fight as a Corps no inch of ground should be surrendered, I had instructed General Anderson that at all costs the lost trenches were to be recovered. There was small need perhaps, as he was not the man to give away anything for nothing in a fight, but my message was sent through to the troops, and I felt those fine comrades would uphold the honour of the Corps. Knowing this, Egerton, although he had already sent off the 39th Garhwalis on their special mission but had no information of their progress, launched a further attack from his right flank.

This attack consisted of two companies of the 2nd Leicesters and two of the 107th Pioneers. The Leicesters effected a lodgment in the enemy's trenches but were hard pressed to retain it owing to heavy bombing, and the 107th were repulsed, but their combined action without doubt considerably disconcerted the Germans and assisted the 39th Garhwalis who were advancing up the hostile trenches from the opposite direction.

This was our first attempt on a large scale in clearing

the enemy out of his trenches by bombing along them from traverse to traverse. It has long since become familiar to every soldier, but in those days at any rate it was new; and considering the primitive instruments at our disposal, some lighted with matches, some with port fires, some anyhow, a large proportion having a tendency to prematurely explode or refuse to light, and all this done on a freezing night with snow and ice in the trenches and half a gale of wind blowing, it was no mean performance.

The result of this long-drawn-out contest was that with the hold gained on our right by the reoccupation of portions of our line by the 107th Pioneers, 8th Gurkhas, 6th Jats, and a company of the Bhopals, and the splendid advance of the 1/39th Garhwalis along the enemy's trenches from our left, the troops from both flanks joined hands and the entire position was restored by 6 o'clock on the morning of the 24th November. The trenches formerly held by the 34th Pioneers and 9th Bhopals were taken over by the Leicesters and 1/39th Garhwalis. Our losses, however, were very heavy.

The enemy also suffered considerably, not only in his advance, but whilst in occupation of our trenches and their vicinity and during our counter-attack. He had many hours in which to evacuate his wounded and remove his dead under cover of night, nevertheless he left behind him a great many of both, showing the hasty nature of his final departure. The recaptured trenches had been knocked to bits by our well-directed guns, and the 1/39th Garhwalis secured two trench mortars, three machine-guns, and a large number of rifles and other equipment, besides four officers and 100 men taken prisoners.

And thus was Corinth lost and won.

It was our first fight within the Corps, and hence deserves to be told in full. We learned many useful lessons which I shall try and epitomise, but first I must tell the story of many gallant deeds by which the results were obtained. Over forty British officers and 1150 other ranks, chiefly Indians, was the price we paid that November day, but the official despatch disposed of the fighting in a few lines and no names were singled out. Few outside the Corps ever heard of it, but it was the Indian soldiers' own fight, and they will often tell of it in the years to come.

Here is the story. The 34th Pioneers had been the first to feel the shock ; and heavily attacked as they were by grenades, soon had their left machine-gun out of action. The enemy broke into the trench but the gun was saved by Havildar Nikka Singh, who, seeing the detachment overwhelmed, picked up and carried the Maxim through a fierce fire into the support trench.

Captain Mackain, who commanded the company to the right, behaved most gallantly. His trench was rushed, but he quickly collected a party and from behind a traverse defied the enemy advance. From this position he shot one German after another with his revolver, keeping them at bay whilst his men maintained a sharp duel. Mackain was at last himself mortally wounded and carried away by Sepoy Ishar Singh, who received a reward, but alas the gallant officer did not live to reap his. This is surely a case for a posthumous reward ! Captain G. E. Wilson of this battalion was prominently brought to notice for his gallantry. He was wounded and taken prisoner, but eventually returned to England.

The attack on the battalion drove the companies back from their trenches partly to support trenches and partly towards and into the trench of the Connaught Rangers on their left. An attempt to retake the lost positions of the 34th's trenches was unsuccessful, and eventually this battalion, and along with them the 9th Bhopals, lost all their line and fell back in some confusion.

Subadar Natha Singh of the 34th behaved with great coolness and retired his men skilfully, gaining the Indian Order of Merit. Lance-Naik Tota Singh and Havildar Pala Singh also received the I.O.M. for bravery, and the same award was given to Sub-Assistant-Surgeon Harnam Singh for devotion to duty at the regimental aid-post. Lieut.-Colonel G. Kelly was killed whilst leading a counter-attack, and Captain A. Masters, the Adjutant, shared his fate also. Subadars Natha Singh (No. 1), Ram Singh, and Jemadar Sundar Singh and sixty other ranks were killed.

Five British and Indian officers and 140 other ranks were wounded and twenty-three missing.

The company of the Connaught Rangers now found themselves enfiladed from their right, but fighting steadily moved along the trench towards the 57th Rifles and finally barricaded themselves and held on. I always admire the short report of Captain G. F. Callaghan, their commander, who merely says, " We resisted them traverse by traverse but suffered considerable losses and could inflict comparatively no injury on them." Again, " Practically all the bombs were wet and useless." True, it was so. We had no provision in our army for such toys. Doubtless the result of

The cankers of a calm world and a long peace.

This flank, as I have already told, was finally made impregnable by Colonel Southey of the 129th Baluchis, who with the 57th and his own battalion never gave the enemy an opportunity of further extending his gains.

On the right of the 34th Pioneers was the 9th Bhopal Infantry. Numbers 2 and 4 double companies were heavily bombed, and with the retirement of the 34th on the left, the Bhopals were temporarily isolated and the battalion was unable to withstand the German rush. One company was surrounded and the entire line of trenches lost. Later on, part of the Bhopals under Captain E. H. Apthorpe joined in the counter-attack with the 6th Jats and helped to recapture a portion of the trench. Their losses were heavy, including two British officers wounded and three missing. Indian officers: three killed, one wounded, and two missing; other ranks, six killed and 208 wounded and missing.

The 58th Rifles on the right of the Bhopals and left of the Black Watch, as soon as it was reported that our line had been pierced, sent up bombs and ammunition to the firing line. Lieut. R. A. Reilly, who carried out this duty, was on his way back when the covered way along which he was moving became exposed owing to the retirement of the 9th Bhopals. He and two of his seven men were killed.

Captain H. L. Baldwin with his company held on to a ditch which enfiladed the covered way; he was in a very trying position but continued there throughout the day, and this good soldier then joined in the counter-attack when he was unfortunately killed. His C.O. wrote of him in the highest terms.

Captain A. G. Lind and his company with its left flank thrown back held on, but a machine-gun was brought to bear on them and with very heavy losses they were forced back. Lind was wounded during a gallant struggle to stem the enemy advance. About mid-day Captain Bull was sent up to replace Captain Willis who had been severely wounded, but pluckily held on to his command and refused to leave till later, when he was ordered to do so. Bull rallied the right company and, assisted by a party of the Black Watch who were on his immediate right, secured this, the last part of the 58th's trench still in our possession, until 4.30 P.M., when the battalion joined in General Egerton's counter-attack. Bull's conduct throughout the day was exemplary, and the Section commander brought him prominently to notice for having held up the German attack on this flank. With him were fifty men of the Black Watch under Sergeant-Major Kennedy and of these I will tell farther on.

This counter-attack led by Major Davidson-Houston, the C.O., was a complete success and a great part of the 58th's trenches were regained. Lieut. L. Gaisford, a lad I knew well, was killed as he leaped into the trench. Major Thomson and Captain Bull were invaluable in keeping the men in hand during all this troubled fighting. It is worth quoting the words of the C.O. 58th regarding their comrades of the Black Watch in this attack, as serving to show the value of example set by the British soldier. He says:

I was also greatly assisted in this advance on the trench, which was done without a halt or firing, by four men of the Black Watch, Privates Venters, Boyd, M'Intosh, and Stewart; these men came with me in the final rush from the road, and by their example gave a fine lead (mark the words) to my Dogra company in front of whom we were. There being nobody at hand when we reached the trenches, I placed them

to hold a sap which had been cut right into our line, and
although bombed they held on till I could get the men
together, after which they helped me considerably, and by
their *sang-froid* and cheeriness, impressed those round them
most favourably.

No higher tribute could be paid to those four splendid
Highlanders.   They all received the D.C.M.
    The 58th in the day's fighting lost three British and
one Indian officer and fifty-three others killed ; two
British and one Indian officer and sixty others wounded.
Lieut. S. Gordon, Indian Medical Service, and Lieut. J.
Milligan were brought to notice for gallantry in rescuing
with the stretcher-bearers many wounded men.   Havildar
Indar Singh was promoted to Jemadar.   Jemadar Hawinda
behaved with great gallantry in carrying in under heavy
fire his British officer.   Both native officers were awarded
the Military Cross.
    Holding our extreme right was the Black Watch.   You
cannot move men of this stamp, no matter who may be
the enemy.   Under ordinary circumstances the battalion
would have been more to its left, *i.e.* in between battalions
of Indian troops, but owing to the fact that our right
touched the French left, I had received orders to have a
British battalion next to them.   Hence it was the case
that the three battalions on their left were all Indians and
it was on these that the Germans directed their attack.
    Such details may appear unimportant to those who
count Army Corps by Divisions and Brigades, but to us
who had the task of holding a given front, they meant
much.   My Generals and I had many things to think of
which needed no special consideration in other Corps.
    The Black Watch were not themselves directly attacked,
but by their assistance the 58th, as already described, reoccupied their lost trenches.   This right section was
commanded by Major J. Harvey of the Black Watch, a
first-rate C.O., who was afterwards given a Brigade and
killed in command of it in Mesopotamia.   Major A. G.
Wauchope of his battalion, always to the fore when fighting was going on, volunteered to proceed to the trenches

and find out the situation, and carried out his mission most successfully.

Company - Sergeant - Major J. Kennedy, with fifty N.C.O.'s and men, accompanied the counter-attack of the 58th Rifles, and this N.C.O. was one of the first to enter the recaptured trenches, ably seconded by Sergeant Wilson, Lance-Corporal Melrose, and Private Swan.

Wauchope proceeded with Lance-Corporal Gorrie, a gallant man who was always volunteering for dangerous tasks, to the firing trench, and thence to Captain Bull, who with his own men and a few of the Black Watch was very hard pressed by Germans, who were hurling hand-grenades amongst them from a distance of only fifteen yards, to which our men could only oppose rifle fire ; nevertheless this fire soon dominated the enemy, who ceased their bomb-throwing.

Wauchope, accompanied by Lieut. N. McMicking, also of the Black Watch, and twenty of his men, immediately charged over the eighty yards which separated them from a German sap, and entering it moved on another hundred yards, the Huns rapidly retiring and leaving rifles, etc., behind them. This small party then returned, and Wauchope made his way to the O.C. 58th, who thought his whole trenches were reoccupied. It was found, however, that there was still a gap of 300 yards on the left of the 58th and between them and the right of the 8th Gurkhas, and this gap was occupied by only four Highlanders, one of whom was lying wounded. Many bombs were still falling and the party was withdrawn ; this portion of trench being soon after filled by the Indians from both flanks. Kennedy, Drummond, and Private Swan received the D.C.M.

Whilst these events were taking place on the right some fine deeds were being done on our left, which finally regained us all our lost trenches. Colonel Swiney with his 1/39th Garhwalis, discarding all idea of a frontal attack over ground white with snow and which showed up every movement, managed after much difficulty to pick a way through ditches and bog and assemble immediately on the right of Colonel Southey's section, where the 57th Rifles

K

joined the company of the Connaught Rangers. Swiney was dead against a frontal attack, and General Egerton left it to him as to how he should move. Present also was a very gallant officer, Lieut. R. G. Robson, R.E., who suggested an advance along the lost trenches with bombs. To prove his opinion, prior to the advance he made a demonstration by moving close to some houses and clearing the Germans out with bombs : an unselfish and gallant act.

The occasion always finds the man, and this occasion found not only a keen battalion but also a heroic figure in the person of Captain D. H. Acworth of that good old Frontier regiment, the 55th Coke's Rifles, and then serving with the 57th Rifles. Robson and Ackworth, with seven Afridis of the 57th (one or two being 55th men attached), and one Connaught Ranger, moved along the trench. The attack was entrusted to two companies of the 1/39th Garhwalis, Major W. H. Wardell's, with Captain S. Orton ; and Captain Lumb's, a third being in support. Wardell was to attack along the trench from left to right, Lumb moving level with him on his right along a shallow depression some fifteen yards away and roughly parallel with the trench. Robson and Acworth started their bombing and continued it for some fifty yards, when owing to bombs running out and for other causes the bombing ceased, and the attack developed into a bayonet advance, pure and simple, by the Garhwalis. The Germans meantime were using bombs very freely.

Wardell's fine attack, after pushing some distance along the enemy trenches, began to lose weight; but here Lumb, finding his own shallow ditch was gradually ending and knowing that his business was to help Wardell, crossed over with a rush and was into the trenches in the midst of Wardell's men. The Garhwalis were now thoroughly blooded and could not be stopped. Traverses fell in rapid succession and prisoners were being gathered up at every turn. The opposition was severe, and time after time as the men sprang up on the parapets or ran along both sides of the trenches they came under heavy enfilade fire.

When the advance was stayed by the reduction in

numbers, Lieut. J. Welchman joined in with more men, and the prisoners being quickly passed to the rear, the Garhwalis under Lumb gallantly pushed on, clearing everything in front of them with the bayonet, till they eventually joined hands with the 107th Pioneers advancing from the right. Dawn broke on our now victorious troops, and the Indians had the satisfaction of knowing that although they had suffered grievously, although some of their comrades had been forced from their trenches, and that no one might ever hear of their work, yet it had been finally completed by the Corps alone.

When Swiney found that the advance was leaving the trenches but sparsely held, he had sent up Captain J. Lane with reinforcements, and as they reached a bend in the trench they were furiously attacked by Germans who held a sap running right into our line. Lane faced this enfilade fire unflinchingly and managed to close the sap with a barricade, thus ensuring the safety of the main trench. The Huns left behind them rifles, tools, and quantities of equipment, some trench mortars and machine-guns in the hands of the 39th, whilst their dead were strewn along both sides of and in the recaptured trench. When I heard it I cheered as if I myself had done the job, although I was safe in a château miles away with my ear to a telephone, but I could not conceal my joy at the thought that my brave Indian troops had not lost an inch of ground.

The losses of the Garhwalis were comparatively light, but the reason was that the work was swiftly and thoroughly done. The gallant Major Wardell who had led the first advance was wounded and missing; Captain Orton was severely wounded; Jemadar Daulat Rawat was killed, and two Indian officers were wounded, whilst among other ranks eighteen were killed and thirty-seven wounded.

Captain Lumb and Subadar Dhan Sing Negi received the Military Cross. Captain Acworth, 55th Rifles, was also given this decoration, and Subadar Jagat Sing Rawat the Order of British India. The I.O.M. was the reward of four of the seven men of the 57th Rifles who accompanied Robson, and the others were given the I.D.S.M.; whilst in the ranks of the Garhwalis several men received the

I.O.M., amongst them a gallant N.C.O., Havildar Alam Sing Negi, and others the I.D.S.M.

The brave Robson was killed a month later, and hence did not live to receive a well-merited honour. Colonel Swiney was promoted Brevet-Colonel for his initiative, gallantry, and skill. And last, but greatest of all who fought that day, was Naik Darwan Sing Negi : first in the advance and first to rush each traverse, wounded in the arm and twice in the head, this heroic son of Garhwal continued to fight to the end, and was the second recipient of the coveted Victoria Cross. How well earned ! In his village of Kabartir, north of the Pindar River, amid the wild regions of the great Himalayas, often will be told the tale of how Darwan Sing upheld the prestige of his race and gained fame for the regiment in which he served.

Colonel Swiney's report is a document which will be preserved in the regiment as a memento of many brave men and the brave deeds they performed that night. Did space permit I would like to name them, but the battalion will treasure them all.

The 39th Garhwal Rifles was raised at Almora in 1887 as the 2nd Battalion of the 3rd Gurkha regiment; became 39th (the Garhwali) regiment of Bengal Infantry in 1890, and received its present name in 1901. A second battalion was added in 1901.

A part of No. 3 Company Sappers and Miners was engaged in the centre section repairing loopholes, etc. Captain E. H. Kelly, R.E., was in command, and finding no officers he took charge of the troops in his vicinity. He was severely wounded by hand-grenades, being hit in the head, shoulders, hand, and leg, but was nevertheless able to reach the support line. The Corps of Royal Engineers never says die.

The Leicesters in their counter-attack with the 107th Pioneers lost Captain H. Grant, killed whilst leading his company in the charge, and 2nd Lieut. M. Seton-Browne was also killed at the head of his platoon just as he had reached the enemy trench. No. 8224 Lance-Corporal G. Grey, Sergeant P. Forster, and three men were brought to notice for their fine example. The latter received the D.C.M.

Major H. Gordon was in command of this attack and received the D.S.O. Throughout the time the Leicesters served with me in France this splendid Corps shared the brunt of every fight in which their Brigade was engaged. Its sterling grit was recognised by none more than the Indian soldiers.

As already described, one company of the Connaught Rangers was fighting next to the 34th Pioneers, whilst six officers and 300 rifles were in support of the 8th Gurkhas in the counter-attack. These latter were met by a heavy cross-fire from machine-guns. Notwithstanding this a part of them reached the objective. Major W. Hamilton, Captain R. G. Eyre, and Lieut. J. Hume, the only officers with one company, were wounded, whilst fifty-five men were killed or missing and fifty-three were wounded, and the detachment had to withdraw. The three officers named above were brought to notice.

The 57th Rifles, who held fast to their trenches on our left, did right good work though sharing none of the glory. The C.O. reported during the fighting: "I am trying to improve my trenches, but have no large-sized spades or shovels. A telephone is urgently needed. We want some sand-bags—most urgent. Also a lot of bombs. Without these and the sand-bags it is difficult sometimes." Splendid fellow! What a commentary on the state of affairs; little he dreamed his words would be repeated for those to read who know nothing of how the fight was waged in the snow-clad trenches of 1914. Ours were held, as a 57th man said to me after the fight, "with our bare hands; we had nothing else." Captain Indajit Singh, the medical officer of the battalion, was killed while coolly carrying out his duties behind the firing line. A brother officer, Major P. Atal, I.M.S., in medical charge of the 129th Baluchis, was also killed with him. Both had gained the respect of their Corps by the fearless discharge of their duty to the wounded.

The 8th Gurkhas, who had suffered so heavily on 30th October and had hardly a British officer of their own remaining, proved their grit on this occasion of their counter-attack by recapturing a portion of the lost trenches. Major K. Cassels, although himself wounded, managed to hold on to

his command and the battalion suffered the further following losses : Lieut. D. S. Macpherson, son of a gallant soldier,
was killed ; Major R. W. Elliott also lost his life ; both of
these officers belonged to the 7th Gurkhas.   Lieut. Peploe,
6th Gurkhas, was wounded and Lieut. C. Maxwell of the
8th was missing.   It is thus made clear how the original
officers of the battalion were fast disappearing.

In this counter-attack the 6th Jats lost nearly 200 men.
Captain Dudley was killed; Lieut. Cockburn earned the
Military Cross for his gallantry in driving the Germans from
traverses ; Captain Moore and Major Dundas were wounded.

The 107th Pioneers had failed at first to reach the enemy
trenches in their attack with the Leicesters, but had eventually reached them and were slowly moving north, where
they met the Garhwalis coming from the other side.
During the fighting Major Bruce and seventeen men were
killed ; Captains Davis, Mangin, Turnbull, and McLaughlin
and Lieut. Wallis were wounded, besides one Indian officer
and forty men.   Subadars Hashmat Dad Khan, and Labh
Singh received the I.D.S.M.

There remains one splendid deed to be recorded, and
that is how a very gallant gentleman died, but left behind
him an immortal name on the list of heroes who have won
the Victoria Cross.

A detachment of the 34th Poona Horse, one of the
regiments of the Secunderabad Cavalry Brigade, had been
sent up as a reinforcement on the 23rd November and was
in the trenches of the Ferozepore Brigade.   A German sap
ran right up to our line and exposed it to fire.   Guarding
the junction was Lieut. F. A. de Pass with a small party.
One of this party volunteered to move along the sap and
reconnoitre it.   It was found that at twelve paces away
the sap turned and there was a loopholed traverse guarded
by Huns.   From this coign of vantage they continued
throughout the day to fling hand-grenades into our trench :
there were no grenades to reply with, and de Pass and his
men had to stick it out, losing several wounded.

He, however, was determined that the Germans should
be turned out, and at dawn next day, with two sowars, he
crawled up the sap, inserted a charge of gun-cotton against

a loophole of the traverse, and the explosion which followed wrecked the traverse and laid bare a wide gap, exposing its site to fire from our trenches.   A grenade hurled at his small party was fortunately ineffective, and for twenty-four hours the enemy was quiet.

The very next day in broad daylight this gallant soul, accompanied by Private C. Cook of the 7th Dragoon Guards, went out and carried in a wounded sepoy under a heavy fire for a considerable distance.

Unbounded courage and compassion joined.

On the 26th November de Pass found that the Germans had repaired their destroyed traverse, from which heavy bombing was again proceeding, and our parapet was being knocked to bits ; moving to the evil spot, he saw a sniper behind the loophole of the traverse and at once tried to pick him off, but was instantly shot dead.   He was honoured in death and gazetted to the Victoria Cross as a reward from the King he had so faithfully served.   The I.D.S.M. was conferred on his companions in peril, Sowars Abdullah Khan, Firman Shah, and Fateh Khan of the 34th Poona Horse.   Private Cook received the Distinguished Conduct Medal.

Colonel Grant, 8th Gurkhas, who commanded the centre section, had a very difficult task as will be readily understood, but he carried it out with resolution.

Brigadier-General Egerton readily undertook the task he was asked to perform by General Macbean.   His two Staff officers, Major Sangster, 2nd Indian Lancers, and Captain Stewart, Cameron Highlanders, well earned the praise he gave them.

The German attack was made by the three battalions of the 112th Regiment of the Twenty-ninth Division, XIVth Army Corps, as evidenced by the killed, wounded, and prisoners, with the 170th Regiment in support; and although their numbers were inferior to the troops we eventually brought against them before our line was re-established, they had the superiority in guns and men on the front first attacked.

During the fighting, although of course I had not been

in the trenches myself, I had followed, as far as this could be done from a distance, the trend of the battle. In the grounds of my Headquarters was a tower, built for purposes other than those to which it was put this freezing night. It was on high ground, in fact the only high ground within range of our front, and from this vantage point I watched from dusk till dawn the progress of the fight, only varying my vigil by constant visits to the telephone in the house to keep in touch with Divisional Headquarters. I can remember no occasion in my life when I felt more acutely the desire to succeed, for where my Corps was in the grips of death was my entire world.

Sir John French sent us his hearty congratulations on the results of the fighting.

CHAPTER X

The fighting east of Festubert had been full of incidents which furnished us with useful material for future operations. The German strength directly opposite the Corps at this time may be taken at about 20,000 Infantry in addition to Pioneers, and an unknown number of guns of all calibres. Ours should have been near that same number, but was, owing to heavy casualties without replacements on any but a nominal scale, very much less. What was found was that the enemy had already achieved great skill in sapping up to our lines, and in this respect was infinitely superior. Having completed his saps, and aided by grenades and trench mortars, there was nothing to prevent his capturing our first lines of trenches, nor for long after this time were we able to employ his methods. The time came when the tables were turned; but you cannot reach the skies while your feet are still on the earth, and ours were deep in the Flanders mud. We also found that it makes for efficiency to have British troops interspersed with the Indians. In this case only on the extreme right was there half a Highland battalion, and on the extreme left one company of an Irish regiment.

But whatever we may have learned, the Huns discovered that the Indian Corps could give back all and more than it got, and we braced ourselves up in the certain belief that although England had been sadly behind in providing us with the means of paying back the enemy in his own coin, she would assuredly make up way, and then would come our turn.

I often said all this to the Indian officers and men, and it cheered them ; they knew our real strength ; they began to realise that we had been caught tripping; and from surprise at first that this should ever have been possible, they gradually became sarcastic at the expense of the Huns. One Jawan (young fellow) even declared that if the Germans would exchange weapons the war would be over in a week. " Not if we kept them as clean as you do," remarked a comrade, and all laughed. I discovered our recruit had been reprimanded that morning for having a dirty rifle on parade.

On the 24th November I attended my first conference at General Headquarters. All the Corps Commanders were present, and although I knew some of them and had casually met others at manœuvres which I had attended when on leave from India (and I may here add that every time I came home on leave I never missed attending manœuvres, British or foreign, as opportunity offered), I felt for the first time in France that I was a stranger. I heard as I came into the hall, " Who is that ? " " He commands the Indians." It was as if some foreign general had suddenly dropped into the sacred haunts of Whitehall in pre-war days. However, I was prepared for it. I knew that most of them would hold out the hand of welcome to our Indian soldiers, and it was satisfactory that at our first meeting I was able to tell the Commander-in-Chief the results of our fighting that very morning. Sir John French and Sir Horace Smith-Dorrien congratulated me on the conduct of all ranks, and I was rather pleased than otherwise that I was not one of those present who might be referred to as Tom, Dick, or Harry.

On the 26th November I wrote to G.H.Q. giving a statement of the strength of the Indian Corps which, including the Secunderabad Cavalry Brigade, then numbered only 14,000 rifles or little over that of a British Division, and was reducing at the rate of about eighty a day; and stating that I could receive no further reinforcements from India before the 5th December, when the Sirhind Brigade should rejoin from Egypt. In addition I pointed out that the British battalions averaged only 700 men each, a pitifully low one for work in this Corps. I laid stress on the fact that there were indications we might be again attacked, and that one Brigade would, before the arrival of reinforcements, have done forty-five days, and all the others thirty-five days actually in, or in support of, the trenches, with only scraps of such rest as could be arranged. I requested that under these conditions the Corps might be given a complete rest of a few days when the reinforcements arrived ; gave full reasons why I considered it absolutely necessary, and suggested remedies for our shortage in numbers and for increasing them. One of these was the addition of Territorial battalions, and I may add that, although G.H.Q. did not at first appear to approve of this, I did get first two, and later a total of six, of these fine battalions, and of them I shall have much to say as I progress. I said plainly that unless my request was agreed to, the Corps would soon only be equivalent to a single Division.

The reply to my letter stated that the condition of the Indian Corps was well known, and I was to exercise caution in its employment, and that the Commander-in-Chief would give such assistance as was possible, and this was outlined ; but I was given no hope of a rest for the Corps as a whole, except such as I could eke out after the reinforcements arrived. I realised the immense difficulties of the Commander-in-Chief ; but I am now writing for those who, knowing nothing of our own difficulties, passed hasty judgement and unfairly criticised men who were in truth doing right good work.

As a matter of fact no rest was given, but the Indian Corps held on to its line for twenty-four days longer, reducing daily and being eventually altogether too weak for its task. As if, however, to strain the rope to the last strand, after the reinforcements arrived, instead of deriving any benefit I was ordered to farther extend my front to include Givenchy and up to the La Bassée—Bethune road. I knew how fatal was such an order, but there was nothing to do but obey. The French Brigadier whom we relieved was surprised at the smallness of the numbers of the relieving troops, and told us his own outgoing strength, which was very considerably higher. Shortly after that a heavy German attack was launched at us, straining the tired-out troops to the limit of endurance and entailing, after three days' hard fighting, the assistance of the First Army Corps from reserve to restore the position.   All that will be described in due course; but why I have gone into detail regarding this matter is that, notwithstanding my having so strongly urged a rest, and written as plainly as a Corps Commander could well do in the field, yet in the despatch describing the operations of the 18th and 19th December I am alluded to as having made an attack on the Germans, because I deemed it to be " a favourable opportunity." Nothing could be farther from the facts. I considered it in truth a most unfavourable opportunity; but my instructions as they read to me, and which I will quote fully, were sufficiently clear to lay on me the definite duty of using every endeavour to make one or more local pushes to the front if I considered this reasonably feasible, and under those conditions I chose what appeared to me to be the most favourable opportunity that presented itself.

I had once drawn attention to the long term of un-relieved duty in the trenches, and again when my front was extended beyond the power of the tired Corps to hold on, and I could do no more.

On 28th November I had the honour of entertaining General de Maud'huy, Commanding Xth French Army, at lunch.   He and his Staff stayed till late in the afternoon, and as usual I never enjoyed anything in France better than visits to or from our Allied officers.

During the rest of the month the usual trench warfare continued, but there was one incident worth recording. On the night of the 27th November a party of the Man-chesters, commanded by 2nd Lieut. S. D. Connell, accom-panied by Lieut. F. E. Buller, R.E., advanced and entered two German saps sixty yards away.   The saps were filled in, but in the subsequent retirement Connell was killed and there were eleven other casualties.   Buller was awarded the Military Cross for his gallantry in returning to bring in a wounded man, during which attempt he himself was wounded.   The O.C. Manchesters after careful inquiry estimated the German casualties as not under forty, including an officer who was bayoneted as he emerged from his dug-out.

On the 1st December His Majesty the King visited the Indian Corps, and the honour was greatly appreciated by all ranks. There is nothing the Indian soldier holds in comparison to a word from his Sovereign, and as the King made frequent inquiries regarding individuals, these of course were henceforth marked men. As soon as I knew that His Majesty meant to start his tour from Corps Headquarters at Hinges, I telephoned to General Maistre in command of the XXIst Corps d'Armee on my right and asked him to attend. The French General had that morning an important local duty in his trenches, but nevertheless he came. I had not been able to tell him on the telephone the reason, as it was essential the news of the King's visit should be kept secret till the last moment; and when he arrived and I explained it to him, he said, " No duty would have kept me from paying my respects to your King. I am very pleased you let me know." His Majesty conversed with him for some time.

The King had all the British and Indian officers introduced to him at each place where they were collected along the route from Hinges to Locon : through slush and mud he tramped, adding joy and strength to his soldiers, and after seeing all the assembled troops who were not on duty in the trenches, and the Divisional Commanders and Indian Princes and Chiefs, I had the honour of motoring His Majesty to a battery in action, where he examined the guns, the men and their dug-outs, and I believe I must have been one of the first officers to have this honour. He has since been among many Corps and batteries, but this was his first visit to the Army in France.

On 4th December I visited General Maistre, and with him went a long tour of the trenches of the XXIst Corps d'Armée. What struck me most was the extraordinarily well constructed communication trenches leading up to the village of Fosse-Calonne. The country was chalky and rolling and as different as a place could be from our own boggy front. I was also struck by the perfection to which the French had brought their village defences. The dug-outs were far more substantial and comfortable than our own ever were at any time : electric power was available, and hence many shelters were lighted with electricity, and every man appeared to be hard at work improving the defences.   The whole organisation was excellent, and the nature of the soil and advantage of having a village in the centre of the defensive line greatly assisted all their protective measures.   The men were full of humour and gave proof of this in one room which was loopholed and only thirty yards away from another held by the Germans. The roof had been damaged by a shell, and through an opening one of the poilus proceeded to display a tricolour flag on the end of a pole, his daily amusement.   On this occasion, however, Brother Boche was not to be drawn. On the table was a gramophone, and another man at once turning it towards the loophole started the " Marseillaise." " If this will not fetch them," he said, " I will try ' God save the King.' "   But the Hun must have been in his mid-day sleep, as nothing would move him, and all was quiet till we got outside, when they started a lively fusillade at a chimney behind us, with what object I could not surmise.

After spending three very interesting hours we returned by another trench, and at an opening near a mound I emerged to find a Guard of Honour drawn up with a band. To my surprise I learnt this was in my honour, and after being saluted, those fine soldiers marched past me.   Needless to say I was more than gratified by this compliment paid to me by an Allied brother Corps Commander.   It is actions like this that bind peoples together, and it is only one of a hundred proofs that our friendship is not on the surface, but deep.   Personally, I shall always look on France as a land where I saw more human nature in its truest form than I have ever seen elsewhere, and like Alexander and Diogenes shall feel that if I were not an Englishman I would be a Frenchman.

On the return journey we went over the ruined village of Vermelle recently taken by the French.   I went through the German trenches and was much surprised to find the comfortable dug-outs of the officers were furnished with every kind of table, chair, and other luxuries. The walls had pictures hung, and there were even good lamps and clocks in niches.   It all seemed so different from our own and gave me the impression that the Huns looked after their comforts far too much.   Shooting was going on and numbers of shells lay unexploded, some of them being English.   By permission of the French Colonel I brought away two kinds of steel loopholes out of German trenches, and eventually these were sent to G.H.Q.; but I kept a periscope.   These I had not till then seen in our own Corps.   The entire village was a mass of ruins, but a statuette of the Virgin near a chapel still stood on its pedestal among the debris.

The Sirhind Brigade, under command of Major-General Brunker, arrived from Egypt on the 7th December, and thus at last the Lahore Division was completed.   With the arrival of this Brigade and considerable drafts from India, I prepared a scheme for giving my troops as much rest as was possible; but it was short-lived, for on the 9th December the Chief of the Staff called and told me the Corps was to extend its front and take over the village of Givenchy and about a mile to the south of it from the French.   I have already told what this meant to us; but there was no option, and on the 11th December we took over the trenches at Givenchy, and as far as the La Bassée —Bethune road.

On the 8th December Sir John French had telegraphed thanking the Corps for a message we had sent him, and said, " I owe them a deep debt of gratitude for the splendid services they have rendered and which have proved of great value in the conduct of the campaign."   Sir John never failed to say a word at the right time.

On 12th December I attended a conference at G.H.Q., and was then informed of the intentions of the Commander-in-Chief to commence an offensive on the 14th December with the Second and Third Corps in conjunction with the French on the left, with the object of reaching the line Le Touquet—Warneton—Hollebeke.   The Fourth and Indian Corps, though taking no direct part in this action, were ordered to " carry out active local operations with a view to containing the enemy now in their front." At this time the French on our right, *i.e.* next to the Indian Corps, also undertook offensive operations.

This was the first of many orders received between this date and 20th December, and, as I shall show, beginning with small injunctions they increased in their scope ; and the loyal endeavour on my part and that of my Generals to comply with their spirit only ended when the enemy launched a heavy attack against several parts of the Indian Corps. Loyalty should claim no conditions, but it does not always meet with its reward. As a matter of fact the offensives undertaken received the commendation of the Commander-in-Chief at the time, as contained in his own operation orders, and would under ordinary conditions have remained at that, and no more would have been heard of them. It was the long-premeditated attack delivered on the 20th December by the enemy which alone brought us into prominence ; and that it was carried out on that date, just after our local efforts, was a mere coincidence, as the German prisoners themselves stated the 20th was the day fixed for it.

On the 16th December it was decided to capture two German saps opposite to the trenches of the 15th Sikhs in the neighbourhood of Givenchy, and then to extend the operation by securing a portion of the German main trenches. The troops selected for this operation were taken from the Ferozepore Brigade.

The 129th Baluchis and 57th Rifles were ready to attack by 8.30 A.M. ; whilst the Connaught Rangers were detailed in support, and a Territorial battalion (the 142nd), lent by the French General on our right, was held in reserve. Major Potter with his company of the 129th was quickly across the thirty yards which separated him from the left sap, and the other company under Lieut. C. S. Browning also reached its objective ; the casualties in this first rush were not heavy, and both attacks pushing up the sap were soon close to the enemy main trench.

But (there was always a " but " in the trench operations of those days) the difficulty now presented itself as to how to reinforce them, as it was impossible to cross the open space swept by a hail of bullets which soon destroyed the wounded who had fallen in the first rush. The attackers were gradually bombed back towards the captured sap-heads. Browning and all his Indian officers were wounded, and the men in the right sap got jammed in on the sap-head but held on till dusk under a heavy fire of grenades, whilst Potter and his men in the left sap also held their position with splendid determination.

A party of the 15th Sikhs who had accompanied each attack were meantime working heart and soul to dig a trench back from the sap-head to our main trench, and the 21st Company Sappers and Miners and working parties of the 34th Pioneers were engaged in the same process to join up with them from our own side. The right sap was the more difficult of the two, and before connection could be established the remnants of our men in the sap-head, fearing that relief would be late, made an attempt to cross the open over the fifteen yards which still separated them from their comrades : the distance was short but the devastating fire which the enemy rained across it killed or wounded every man as he ran, and the Hun had his revenge in the recapture of his lost ground.

Potter in the left sap was more fortunate, the new communication trench being completed by dark, when he and his men withdrew into our own line. His cool bearing and gallantry were never more conspicuous than on this day, and though he was missing a few days later during an attack, his name will live in the history of his Corps.

The casualties were heavy. In the Baluchis Captain Ussher, Subadar Adam Khan, and fifty men were killed; Lieut. Browning, Captain Money, two Indian officers, and seventy rank and file were wounded.

Writing of the 129th Baluchis brings to mind one or two good stories of that battalion. Early in November, for purposes of identifying enemy corps on our front, C.O.'s were asked to secure a few prisoners. One afternoon Sepoy Abdulla Jan, a Mahsud, asked permission of his section commander to cross " No Man's Land " and enter a German sap. This was refused, but shortly after, no N.C.O. being near, Abdulla slipped over the parapet, ran

L

across to the sap and jumped in. There was a Hun in it all right but, possessing no rifle, he promptly bolted. The section commander, having meantime returned along our trench, looked over the parapet and saw our gallant friend ; he shouted to him to return, which the man did very quietly, and on arrival, being asked what he was at, replied that he was trying to get hold of a German rifle and did not think it worth while bringing in a mere man without it. His native instinct had got the better of his discretion, as a Mahsud in his own hills will risk his life to steal or otherwise procure a good firearm. On being told a rifle was as nothing in value compared to a man, he at once volunteered to go out again and capture one, and was much disgusted when his request was refused.

These Mahsuds were on their first trial in our regular Corps, and in some respects showed aptitude for trench warfare. As soon as our roughly-made hand-grenades began to be issued they asked to be allowed to use them, and the gallant Robson, R.E., of whom I told in the attack by the 39th Garhwalis on November 23, gave them several lessons in their use. The men were quite delighted, and parties often went out and bombed German saps and entirely stopped the Huns working on that particular bit of front. I have one more story of the 129th Baluchis.

The C.O., being in need of a change in his menu, one morning sent his Afridi orderly and a signaller to find a chicken ; no special method of procuring it was prescribed, except that the men were to leave by the communication trench. Some hours later the signaller returned with the chicken and reported that the orderly had been arrested by the Provost-Marshal for looting an empty shop (mark the words). This was followed by another report from the Staff Captain. Next morning, to the C.O.'s surprise, the orderly turned up as usual. Asked by what means he had returned he quietly said, " I told the officer that I was taking the things for you " ; and later a large bundle arrived from Brigade Headquarters addressed to the C.O. and on it a label, " Herewith your property." The contents comprised a bedspread, two blankets, a box of china basins, knives, forks, a lady's parasol, and a pair of stays. When asked what the stays were for he replied, " They make very good hockey pads." Such were some of the lighter sides of trench warfare.

However, stern events were now ahead of us, and the Corps was about to bear the brunt of a heavy German blow. On the 17th December, the operation orders from Chief of Staff, G.H.Q., stated that it was the intention of the Commander-in-Chief to " attack vigorously all along the front " on the 18th, with the Second, Third, Fourth, and Indian Corps, and a further paragraph directed that these Corps " will demonstrate and seize any favourable opportunity which may offer to capture any enemy trenches in their front."

It is hard to reconcile the two operations contained in the selfsame order. To " attack vigorously " is clear enough ; to " demonstrate " is to make only a show of doing so. How can you do both at the same time ?

This order was issued from G.H.Q. at 9 P.M. on the 17th December. My orders based on it were timed 2.45 A.M. on the 18th, and the operations planned were ordered to commence at 10 A.M. on the same day. At 10.15 A.M. G.H.Q. issued instructions that the efforts of the Second, Fourth, and Indian Corps should be concentrated only on such objectives as were reasonably feasible. At the risk of going into technical details for a moment, I must give the orders in their sequence so that military readers may realise the difficult conditions under which I had to carry on operations until the German attack came on us. On this same date (December 18) another order from G.H.Q. issued at 4.15 P.M. said the Second, Third, Fourth, and Indian Corps would continue to demonstrate on the 19th December along the whole front and seize every favourable opportunity which may offer to capture any of the enemy's trenches.

Now in order to capture enemy trenches it is necessary to make elaborate and detailed arrangements. You cannot issue orders the same as you might do in open warfare, and indeed it is the carefully-thought-out and elaborate plans adopted since those early days that have turned this trench warfare into an exact science, and why two years later even less highly trained troops, assisted, it is true, by an overwhelming Artillery fire, grenades, howitzers, etc., were able to carry out their programme with something approaching mathematical exactitude. But all this was different in 1914; we had then to do our best without these aids and to take the consequences.

I have often thought how different might have been the results of some of the many attacks carried out by Indian troops had we arrived " After " instead of " Before " unlimited ammunition and all the other helps to victory had come to be looked on as part of the absolute necessaries for any advance.

A distinguished General said to me in 1917 : " When *you* were in France it was a crime to say it was necessary to success to have a large gun support; now any one volunteering to carry out an enterprise except with an unlimited amount of shells would be looked on as a fool and take his *congé* at once." What a pleasant change !

On the 18th and 19th, operations were carried out by the Indian Corps as will shortly be narrated, and G.H.Q. was of course kept fully informed. On this latter date the Commander-in-Chief's orders were as follows :

Issued at 6 P.M. The operations conducted yesterday were attended in several cases with marked success. Although the ground gained has not in all cases been maintained the balance of advantage rests with us and promises well for further progress. It is the intention of the Commander-in-Chief that the Second, Third, Fourth, and Indian Corps should continue until further orders to prosecute similar enterprises under Corps arrangements, taking every possible measure to consolidate and " extend " [my inverted commas] all successes achieved.

Such were the orders received by me from the 12th to 19th December inclusive, and it was in accordance with them that the operations of the Corps, now about to be told, were carried out. As will be seen, we succeeded in occupying a portion of enemy trenches and sap-heads, and captured two machine-guns and some prisoners, and, as I said before, but for the German attack on us the following day, our job would probably have been considered as very successful.

Details were, of course, left to Divisional Commanders, but the responsibility was mine, for I could have altered or refused to sanction them. In the case of the Meerut Division matters were allowed to stand as proposed. In the case of the Lahore Division for their attack on 19th, General Watkis proposed an attack on a front of 1000 yards. I reduced this to 300 yards, leaving the choice of the part to be attacked to him. We had neither the men nor the guns for the larger attack, and our orders limited us to distinctly minor operations.

The Commander-in-Chief's despatch on this battle stated that the losses in the Meerut Division after the first attack on the 19th December and subsequent return to its own trenches were " considerable," but the total casualties amounted to eighty-two, including officers. The Lahore Division fought for several successive days before the German attack was launched, and during this time lost very heavily, especially in officers ; but in both Divisions not a single regimental officer in the Indian Army was " mentioned " in the body of the despatch, and only two in the British Service.

At this time our distribution was as under. The French on our right had their extreme left on the Bethune —La Bassée road. From this road to the canal was held by the Connaught Rangers of the Ferozepore Brigade, and the remainder of this Brigade held the trenches as far as east of Givenchy. The Sirhind Brigade was on their left and extended the line keeping parallel to the Festubert road, up to within half a mile of the cross-roads at La Quinque Rue. This completed the front of the Lahore Division ; and the Meerut Division, with the Seaforth Highlanders of the Dehra Dun Brigade on their extreme right, was distributed as follows : Remainder of this Brigade in position as far as the cross-roads on the Rue du Bois, the line passing through what was commonly then known as " The Orchard," though this name later caused some confusion, owing to the fact that several other orchards existed. The Garhwal Brigade was on the left of the Corps, and held trenches as far as the cross-roads south of Neuve Chapelle.

Both the Lahore and Meerut Divisional Commanders had arranged local offensive operations to give effect to the orders of the Commander-in-Chief, and these were put into execution on the morning of the 19th. The portion of German trench to be attacked by the Lahore Division was just opposite the junction of the Ferozepore and Sirhind Brigades, and the attacking troops consisted of one battalion from each Brigade.

The Meerut Division had selected as its objective the German trenches near the " Orchard," and opposite the 6th Jats on the left of the Dehra Dun Brigade. The attacking troops consisted of one and a half battalions of the Garhwal Brigade.

Both attacks were accompanied by a complement of Sappers and Pioneers. A biting cold wind blew over the trenches, making it impossible to get any warmth into the body, as the Meerut Division party, which advanced first, left its trenches.

Half an hour after midnight the Leicesters moved to the salient whence would start the attack, and by 3.30 A.M. deployed and began the advance. The battalion was commanded by Lieut.-Colonel Blackader, and he had under him a splendid body of officers and men. The remainder of his troops consisted of half of the 2/3rd Gurkhas, a company of the 107th Pioneers, and a party of Sappers.

Immediately the advance began machine-guns swept the area, but, although held up by barbed wire and a hedge, Captain Romilly, who was with his company on the left, stopped at nothing until they had entered the Hun trench and captured two machine-guns. The enemy, not caring to face this class of men, had bolted as we neared the objective, but the Leicesters once started are hard to stop, and into the hail of another gun which had opened on them went the men from the Midland County. Again the bird had flown, but a second trench was ours and was only abandoned when it was seen that it was too far in advance and under our own Artillery`fire. The captors took up their position in the first trench and at once put it into a proper state of defence.

The right company of the Leicesters with equal determination had soon made themselves masters over 100 yards of trench, but in bombing along this found it led into the main trench, and when within only a few yards of this, seven of the eight bombers were put out of action. A barricade was erected and, being reinforced by their own men and some of the 3rd Gurkhas, they held on. This, however, left a gap between the right and left attacking companies, which Major Dundas and his Gurkhas, with splendid élan, endeavoured to bridge. The enemy, however, held this portion of the trench strongly, and although driven back with grenades and bayonets, still remained in possession of a considerable part of it. The Gurkhas suffered from a close enfilade fire, but consolidated their gains.

In the result the trenches captured by the Leicesters on the right were lost, as the enemy employed machine-guns to cut away the barricades and followed up with unlimited bombing. New barricades were constructed but shared the same fate, and, as Dundas on the left found it impossible to advance farther, and all ranks were under heavy minenwerfer fire, a withdrawal of the right attack was carried out deliberately and in good order. The left company held on all day to the captured trenches but was withdrawn by 8.30 P.M., having done its duty well.

Meantime General Anderson, commanding the Meerut Division, had with his usual energy been doing all that was possible to enable the Leicesters to hold on ; an attack by portions of the Dehra Dun Brigade had been arranged, but the Germans, now thoroughly roused and angry, and having made their preparations for the attack they had planned for the next day, the 20th, began a very heavy bombardment of our trenches, specially selecting the " Orchard " portion of them, on which shell-fire was concentrated, damaging everything in the vicinity, blowing men to bits, and rendering any hold on them quite impossible. At the same time it was reported by aviators that numbers of the enemy were concentrating on this and other fronts, and everything pointed to a counter-attack. During the fighting I had placed troops as necessitated from the Corps Reserve at the disposal of the G.O.C. Meerut Division.

It has always been a wonder to me how in these winter days of 1914 the Indian troops did their work so well. If any man trusted them to fight, I did : but I knew their limits. What surprises me as I look back on it all is that they stood the strain as they did. It was in truth a prolonged feat of arms.

The result of this destructive fire was to render the " Orchard " untenable, and a new line fifty yards farther to the west was taken up and put into the best state of defence possible, but this was only done late in the evening and after the Brigadier had reported the impossibility of holding on any longer ; a few Scouts still remained in the destroyed trenches. Orders were got ready for a combined counter-attack the next morning, but before this could be carried out the prepared and due Hun attack was launched and a new phase in the operations begun.

The following are amongst those who were brought to special notice during these operations : Colonel Blackader, who led his battalion and withdrew it skilfully ; Major Knatchbull, Captain Romilly, and Lieut. Tooley, all of the Leicesters ; No. 6275 Private Buckingham, for great gallantry (and it is pleasant to record that this brave soldier later in the war won the V.C.) ; Sergeant Sutherland, Lance-Corporal Brakes, and Private Crisp ; and if all the names of other brave Leicester officers and men were recorded here and whenever the battalion was engaged they would fill many pages. Captain Lodwick, 3rd Gurkhas, who with his machine-gun team rendered good service ; Rifleman Thaman Gharti and Major Dundas of the same battalion came in for high praise ; and Captain C. D. Bamberger, R.E., who was killed, would have assuredly been rewarded had he survived.

We had on the left made our demonstration—or give it any other name. We had certainly succeeded on this flank in holding the enemy to his ground and prevented him sending away troops to other parts of his front. We had captured a few prisoners and machine-guns, and now we were doing our best to hold his attacks.

CHAPTER XI

BEFORE beginning the story of the Lahore Division's share in this fighting, it is well to state that the Indian Corps had received meantime two notable additions to its strength. The 4th Suffolks was the first of the Territorial battalions to join us. I saw them on parade and told them how glad I was to have them with us. I explained how it was proposed to employ them, and particularly noticed their physique and workmanlike appearance. I had but little acquaintance with the Force, and had never soldiered with any but regular British troops in my life, and hence I was able to take an impartial view.

The next to join us was the 4th Seaforths, another of that wonderful Army which leapt from the dim shadow of neglect into the fulness of the shining light of war, and gave England immediate proof of the truth that though we are the least military we are the most warlike race on earth. This battalion was intended to learn its trench work from the sister regular battalion of Highlanders, forming part of the Indian Corps.

Immediately after their arrival I saw them at Vieille Chapelle, December 20. Even whilst I was going round and talking to the officers and N.C.O.'s, the angry and increasing roar of guns was growing louder, and just as I had finished explaining how they would at first be employed by platoons in the trenches, an orderly arrived with a note to say the German attacks were in full swing and my presence was required at my Headquarters. These days of telephone warfare have destroyed the glamour, such as is left of it, for Generals. It is difficult to get away and see something of the fray oneself, but it amused me to think after all my explanations and injunctions that this corps was in fact to learn its lesson in the thick of the fighting without any preliminary practice at all. Thus the 4th Seaforths, under their fine commander, MacFarlane, marched away from the ground and their next halt was in the second-line trenches running south from La Couture. The officers and men all looked like fighters, and, as will be related later, they did not belie their looks and rendered grand service throughout.

In accordance with the general plans for the local offensives, Lieut.-General Watkis, in command of the Lahore Division, had also directed an attack, on December 19, against a front of 300 yards of German trenches N.E. of Givenchy, as already stated. The attacking companies were drawn from the Highland Light Infantry and the 4th Gurkhas, the latter being on the right, and this formed the left of the combined Divisional attack, and was commanded by Colonel Ronaldson, H.L.I., a good soldier. The Ferozepore Brigade was on the right of the Sirhinds, and the 129th Baluchis were to have furnished the companies to complete the attack which was being delivered from the point of junction of the two Brigades, but this battalion, after its hard fighting on the 16th instant, was not fit for another thrust and was replaced by the 59th Rifles of the Jalandar Brigade.

The Sirhind attack was delivered at 5.34 A.M. after a very brief Artillery preparation from field-guns and howitzers. I have seen this criticised in Sir Arthur Conan Doyle's most interesting book, *The British Campaign in France and Flanders*, 1914, but it is necessary to remember that our ammunition supply was very limited in those days and commanders occasionally preferred a very short bombardment and a bigger reserve to meet the counter-attacks, and to enable our men to hold on and consolidate, or cover their retirement should such become necessary. In any case the assault was completely successful, two lines of trenches being taken. Though the distance was considerably over 150 yards, our casualties in this first rush were few and over seventy prisoners fell into our hands. The attack was made in four lines, the first being under the command of Major B. U. Nicolay, 4th Gurkhas. He was wounded next day, but commanded here with skill and behaved under trying circumstances with the utmost coolness. He reported that the conduct of the H.L.I. and 4th Gurkha detachment was admirable and described the conditions, which, shortly explained, were these: The captured trenches were about 200 yards long, straight and without traverses, and they were found after some time to be under enfilade fire from the higher ground on the right rear near Givenchy village. The trenches became overcrowded and the saps between our own trenches and these were not finished. Colonel Ronaldson reported that had it been possible to join these up the gains would assuredly have been retained. Nicolay and his command held on throughout a long and very trying day, and then, seeing the hopelessness of the position, retired, with all the wounded, towards dusk. The captures of the day were lost and we were once more back in our own trenches.

Captain Cramer-Roberts, 4th Gurkhas, behaved with splendid gallantry in carrying back a message over the open; he was thrice wounded but nevertheless persevered, and just managed to reach the trench and give his information to Colonel Ronaldson. He received a D.S.O. The name of Major Gardiner, R.E., was prominently brought to notice for good work.

Our bombs had run out early in the day and the only others available were a few found in the captured German trench, which Nicolay used with good effect on their former owners. An incident occurred in front of the H.L.I. advanced platoon which was already in those early days opening our eyes to Hun methods. A German officer advanced with a white flag, and his men, who had put on some of our Balaclava caps, under this protection hoped to deceive us. They gained but a temporary advantage and were soon found out, many being hit, and had thus added one more deed to their scroll of shame.

After dark over thirty machine-guns concentrated their fire on the H.L.I. trenches, foreshadowing the preparations which were in the making for the attack next day.

In the H.L.I. Captain Pringle and Lieut. Anderson

were missing and Lieut. Kerr was killed. Sergeant Whitton, H.L.I., was strongly commended by Major Nicolay, who also brought to notice the names of Subadar Durga Gurung, Havildar Hara Sing Thapa, Naik Dharmraj Gurung, and Rifleman Jangia Thapa, Cramer-Roberts' orderly. Correspondence found in the enemy's trenches showed that we had been opposed chiefly by portions of the 3rd, 13th, and 56th regiments, XIV. Division of Prussians.

Captain Inglis, Adjutant of the 4th Gurkhas, had guided the troops to their rendezvous, and had then insisted as a reward on accompanying them in the assault, and was killed. A good specimen of those splendid British officers of which the Indian Army can boast so many.

Lieut. C. H. Anderson, H.L.I., one of those glorious spirits who are well described in the Book of Job : " He saith unto the trumpets, Ha ! Ha ! and he smelleth the battle afar off, the thunder of the Captains and the shouting," rushed on to the German Reserve trench, which he and his Highlanders took in their stride, and shouting, " We are going to capture Chapelle St. Roch," those brave men went into the darkness, through the pelting rain and storm, and were no more seen.

> From scenes like these old Scotia's grandeur springs.

The 59th Rifles, who attacked on the right, were only able to reach the main German trench with a few men. Their task was a difficult one as they had only just reached the front to relieve the 129th Baluchis, and it was a wild stormy night with heavy rain and the ground was unknown to them. It would have been better to have told off another corps for the purpose, but the G.O.C. Division found it was the only way to carry out his orders.

One company joined with the H.L.I. on their left ; a platoon of another company lost direction and went away to its right. The result was that a number of men eventually got into the two saps on the right and left of those attacked and held on. These two saps ran almost the whole way between the German lines and ours. A bit which was incomplete in the right sap was eventually, after many hours, joined up by the Sappers and Miners, thus enabling a party of the 129th Baluchis who were holding the main trenches to relieve the 59th. In this affair Jemadar Mangal Singh of the 59th behaved with great gallantry and received the I.D.S.M.

After the first advance the fighting was of a very confused nature owing to the darkness, rain, etc., and the reports that can be pieced together are not sufficiently clear to enable me to form a connected story. This, however, is certain, that considering the general mix-up in the dark, many deeds of bravery were performed, and although the attack did not succeed in capturing any length of German trench, and thereby exposed the right of the trench which had been captured to a flank attack by the enemy, the 59th Rifles, well directed by their officers, made every endeavour to accomplish their task.

Captain B. Anderson of this battalion, whom I had once seen lead a charge against a band of Ghazis across the Indian border, was here again leading his men, but on this occasion, unlike the Ghazis, who died fighting to a man, the Germans turned and ran. Lieut. J. G. Atkinson was killed. Lieut. W. A. McCrae-Bruce by his personal disregard of danger set a splendid example which kept his men together in the turmoil.[1]

Havildar Dost Mahomed and Havildar Abdul Wahab were awarded the I.O.M., and a small party of men whose names cannot be recorded, for they all perished, behaved splendidly, refusing to retire because the body of their officer, Lieut. Bruce, had not been recovered.

Captain H. N. Lee and R. C. Gilchrist were killed during the attack on and capture of the left sap, whilst Captain Scale was wounded and the battalion had over 100 other casualties. Lieut. Scobie received the Military Cross for his share in holding on to the left sap. Lieut. Kisch, R.E., did excellent work under a heavy fire.

An attack on a German sap-head by two platoons of the 1st Gurkhas had been ordered to be carried out at 5.30 A.M. this same day, and the officers to accompany it were Captain T. Burke and Lieut. L. B. Rundall. The latter was

[1] I was rejoiced to see in the *London Gazette* of 4th September 1919 that this very gallant officer had been given the Victoria Cross.

the younger of two sons of Colonel Rundall, an old friend and comrade of mine who had served on my Staff. I knew both boys, and all three of these fighting soldiers belonged to Gurkha regiments. The elder brother was a Captain in the 4th Gurkhas and both were killed on this and the following day, behaving as British officers do when stern work is in hand, and leaving a name which will be cherished in the Gurkha Brigade.

This attack could not be launched in time, owing to various causes, and orders were issued cancelling it, but for some unknown reason the assault was carried out at about 10 o'clock. As usual, the two brave fellows rushed forward at the head of their men and were met by a hail of fire and the leaden scythe mowed them down. About fifty took part in the assault, of whom half were killed or wounded, both British officers being among the former.

This brings the story of the Lahore Division's attempts on December 19 to engage the enemy and help our other Army Corps and our French Allies who were operating on our right to an end. As I said before, in themselves, though described at length, they were only local offensives, but they were unfortunate in as far as they had severely tried our already tired troops on the very eve of the prepared German attack. In war the man who can truly forecast events is of more value than many legions of soldiers. All one can do is to endeavour by every means in one's power to carry out the Commander - in - Chief's plans. Both Divisions had done their duty.

The Meerut Division after the fighting on the 19th December was disposed as under : Garhwal Brigade back in its own trenches ; to their right the 6th Jats, the left battalion of the Dehra Dun Brigade, held their line with the right thrown back so as to connect with, and conform to, the retired line of the 2nd Gurkhas behind the " Orchard " ; the Seaforth Highlanders formed the right of the Brigade to near the " Picquet " house, from which point the Sirhind Brigade of the Lahore Division continued farther still to the right.

About 9 A.M., December 20, the attack on the Meerut Division was started. The 2nd Gurkhas and the Seaforths

—old and trusted comrades—were singled out, and a heavy bombardment and Infantry advance told the Division that a day which was to be an important one for the Indian Corps had begun.   Half an hour later word reached General Anderson that the Seaforths' right was in the air owing to the retirement of the left of the Sirhind Brigade and that they were being heavily attacked from this flank and at the same time bombed on their left owing to retirement of part of the 2nd Gurkhas, which exposed them to the enemy's bombers.

The Seaforths never lose an inch of ground without making the attackers pay a heavy toll, but they were now fighting against great odds, hand-grenades, machine-guns, and trench mortars, with both their flanks in the air.   One company was driven from its trench, but not until fifty per cent of the enemy lay dead in it.   Captain the Hon. St. Clair was killed just as he had skilfully withdrawn into and was holding a communication trench.

The 2nd Gurkhas were again put to a severe test this day ; bombed and overmatched, they were driven from their newly-occupied trenches ; followed up with hand-grenades and harried they retired, but always took their toll in the retreat and finally drew up in a retired position under Major Boileau, a soldier with an extraordinary personality.   I cannot better describe him than in the words of one of his own Gurkha officers, " Asal Jangi Sahib " (a truly brave gentleman).   With him was Major Watt, another staunch fighter.   During this fighting the Gurkhas were pushed back a long way and were glad indeed to meet the 9th Gurkhas coming up to their assistance.   To do what is set you is of course the best proof that you are competent to do it, but I have found in life that some-times though you may fail in the eyes of your judges, you may nevertheless have done everything that was possible. Those gallant Gurkhas deserved success, and I would as soon have them by me in a tight place as any battalion I know.

It is instructive to note that at this moment N Battery, R.H.A., from the Secunderabad Cavalry Brigade, came into action and helped materially by its fire across the front.   This was the only calibre of gun (13-pounders) for which we were not limited to a certain number of rounds of ammunition, and the confidence this inspired, with the excellence of the fire itself, was equal to many heavier batteries. Think of it, the warriors of later times! An Army Corps was rejoiced at the advent of six guns, manned by the pick of the Army, and instead of wondering how it was going to be done, considered themselves fortunate and bound to win. Unlimited ammunition! although only for six guns it is true : but the surprise caused by the advance of the first six tanks in later days was as nothing compared to that of the General who found himself with six real guns and plenty of rounds for each. " Tempora mutantur, nos et mutamur in illis."

To fill the gap between the Seaforths and the retired line of the Gurkhas, the 58th Rifles were ordered up ; half the 41st Dogras was also placed at the disposal of the G.O.C. Dehra Dun Brigade, and half the Black Watch to form a link between Seaforths and the retired left of Sirhind Brigade.

It was now 1 o'clock, December 20, and in order to retain the thread of the story and make the movements of both Divisions coincide, I will leave the Meerut Division and relate the occurrences which had taken place in the Lahore Command.

Simultaneously with the attacks already described on the Meerut Division, the Germans started their operations against the Lahore Division, and from the early morning of the 20th December the trenches were subjected to a fierce fire from guns and mortars, and then followed a series of mine explosions under the trenches occupied by the Sirhind Brigade. Soaked with rain which had lasted through the night ; wearied by the previous day's trials ; standing in bog knee-deep with the mud slipping in as fast as it could be shovelled out of the trenches, and with numbers totally inadequate to the front held, the British and Indian troops began the resistance which lasted for twenty-four hours without any extraneous help, and continued it for another twenty-four hours until in part relieved by fresh troops of the First Army Corps; when first the Lahore and later the Meerut Divisions were withdrawn, with difficulty lasting out the ordeal. The wonder is not that they were literally done up but that they were able to hold out as they did.

And the men who came to their relief, what of them? They were some of the finest troops in our Army, the famous First Corps of Mons and Ypres fame: with double our reduced numbers, fresh from a rest in reserve, full of fight. Guards, Highlanders, Irish and English: neither Germans nor anybody else could have withstood such a gathering; and as they looked at our tired-out men, amongst them a few British battalions of their own countrymen, as fine soldiers as themselves, battle-stained and mud-grimed, I do not believe there was one amongst the brave new arrivals who did not own that the Indian Corps had indeed had a hard task and done its duty well.

The fight that followed showed them that it was a determined foe they had to deal with, and 2400 casualties in their own ranks before the line was more or less restored was evidence of the hard fighting which had taken toll of over 4000 British and Indian soldiers.

However, to my story. The right of the Sirhind Brigade was the first to bear the brunt, and here a half-company of the H.L.I. and a double company [1] of the 4th Gurkhas suffered very heavy losses, being buried or blown up by the well-engineered explosions. The day had not then arrived when we were able to detect and counter this underground warfare; it was new to the Indian Corps at any rate, nor had we the appliances to put it into use.

Amongst the survivors of these first explosions was Colour-Sergeant Brisbane, H.L.I., who had served with me in Ashanti fourteen years previously. I had met him later in India, and on this day we were once more separated, for after holding on to the last, he with his officer, Lieut. D. Barry, and some others were captured by the enemy. May we meet again!

Another double company of the 4th Gurkhas made a stout resistance against heavy odds, but were driven from their trenches, and at about 1 P.M. these were occupied by the Germans, who were coming on in massed formation.

[1] Indian battalions were in these days formed in eight companies

M

During this fighting, which ended in many hand-to-hand encounters, Captain A. M. Rundall of the 4th Gurkhas, brother of the Lieutenant whose death I described in the previous day's fighting, led a bombing party in a counter-attack, himself killed two Germans, and died fighting at the head of his few men.

> A glorious tale indeed to tell,
> 'Neath thousand blows one hero fell.

The machine-gun detachment of the 125th (Napier's) Rifles at this stage rendered gallant service, and with that of the 4th Gurkhas was practically destroyed.

Captain R. C. Yates of the 4th Gurkhas with the greater part of his company was also overwhelmed. It was reported to me after this action that, whereas the Germans used hundreds of bombs which almost invariably exploded and caused great damage, our own home-made articles constantly failed to light or dropped harmless, being wet and unprotected from the slush and rain.

Farther to the left of the Sirhind Brigade was a double company of the 1st Gurkhas commanded by Major C. Bliss, and a company of the H.L.I. under Major T. F. Murray, and they had between them four Maxims. Following heavy mine explosions this section was also attacked by great numbers of the enemy, who notwithstanding heavy losses, caused especially by our machine-guns, rushed in and made themselves masters of the trenches.

Murray and Captain W. Cameron with their men made a fine stand and were reported killed. Lieut. R. Guthrie-Smith, also of the H.L.I., was killed and Lieut. C. Pitts-Tucker, whilst crossing the open with sorely needed reinforcements, was wounded, and most of his party shared his fate or were killed. Tucker was being carried in by two gallant comrades, Corporal A. Barr and Private J. Carmichael, when he was again hit and killed. Both men received the D.C.M.

About 11 o'clock General Watkis ordered up his reserve, and two French Territorial battalions which were at his disposal, to the neighbourhood of Givenchy; the 47th Sikhs to move up in reserve of the Sirhind Brigade, and

General Carnegy, commanding the Jalandar Brigade, to make a flank attack from Givenchy to retake the lost trenches of the Sirhind Brigade. During the defence of the left section by H.L.I. and 1st Gurkhas, just described, Lieut. W. Stewart, H.L.I., with seventy men and two Maxims, held on in the support trench. His party was very much in the air, but showed splendid grit, tired and over-worked as they had been for two days; but with the help of forty men who reached him at dusk he held on for nearly twenty-four hours until relieved by troops from the First British Division. He was awarded the D.S.O.

The assistance rendered by our Artillery at this stage, and indeed throughout these operations, was the theme of high praise from all ranks of the Infantry, and well was it deserved, for without it the H.L.I. and Gurkhas would have been destroyed by the advancing mass of troops.

The 1st Gurkhas, like the H.L.I., were being severely handled and the enemy had driven a wedge into their line. Major Bliss was mortally wounded while leading a bayonet charge which succeeded in affording our sorely-tried men a short respite; Captain H. Momey was killed; but numbers prevailed, and the Germans having gained a footing on flanks and centre, and using large numbers of grenades, forced the Gurkhas back into their support trenches, and quickly following up established themselves in all our advanced lines. Festubert was reached before the retiring line could be thoroughly joined up, and some of the troops had by this time become much disorganised.

Seeing that General Watkis had his hands more than full, and being apprehensive of further retirement, I had placed the Secunderabad Cavalry Brigade and Jodhpore Lancers, acting as Infantry, and the 8th Gurkhas from the Meerut Division, at his disposal, and to these was added the 47th Sikhs; the whole under General Macbean.

This brings the narrative up to an hour after mid-day of the 20th December, at which time news was received that the left of the Ferozepore Brigade had been driven back and that Givenchy was being heavily attacked.

The Artillery was working with a precision that spoke volumes for them, and I felt assured that, come what might, the gunners, most of whom I had known well in India, would answer to any call, and prove as ever that their motto is well called " Ubique."

Of the Indian battalions of the newly-arrived Sirhind Brigade two were Gurkhas and the third was the 125th Rifles. The 1st Gurkhas (King George's Own) was raised in 1815 from soldiers who took service with the British after the fall of Malaun. It went through many changes of name and shared in many campaigns from Bhurtpore and Aliwal to Tirah. In 1910 it received its present title. A second battalion had been added in 1886.

The 4th Gurkhas was raised in 1857 as the " Extra Gurkha Regiment." Its battle honours date from " Ali Musjid and Kabul, 1879," to "China, 1900." A second battalion was added in 1886.

The 125th (Napier's) Rifles was raised in 1820, largely from men who had served in the Peishwa's Army. The battalion received several titles connecting it with the old Bombay Army from time to time, until in 1903 its present designation was conferred upon it. It had served under Napier at Meance and last seen service in Burmah 1885–87.

My story of the action of the Meerut Division stopped at about this same hour, and it is convenient to take a retrospect and see how the Army Corps stood exactly at this time in order to better follow the battle. Beginning with our right, the Ferozepore Brigade was next to and on the left of the French XXIst Corps d'Armée, the Commander of which had placed two Territorial battalions at the disposal of the Lahore Division. The right battalion of the Ferozepore Brigade, the Connaught Rangers, held the trenches south of the La Bassée Canal. On their left, covering the east of Givenchy, were the greater part of the 57th Rifles and part of the 9th Bhopals ; these troops had not so far been attacked. The 129th Baluchis was the left battalion of this Brigade and, as I said, had just then been reported as retiring. Continuing to the left stood the Sirhind Brigade, lately arrived from Egypt, and hence fresher for work than others. The 4th and 1st Gurkhas and H.L.I. held the front ; companies of the Highlanders being interspersed in the Gurkha ranks. The

machine-guns of the 125th Rifles of this Brigade were also
up in the trenches.   This ended the line held by the Lahore
Division, and the movements of the Divisional reserves
have already been explained.   As will have been seen
from the description of the fighting, this whole Brigade had
been driven back and held a now considerably retired line.

Carrying on our line to the north, *i.e.* farther to the
left, the Meerut Division had on its right the Dehra Dun
Brigade, of which the Seaforths occupied their old position,
near the Picquet House, and though being severely attacked
were holding on in the most gallant manner.   On their
right rear was half of the Black Watch which had been

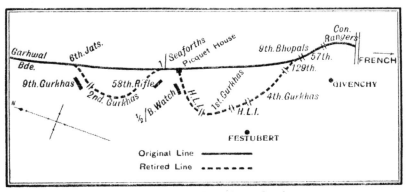

From a rough sketch made at the time.

sent up to establish connection between the Seaforths
and the now retired Sirhind Brigade.   To the left of the
Seaforths were the 2nd Gurkhas, considerably drawn back
by their retirement ; and as a connecting link to fill the
gap the 58th Rifles had been ordered up by General
Anderson.   Still farther to the left were the 6th Jats,
forming the left battalion of the Brigade, with their right
skilfully thrown back so as to keep connection with the
retired Gurkha line.   Finally, the Garhwal Brigade completed the Meerut Division and was holding its original line.

To continue the story of the Meerut Division from 1 P.M.
on the 20th, where I left them.   At this hour the 2nd
Gurkhas were holding a line a quarter of a mile south of
La Quinque Rue, and the Seaforths had recaptured a lost

trench on their left, and were bombing the Huns out of their right, greatly hampered by a heavy fire from the Picquet House, from which the left of the Sirhind Brigade had been driven. The Germans were in occupation of the old 2nd Gurkha trenches ; the 41st Dogras were in Brigade reserve, and the 107th Pioneers, half of the Black Watch, and 4th Indian Cavalry were in Divisional reserve at Le Touret. The Garhwal Brigade was being heavily attacked by shell fire and trench mortars, but was holding its own well. All available machine-guns were sent up to assist this Brigade.

Lieut.-Colonel Roche, 6th Jats, as senior officer on the spot, was in command of his own Corps and all neighbouring reinforcements, and took prompt measures to consolidate his position, and held it throughout this and the next day.

The fighting Major Wauchope with half his Black Watch had succeeded by 11 P.M. in re-establishing touch with the Sirhind Brigade on his right and the Seaforths on his left, and by this manœuvre completed the line of the Meerut Division. The Germans had pushed in deep in front of the 2nd Gurkhas, but their triumph was only to be a temporary one.

As the attacks all along our front had assumed big proportions by the afternoon of the 20th December, and I was only too well aware that the Corps was, after its long tour of trench work since the end of October, quite unfit for a prolonged struggle, I had asked G.H.Q. for two Brigades from the Indian Cavalry Corps, which on foot might furnish the strength of two battalions, and also for a Brigade from the First Army Corps then in Army reserve, and these were at once given me, and two additional Brigades from this Corps also arrived and were all employed the next day, thus making an extra Division. I informed the G.O.C. Meerut Division that one of these Brigades would reach him next day.

By 3 A.M. on the 21st, the Dehra Dun Brigade reported the enemy massing on its front, and at 7.45 A.M. the G.O.C. Division learnt that a counter-attack by the left Brigade of the Lahore Division had been unsuccessful. At this stage General Keary, commanding the Garhwal Brigade, suggested a counter-attack by the Dehra Dun Brigade, which he would support from his side with his reserve battalion, the Leicesters; this attack did not mature as the Dehra Dun Brigade was too exhausted to carry it out. By this time the Seaforths on the right were being very hard pressed, and half of the 107th Pioneers were sent to their assistance, whilst the remainder of this battalion and the 4th Indian Cavalry were called up and placed in a second line of trenches.

This remained more or less the position until the arrival that evening of General Westmacott's Brigade from the First Army Corps. Owing to unavoidable delays in bringing this Brigade up, its attack was not commenced until late in the evening. One battalion of the Royal Sussex regiment was to relieve the Seaforths whilst the Loyal North Lancashires and Northamptons attacked the lost " Orchard " positions.

By 10.80 P.M. on the 21st a report was received that this attack had taken the supporting trenches west of the " Orchard " and was progressing favourably, but the trenches about it were untenable and the attackers eventually took position just west of it.

The Dehra Dun Brigade and the other Corps assisting in this part of the line had now been fighting without a break for seventy-two hours in rain and mud, and were much reduced in numbers. They had lost the " Orchard," but by the action of the troops in that neighbourhood, especially of the Seaforths, the pivot at the Picquet House was still retained and acted as a hinge the flexibility of which meant that the Meerut Division's line, though deeply indented, was still intact. By 7 o'clock on the morning of the 22nd December the bulk of the Dehra Dun Brigade, as also the 58th Rifles and Black Watch, had been withdrawn for a well-earned rest, and the newly-arrived British Brigade had occupied their places in the trenches.

At 10 A.M., 22nd December, after General Anderson had arranged for the handing over of the right of his command to the First Army Corps, an Artillery observing-officer reported that there was something wrong in front of the " Orchard," now held by the British troops, and that a retirement was taking place there. If fresh Britishers found it necessary to temporarily give way, it only shows the pressure that our men had been faced with for two long days.

Tired out as they were, orders were at once given for the still fit Indian Corps battalions to move up again and the others to stand fast. The *contretemps* was put right by the G.O.C. 2nd British Brigade before 10.30 o'clock; and at this hour on the 22nd December, the second shortest day of the year, but, like the 21st, the longest in a fighting sense, the worn-out troops at last found some rest, although still retained ready in case of need. The Divisional Commander in reporting his positions wound up with the words: "The worn-out Seaforth Highlanders and 58th Rifles are now in reserve."

At this point, 1 P.M., 22nd December, I will leave the Meerut Command and describe the heavy fighting which was all this time going on in the Lahore Division in and near that place of ill omen yclept Festubert. Before doing so I will turn from the general story and record a few of the names of those heroic soldiers who throughout these days had maintained the traditions of the British and Indian Armies. I often feel, and I say it in truth, that the rewards of Senior Generals are seldom their own, but rather the work of subordinates of all ranks; and if I had the power I would issue gazettes notifying them somewhat as follows, taking as a sample an Army Corps :

In recognition of the fine fighting qualities displayed by the —— Army Corps during the battle of ——, the G.O.C. in Command is awarded, etc.

I have received many honours from three Sovereigns. I should have received none had it not been for the officers and men who had to carry out orders at the risk of their lives, whilst I only issued them. It was comparatively easy in this trench warfare to say " Promite vires," when you yourself were safe. He who has to make decisions under stress of danger is the hero, and not the man FAR behind the guns.

In writing this story I have relied chiefly on orders

and reports I was able to get copied in France, and on my own diary very carefully kept from day to day, together with letters and information from friends since, but I have not had access to all the War diaries of Brigades and battalions, etc. I cannot therefore pretend to describe in any detail the doings of all those whose work I saw daily, and can only record such matters as I have some knowledge of. If, therefore, omissions occur I can only regret it.

Lieut.-Colonel Widdicombe, who commanded the 9th Gurkhas, did excellent work; he arrived at a most opportune moment, reinforcing both the 2nd Gurkhas and 6th Jats during the early fighting on 20th December. Captain Laing of the Seaforths, leading a bombing party with great gallantry, rushed and recaptured several traverses in a trench evacuated by the 2nd Gurkhas, and in which the Huns left over twenty dead. Lieut. I. M. Macandrew of the same regiment rallied some of the men of the British Brigade as they retired from the "Orchard" on 22nd, led them in a bombing attack, and after killing several of the enemy this gallant young officer and ten of his men were themselves killed. Colonel Ritchie, ever staunch and brave, Captain Wicks, a very fine soldier, and Captain Laing, all of the Seaforths, received distinctions. In this fighting the Seaforths suffered 175 casualties out of 700 engaged.

Major A. Young of the 1st Gurkhas, Brigade Major of the Garhwal Brigade, had died of wounds on the 14th—a great loss to the Service. Major Wauchope, Black Watch, was again wounded, and the regiment had to record severe casualties.

In the 58th Rifles, Captain M. A. R. Bell, 54th Sikhs (attached), whom I had known for many years, was killed, a very earnest soldier. Jemadar Mardan Ali and twenty-five others were also killed and thirty-two were wounded. The losses in killed, wounded, and missing throughout the Divisions bore witness to the nature of the struggle in which they had been engaged.

CHAPTER XII

THE narrative of the Lahore Division brought us to after mid-day of the 20th December, at which hour the 129th Baluchis, on the left of the Ferozepore Brigade covering Givenchy, were retiring and their trenches were in occupation of the enemy, and the village was being attacked. In consequence General Carnegy's orders were cancelled, and he was directed to secure this place ; and two batteries from the Fifty-eighth Division were placed at Watkis's disposal by the French.

By 3.30 P.M. on the 20th the Manchesters under Colonel Strickland, with a company of the 4th Suffolks in support, started their attack for the recovery of the lost Givenchy trenches. By 5 P.M. this gallant battalion, fighting often with the bayonet, had cleared the Huns out of the village and recaptured the trenches to the north - east; but they still retained possession of those to the north of the village ; whilst to the east and southwards the company of the 9th Bhopals, the 57th Rifles, a portion of the 4th Suffolks, and the Connaught Rangers held their lines intact.

On the Sirhind Brigade front the right section at 3.30 P.M. was holding its reserve trenches ; farther to the left, notwithstanding its considerable retirement, touch had been more or less established with the right of the Meerut Division, and the retired line of the Brigade was intact, though somewhat disorganised. The enemy at this stage did not appear to be making a further attack on this front.

Meantime General Macbean. with the Secunderabad

Cavalry Brigade, consisting of the 7th Dragoon Guards, 20th Deccan Horse, 34th Poona Horse, and Jodhpore Lancers, under Brigadier-General Wadeson, and in addition the 8th Gurkhas and 47th Sikhs, had been ordered to move to a position near Marais and counter-attack. This movement was delayed from various causes, and it was not till midnight that the advance was actually carried out by the 7th Dragoon Guards and 47th Sikhs.

It was a hopeless attempt; the ground was deep in mud and a network of ditches, and the enemy's fire very heavy. Nevertheless these gallant troops actually reached and entered our abandoned trenches, but were then subjected to a heavy flanking fire and occasionally to that of our own guns. Under such conditions it was no wonder they were driven back to their starting-point and suffered severely. Amongst the killed was Colonel H. Lempriere, commanding 7th Dragoon Guards, a very gallant gentleman and hard to replace. Captain J. L. Mansel was killed leading a rush on enemy machine-guns. Lieutenants R. L. Mann and S. Bryce were missing. The total casualties of the 7th Dragoon Guards during the short time they served with the Indian Corps amounted to twenty-six killed or missing and forty wounded. Sergeant R. Snelling and Private J. Crackett received the D.C.M.

Another counter-attack was carried out about 5 A.M. on the 21st December, under command of Colonel Grant, 8th Gurkhas. The troops under his command now consisted of the 8th Gurkhas, 47th Sikhs, 7th Dragoon Guards, and Jodhpore Lancers. Stumbling under a pitiless rain, over the ditches and through mire, this attempt, like the first, was unable to achieve its object, and eventually a retirement had to be carried out.

To return to Givenchy, where the Manchesters had retaken a great part of the village, General Watkis had sent the 59th Rifles to reinforce Carnegy, who had already despatched a company of the 4th Suffolks and one company of the 142nd French Territorials to Givenchy, as a support to Strickland in the attack he was about to make on our advanced abandoned trenches to the north of that village.

This attack was launched about half-past six on the morning of the 21st December, and carried out with the *élan* which distinguished that fine corps, the 1st Manchesters. All that men could do was done, but the hail of fire from machine-guns, etc., made it impossible to advance far. By 11 o'clock the enemy, after a severe bombardment with shell, pushed home an Infantry attack which forced us back from the village. Still the Manchesters again and again made vigorous counter-attacks, though enfiladed and gradually becoming enveloped, until at length after severe bayonet fighting the battalion was pushed back and Givenchy practically lost. Their heroic conduct had, however, saved the position in this part of our line, and held the enemy at bay just long enough to enable the fresh troops of a Brigade from the now arriving First Army Corps to stem and turn the tide. As the Manchesters met the Cameron Highlanders coming up, they must indeed have been thankful that their stubborn fight had enabled their Army Corps to still maintain its front and an almost lost local battle to be turned into a glorious episode.

The battalion in this fighting had two officers (Captain L. Creagh and Lieut. S. Norman) and sixty-four men killed, and forty-six missing, whilst three officers and 124 men were wounded. I have known many splendid Corps in the Army but not one to beat the 1st Manchesters, and I felt that a brilliant future awaited Strickland. He has since risen to Major-General and is a K.C.B.

At dawn on this morning I had ridden from Hinges, my Headquarters, to see one of my Generals, and on my way back I met a brigade of the First Army Corps now arriving to help us; it was marching towards Givenchy. I can never forget my feelings as these splendid battalions moved along—young, vigorous, fresh from a rest in reserve: 1000 strong each, eager for the battle, they were the very embodiment of certain victory, and I could not but feel proud of my own brave Corps, many of whom I had just seen, literally caked in mud and slime, worn out after long weeks of vigil and toil in the trenches, sadly needing some sleep and rest; battalions worn to mere skeletons in strength, a few with no more than a full company in the fight.

But notwithstanding all this they were still holding on, still keeping the flag flying and doing their duty. I would fain have wished the addition of some of the newcomers to my own Army Corps ; they were my own flesh and blood, with great traditions and a great cause which all understood; but I would not have changed places with any living man. It was enough for me that I was Commander of the Indian Corps, and that that Corps was so nobly acquitting itself under extraordinary difficulties.

As stated before, the trenches to the south and east of Givenchy had during the battle been held by the Connaught Rangers, the 57th Rifles, and a company of the 9th Bhopal Infantry. During the 20th December the 57th and 9th were subjected to attacks which succeeded in laying the flank of the 57th open to enfilade fire and obliging the left to retire. Here my old friend Subadar Arsla Khan of the 57th was again to the fore, and by a plucky reconnaissance obtained useful information regarding the German barricades, and surprised and shot several Huns. Later, on the 22nd December, this fine Indian officer, a Malikdin Khel Afridi, led a charge on a party of the enemy, killing two officers and a number of men. He has many orders and distinctions for various campaigns.

After the Manchesters were forced back from Givenchy, on the afternoon of the 21st December, the pressure on this portion of our trenches increased very considerably and was only relieved by the arrival of a Brigade of the First Army Corps, and by nightfall the position was secured. On the 22nd December the whole of the trenches east and south of Givenchy were taken over by the First Corps, and our troops, at last relieved from their long vigil, were able to gain some urgently-needed rest.

My story left the Meerut Division at 2 P.M. on the same date, and just after it had been relieved by the First Army Corps, and although the Meerut troops remained at the disposal of that Corps for a few days longer until a new alignment had been taken up, they were not called on to make further efforts, and eventually, like the Lahore

Division, were able to get back to billets and enjoy a sorely-needed rest and to re-equip themselves.

By 1 P.M. on the 22nd December one Division of the First Army Corps had arrived and taken over a great part of our trenches, and the Second Division was in process of relieving the remainder of my Corps, and the responsibility was gradually becoming involved, hence I asked the G.O.C. First Army Corps to assume the command whilst I withdrew all the relieved battalions and Artillery. This he agreed to, and the Indian Corps was withdrawn.

During this long-drawn-out battle the losses of some battalions had been very severe. In the Sirhind Brigade alone, on which fell the main German onslaught, the H.L.I. had lost ten officers and fifty-four men killed, 276 men missing (mostly killed), and sixty wounded, and the total casualties numbered 400, about fifty per cent of those in action.

> Such monuments shall last when Egypt's fall.

The 1st Gurkhas suffered well over 200 casualties, including six British and Indian officers, and the 4th Gurkhas had seventeen British and Indian officers and a total of 300 of all ranks. In the 4th, Jemadar Lachman Sing Thapa, the Gurkha Adjutant, was amongst the killed, and Captain M. Wylie was missing.

To suffer such losses and be again ready for battle within a few weeks needs discipline of a high order, and I was lost in admiration of those gallant corps, which I had inspected only a few days previously in their full war strength, and saw again after their arrival in billets. The ranks were sadly thinned, but there was no sign of despondency and only determination on their faces. " Give us their hand-grenades and trench mortars," said a Gurkha havildar to me, " and you will see some fun."

During the attack by the Secunderabad Cavalry Brigade Captain Alan Ross, 20th Deccan Horse, performed a very gallant action, which in any other war would have been rewarded with a Victoria Cross; but I was informed that in France it could not be given to officers for saving life alone. Ross was one of the hardest men I ever knew : a brilliant polo player and a strong rider all round. He had been my own A.D.C. years before in India. Seeing an Indian officer was wounded and lying in the open, he with two of his N.C.O.'s, Duffadars Shankar Rao and Sardar Singh, ran under a terrific fire and carried him back. On reaching a ditch they lay down, and seeing the Indian officer was too badly hit to be moved further, Ross ran back, still under heavy fire, and fetched up a stretcher, in which they placed the wounded officer and got him away. Ross received a D.S.O. and his two companions the Indian Order of Merit.

Captain W. H. Padday, 47th Sikhs, was killed whilst bombing up a trench with some of his men. The 20th Deccan Horse, a Corps which I had known in years past when I commanded the Secunderabad Division, suffered over eighty casualties, including Captain J. S. McEuan and Risaldar Mir Hidayat Ali killed; Captain C. A. Mackenzie, Risaldar Major Jharmal Singh, and one other Indian officer and thirty-five other ranks killed and missing; besides these, five officers and thirty-seven men were wounded. The 47th Sikhs, of whom I shall often have to write, had 130 ; the 34th Poona Horse fifty, including Major C. Loring, 37th Lancers, attached. The Jodhpore Lancers in this, their first fight as a unit on the Western Front, suffered eleven casualties. In the 8th Gurkhas one Indian officer was killed, and there were twenty-two other losses.

Generals Watkis and Anderson, in admirably written and concise reports, gave a very clear summary of the events which had been crowded into the four days' fighting, and it is interesting to note the chief points brought out. After giving full credit to all who deserved it and not concealing faults such as must occur in all battles, in the Lahore Division Watkis brought specially to notice Major-General Carnegy, commanding the Jalandar Brigade, for his thorough grasp of the situation ; General Brunker, Sirhind Brigade ; and General Egerton, Ferozepore Brigade. He gave the greatest praise to Colonel Strickland and his fine battalion the Manchesters. Colonel Cauteau of the 142nd French Territorial regiment was reported as rendering valuable and noteworthy service; and Capitaine Salles, also of the 142nd, for gallantly leading a counter-attack, although twice wounded.

Anderson specially commended the Seaforths and 58th Rifles, whose " action, sustained over a period of three days and nights under extremely difficult conditions, was worthy of the highest possible commendation and reflects the greatest credit on officers, N.C.O.'s, and men of both regiments."

The Ambala and Sialkote Cavalry Brigades had been brought up as reinforcements late during the battle ; the former suffered thirty casualties.   I had known both these splendid Brigades when commanding the Northern Army in India, and only regretted that this trench warfare gave them no opportunity of riding down the Huns, who assuredly would have had cause to remember that the Cavalry arm in India has a sword even sharper than the boasted German weapon.

It is one of my cherished recollections that our gallant French Allies did not fail to place on record their great regret at the departure of the Indian Corps from their immediate vicinity.   For two months we had been able to afford each other assistance in men and guns on many occasions, and our relations had been those of friends and comrades.   General de Maud'huy, commanding the Tenth French Army, and General Maistre, commanding the XXIst Corps d'Armée, wrote most cordial letters, wishing us every success as the war progressed and congratulating the men on their having so long victoriously sustained the " particularly difficult " conditions, especially of terrain, under which they had fought.

It would be impossible to serve with finer soldiers and gentlemen than composed the Army of France.

The battle was over, India had paid her dues, and this is what the Commander-in-Chief recorded :

The Indian troops have fought with the greatest steadfast-ness and gallantry whenever they have been called upon.

In these words Field-Marshal Sir John French summed up in his despatch of the 2nd February 1915 his opinion of the conduct of the Indian soldiers from the time they joined the Army in France until the close of the battle of Givenchy.

In his admirable book, " 1914," the great Field-Marshal has written on page 196 :

Much has been said and written about the work of the Indian troops in France, and various opinions have been expressed. For my part I can only say that, from first to last, so long as they were under my command, they maintained and probably surpassed even the magnificent traditions of the Indian Army. In a country and climate to which they were totally unaccustomed, the exigencies of the moment required that they should be thrown into action successively by smaller or greater units before they could be properly concentrated.

I shall always gratefully remember the invaluable assistance they and their Commander, Sir James Willcocks, rendered under these difficult conditions in the most critical hours of the First Battle of Ypres, especially the Lahore Division, commanded by General Watkis.

This finally disposes of any criticisms of the Indians by lesser luminaries. No one had better opportunities of realising the difficulties connected with their employment in Europe during a very trying winter. No one was more generous in his public utterances and despatches to the soldiers of India. There was, it is true, another side to this picture, but I will refrain from the narration of such incidents, for I realise the enormous difficulties the Commander-in-Chief had to face and the unflinching courage and steadfastness with which he faced them ; and I am convinced that no other soldier in our Army would have succeeded, to the same degree, in those tempestuous times.

The Indians were but a small unit in his complicated command, and that he has for all time plainly recorded his opinion is sufficient to disprove the criticisms of any others who are not possessed of his soldierly instincts.

This story of the Indian Corps is only a personal narrative and the opinions expressed in it may not be convincing to all who read it ; however, it has one merit, and that is, it is compiled from notes and diaries kept by me from day to day, and in which I recorded the opinions

N

and doings of the principal actors as I observed them at the time, and not from hearsay or memory alone.

We were now billeted in and about Lillers, and the first change in the reconstruction of the Army came at this time. Sir Douglas Haig had just received his well-merited promotion to General for his fine work as a Corps Commander during the retreat from Mons and the First Battle of Ypres. Two Armies were created, and he was appointed to command the First Army. I had up to then been senior to him, but now found myself junior and under his immediate command, as under the reorganisation the Indian Corps was attached to the First Army.

To the British soldier such supersession is a natural consequence of promotion for distinguished service in the field. To the Indian soldier it means something very different, when suddenly thrust on him in the field, and so it was in this case. To him his commander is everything, and he looks to him as at any rate his local commander-in-chief, and when he learns one morning that another, till then his junior, has been placed over him, he concludes something is wrong. Had the Corps gone to the Second Army, the Indians would have neither known nor cared what promotion had taken place, for Sir Horace Smith-Dorrien in command of it was already senior to me, but as it was I can best describe how they took it, in the words of an Indian officer who said to me, " Now we know the Government is displeased with our conduct in the recent battle." They have very strong opinions in some matters which cannot easily be shaken.

Putting aside any personal feeling, in this case it was a pity it happened, for it wrongly gave them to understand that it had been done with a purpose. Of course the necessities of the Army as a whole were far superior to any personal considerations, but I should have been glad if it could have been otherwise arranged. However, it was now an accomplished fact, and from that day to the day I left France no man ever rendered more loyal or whole-hearted service and support to his superior officer.

The first duty, now we were in billets, was to overhaul thoroughly, refit, and practically reconstitute the entire

Corps. Our numbers had fallen very considerably below war strength, but this was partly remedied by adding Territorial battalions ; these were brought on to the strength as they became available, until eventually five of our Brigades consisted of one Regular British, one Territorial, and three Indian battalions, and the sixth Brigade had a battalion of the Special Reserve ; but even with these additions, owing to the limited reinforcements from India, the shortage in the Regular British battalions, and the weakness of the Territorial units, which occasionally amounted to no more than half war strength, the total of the Indian Corps, consisting of thirty-two battalions of infantry, was under 21,000 rifles when we again took over our trenches on the 15th January.

I have already told of the arrival of some of these Territorial battalions, but I would again repeat that they were to us all the surprise of the war—splendid officers and men suddenly transferred from civilians into veteran soldiers. They will enter frequently into this story.

Great changes took place in the commands of the Brigades, which will be seen by reference to the lists farther on, and I was indeed sorry to bid farewell to gallant comrades with most of whom I had served in India and for whom I had the greatest respect as soldiers. I have already explained the reasons for this, and so will not repeat myself.

Lieut.-General Watkis, who had commanded the Lahore Division throughout the past trying months and had borne the chief responsibility during the battle of Givenchy, was given the K.C.B., a well-merited honour.

The weather during January 1915 was very trying, being a succession of rain, storm, and snow, but this did not prevent us from carrying on systematic training of every kind—attack, defence, trench work, practice with grenades and mortars, then still in their infancy, and night operations. Route marching was done daily, gradually increasing until the men's feet had recovered somewhat from the results of immersion in mud and snow. It was a real pleasure to watch the transformation taking place ; limbs long dormant in the trenches were restored to their natural functions, and the knowledge that the worst was over and a warmer season would come at its own proper time, cheered all ranks. It was a very busy time for us all, but there is nothing like hard work to keep men fit and happy, and the absence of it kills all joy.

Personally I have seldom been more busy in my life ; rain or storm I invariably rode from ten to fifteen miles a day, and often a lot more ; and although this may not appear much it was a great deal through those bogs and along those cobbled and slippery roads. By the middle of January two Brigades had returned to the trenches, and before the 24th of the month the whole Corps was finally re-established once more about our old haunt, Neuve Chapelle. The arms, clothing, and necessaries had been thoroughly overhauled, boots refitted and extras issued, and when we again entered the trenches I do not think there were many individuals either in units, departments, or even among the followers, whom I had not seen. It gave us a fresh start, and the many new officers who had joined got to know something of their men.

On the last day of 1914 I gathered together nearly all the British and Indian officers in the Army Corps ; it was a damp, misty day, but they came to my headquarters at Lillers by motor, lorry, or on horseback. It was a pleasant gathering, full of interest to us all. Amongst those present were a large percentage who had served with me in the field, a few in the Soudan and West Africa, and a great many on the Indian frontiers, and practically all had been under my command at one time or another as Brigadier, Divisional and Army Commander. Many a time also had I had the pleasure of entertaining them as my guests in other climes, and now they were assembled under one roof and under such different circumstances. It was for me a solemn occasion, for since we had last met at Orleans many had gone for ever, and I knew before we could meet again their ranks would be still further thinned. But no such passing thoughts prevented us from being a cheery party, and all Corps were enabled to exchange greetings, and fight their battles over again. I also took the opportunity of explaining to many of the Indians, who asked me about the recent changes, that the Indian Corps now formed part of a larger Army, and was under the command of a very distinguished soldier, who would assuredly lead us to victory. I am sure they felt relieved, for the notion had got abroad that they had fallen in the estimation of the Commander-in-Chief.

Any exotic when first transplanted must in its new soil be watched if it is to be a success ; this was our task with the Indians, and it was succeeding by degrees, and at this gathering this was evident. They had been plunged into Europe, but Asia was assimilating itself with its new surroundings. It was a far more difficult task, however, than was realised by some of our superiors, who merely issued orders and expected them to be carried out. They did not realise that the pawns in the game had peculiarities and characteristics which must be respected, if they were to continue as a tangible entity. These matters were left to those of us who understood the material we had to deal with, and it is fortunate in some ways that it was so ; for as time went on nothing was more evident than the fact that in the First Army the Indians were merely looked on as so many thousand men, who must just take their place in a certain portion of the line and carry on irrespective of their constitution or the changes which time was working in their ranks. But it was absolutely necessary for us in the Corps not to forget these things, and to so arrange that the machine would work smoothly and prove efficient on the day of battle.

It was a fine test of the value of the British officer and he came well out of it, and proved that the officers of the Indian Army are second to none in positions of responsibility and trust.

CHAPTER XIII

When I look back on those winter days of 1914–15 I recall the names of many of our great Indian soldiers, and it comes home vividly how much they had done for our power in the East, and how they had gained the confidence of the Indians. It was men like John Nicholson, Edwards, Outram, Hodson, and Lord Roberts who had won the devotion of the men and tempered the steel they used, and it was their example that in this twentieth century had enabled England to call to her aid thousands of loyal men from far across the seas, to fight her battles within a few hours' journey and within gun-sound of her own shores. It is an extraordinary story, and one which we will do well to ponder. Here was a great country with 48,000,000 of inhabitants, and yet it was found necessary to summon a few thousands from Asia to defend our cause at our own gates. I have heard it said that the Indian Corps was only sent to France to give India a chance of taking her part in our Empire war; maybe that was partly the idea of those who first originated it, but the fact remains that the arrival of the Army Corps, just when it did come, was the respite so sadly needed by the brave men who had wrought deeds of almost superhuman devotion, but were then outnumbered and all but overwhelmed by the German hordes.

Be that as it may, what has our country to say to the fact that whilst our Indian soldiers were playing the part they did, millions in this island were waiting on events? Lord Kitchener's call had rung like a trumpet through the land, but there had not yet been time for the New Armies to be trained. Who then could be sent to stem

182

the tide of steel that was rolling in billows against the battered granite wall in Flanders ? There were none, save those few thousand British and those loyal Indian soldiers just arrived from the East. There are always critics enough to say that what was done might have been done better, but these stay-at-home strategists and tacticians must answer the question, why they were doing nothing themselves to help in the trenches, and why did so many hundreds of thousands continue to do nothing but talk, until they found themselves forced by conscription to do their duty ? And meantime who was helping (even though it was only in small numbers) to defend their country for them ? Helping with ungrudging valour, and as recompense but a few hard-earned shillings a month.

When the tongues of controversy are lulled, and we can look back on facts without bitterness, there will be but one verdict as to the fine spirit and loyal devotion to duty displayed by the Indians in the hour of England's need.

It was my proud privilege to command these men, and it is my highest reward that I had their confidence ; I ask no other. It was palpable to me after the formation of the New Armies that whatever might be the outcome of our doings in France, my own days as Commander were assuredly numbered. It would in my belief have been the case with any man in command ; that it fell to me was chiefly because I happened to be the man.

It is of interest to note here that Lord Roberts, during his visit to the Corps, had given me some very valuable advice, and promised that he would bear me out in anything I did acting on that advice. I followed it out, for it was the only way in which the best could be got from the Indians. Alas ! he did not live to help, when his help was sadly needed ; and though it eventually led to my being relieved of my command ten months later on, I do not regret it for a moment, for it was my duty ; and in the consciousness of having done that lies a man's greatest reward. I will quote some of what he said from my diary of the same day. He told me that it was absolutely necessary to remember that the Indians must be used with discretion and not flung into battle indiscriminately.

He gave me his reasons fully, and told me it was my duty
to keep those in higher command reminded of this, and
that even if it was an unpleasant task, it still must be done.
He added very positively that it was only fair to the Army,
to the Indians themselves, and, above all, to the British
battalions in the Brigades, who, he added, " will have to
bear a heavy burden in any case."

No words of mine could possibly sum up so truthfully
and exactly just what was necessary, and to those who
know the trials they endured, it will be clear that these
were the only conditions on which the Indian soldiers
could be asked to give of their best in Europe.

I write this four years after the event, and hence any
spirit of personal recrimination has, I hope, disappeared;
but what can never disappear is the sense of wrong done
by the public to the men who served under me, and served
so well.

For, what were the facts ? Whilst the British forces
were daily improving in man-power, we were going down-
hill; whilst the type of British recruits was daily getting
better and the best manhood of these islands was gradually
being drafted into their ranks, ours were deteriorating.
Whilst in England the whole country was watching and
encouraging her men to join up, India was kept in the dark
regarding the doings of her soldiers and we had to take
whatever was sent us.   The whole conditions were different.

So long as we remained an Army Corps under the
Commander-in-Chief, Sir John French, he frequently saw
the men and spoke to them in words of warm praise, and
even after the Armies were formed he still came more than
once and inspected the Brigades on parade; but as a part
of the First Army the rank and file never saw their Army
Commander, except in company with the Commander-
in-Chief, and on more than one occasion the Army Corps
was omitted from any share in the credit it had earned
in hard-fought actions.   Indians are very quick to grasp
such facts, and many of their British officers strongly
resented but loyally accepted the situation.   As this
story proceeds, it will be seen that what I have stated
above is the simple truth, and it will be readily understood

that under such conditions service in the field loses much of the glamour which all soldiers associate with it, and which even the muddy trenches of Flanders could not obliterate; and men naturally keen to do their utmost become by degrees less zealous in the cause.

On 6th January I was informed that Lord Kitchener hoped to be able to send us three fresh battalions from Egypt, but this he was unable to carry out until much later. On 7th January Sir John French inspected two of our Brigades; it was a stormy day with heavy rain, but the Field-Marshal said a few words to each battalion, which I translated to the men, and their pleasure was manifest. Lord French is a very eloquent speaker to soldiers; he knows what to say and how to say it, and it is easy to translate it into the language of the East.

It is a special pleasure to tell of the intense interest taken by Lord Kitchener in the Indian Corps; from start to finish as Secretary of State it is not too much to say that without his guiding hand and his determination we could never have been kept going so long in France. Nothing was too small for him personally to look into; nothing we wanted and which he considered necessary was overlooked. His one great idea, as far as the Indians were concerned, was that as he had initiated their employment in Europe, so he would see it through. As I shall tell in this book, at different times he brought his great personality into play, and insisted on the Indian Corps being recognised and kept up. Notwithstanding any opinions that may already have been or may in the future be formed as to his keeping the reins of office in his own hands, I maintain in our case, no other man could have conducted the business as he did, and no other man could have more staunchly upheld the name of India and its Army.

I had served under him as a Brigadier and a Divisional Commander during the whole of his seven years as Commander-in-Chief in India, and twice commanded frontier expeditions during that time, besides frequently having been his guest; but I never realised until we came to France how deep-rooted was his affection for our great

Eastern possession, and how wide was his sympathy with its people and Army. Many times during the first year of the war I was sent for, and every possible aspect of our employment was discussed by him, and it will probably surprise some as I tell of the opinions he had formed, and his plans for employing the Indian troops as an Army Corps. After the lamented death of our Colonel-in-Chief, Lord Roberts, it became evident that Lord Kitchener meant to take his place as our special friend.

During the rest we enjoyed after Givenchy I find many notes made by me, some of which may prove of interest to those connected with the Indian Army.

Campaigning as we were in a friendly country I was altogether against allowing punishments to be inflicted on either British or Indians, which might give a false impression to our Allies, or make it appear that there was a difference in our methods of treating different classes of our soldiers. Whatever may be thought of field punishment or of flogging, I am convinced that to administer the former to Britishers, and thus make them a mark of contempt to the Indians, is altogether wrong. In the same way to flog Indians (which was permissible under the Indian Articles of War) in France could only bring unmerited disgrace on them as a race. There are of course crimes for which flogging is a very suitable punishment, but this should, like a death sentence, be inflicted only in very rare cases.

However, the law was laid down, and all a commander could do was to mitigate sentences which he considered harsh. With this in view I very early stopped field punishment being carried out in or near any public place, and reserved all sentences of flogging, which could by law be inflicted by junior commanders, for my own confirmation, and except for most disgraceful conduct this punishment was in abeyance in the Corps in France.

Some of the Indians, contrary to my expectations, developed a taste for learning French. Their efforts frequently led to amusing incidents. On one occasion I was passing an officer's private servant, who was ordinarily a strict Musalman, and would of course never eat meat

that had not been *hallaled, i.e.* killed in the orthodox style
by having its throat cut. I observed that his platter
contained some beef, which was not then part of the Indian
ration, and asked him how he came by it. " Oh, I bought
it at a French butcher's." " But," I said, " it has not been
hallaled; how can you eat it ? " My friend, however,
explained that he had picked up some French, and that
the " Miss Sahib " (young lady) in the shop had told him
it was, and proceeded to repeat the conversation. " I went
into the shop and said, ' Beef, Miss,' and she said, ' Oui.'
I then put my finger to my throat and ran it across to
explain that it must be *hallal*, and she at once said, ' Oh,
oui, oui,' so you see it has been properly killed." That
Indian was not for being too orthodox in a foreign land,
and that young lady had evidently learned something of
Oriental customs ; but the story got about and less meat
was purchased from the stall after that.

At first the Indians found it very difficult to distinguish
between French and the German deserters, or prisoners
captured. A story is told, which I believe is absolutely
true, of a German deserter who managed to crawl through
our front line, and finding himself among Indians, lay
hidden till dusk and then warily proceeded along a path
towards our rear in the hope of coming across a Britisher.
He was afraid the Indians would, according to what he
had been taught by his own officers, soon make mincemeat
of him ; however, his luck, as he explained, was all out,
and as he walked along he saw two Gurkhas coming from
the opposite direction. Bracing himself up for the tragedy
he imagined was on the point of being enacted, he
approached with as much *sang froid* as he could muster,
but to his surprise the two men, taking no notice whatever
of him, passed on. Our friend breathed once more and
felt sure the next man he met would be a Britisher ; but
no, his luck was still out, and he beheld to his dismay a
solitary Gurkha, by whose side hung the terrible *kukry*,
the weapon with which according to German ideas these
lusty inhabitants of Nepal were wont to carve up their
victims, or decapitate them with a single stroke.

Nothing could save the Hun now, and he advanced

trembling from head to foot, for surely the other two had only left him alive through being engrossed in conversation and hence not having noticed him. He moved on saying his last prayer, when the little Gurkha suddenly realising his position pulled himself together and came to attention. The last hour of the deserter had at last come ; the hand of the man from Nepal went first to his side ; it must be the terrible *kukry* he was about to draw, but instead of ending the career of the German our Gurkha gave him a smart salute. The deserter, wondering whether he was indeed face to face with his brutal and ferocious foe or in a dream, breathed freely and went on his way.

At last to his great relief appeared a British soldier, and he now thought all was well. Imagine his final surprise when he was hailed with, " What the something are you doing here ? " and at the same time he felt a bayonet point unpleasantly close to his hinder parts. He went calmly to the guard-room ; he had changed his mind about the bloodthirsty Indians.

One more story of Indians and Germans. One night a British officer was out scouting in front of his Corps in " No Man's Land," accompanied by his Indian orderly. The pair had very stealthily approached the enemy trench and were within a few yards of it, when a German, who had been watching unknown of course to them, covered the officer with his rifle and said, " You are a brave man and I do not wish to shoot you; go back." They went back ; but this time it was the sepoy's turn to wonder why he had been told that the Boches were such fiends.

On the 14th January 1915 two of our Brigades, as I said before, again took over trenches, and by the 24th the whole Corps was once more holding a front which extended from a point west of Neuve Chapelle on the north to the vicinity of Givenchy on the south, connecting there with the First Army Corps.

At this time our strength was close on 21,000 rifles, 900 sabres, and 120 guns. During February I learned that it was the intention of Sir John French at an early date to carry out a big operation in the vicinity of Neuve Chapelle, and that it was to be the good fortune of the

Indian Corps to take a prominent part in it.   The battle of Neuve Chapelle is what resulted, and that I shall shortly describe.   But before doing so I will deal with certain matters which affected the Indian Corps, and which may be of interest to my readers.

The enormous amount of correspondence which had to be carried on not only gave me an insight into the complications which attended this somewhat intricate command, but as I look back on it all I see more plainly than I could at the time that my work as Indian Corps Commander was doubled as compared with other Corps Generals.   In this connection I remember well the remark of one of them, who was paying me a visit, and seeing the pile of letters already written and still to be answered, on my table, said, "I would not change places with you for anything ; you appear to have one enemy in front and God knows how many behind you."   He was not so far from the truth.   Still I would not have changed places with him, for although the writing work was onerous and generally kept me up till all hours, it was very interesting ; and one felt it was all so new.

Amongst the officials with whom I had to carry on a correspondence, or to whom I sent personal accounts of the Indians, were the Secretary of State for War, Secretary of State for India, the Viceroy of India, and the Military Secretary, India Office.   These were high officials, but as I recall the piles of other letters I received and answered, it surprises me how many people took an interest in or wished to ascertain a hundred things concerning the Indians in France.   The command was a military one, but the amount of semi-political work combined with it could seldom before have fallen to the lot of a soldier in a comparatively junior position in the field in Europe.

One of the points that up to this time had most disconcerted people in India, both British and Indian, but chiefly the latter, was that they received no news of their people.   High officials in India, and some of them in this country, constantly wrote urging me to let something be known of the doings of the Corps, but those were the days of secrecy, and recruiting in India was much hampered.

It was not common sense to imagine that India would rush to furnish the large number of recruits necessary to maintain her contingents, unless the people were at least told whether Sikh, Dogra, Gurkha or whoever it might be was in Europe or in some other continent. You cannot describe troops from that country as " Midland " or " Highland," and thus give a clue; for the battalions were largely composed of men of several nationalities and religions, formed in companies or double companies, and without mentioning the number of the unit no one could tell what a man belonged to. Yet it was looked on as criminal to name a corps in any of our communications; whilst the Germans knew exactly to a man what we had in France.

Should Indian troops again be employed in Europe, which I hope may never be the case, the authorities concerned will have enough to go on, to avoid the blunders made during the war in the matter of reinforcements, drafts, and reserves. From the first weeks onwards these questions were a puzzle.

Imagine a cold winter's day in Flanders; a biting wind, perhaps snow falling, and a hundred odd, unwilling and unfit reservists from the tropics, standing shivering. The sound of the guns was more or less incessant; overhead passed one or more aeroplanes; an occasional burst from an anti-aircraft gun gave colour to the scene, and you have a picture of more than one inspection of reservists I carried out. It was unfair to the men themselves, still more to the Corps, and most unfair to those who had to include them in their ranks and show a battle strength of so many hundred men on paper.

Of course these remarks apply chiefly to reservists, and some other drafts; there was the other side of the picture. Whole double companies occasionally arrived from other battalions, splendid fighting material and glad to be with us; and although this meant weakening the units they came from, that was another story with which we could not concern ourselves. As time wore on, India found it necessary to fill our gaps as far as was possible from all classes and parts of the country. There were at times in a single battalion men collected from nine to eleven different units, and to those who know the Army, its composition and its regimental system, it will be very evident how impossible it became to keep battalions to a proper standard. Had this been the case with the Indian ranks alone, the British and Indian officers could have worked great changes, but these had themselves disappeared in large numbers and been replaced by newcomers, some with a little and many without any experience whatever of the classes they were posted to.

Towards the end of January a question was raised as to the reduction of British officers in Indian battalions. I was surprised to receive a letter through G.H.Q. asking if this could not be done. Considering our losses in officers and the absolute necessity of keeping these up to at least the number then fixed, viz. twelve combatants per unit, I found no difficulty in proving that not only was no reduction possible, but if efficiency was to be maintained an increase was necessary. I presume the suggestion was only made owing to the great shortage that then existed and the difficulty of finding replacements, but there was no question as to the answer, more especially as I was well aware that a great number of Indian Army officers were being employed on Staff duties in England or with the New Armies then in course of formation.

During the winter months I received several letters from General Sir Dighton Probyn. He of course took the greatest interest in the Indians, and in one he said to me, " I wish I could reverse the figures of my age and make myself twenty-eight instead of eighty-two. I would then beg of you to take me as anything, trooper or mounted orderly," and added that the shirkers would have a miserable existence to the end of their days, after the war.

During January and February 1915 hardly a day passed without my seeing one or more units, or sometimes a whole Brigade. Often did I enter the billets and barns, to be greeted by a chorus of cheers and shouts, and the Indians would gather round and ask how the war was getting on. I frequently took with me some of the presents received from friends in England or India, and the varied class of these sometimes caused great amusement. One kind lady had sent several coloured waistcoats for " the dear Sikhs," as she styled them. Amongst these ornate articles was one made up of patches of every hue under the sun ; it was an extraordinary garment and was trimmed with gold lace. Seeing a party of Sikhs in front of a barn, I stopped and asked them if they would like some presents from England, and if so to come to the car and receive them. All but one sulky-looking fellow came up and I asked why he did not come. They all said, " Oh, he is a pessimist ; he thinks the war will never end ; of what use is anything to him ? " I at once took the coloured garment in my hand, and went up to the man and in his own language asked him, as a favour, to accept it at the hands of his General. The sepoy took it in a rather surly manner and opened it, but even his torpor gave way when he saw the gorgeous coat. All the others roared with laughter, in which he joined heartily, and putting it on said, " General Sahib, you have altered my ideas of the war, for this proves that people must still be full of humour in England, and not as I have heard despondent. I will send it home to my village, and attach a card to it : ' Taken by me —— Singh in single combat with the German Emperor and presented to me on a full - dress parade by the Commander - in - Chief in France." They told me afterwards that he had become an optimist and very keen all round.

Against 12th February I find in my diary : " General Robertson came to see me and stayed an hour—he is a genius." I do not think I was far wrong. I only wish I had got to know him years before, for what I found was that I was a stranger in my surroundings, and nothing more brought home to me the position of the Indian soldiers. They too were strangers, and far more of course than I could ever be, for even their language was a different one. In those days the New Armies had not begun to arrive ; the old traditions still survived, and many of the *élite* in the higher ranks still looked on any innovation, such as the introduction into their ranks of a bushman from Asia, as something which must perforce be tolerated but not encouraged.

CHAPTER XIV

On the 27th February 1915 I arrived in England on ten days' leave, my first from France, and as I had not been home for over two years it was a pleasant prospect. I did not, however, get my full leave, as I was recalled on the fourth day, but I could well afford to give it up for it was in order to receive the decoration of " Grand Officer of the Legion of Honour " which the French Government had conferred on me. It was very good of Sir John French to recommend me for this, which I prize as one of my highest rewards. My four days were very busy ones, and I had the honour of being summoned to see His Majesty, who made inquiries regarding his Indian soldiers, and sent them a most encouraging message. Lord Crewe, then Secretary of State for India, asked my views on many matters connected with Indians, amongst others the question of granting them commissions on the same footing as British officers. I have already written of this. I had the pleasure of a long talk with Mr. Lloyd George whom I met for the first time. When I left I had, like vast numbers of his countrymen, no other opinion than that I had conversed with one of the greatest living men. His assurance that all would be well, and his magnetic manner, sent me away more convinced than ever that he would be the man who would eventually guide us to a victorious peace.

Next day I dined with Neil Primrose, who had been serving on my Staff in France, and there met Colonel Winston Churchill and many others prominent in politics. Much of the talk turned on the Indians, and all were most enthusiastic in their admiration of their loyalty. What, however, struck me most was the note of something approaching pity more than one of them manifested at their hard lot. Now there were no grounds for such; the men were, of course, undergoing great hardships, but so were others, and if the ordeal was harder for them to bear it was only the luck of war. What I and many others of the seniors in the Corps felt was that people in England believed that the Indians could not stand the severe climate. They, like other mortals, were open to criticism, but did not ask for pity and resented it, and I was always very careful to keep my lips closed as to this phase of the situation when the native officers and men asked me (as they always did) what I had heard about them in England.

The following day I lunched with Winston Churchill, and later had him as my guest for half a day in France. I had first made his acquaintance after my return from Ashanti in 1901, and every time I have met him since I like him better. There is something very taking in his character; he always appears to be quite sure that whatever he is doing is the best that can be done, and I think he is generally right. I have met many others who claim to be like this, but are in reality anything but sure. It is a treat to talk to him, and if I were a young man with life before me I would sooner serve with him than almost any one I know.

On the 2nd March I dined with Lord Kitchener; the only other person present was Colonel FitzGerald and he left immediately dinner was finished. I had the benefit of a very long talk with the great Field-Marshal, and some of this I will relate for it is of great interest. The chief point he dealt with was the shortage of shells and the necessity for economising ammunition in the field. He urged me to let it be quietly known to my senior officers that it was criminal to waste a single round; he said all would be well in due course but at that time he could not possibly supply the wants. He particularly pointed out that what we called " registering " and what he called " shooting into the mist " must be limited to absolute necessity alone. I was much impressed by this insistence on economy of gun power, and his clear assurance that we might find ourselves without shells unless this warning was observed. He made no mystery of it, and as I was leaving urged me once more to do all in my power to keep down the expenditure both of ammunition and money. "Each individual can help in his own degree," were his parting words. I knew, of course, we were very short of shells, but after what he said I was more than surprised long afterwards when I read that he had not let this be understood.

Another subject which Lord Kitchener discussed was the question of compulsory service. He was entirely in favour of it, but said his great difficulty lay in the fact that he knew he would never get a fair chance. "They will exempt hundreds of thousands in what are called indispensable positions and will only leave me the chaff." I suggested that if he once told the country he must have the men, would he not get them; and he replied, "You little know all I shall have to fight against. I do." Judging by all the wrangling that went on before compulsory service became a reality, his words sound prophetic now.

Regarding the Indians he spoke very fully. He did not say it in so many words, but his meaning was quite clear, and that was that whoever might try and get rid of them, he meant to keep an Indian Corps in France in name at least, if not in numbers, but that he would entirely relieve units as they dwindled, and replace them from Egypt and elsewhere. At a subsequent interview I had with him four months later he put this very forcibly and gave his reasons, as I shall tell.

The months of January and February had passed in what were called quiet conditions, and during the first days of March we were full of preparations for the coming battle before Neuve Chapelle. Previous to this battle, in conjunction with all my Generals and my own Staff, I had very carefully considered the question of man-power in the Indian Corps, and I feel justified in stating at some length the conclusions we had arrived at, and the many battles royal that they raised. I am convinced I was right, but I was accused by the highest authorities at the time of a lack of appreciation of the situation as it existed.

In order to explain myself I will not only state what actually occurred early in March but will carry on the story to its final solution in August 1915, when, to my surprise, I was summoned to England only to be told that certain propositions were before the Government, which I found if adopted would entirely coincide with my own made five months previously, and would in point of time be exactly what I had recommended. I am writing from my diary kept up daily and make no error in details. To those who were associated with me in the task of commanding the Corps it will be as plain as it was at that time, that it indeed needed patience of a degree with which nature had perhaps insufficiently endowed me, but which perforce I had to adopt ; and a spirit that refused to be subdued even when opposed to the highest military and political authorities in the field and at home. Even if I am considered egoistic, I must again say that I had one great advantage, and that was I knew what I was talking about.

Armageddon has shown up the impossibility of attempting to rule the East under purely Western methods, and has plainly manifested the need of first acquiring some knowledge of what you are undertaking, before you rush things to a hopeless standstill.

The many causes I have stated had by March 1915 told so severely on the Corps that on 8th March I summoned a Conference of all my Generals and their senior Staff officers as well as my own Army Corps Staff. On this occasion the whole question was gone into and discussed, and it was unanimously agreed that I should represent to the Commander-in-Chief that it would be wise to relieve the Indian battalions then in France as soon as this could be conveniently done, but in any case before another winter set in. I knew that our reinforcements would dwindle, and later on I had it on the authority of the Government of India itself that there might be a considerable break in our receiving any at all.

Accordingly I made my recommendations, and at the same time told the Brigadiers to inform their C.O.'s that I had done so. It was the eve of Neuve Chapelle, and from many trusted Indian officers I learned that they had been much impressed by the news that they were anxious to join in the coming battle and ready to remain on, but they plainly saw they would lose their good repute unless reinforcements were sent in large numbers, and one officer put it, " These miserable reservists were sent away from India so as not to frighten the young recruits." The truth was that every officer and man saw clearly that the Corps would soon dwindle to a mere handful of men, and they also knew that, under the system then prevailing, it was impossible to maintain their numbers at anything approaching efficient fighting strength.

All kinds of remedies were already being adopted, and occasionally complete companies from other battalions in India were sent to us and these were generally good. Of course I knew the times were pressing, the need great, and the arrangements for reinforcing us *nil*, but that is just why I felt convinced the game would very soon not be worth the candle. We had held our trenches for five months, we were on the eve of a big battle in which I was sure the Indians would give a good account of themselves, and our Territorial and New Armies were lining up and would, by the time we could be relieved, have arrived in thousands, with more ready to follow. Then, again, it was plain that the Indians would be sadly needed in other parts of the world, where they would prove invaluable and be nearer their own natural bases. Moreover, in France there could be no chance of leave or relaxation for them under any circumstances, whereas in Egypt they could quickly be re-formed, strengthened, and again made fit for service under more congenial skies, and at the same time others who had not then had the good fortune to see fighting would welcome the opportunity.

It was also an important consideration they should be given to understand that the transfer was in no way intended as a slight on them, but was being carried out on sound principles and with the object of making the best use of them in the many theatres of war. A hint that this was the intention of Government would have been welcomed by all ranks, whereas to do it suddenly for any cause would rankle in their minds and never be understood. Everything pointed to the wisdom of allowing them to leave France as soon as the gap they had filled was completed by Britishers. This was my conviction and is stronger to-day than it even then was.

However that may be, I had indeed fallen on a hornet's nest. G.H.Q., of course, had other expert advisers to assist them in their decisions, but experience gained in India was somewhat discounted when the game was being played for the first time in Europe, and only those who were actually playing it could give practical advice.

My papers teem with suggestions for remedying the shortage of men in the Indian battalions. Over and over again did I adjust the Brigades, mix up units, reduce the strength of Brigades, and use every device to still retain the name of the Corps as " The Indian Corps." In June I received an order by telegram to proceed to London where I again saw Lord Kitchener. On this occasion he said to me, " I will never allow the Indian Corps to lose its designation ; it would be a disgrace to India."

Time soothes all things, and as the months passed the battles of Second Ypres, April 1915, and Festubert, 15th May, were fought, and in both the Indian Divisions largely shared. I had made up my mind that the same Army Corps was to remain in France. I had no illusion as to my own future ; after 8th June I saw it must come to an end, how or when I could not guess, but I believed I had the confidence of Lord Kitchener and that was my bulwark. To my surprise, in August I was summoned to London and told to go straight to see him before seeing several other notabilities. He informed me that the Cabinet had decided to send the whole Indian Corps to Egypt and elsewhere and that he did not wish it. He asked me my opinion and I reiterated my previous recommendation, but added that if he could replace our old units by fresh ones and complete our numbers the Indians could certainly remain. He again impressed on me the necessity of keeping an Indian Corps in Europe ; said that India would never forgive us if we removed the Corps as a body, and asked me to state my opinions to all whom I interviewed.

Now if there was one man for whom I would do anything

in my capacity as Corps Commander that man was Lord Kitchener. In any circumstances, moreover, it was better to stick to a decision once made than to go on vacillating and thus disconcerting and needlessly annoying brave men, who cannot understand being made the shuttlecock of politicians. I will not go into further details. I had several other interviews during my short stay. I was once more in the Maelstrom of Scylla and Charybdis and went back impressed by two things : one was that if the Indian Corps remained it would be at Lord Kitchener's wish alone ; and if it left it would be for reasons other than those I had gathered at my various interviews. However events followed rapidly ; Mesopotamia, Palestine, and East Africa swallowed up the two Divisions, but not before my own tenure of command had abruptly terminated.

CHAPTER XV

AT the end of February 1915 Sir John French had come to a happy decision and that was to attack the enemy at some selected point. I cannot enter here into the reasons, or discuss the general military situation; suffice it to say that the centre of the objective was to be the village of Neuve Chapelle, and that it was the good fortune of the Indian Corps to be in this line, with its left or northern flank resting opposite to it. Amongst the reasons assigned by him was one which was particularly apposite to the occasion, viz. "the need of fostering the offensive spirit in the troops after the trying and possibly enervating experiences which they had gone through of a severe winter in the trenches."

This, in itself, was indeed a very weighty reason for giving all ranks an opportunity of stretching their limbs. For over five months on and off we had lived a tedious life. Our reveille was the morning hate; our weary day, a long-drawn-out and slow process of avoiding shells, which we could seldom reply to for there was little ammunition to do it with; our evenings, an interminable gloom lighted up by German Véry lights and other fireworks, and our nights a long vigil of tired men, waiting in muddy trenches for the dawn. No wonder then that the prospect of an advance, preceded by what we knew must be a sharp fight, cheered all ranks and revived their spirits. Nothing struck me more during my year in France than their evident delight when they became aware that the inertia of the trenches was to give place to something more active. As a Sikh native officer said to me on the day preceding the battle, " Sahib, we shall have a chance of proving that the Indian

Army can fight and not only do sentry-go in the *khandak* (trenches). We shall again be able to cry, *Fateh* (victory)."

Our left rested on the right of Rawlinson's Fourth Corps, on the La Bassée—Estaires road, and our right on the Chocolat Menier Corner, from which point the line was carried on by the First Corps past Givenchy.

Since those early days of the war so many attacks have been made on a colossal scale, and such detailed accounts of them have been published, illustrated, and placed on the stage, that it would be superfluous to describe what was done by way of preparation. But it is an erroneous idea to imagine that in those days details were neglected or only cursorily gone into. Nothing could have been more minutely arranged to the very smallest item ; no Staffs ever more thoroughly studied, checked, and elaborated essentials than did those of the Corps. From the big guns down to the men's boots nothing was neglected by the Staff, commanders, and other regimental officers. Indeed, as I now study the orders issued I realise that, although frequently making bricks with but scanty straw, each blade of that straw was utilised to the greatest advantage.

Times gradually changed, until the British Army was equipped as no army ever was before or probably will be again, but the improvements were gradual, the Staff work enlarged with the experience gained, time was given officers and men to go into the battle-line after a thorough training in the requirements of trench or open warfare, and everything improved until there was little room for improvement left. In the Neuve Chapelle days, with all our shortage of shells, grenades, etc., there was no shortage of endeavour, and in that respect indeed there was even more need to husband our resources and make the best use of them. Even so, and considering that we had been at war for seven months, it reads strangely in the official reports of the Indian Corps that in the case of two Territorial battalions attached to our brigades, and both of whom fought splendidly, " Owing to the —— and —— battalions having only just arrived, and not being in possession of any telephone equipment or trained signallers, communication during the battle had to be carried on by messengers alone."

Yes, times indeed changed, but there never was any difference in the fighting spirit of the officers and men ; they remained as they were from Mons to the Marne, from Ypres to La Bassée ; the same immortal souls, if anything, even braver, in the hour of sore trial, outnumbered and outgunned, than in the later days of triumph when the Huns at last began to realise that

> This England never did, nor never shall,
> Lie at the proud foot of a conqueror.

The object of the operations, as laid down in the First Army operation orders, was " to force the enemy's lines in the vicinity of Neuve Chapelle, and drive back any hostile forces from the line Aubers—Ligny-le-Grand, with the object of cutting off the enemy's troops which are now holding the front between Neuve Chapelle and La Bassée." The orders of the First Army were always clear and distinct, and I never experienced any difficulty in thoroughly recognising their object. It was sometimes the execution, with the very limited number of guns and ammunition, that was the difficulty. At Neuve Chapelle, however, we were locally and temporarily superior in both guns and men, and had we succeeded in gaining more than our first objective we could have advanced our line to the Aubers Ridge. Suppose we had done this, the question arises, was it possible to retain the advantage ? Judging from what immediately followed the battle we certainly could not have done so.

Events have since proved that, given sufficient gunpower and good troops, it is always possible to capture the enemy's first and supporting lines, but subsequently you must have unlimited munitions to hold your gains or push on farther. We had not got the munitions, and did not receive them till long after, and hence any advance up to or beyond the Aubers Ridge would have resulted in a Pyrrhic victory. In this connection it makes one think how different were our ideas in those days, compared with those formed after two years of war, and when experience had proved that bravery without munitions may enable an Army to hold its own even against immense odds, but it cannot turn defence into the offensive, except on a local and minute scale. As I write this three years have elapsed since the battle of Neuve Chapelle, but our trenches are still on the very same spot we gained that day, and our gallant fellows, though but few, if any, of those who fought are still there, look out on the very same ridge and the remnants of that same Bois du Biez which cost us dear to attack but which we never reached. Nevertheless it will ever remain a great day and a great memory, for if we did not get as far as we had hoped to do, we taught the Huns a very sharp lesson, and, as far as the Indians were concerned, they learned that alongside the British soldier they could enter the jaws of death and triumph.

The objective assigned to us was the Bois du Biez, a wood of considerable size, lying just beyond and to the south-east of Neuve Chapelle, whilst Rawlinson's Fourth Corps was directed on Aubers and La Cliqueterie Farm. Farther to the south the First Corps was to assault the enemy's lines north-east of Givenchy, and the Canadian Division was to co-operate by a fire attack along the entire front. The map will show how the river Des Layes formed a considerable obstacle between the village and the Bois du Biez, being from six to ten feet wide and from three to five feet deep, and along this stream the Germans had constructed strong bridge - heads and trenches.

At Neuve Chapelle we were to experience for the first time the scientific employment of 18-pounders for wire cutting, and three Brigades were detailed for this purpose. The success achieved by the guns in demolishing these obstacles was in those days a revelation to us ; nothing could have been better done, and wherever the Infantry took the right line as laid down, the attack succeeded up to all expectation. The G.O.C. First Army had frequently impressed this on me and he was right. The pioneers and sappers and miners had done their work very thoroughly under the direction of Brigadier-General

Nanton and every preparation had been completed before the battle opened.

Surgeon-General Treherne, who had served with me on the Indian Frontiers, had arranged the medical side of the operations with a thoroughness that could not have been exceeded, and which earned the gratitude of the Indian soldiers; and last, but not least, my Chief of Staff, General Hudson, had worked out all plans and orders with such scrupulous care that when the battle commenced I felt it was already half over, for each and all knew what was to be their share in it.

A readjustment of our line had been carried out during the night of 28th February/1st March, whereby the front of the Corps extended from Chocolat Menier Corner through Port Arthur to the La Bassée—Estaires road. This front was occupied by the Meerut Division with one Brigade, the two others being in reserve. The Lahore Division, less one Brigade in Army reserve, was in Corps reserve.

About this time the heavy artillery of the Indian Corps (excepting the 2nd Siege Battery, 6-inch howitzers), and with certain additions, was grouped under Brigadier-General Franks, R.A., as No. 1 Group G.H.Q. Artillery. This group was ordered to support the operations of the Indian Corps. The remainder of the Artillery of both Divisions was gradually brought into action into positions selected by Brigadier-General Scott, R.A., attached to Corps Headquarters. The moves were completed by the evening of 7th March.

The system under which the artillery was disposed was as follows :

3 18-pr. Brigades to cut wire on front to be assaulted.
2 18-pr. Brigades to cover the southern section, which was not attacking.
1 18-pr. Brigade partly building curtain of fire on roads and approaches from the Bois du Biez, and partly in observation.
1 Brigade 4·5-inch Howitzers ⎫
1 Brigade 6-inch Howitzer ⎬ destroying enemy trenches.
Siege Battery ⎭
1 Section 2·75 inch actually in fire trenches for close support of Infantry attack.

The above were the objectives for necessarily the first phase, but the subsequent objectives laid down did not involve a change of position for the batteries.

Considerable engineering preparations had been made in advance, such as provision of cover for the assaulting Brigade to form up in, improvements to communications, and provision of light bridges, etc., for crossing obstacles.

The Lahore Division had moved forward on 7th March and concentrated in the area Calonne—Lestrem—Robecq, the Meerut Division concentrating its troops still farther forward in order to provide the necessary accommodation.

By the morning of 9th March the Corps was disposed as follows :

CORPS HEADQUARTERS.   Report Centre, La Cix Marmuse.
MEERUT DIVISION.   Report Centre, Vieille Chapelle.
    Dehra Dun Brigade, La Couture.
    Garhwal Brigade, Richebourg St. Vaast.
    Bareilly Brigade, Holding front line.
LAHORE DIVISION.   Report Centre, Lestrem.
    Ferozepore,
    Jalandar,   }Farther back.
    and Sirhind Brigades.

The Artillery of both Divisions was in action under the orders of the Meerut Division.   The Cavalry, Sappers, and Pioneers were with their respective Divisions.

The 125th Rifles and 1 Company 34th Pioneers had been placed temporarily at the disposal of the Fourth Corps for the road work which would be necessitated by an advance.   The recent addition of some battalions of the Territorial Force had necessitated a reconstitution of Infantry Brigades.

On the 10th March the composition was as under :

LAHORE DIVISION
Major-General KEARY (Indian Army).

SIRHIND BRIGADE.—Brigadier-General Walker, V.C. (Indian Army).
    1st Highland Light Infantry.
    4th Liverpools (Special Reserve).
    15th Sikhs.
    1/1st Gurkhas.
    1/4th Gurkhas.

JALANDAR BRIGADE.—Brigadier-General Strickland, Manchester Regiment.
1st Manchesters.
4th Suffolks (Territorials).
47th Sikhs.
59th Rifles (Frontier Force).

FEROZEPORE BRIGADE.—Brigadier-General Egerton (Indian Army).
1st and 2nd Connaught Rangers (one unit).
4th Londons (Territorials).
9th Bhopal Infantry.
57th Rifles (Frontier Force).
129th Baluchis.

DIVISIONAL TROOPS.—
15th Lancers.
34th Sikh Pioneers.
20th and 21st Companies Sappers and Miners.

MEERUT DIVISION

Lieut.-General ANDERSON, late R.A.

GARHWAL BRIGADE.—Brigadier-General Blackader, Leicestershire Regiment.
2nd Leicesters.
3rd Londons (Territorials).
1st and 2nd Battalions 39th Garhwal Rifles (one unit).
2/3rd Gurkhas.
2/8th Gurkhas.

BAREILLY BRIGADE.—Brigadier-General Southey (Indian Army).
2nd Black Watch.
4th Black Watch (Territorials).
41st Dogras.
58th Rifles.
125th Rifles.

DEHRA DUN BRIGADE.—Brigadier-General Jacob (Indian Army).
1st Seaforths.
4th Seaforths (Territorials).
6th Jats.
2/2nd Gurkhas.
1/9th Gurkhas.

DIVISIONAL TROOPS.—
4th Cavalry.
107th Pioneers.
Nos. 3 and 4 Companies Sappers and Miners.

Aeroplanes and flying machines in general were few and far between in those days as compared with later times; nevertheless our airmen had even then shown what these neoteric implements could achieve in the hands of brave men in war. The Germans were completely taken by surprise when our attack began, and this was in a very great measure due to the fearless daring and persistence of our aviators, who had left nothing to chance. Although I have little to tell in this book of the Air Service as it then was, it is a fact that the Sepoys, when they first realised the objects and witnessed the extraordinary daring of aeroplanes, felt that their epic of the Mahabharat (Great War) was about to be repeated.

And so the Indian soldiers were, for the first time in history, on the eve of an offensive battle against the most highly trained and organised army of Europe.

For those who merely looked on an attack in force as an incident of the Great War, the coming battle may have been only a new phase in the struggle; for me as Commander of the Corps it meant much more. I was standing on the brink of an experiment which might have momentous consequences. I was responsible, in my own way, for important issues; I was, on a very small scale it is true, but nevertheless in a somewhat similar position to the first Japanese General who met and overthrew his Russian opponents. It was a question of the East versus the West, and although I felt sure of my brave men, it remained to be proved how the East would take it.

The night of 9th March 1915 will ever remain one of my most inspiriting recollections. I can recall every moment of it; I did not sleep long, but I thought a lot; I did not doubt, but the thing had to be made good.

Many beside myself thought much that night, but I wonder if one felt a greater joy than I did as I realised that a life's work was to be tested. That life had been mostly spent in India, amongst Indian soldiers, and when dawn proclaimed that the supreme moment was at hand, I walked into the small garden of my dwelling and felt with Thomas Jefferson

That all men are created equal.

Although the night of the 9th March had been cloudless up till about midnight, the morning broke cold, damp, and misty. I stood in the drizzle with my friend Khwaja Mahomed Khan, A.D.C., and as the watch marked the hour for the intense bombardment, I said to him, " This is a great hour in Indian history. Praise be to Allah." And he replied, " Allah is with us, the Germans' turn for a thrashing has arrived."

The Lahore Division during the early morning of the 10th March moved up to Vieille Chapelle — La Couture and the area La Tombe Willot—Les Lobes—Zelobes, the Ferozepore Brigade remaining in Army reserve at Calonne.

After some preliminary registration the previously arranged Artillery bombardment commenced at 7.30 A.M. For the first ten minutes three Brigades of 18-pounders fired at the enemy's wire entanglements, which they succeeded in demolishing pretty completely, as we afterwards found. For the remaining twenty-five minutes of the first phase of the bombardment the 18-pounders (eighteen batteries) were covering the area held by the enemy and the southern flank, so as to prevent the arrival of reinforcements. During this same period of twenty-five minutes the 4·5-inch and 6-inch howitzers shelled the trenches which were to be assaulted.

The frontage attacked was 600 yards, the obstacles being *chevaux de frise*, thickly wired, generally in one but sometimes in two rows, and a certain amount of low wire entanglement. The depth of the obstacles varied from 6 to 15 yards, but owing to their being opposite one side of a salient only a limited number of batteries could be brought into action, so that the line of fire was direct. The 9th and 13th Brigades took position at ranges averaging 1800 yards. The 4th Brigade was disposed at an average range of 2500 yards, the line of fire being oblique.

The method of attack was that in each battery of

the 9th and 13th Brigades fire was concentrated on numbers 2 and 5 guns, whereby two lanes per battery, or twelve in all, were to be formed.

The 4th Brigade concentrated three guns on each alternate lane position.

The allowance of ammunition was 50 rounds per gun, and was fired in ten minutes.

Thus twelve lanes were formed, six by having 150 rounds and six by having 300 rounds expended on them.

The Garhwal Brigade, which had the honour of being detailed to carry out the first assault, was commanded by a fine soldier, Brigadier-General Blackader. I had first met him when he commanded his battalion of Leicesters in India, and from that day onwards I had learned to respect him and to trust in his judgement. The manner in which he handled his Brigade at Neuve Chapelle was good to see, and his report on the three days' fighting is concise, and written as brave and modest men write.

In support of the Garhwal was the Dehra Dun Brigade, commanded by Brigadier-General Jacob.

The Bareilly Brigade continued to hold the original trenches, and in command of it was Brigadier-General Southey, Indian Army, in whom I reposed the utmost confidence.

Whatever the qualifications of other brigade commanders in France, I certainly was fortunate in those who directed their brigades at Neuve Chapelle.

And all is now ready for the great attack. In such moments men think and act according to their own peculiar natures; the Oriental's thoughts are generally quite different from our own. I asked a sepoy I had known for years, and who came out of the battle scatheless, how he felt just before the assault. This was his reply: " My right-hand comrade had been looking at a rough map with the names of the villages and trenches marked in Hindustani. I could read the names, but did not understand the map; so just before we started I made up my mind to go to my British officer after the battle and get him to teach me. I had no time to think of anything

P

else, for just then we advanced." Splendid fellow! I am
glad I was not the first German who came across his path;
but his simple story impressed me much. He was not
wondering what was going to happen; he was just going
to death, if Ishwar so ordained, and if he lived he was
going to improve his military value.

The half-ruined village of Neuve Chapelle, about to
be turned into a shambles for the third time, lay but a
few hundred yards to the front; boggy fields, torn hedges,
and numerous ditches blocked the passages of the attackers,
and the Aubers Ridge beyond looked down on the dead
level country, so soon to mark the triumph of the Asiatic
over the Teuton.

At 8.5 A.M. precisely the Garhwal Brigade rushed to
the assault of the enemy's trenches opposite the front he
had been holding along the La Bassée road. The order
of battalions from right to left was:

1/39th Garhwal Rifles	(Colonel Swiney).
2nd Battalion Leicesters	(Lieut.-Colonel Gordon).
2/3rd Gurkha Rifles	(Lieut.-Colonel Ormsby).
2/39th Garhwal Rifles	(Lieut.-Colonel Drake-Brockman).

The 3rd London Regiment was in Brigade reserve.

The assaulting infantry (except the 1/39th Garhwalis)
reached their first objective without a check, and by 8.30
had pushed through to the east side of the road joining
Port Arthur with Neuve Chapelle.

The 2/39th, the left battalion of the Brigade, and
therefore the one nearest the right of the 8th British
Division, which was attacking on our left, was met by
some rifle and machine-gun fire but had soon reached the
fourth German trench. Scouts were at once sent forward, and the consolidation of the position commenced.
Simultaneously the advance was continued to the out-
skirts of Neuve Chapelle, where three machine-guns and
300 prisoners fell into their hands.

In this advance Naik Jaman Sing Bisht won the
Indian Order of Merit by fine leading, and Havildar Buta
Sing Negi was awarded the same decoration. Rifleman
Gobar Sing Negi received the Victoria Cross for con-
spicuous bravery and under circumstances so similar to

those which had won it for his Garhwal comrade of the
1st battalion, viz. Naik Darwan Sing Negi, on the 23rd
November 1914, near Festubert, that it would appear
the soldiers from Garhwal firmly believe that the bayonet
is the best weapon for use in the trenches. He was the
leading man of the bayonet detachment which accompanied the bombing party; was first to rush each
traverse, and besides himself bayoneting several Germans
drove back many more who finally all surrendered. Death
claimed him before he could receive the Cross which he
had so bravely won, but it was awarded posthumously,
and his family get the monetary award; whilst his name
will remain a beacon to attract for years his fellow hillmen to the 2/39th Garhwal Rifles.

Jemadar Ghantu Sing Negi was killed and over 130
casualties were suffered by the battalion.

The 2/3rd Gurkhas carried the trenches to their front
and secured two machine-guns. Having arranged for one
company each from the 2/39th and Londons to consolidate the line gained, the Gurkhas pushed on, wheeled
to the right, crossed the Rue du Bois and reached the
old British trench east of Neuve Chapelle. Quickly
entrenching they gained touch with the Rifle Brigade of
the Fourth Corps on their left. Major A. Tillard on his
own initiative carried the attack still farther forward
towards the brewery and captured several prisoners.
The Indian Order of Merit was conferred on Subadar
Bhim Sing Thapa, Lance-Naik Harak Sing Gharti, Subadar
Major Gambhir, Sing Gurung, Havildar Bahadur Thapa,
and Rifleman Gane Gurung. This latter gallant fellow
was the hero of a melodramatic affair. The 2nd Rifle
Brigade from the Fourth Army Corps met the Gurkhas in
the village, and the first thing seen was my friend Gane
Gurung, with his bayonet very close to the stern of a
German, who with seven others were being driven off as
prisoners, having surrendered *en bloc* in a house to the
little Gurkha. Lieut.-Colonel Ormsby was made a C.B.

The 2nd Leicesters also advanced without a check
and by 8.30 A.M. had gained the road parallel to and east
of the Estaires—La Bassée road, where the battalion began

to entrench itself. It was found, for reasons which will be related, that between their right and the left of the 1/39th a considerable gap existed. Captain Romilly, using his revolver freely and followed by a platoon of the Leicesters, bombed back the Huns for over a hundred yards of trench and then with the assistance of Captain Hobart, R.E., and some sappers who came up opportunely, erected a barricade. Hobart was awarded the Military Cross, Sapper Sheikh Abdul Rahman the I.O.M., and Colour-Havildar Chagatta, who had previously won the I.O.M., was given the Russian Cross of St. George.

Romilly received a well-earned D.S.O., and Captain D. L. Weir, also of the same battalion, a Military Cross. The Leicesters are all brave, but conspicuous amongst them on this day was Private William Buckingham, who, regardless of an inferno of fire, carried in several badly wounded men. In doing this he received two severe wounds himself but escaped with his life and was awarded the Victoria Cross. Poor fellow ! he no longer lives to enjoy his reward ; he has added one more to the immortal dead along the Somme. Several D.C.M.'s were also awarded to N.C.O.'s and men of this fine fighting Corps.

In none of these assaults so far had any serious check been caused by the enemy's wire entanglements, these obstacles having been destroyed by the artillery, and only in the case of the 2/39th had any considerable fire been met before the first trench was reached.

The 1/39th Garhwalis did not fare so well ; their assault unfortunately took a wrong initial direction, and instead of keeping their left as ordered on the Rivière des Layes, swung away to the right. Nevertheless, in face of a heavy rifle and machine-gun fire they reached close up to the German trenches, but the obstacles had not been destroyed by our artillery, as they were not included in the marked zone, and consequently the impetus of the rush was broken.

During this check the battalion suffered considerable casualties in British officers and Indian ranks. But although the initial error cost them dear, it was the occasion for proving the grand material of which these fine

Garhwal Rifles are made.   On no occasion in the history of the Indian Corps in France was it better proved what Indians led by British officers will assuredly achieve, provided the men have been properly trained.   The capture of the enemy's trenches here became a terrible struggle, but the 39th would take no denial.   Captains Owen, J. E. Murray, R. J. Clarke, and Sparrow were killed, whilst Captain Kenny and Lieut. Welchman actually reached and entered the trenches before they also shared the same fate.   Six out of the total of twelve British officers gave their lives in a few short moments, and Major MacTier of the 2nd Battalion, who had been sent to replace Colonel Swiney (wounded), was also killed later on.

Faithful unto death.

The check created a gap between the left of the 1/39th and the right of the Leicesters.   In this gap the Germans held out, and it took much time and was not without considerable losses that their trenches were finally captured.

The Leicesters seeing how matters stood immediately set to work to clear up the situation, and a party under Captain Romilly, as already related, using bayonets and hand grenades, gradually forced the enemy back along his trenches.   Lieut. G. A. Cammell, R.F.A., on forward observation duty, seeing the British officers were being mown down and that some hesitation was occurring in the advance, and his telephone communication having been destroyed, dashed forward and headed the charge, with some Garhwalis by his side ; he and a few of the Riflemen were almost immediately wounded, and fell, but here again another gallant soldier, Corporal V. Thompson, 2nd Black Watch, was quickly on the scene to save the officer, and carried him back, being himself wounded while doing so.   It is pleasant to record that the D.S.O. and D.C.M. were promptly bestowed.

Colonel Swiney, the Commander of the 1/39th, who himself related to me the doings of his Corps on this day, a brave and modest gentleman, was also severely wounded during the morning ; but what he did not tell me was that he remained on for many long and weary hours, till loss of blood forced him to leave his command. Subadar Kedar Sing Rawat and other Garhwali officers did very fine work after the British officers had been killed and wounded.

Further help was needed before the end could be attained, and this came from the Dehra Dun Brigade, whose G.O.C. placed two companies of the 1st Seaforths at the disposal of the Garhwal Brigade, and these, together with two companies of the 3rd Londons and one company of the 1/39th from Port Arthur, finally succeeded in carrying the trenches.

The Seaforth advance was brilliantly seconded by the 3rd Londons and a company of the 39th, who carried out a frontal attack with the bayonet in a most dashing style, but of course with heavy loss. The 3rd Londons, especially in this their first fight, literally covered themselves with honour, and I never heard their name mentioned thereafter except in terms of the highest praise by all ranks of the Army Corps.

The 1st Seaforths carried out its advance, as it always did, with the *élan* and thoroughness of the pick of the " Old Contemptibles." Captain Wicks, once on my Staff in India, was wounded, one of the very best all-round men I ever knew. Captain R. Murray was wounded and died the next day. 2nd Lieut. C. H. Kirkaldy was killed, and in this short attack the battalion suffered over seventy casualties. Three N.C.O.'s and men received the D.C.M.

I recall a story of the Seaforths during one of my expeditions on the North-West frontiers of India in 1908. A brigade, after carrying out some punitive measures on a large village, was retiring over an open plain scored by deep nullahs. The Seaforths formed the rearguard. The Afridis, as usual, were following and firing whenever opportunity offered, but on such ground they had no chance and were kept at a respectful distance. After the expedition was over the chiefs all came in to hear the terms of our Government. I asked an old warrior why they had not followed us more closely on that day. His answer was: " We did not like those Highlanders; they looked as if they wanted us to come on, and we had no intention of obliging them." He was right; the Seaforths moved deliberately throughout as if they were spoiling for a fight. It was on this same day that my gallant friend Major Hon. Forbes Sempill, their C.O., was killed, and the battalion would have given a good deal to have had its revenge.

The assault of the 3rd Londons was, as I have already said, a "most dashing" one. Officers and men vied with one another to be first into the German trenches. Wherever they all came from I cannot say, but blessed indeed is the city that can pour forth such men at the call of their country. 170 casualties marked their share in the battle. Captain Moore received the Military Cross, and a few N.C.O.'s were awarded the D.C.M.

The result of all these operations was that the gap in our advance was closed, and many wounded Germans surrendered.

The 1/39th Garhwalis paid dearly on this day. By the time they had reached the objective assigned to them in the assault the battalion had been severely mauled, and its subsequent losses brought its total casualties to 330 out of a strength which did not exceed 600 all told. Every British officer was either killed or wounded before the fighting at Neuve Chapelle ended.

Captain J. Taylor, I.M.S., in medical charge of the battalion, was awarded the D.S.O. on Colonel Swiney's special recommendation for gallant conduct and devotion to duty.

During the attack of the Garhwal Brigade the Dehra Dun Brigade had moved up in close support. At 10.45 A.M. the Jalandar Brigade also was ordered to move to Richebourg St. Vaast, and later, at 2.30 P.M., the Sirhind Brigade was ordered to Vieille Chapelle and La Couture.

By 11 A.M. the Dehra Dun Brigade (less 1st Seaforths, detailed to assist the 1/39th Garhwalis' advance) was ready to issue from the trenches along the La Bassée road and to advance to the attack of the Bois du Biez. Since, however, at that hour the enemy was still holding out in the trenches between the Leicesters and the 1/39th Garhwalis (who were isolated) this attack was postponed. The delay was most unfortunate, as had it been carried out on the heels of the first assault, great results might have been achieved.

As will be seen later, even as it was the Bois du Biez might have fallen to us, but the inability of the British Brigade of the Eighth Division, on our left, to advance prevented it, and on this and the following days for the same cause an advance into the Bois du Biez became an impossibility, as our left flank was entirely enfiladed.

As I stood that morning expectantly by the telephone, awaiting the first news of the results of our assault, it seemed as if ages were rolling by, but when the news came, it was one of the moments I often live again. " Practically all our first objectives captured." " Hurrah ! " I shouted, and with such energy that, as the French women at the back of the house afterwards told me, they thought a bomb had burst inside. And so it had ! The bomb was the birth of a new life for India ; the story that the cables would bear throughout the world, viz. that the Indians, led by British officers, could drive Germans from their own deliberately selected entrenchments. That the men who had fought against us from Seringapatam to Assaye, at Moodkee and Chillianwala, at Delhi, Lucknow, and Tirah, all classes, creeds, and clans, had banded together under the Union Jack, and trusting in the inviolable word of England's King and the proven valour of their white leaders, had inaugurated a new era in the history of Hindustan.

At 3.15 P.M. orders were received from the First Army to push on to the Bois du Biez, and instructions were issued for the Dehra Dun Brigade to advance, supported by two battalions of the Jalandar Brigade (the 1st Manchesters and 47th Sikhs), which had now come under the orders of the Meerut Division. The deployment for attack along the road running south-west from Neuve Chapelle was not completed until 4.30 P.M., and it was nearly dark by the time the troops reached the line of the river Layes. By 6.30 P.M. a portion of the Brigade had reached the western edge of the wood, guided in the pitch darkness by a burning house on its extreme north-west corner.

The leading companies of the 2nd Gurkhas under Major Watt and Captain Dallas Smith crossed the road, occupied some houses, and commenced to dig in at the edge of the wood. Major H. Nicolay was killed during this operation. A portion of the 9th Gurkhas on the left of the 2nd Gurkhas also reached the wood. In this advance both battalions moved with the greatest steadiness under rifle and machine-gun fire from both flanks, but although suffering casualties, had soon placed portable bridges across the Layes river and reached the farthest limit attained during the battle. Subadar Mehar Sing Khattri, 9th Gurkhas, was awarded the I.O.M. for his daring leading, and Major Watt was gazetted a D.S.O. Of the conduct of the 4th Seaforths, who were in support of the Gurkhas, General Jacob wrote: " The 4th Seaforths (Territorials) showed itself to be the equal of any Regular Regiment."

The Germans, realising the position, now made a special effort to turn our left flank, but the 9th Gurkhas were equally determined that the attempt should fail, and Lieut. Murray, with a machine-gun, very opportunely stopped the movement. He received the Military Cross for his gallant conduct on this and subsequent days.

At 8.7 P.M., 10th March, Jacob, after a consultation with his Battalion Commanders, decided to withdraw from the wood to the line of the Layes. This operation was rendered necessary by the fact that the British Brigade on our left was unable to make any further advance beyond the line of the old British trench, which they had captured earlier in the day. The left flank of the Dehra Dun Brigade was therefore entirely in the air and exposed to machine-gun fire, and to have held on to the wood would only have meant being cut off and adding another long list to the " missing."

The First Army Commander considered that Jacob should have held on, but he was not in a position to judge, and the decision to get back to the Layes was, in the opinion of all those cognisant of the real state of affairs, a correct one.

The position was in fact somewhat similar to that of the 8th Gurkhas six months later at the fight near

Mauquissart during the battle of Loos.   In this case the 8th gallantly held on till it was too late to retire, and paid a terribly heavy toll.

During the move back from the wood the following riflemen of the 2nd Gurkhas behaved with great courage and received the I.O.M. : Hastobir Roka, Partiman Gurung, Ujir Sing Gurung, Manjit Gurung, and Jagtia Pun.

At the time the point regarding the position in the wood was much discussed, and it is only fair to the battalions concerned to say that they did all they were asked to do. If any man could have remained, without quite needlessly undue risk, that man was General Jacob.   I quote from his report : " If the Eighth Division had been able to co-operate with me, I would have been able to maintain myself on the edge of the wood.   As it was I found myself with my left flank enfiladed.   The right flank of the Brigade was also in the air.   My information showed me that the wood was held by the enemy."   He then states that he intended to continue the advance next morning and had issued his orders for this advance, but that it was impracticable unless the Brigade on his left also co-operated.

The situation at 9 P.M., 10th March, was as follows :

MEERUT DIVISION

Dehra Dun Brigade (less 1st Seaforths).—On line of river Layes south-east of the village of Neuve Chapelle.   Both flanks in the air.

Garhwal Brigade (plus 1st Seaforths).—Holding and strengthening a line parallel to and about 200 yards east of the road running from Neuve Chapelle to Port Arthur, with the right practically on the La Bassée road.

Bareilly Brigade.—In original trenches along the Rue du Bois.

LAHORE DIVISION

Jalandar Brigade (temporarily at the disposal of Meerut Division). —In and about the Rue des Berceaux and in Neuve Chapelle.

Sirhind Brigade.—Vieille Chapelle and La Couture.

Ferozepore Brigade.—Calonne.

The night of 10th March passed without any particular incident, but work went on incessantly in strengthening all positions gained.

The Garhwal Brigade, divided into three sections, had its left in touch with the Rifle Brigade on our left, which battalion was, however, some 200 yards farther to the rear. The left section was commanded by Lieut.-Colonel Ormsby, 2/3rd Gurkhas, a soldier who loved his battalion but had the great virtue of never concealing any faults of his men, and from him I often obtained the greatest assistance in matters of discipline.

Lieut.-Colonel Gordon, 2nd Leicesters, had charge of the centre section, and where that Corps was stationed there was never any chance for the enemy.

Lieut.-Colonel Ritchie, 1st Seaforths, commanded the right section, consisting of his own battalion, the 3rd Londons, and the 1/39th Garhwal Rifles. Ritchie was a most reliable officer, and in a short report written on the spot, the Brigadier had added: " I am much indebted to Colonel Ritchie for the efficient organisation and command of his section."

Orders had been issued from First Army at 3.45 P.M. placing one battalion of the First Corps at our disposal. This battalion was to be employed in working down the enemy's trenches, parallel to the Rue du Bois, starting from near Port Arthur, but for various reasons this order was cancelled at 12.45 A.M. on the 11th.

CHAPTER XVI

THE attack of the Dehra Dun Brigade was to have been renewed at 7 A.M. on the 11th March and all orders had been issued. By 6.30 A.M. the Jalandar Brigade had commenced to arrive at Neuve Chapelle in support of Dehra Dun, but there was still no sign of any advance by the British Brigade on our left.

At 8 A.M. General Jacob himself visited the Rifle Brigade, but was informed by the C.O. that "he had distinct orders not to attack without further orders." The 2/39th Garhwalis, who had been detailed to move to the right to protect the flank of the Brigade as it advanced, reported themselves in position, and that the enemy was crowding into the trenches straight to their front, whilst the houses and edge of the wood were manned with machine-guns and men.

The 2nd Gurkhas were being enfiladed from their left, and the 9th Gurkhas facing the Germans at 100 yards with the river between them, were held up. The mist during the morning made observation very difficult, and it was not possible to bring artillery fire to bear on the points whence the attack was being retained.

During the morning of 11th March Jemadar Shibdhoj Mal of the 1/9th Gurkhas won the Indian Order of Merit for bringing in, with the help of some of his men, several wounded, under very heavy fire.

By 12 noon on the 11th it was found that the attack of the Dehra Dun Brigade could not continue under the conditions, and I issued orders for it to be renewed on the Bois du Biez at 2.15 P.M., with the Jalandar Brigade in support. Both Brigades got into preparatory formation, but the same causes prevented an advance.   As it gradually became apparent that nothing further could be done that afternoon, fresh orders were issued for the relief of the Dehra Dun Brigade and for the attack to be renewed on 12th ; the Sirhind Brigade of the Lahore Division being placed at the disposal of the Meerut Division for the purpose. This Brigade had been ordered up at 7.45 A.M. to Richebourg St. Vaast.

The Dehra Dun Brigade eventually moved back after nightfall to the vicinity of Lestrem, in Army reserve, and the Ferozepore Brigade was directed on Richebourg, to arrive there on morning of 12th. The First Army had sent a message saying that the Indian Corps should keep in touch with Eighth Division, but this had, as already explained, been done all along, the 9th Gurkhas being in touch with the right of the Rifle Brigade, which corps was directly behind their left. Some confusion existed as to the dividing line between them, the two attacks overlapping, both Brigades having been given two common objectives.

Throughout this day the Dehra Dun Brigade had been subjected to constant shell fire and suffered considerably. Whilst this delay was being caused, some platoons of the 4th Seaforths rose up and doubled forward, and in doing so had to pass through a heavy machine-gun fire, but nothing ever dismayed that gallant Corps, which was reported by the Brigadier as advancing during the battle " with a confidence and self-reliance that left little to be desired."

The C.O., Lieut.-Colonel MacFarlane, and the Second in Command, Major Cuthbert, were both severely wounded. I can see them now as I first saw them in France : two gallant gentlemen who at once gave me the impression of being real " cool-headed Scots," who would enjoy nothing more than a tough scrap with a good few Boches.

I will revert to the Bareilly Brigade, which, as already narrated, was holding our original front trenches, and had divided their line into two sub-sections. Before the opening of the battle, advanced picquets had been withdrawn and all houses in the Rue du Bois evacuated, in case they should be shelled by the enemy. The main line of defences had been fully manned, and Brigade reserves were in position by 4 A.M. on the morning of 10th March.

Port Arthur was evacuated by the garrison for the period of our obstacle and wire-cutting bombardment, but rifle and machine-gun fire was maintained. A German aeroplane which had made an early trip over our lines had spotted the gathering of troops, and shortly after a rain of shells was poured into the redoubt, and caused many casualties. The Leicesters and 1/39th suffered somewhat severely, and the 2nd Black Watch also had over thirty.

Communication trenches to connect our own line with the captured German works had been pushed forward, and three companies of the 4th Black Watch moved up to take over the *points d'appui* which were being established. Shortly afterwards this battalion was withdrawn, but it reads strangely, in the light of after events, that "it was found difficult to keep proper communication with this unit as it had no telephone equipment."

I must digress a moment. "No telephone equipment!" Think of it, those who later on fought so bravely but under what different conditions. The Indian battalions at least had their ordinary equipment, though at first on a very meagre scale, and if we owed nothing else to the parsimony of the Indian Government in connection with all things militant, we nevertheless owed them one debt of gratitude, and that was, that perhaps of all the troops in the field in France during the winter of 1914–15, the Indian Corps felt least the lack of necessaries, simply because it never realised that a shortage existed ; for when things were at their very lowest ebb they still were in excess of anything we had been accustomed to in India, even in our palmiest and most festal Durbar days.

Before this war I never discussed with Indian officers the policy of the Government of India in regard to the Army. They knew the position fairly well, but with an inborn good feeling they seldom ventured to do anything more than touch casually on what was notoriously the intense stinginess practised towards the soldiery. If any of those high dignitaries yclept Members of Council should read anything I write, they may perhaps feel a passing shame in the thought that whilst they themselves, to use a slang phrase, always " did themselves well," soldiers of all ranks below at any rate that of Major-General were treated as outcasts in a financial point of view, at all and every large political or social gathering, at which the civilians lived in luxury, sometimes casting an eye of patronage on their military " brethren," whilst the latter, who had perhaps been undergoing very severe training at manœuvres, and had only arrived in Durbar camps at the eleventh hour (in order to make a show in scarlet and gold for the glorification of the aforesaid civilians), were consigned to some outlying sandhills and told to shift for themselves: no water supply prepared, no wood at hand for fires, and no preparations for sanitation.

Yes, I have in my mind some very vivid recollections of many such scenes, and they are recalled to me by the remembrance of incidents at Neuve Chapelle. On this occasion the fault lay not with India, but that it passed almost unnoticed in the Corps was, as I have said, because the members of that Corps had been bred in an atmosphere of civilian selfishness so abysmal that they failed to realise they were no longer in the shiny East, but were actually considered as good as their fellows, and would be so treated.

During the fighting, 10th to 11th March, the Dehra Dun Brigade sustained over 570 casualties. General Jacob and Colonel Widdicombe, 1/9th Gurkhas, were given the C.B., and Major Boileau, 2/2nd Gurkhas, was promoted to Brevet Lieut.-Colonel.

The attack on 11th March was to have been supported by the Jalandar Brigade, but, as already described, it could not be carried out, and the Jalandars in consequence remained out in the preparatory positions they had assumed for the advance, under a heavy shell and rifle fire. Brigade Headquarters here had no luck: three different tumble-down houses selected were shelled in turn, till at last four of the signalling section were wounded by one projectile which plumped into the room they were working in.

This Brigade underwent a two days' fiery ordeal, both in support and in moving up to Neuve Chapelle. They had been very exposed and subjected to a ceaseless fire from big and light guns, in addition to machine-guns and rifles, and nearly 600 casualties resulted. Some of the units became much disorganised and broken up, but in Brigadier-General Strickland they fortunately possessed a commander whom no losses could deter. I remember well his quiet verbal description of the whole incidents, and his unfaltering faith in his Brigade, happen what might. Included in this was his own battalion of Manchesters, a model Corps.

At 8.30 P.M., 11th March, the situation was as follows :

MEERUT DIVISION.—At original Report Centre at Vieille Chapelle.
  Dehra Dun Brigade.—Marching back to La Couture.
  Garhwal Brigade.—Holding line gained on the first day.
  Bareilly Brigade.—Holding original line on the Rue du Bois.

LAHORE DIVISION.—Headquarters at La Couture.
  Ferozepore Brigade.—South of Lestrem.
  Jalandar Brigade.—Vicinity of Rue des Berceaux.
  Sirhind Brigade.—In Neuve Chapelle.

During the night Neuve Chapelle was heavily bombarded by the enemy.

The Jalandar Brigade did not long remain in their new situation, as at midnight they were warned to be in position by 7 A.M. on 12th March, to carry out a fresh attack in conjunction with the Sirhind Brigade.

Before relating the story of this advance I must tell of a great counter-attack made by the enemy. About 5.30 A.M. on the morning of 12th March, as darkness began to give place to light, the Germans launched an attack, which covered the whole front of the Garhwal Brigade and partially enveloped its right. Preceded by a heavy shell fire on Roomes trench and almost immediately after on the Crescent and Port Arthur, the massed enemy came on. The 5th and 18th Brigades R.F.A. soon found their targets, and masses of Germans were literally mown down by their fire and that of every rifle and machine-gun in the vicinity. The garrison of the " Orchard " also opened fire. The waves came on until within 100 yards of our trenches, when they melted away, leaving many hundreds of dead and more wounded strewing the ground in front of the Brigade.   On this day the Indian troops had a real taste of killing, and a sepoy said to me, "It was like a hot-weather dust storm in India and looked as if it must pass over us; but at the very moment of reaching us it was as if a fierce rain had suddenly extinguished it."

Captain Lodwick, 2/3rd Gurkhas, the machine-gun officer of the Garhwal Brigade, was awarded the D.S.O. for personal bravery and the manner in which he had used his massed guns.

On the right of the 1/39th the Germans tried to work up the trenches and eventually came into the open; here they again met with a tempest of fire and were literally wiped out.   Lieut. Mankelow, machine-gun commander of this battalion, was in great measure responsible for their repulse.   He was awarded the Military Cross.

The enemy consisted of various units of the 6th Bavarian Reserve Division and troops from the XIXth Corps, who had been rushed up from Roubaix and hastily pushed into the counter-attack.   Another attempt made by them about 9 A.M. was also repulsed.

At 7.15 A.M., 12th March, Captain J. Inglis, 2nd Black Watch, had by a very smart local attack from the Crescent rushed and captured seventy prisoners.

During the 11th–12th March, the 2/8th Gurkhas were employed in carrying ammunition from the Brigade reserve to forward depots in close proximity to the trenches. General Blackader reported that this duty was admirably performed under heavy shell-fire.   I am glad to record this here, as this battalion had met with very ill-luck immediately it entered the war zone in October 1914, and was again in September to go through a thrilling experience, one which practically destroyed it but has perpetuated its name.

Another instance of the shortage of war material in those days I can recall.   The 4th Londons, when pushed up on one occasion to replace the 41st Dogras, had to move up into the trenches without telephones or operators, and communications had to be maintained by orderlies alone.

Q

By 6.10 A.M., 12th March, headquarters of the Jalandar Brigade were established in Neuve Chapelle, and units gradually arrived there. As already told, they had suffered very heavy losses, and it speaks well for these gallant officers and men that, with nearly 600 killed and wounded out of 2600 actually engaged, and having had to take their punishment whilst in a semi-passive state themselves, they were ready, nay eager, for the attack which was now at hand.

The final orders to the Meerut Division had been issued at 3 A.M. on 12th, directing the attack on the Bois du Biez to be resumed at 11 A.M.; the Jalandar and Sirhind Brigades of the Lahore Division being placed at the disposal of General Anderson.

It will be readily understood by all soldiers that in a battle of this nature the mixing up of brigades and their transfer temporarily from one division to another, was unavoidable. The objective remained almost always the same; the Divisional Headquarters were more or less fixed, and the necessity of relieving tired units was imperative, and so long as the objective had not been obtained it was essential that unity of command should not be broken. Later in the battle, as will be seen, the main attack was placed under General Keary's orders, who by that time had his whole Division (Lahore) under his own command.

The combined attack of these two Brigades was made under the orders of Brigadier-General Walker, V.C., Indian Army, then in command of the Sirhind Brigade. He was an old 4th Gurkha officer, had served his life with that race of men, and wore the Victoria Cross for conspicuous gallantry in Somaliland.

The formations ordered were as follows. The attack was to be made on a two-brigade front, Sirhind on the right, with the 1st Highland Light Infantry and the 1/4th Gurkhas in front line, and the 1/1st Gurkhas and 15th Sikhs in support. The Jalandar Brigade on the left of the Sirhind had on its own left the 1st Manchesters, in touch with the 25th Brigade, 8th Division, Fourth Army Corps; next on the right was the 47th Sikhs, fine fighters always; and on the right of all, the remnants of the Suffolks and 59th Rifles; leaving

no troops to form a Brigade reserve.   The frontage allotted
to the Brigade made a total of about 900 yards.

The hour for the attack had been fixed for 11 A.M., but
an order from the First Army postponed it for two hours,
on account of the difficulties of registration due to the
misty atmosphere.

Bavarian prisoners of the 16th and 21st Regiments
who had surrendered, stated that the enemy in the Bois
du Biez had been strongly reinforced that morning;
however, Germans kept coming in all day and surrendering
in small parties; they stated they had had no food, and
looked cold and hungry.

I several times personally interviewed German prisoners
during my year in France, but I seldom came across the
truculent specimens one reads of; most of those I saw
appeared very glad to be on the British side of the trenches,
and of one, at least, after this battle, I have an amusing
story to tell.

About 11 A.M., 12th March, the Brigadier received a
report from one of his battalions, the 4th Suffolks, that
this unit then consisted of but 140 rank and file, and at
the same time the 59th Rifles reported a total strength of
125 men.   The shortage had been caused largely by the
casualties both battalions had suffered, but also by the
fact that many of the men were wandering about dazed
by the intense shell-fire, and unable to follow their units.
Some gradually rejoined, but meantime, as the hour for
the attack was nearing, Strickland was obliged to readjust
his formations, reducing frontage and bringing his reserve
battalion, the 59th Rifles, into the first line, thus dispensing
with a Brigade reserve altogether.

No reserve! and two battalions numbering 270 men
between them: the Corps was often expected to make
bricks without straw.   This reminds me of a native of
India who once explained to me, that the reason why the
old Mogul emperors used very small bricks for all the
monuments round Delhi, was that they cost less than large
ones.   Perhaps he was thinking of the Government of
modern India.

At 1 P.M., 12th March, it was reported that the attack

of the 25th British Brigade on our left had progressed 100 yards. Just previously about a hundred Germans hurried across from their lines and surrendered. By 2.10 P.M. the Jalandar Brigade was held up, as it found itself in advance of the British Brigade on its left, and was now under a severe enfilade and oblique fire from machine-guns and rifles.

Nevertheless, some 200 yards had been gained, but any further advance became impossible, as the left flank was entirely exposed to a hail of bullets. The right of the Brigade made slightly more progress, but to no appreciable extent. In two lines the Manchesters pushed through a heavy fire and reached our most advanced positions, losing considerably *en route.*

The 47th Sikhs, next on the right, advanced with their usual stoicism. Six British officers were wounded in quick succession, but the officers of this good Khalsa regiment feared nothing; perhaps more caution was needed (?) but praise be to God, such men are not uncommon in the Indian Army. Subadar Harnam Singh and Captain A. M. Brown were killed. The I.O.M. was the award of two gallant men, Sepoy Rur Singh and Havildar Gajjan Singh. The Subadar was posthumously awarded the Order of British India.

In the 59th Rifles the C.O., Lieut.-Colonel Eliott-Lockhart, was wounded whilst moving up to the trenches, and died of his wounds. He had done his service in that fine corps the Guides, and had only recently got his new command. He was one of the most refined, gallant, and attractive men you could meet. In him we lost a tower of strength, and his battalion deeply felt the blow. Captains P. Hore and T. Reed shared the fate of their colonel. The first-class Order of Merit (a very rare decoration) was conferred on Sepoy Zarif Khan. I knew Zarif well.

The 4th Suffolks on the two days 11th and 12th March lost Captain S. Garrett, Lieut. H. Row, and twenty-six men killed, while four officers and 174 other ranks were wounded. When I first saw the Territorial battalions which were sent to the Corps, I wondered how they would get on with Indians. After their very first fights, wherever they took place, I ceased to wonder. I then knew very well, for there is no one the sepoy more quickly likes than a fighting Englishman, and he found them in plenty.

The attack of the Sirhind Brigade was made with two battalions in front line, 1/4th Gurkhas and 1st Highland Light Infantry, supported by 15th Sikhs and 1/1st Gurkhas, the last in reserve. The 4th Liverpools were held in hand for any special work.

The H.L.I. swept over the open ground, nor stayed their advance until they were in the German trenches after a sharp bayonet duel, capturing nearly 200 prisoners. The losses of this battalion at Neuve Chapelle were very heavy. Of the officers eight were killed, five wounded, and among other ranks there were 240 casualties. Sergeant-Major A. G. House and a few N.C.O.'s and men were awarded Distinguished Conduct Medals, and they were indeed well earned. I mentioned six officers in my despatch, but was unfortunate in not being able to procure any rewards to mark their gallantry, although I made every effort to do so. Of these Captain W. Stewart had already been awarded the D.S.O. at Givenchy in December 1914.

The 4th Gurkhas did not have full opportunity on this occasion of showing their mettle, but in the performance of very gallant deeds Major D. Young was killed, and Rifleman Wazir Sing Burathoki and Jemadar Gangabir Gurung earned the I.O.M. Captain Collins was awarded the D.S.O. for conspicuous bravery, when with his company he rushed a German trench, accounting for a large number of prisoners, besides many killed.

The 1/1st Gurkhas lost their Adjutant, Captain G. S. Kennedy, and suffered a total of seventy casualties.

In the 15th Sikhs an old comrade of mine, Subadar Gajjan Singh, was killed.

In writing the story of any action in which one has been in command of a part of the attacking troops, it is only natural to try and confine criticism to one's own restricted front ; but in order to explain matters it is also necessary to refer to those who were co-actors in the drama. In this battle there is no sort of doubt that the advance of the Indian Corps, after the initial success in rushing our objectives in Neuve Chapelle, was severely handicapped by the inability of the Eighth British Division of the Fourth Corps to make more rapid progress. All I know is that the most gallant attempts to advance of the Brigade on our immediate left, after the capture of the ground gained in their first assault, proved unavailing ; and in consequence, for long hours, running even into days, we were unable to push our advantage.

This is not the opinion of one person, but the verdict of every Brigadier of the Indian Corps engaged in this part of the battlefield ; explicit reports which I have in my possession give the exact hours in explanation of my statement.

It was a pity it was so, for had the troops on our left been able to push on, the First Army might have made a greater success of Neuve Chapelle than it turned out to be, and it is well to point out that the Indian Corps, during its year in France, did occasionally carry out its instructions, but did not always receive the credit in its own Army. Read the remarks of First Army attached to the Order of the Day issued by the Commander-in-Chief after Neuve Chapelle, and compare it with similar Orders of later times. But the Indian Corps had not come from the Dominions ! Did the words " British soldiers " include Indians ? I wonder.

It was different with the Commander-in-Chief, who did us the honour of specifically mentioning the " Indian Corps " by name in his despatch of 5th April 1915.

The only comment made to me by the First Army Commander regarding the battle was, that if the Brigadier in front of the Bois du Biez had been a tactician, he would never have left the wood once he had gained a footing in it. Perhaps his vast experience since those early days may make him take a more lenient view of our shortcomings in 1915. In any case that same Brigadier rose to the rank of Lieutenant-General in France.

To resume my story. At 4.40 P.M. on the 12th March General Strickland was informed by Walker that there would be another artillery bombardment from 5 to 5.15 P.M., at which hour the infantry would again attack.

During this period the O.C. 47th Sikhs reported that his unit then consisted of but five British and seven Indian officers, and about 130 men "as far as he could ascertain"; whilst the Manchesters reported the battalion as "very much reduced."

By 5.45 P.M. on the 12th it was rumoured that the Sirhind Brigade had reached the Layes river, and it was enjoined on all units that the attack should be carried out "vigorously," as the British Brigade on our left was to assault at the same hour. For various reasons the bombardment did not take place, in fact, till later, and at 6.5 P.M. the Jalandar and Sirhind Brigades made their attempt to advance. Meantime, General Keary, commanding the Lahore Division, had taken over all the troops of his Division, and issued orders for the capture of the Bois du Biez "at all costs." Still no advance was made on our left, and after covering a very short distance the forward rush was again stayed by the deadly oblique and machine-gun fire from the German trenches. Casualties were accumulating, and the wearied troops were getting done up after their trials of two whole days without rest.

However, I received fresh orders at 7.20 P.M. for an attack by the whole of the Lahore Division. Without going into details which would interest no one, these orders were found to be impracticable during the hours of darkness, over unknown ground, and I most reluctantly felt obliged to hold them in abeyance. I feel sure the G.O.C. First Army when he found what the situation really was, agreed with my decision. At 10 P.M. orders were received to suspend further forward operations and to consolidate our gains. The Jalandar Brigade was withdrawn to the Rue de Berceaux, where it had already once moved back the previous day.

The battle was fought and won. We had not done all that was hoped for; we had not captured the Aubers Ridge (nor did we succeed in doing so until three years later), but as far as the Corps was concerned we had shown that Indians will face any enemy.

How changed are some of our notions regarding the enemy, and how different became our orders as the war went on, from those which prevailed before Neuve Chapelle. I recall how, after a conference held before the battle, I left with the impression that Army Headquarters would shortly, in all probability, be advanced some miles. Places were named; the *moral* of the Germans was placed at a low ebb; and perhaps to encourage all ranks, perhaps because the higher authorities really believed it, the general impression left on me was that the Hun was on the eve of receiving a blow so severe that it would be with difficulty he could recover. Second Ypres, Loos, the Somme, Verdun, Amiens, and other *mighty battles had not then been fought.*

As an indication I will quote only one message received by me during the battle. It was issued at 3.6 P.M., 12th March, by the First Army:

Information indicates that enemy in our front are much demoralised. Fourth Corps and Indian Corps must push forward at once regardless of the enemy's fire, using reserves as may be required. Fifth Cavalry Brigade has been ordered on Pietre. Second Cavalry Division has been ordered up.

How often was that splendid cavalry "ordered up"; but although always ready to do or die, the day was still far distant when the sabre and lance could be used to destroy the " much demoralised " enemy.

Neuve Chapelle was the biggest battle up to that time in which Indians, as a body, had ever taken a share. It marks the beginning of a new era in the history of that wondrous land; it proved the solidarity of our Empire in the East; it opened new fields to the peoples of Hindustan, and it was a living proof of the genius of our race to weld into one Imperial whole, people so diverse in colour, race, and creed. Are we on the eve of undoing our own great work? Are we, in our desire to grant equality to all and every race, rushing towards the goal of an ultimate dissolution? In the words of the African proverb I would say,

Softly, softly, catchee monkey.

The total casualties of the British Army in the battle amounted to nearly 13,000 officers and men; of which the Indian Corps sustained a loss in killed of forty-one British and twenty-two Indian officers, 364 British and 408 Indian other ranks. Wounded, ninety-one British and thirty-six Indian officers, 1461 British and 1495 Indian soldiers; whilst the total reported as "Missing" numbered 315. When the actual numbers engaged are calculated it will be seen that the Indian Corps bore its full share of the losses.

The net result of the operations was to advance the line held by the Indian Corps by about 1000 yards at its northern extremity, and to straighten out the dangerous salient known as Port Arthur—a point which had always been a considerable source of anxiety to the various Corps who had been responsible for holding it. The losses inflicted on the enemy by the Indian Corps amounted to five machine-guns captured, twelve officers and 617 men prisoners. Their losses in dead amounted to 2000 on the front captured by the Indian Corps. After the battle I viewed the ground to our immediate front, from a ruined tower near the trenches, and in places it was thick with bodies.

Every Brigadier engaged brought prominently to notice the excellent spirit that had prevailed throughout all ranks, and it was a great pleasure to me to visit every unit, combatant and non-combatant, that had in any degree shared in winning our first Indian offensive victory. The delight of the men was very visible, and the toils and hardships of the long weary winter were soon effaced.

Of the units engaged, some I have not so far in this book particularised. The 41st Dogras was serving its maiden campaign. Raised at Jalandar in 1900, by an old brother officer of my own, as the 41st (Dogra) Regiment of Bengal Infantry, the battalion received its present title in 1903. It was a class regiment, and suffered very heavy losses only eight weeks after Neuve Chapelle.

The 107th Pioneers was originally raised in 1788, as the 4th Battalion of Bombay Sepoys. In 1900 it was turned into a Pioneer Corps and became the 107th Pioneers in 1903. Mysore, Seringapatam, and other famous names record its war services.

The 9th Gurkhas was raised in 1817. Till 1894 it bore the name of the Bengal Infantry in one shape or form, but in that year became Gurkha Rifles, and its present designation dates from 1904, in which year also a second battalion was added. Amongst their battle honours are Bhurtpore and Sobraon.

The 15th Lancers (Cureton's Multanis), the Lahore Divisional Cavalry regiment, was raised in 1858 by Captain Cureton and was then known as the " Multani Regiment of Cavalry," and received its present designation in 1903. It was composed of four squadrons of Musalmans from the Derajat and Cis-Indus. The regiment fought in Afghanistan 1878–80.

During the fighting many acts of distinguished bravery besides those I have described could be recorded had I space, but a few must be mentioned. Naik Khan Zaman of the Lahore Divisional Signalling Company was brought to notice for his extraordinary coolness in repairing telephone lines under very heavy fire. Lieutenant Steven, 4th Black Watch, most gallantly headed a successful charge on a German redoubt. He received the Military Cross. Corporal W. Gurdon of the Calcutta Volunteer Rifles proved himself a very gallant soldier. He was doing duty with the Meerut Signal Company and was awarded the D.C.M. Private Duffy of the Highland Light Infantry brought in several wounded under a very galling fire, and received the D.C.M.

The Fourth Army Corps, which with the Indian Corps carried out the attack on Neuve Chapelle, was then commanded by Lieut.-General Sir Henry Rawlinson. Of all the Corps Commanders I knew him best, and working with him was a real pleasure. He is so straight and fearless, two unsurpassed qualities in a great leader, and such he has indeed proved himself in the Great War.

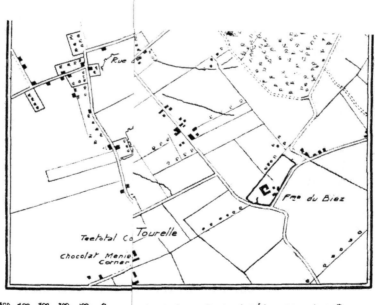

Rue d...

Teetotal C... Tourelle

Chocolat Menie...
Corner

Fme du Biez

500 400 300 200 100 0

...solidated by Garhwal B'de. March 10th 1915
...ra Dun B'de 6·30 p.m. ---do----do--
...sc ------ do-- from 9 p.m March 10th
to 9 p.m March 11th 1915

NEUVE CHAPELLE   10ᵀᴴ ᴛᴏ 13ᵀᴴ MARCH 1915.

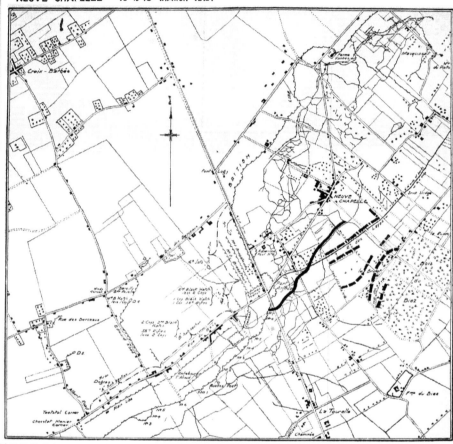

SCALE OF YARDS.

Approximate line reached and consolidated by Garhwal B'de.   March 10ᵗʰ 1915
--- do ------- do ------ by Dehra Dun B'de 6.30 p.m --- do --- do ---
--- do ------- do ------ held ------ do -- from 9 p.m March 10ᵗʰ
to 9 p.m March 11ᵗʰ 1915

CHAPTER XVII

NEUVE CHAPELLE will always remain a great name with Indians, for they fought right gallantly; they fought as a Corps, with a definite objective, and they gained a decided victory over the highly trained army of Germany. We were superior in numbers on the actual front attacked; we had, it is true, a superiority in guns, and the attack came as a complete surprise to the Huns; nevertheless, theirs was at that time the most efficient army in the world, flushed with success, believing itself invincible, and professing to despise the Indian soldier. The German race, no matter what its writers may say in the years to come, will, so far from despising, respect the soldiers of India, who have established for all time on the sodden plains of Flanders and in many other theatres of the Great War a reputation that cannot die.

On the 14th March Sir John French sent me the following telegram:

I have cabled following to Viceroy of India. Begins. "I am glad to be able to inform Your Excellency that the Indian troops under Sir James Willcocks fought with great gallantry and marked success in the capture of Neuve Chapelle and subsequent fighting, which took place on the 10th, 11th, 12th and 13th of this month. The fighting was very severe and the losses heavy, but nothing daunted them; their tenacity, courage, and endurance were admirable and worthy of the best traditions of the soldiers of India. Message ends." Please make this known to the Corps under your command. Accept yourself, and repeat to all troops, my warm and hearty appreciation of their services and my gratitude for the help they have

235

rendered, which has so much conduced to the success of the operations.

Such a generous tribute to the Indian Corps coming from the great Field-Marshal immediately after the battle was equal to a strong reinforcement, and his appreciation of my own efforts was not only the highest reward I could have received, but determined me to hold fast to my command under any circumstances.

On the 15th March I received the following telegram from Lord Hardinge, Viceroy of India:

"I have just received from Field-Marshal Sir John French a telegram informing me of the great gallantry and marked success with which the Indian troops under your command fought in the capture of Neuve Chapelle and subsequent operations which took place on the 10th, 11th, 12th, and 13th of this month. Stop." I shall be glad if you will be so good as to convey to the Indian troops on behalf of myself, the Commander-in-Chief, the Government, and the people of India, our warm admiration of their gallant behaviour and our confidence that they will ever maintain before the enemy the best traditions of the Indian Army. Viceroy.

Naturally all ranks were very pleased, and the Indian officers especially so.

During the battle I had ridden into the village of Richebourg St. Vaast, and came on a company of my old friends the Guides, just arrived as a reinforcement from India. The village was at the time being shelled, but our meeting was all the more opportune. I spoke to the men and had a handshake with the Indian officers. One of the sepoys, who had once served as my orderly in the Peshawar Division, said as I rode down the ranks, " General Sahib, if you are in need of an orderly I am with you, but I must just see one *pukka larai* (real fight) first, then I am ready to come." The Connaught Rangers were also in the village, and as I passed them they raised a loud yell; it was splendid seeing the gallant Irishmen just spoiling for a fight.

On 21st March I visited the trenches in Neuve Chapelle and returned *via* Richebourg. The high tower of the church had always been a great landmark for the Corps, and as I passed it I remarked, " I wonder how much longer it will stand." I had not long to wait, as a few moments later an 8-inch shell struck it fair, and our well-known landmark disappeared.

On the 24th I was riding out to make some inspections, when I came on a party of Japanese officers going round the 4th Gurkhas drawn up on the side of a road. I watched for some time, and could not but notice the similarity of build and stature of the two races. A few days later the veteran General Sir Partab Singh came to see me. His visits were always most welcome, and his advice *re* matters connected with the Indians most valuable. He always kept a few hog spears, much the same as cavalry lances, and used to assure me he would never be happy until he had used one on the Boches. His wish was probably gratified when the Jodhpore Lancers charged the flying Turks and Germans in Palestine in 1918.

On 28th March I inspected a motor machine-gun battery which had been sent to the Corps. It looked smart and workmanlike, and I felt as if England was really waking up and meant business in earnest. My thoughts wandered away to the very early days of the war, and that night I earnestly prayed to God I might be allowed to remain in the field and see the day when the British Army would be equipped as well as and even better than our enemies ; and then, and then, alas ! my diary for this day notes : " Was on horseback all day." I can recall every hour of that day, for I saw a great many units, and each one gave me signal proof of its respect. What more could a General wish ?

My horses were my great delight, and were kept fully employed. " Arabi " and " Guide " were old Indian friends, and recently I had added a remount. He was a fine jumper, and if by any chance I was not using one or all of them, my son, who was one of my A.D.C.'s, was always ready to take them on, as well as his own. The constant work kept us all fit, and I seldom had one sick or sorry.

My brother, who was a retired Colonel in the Indian Medical Service and had rejoined for the war, paid me a visit in April. He came on sanitation duty, and we visited several of the field hospitals and billets together. He had a very wide experience in his profession, and I was glad to learn that he considered our sanitary arrangements admirable. He made many valuable suggestions, and his short stay did a lot to enliven me.

On 9th April I saw the 40th Pathans, just arrived from China. The battalion looked splendid. The rain came down in buckets, but I was never in happier mood; for here was a whole battalion ready for the fray and up to war strength : a rarity in the Corps and enough to rejoice the heart. A fortnight later they received their baptism of fire at the second battle of Ypres. Colonel Rennick, their commander, fell mortally wounded, and his last request was that his orderly might be with him when he died. Brave man ! his wish was gratified a few hours later. 320 casualties out of a total strength of 750 made up the debt paid by the Pathans in three days' fighting within a month of their joining the Army Corps.

The 40th Pathans were originally raised in 1858, and underwent many changes of name and constitution. In 1890 they were named the 40th (Baluch) Regiment of Bengal Infantry, and later again designated as " Pathan." The Corps received its present title of " 40th Pathans " in 1903, and was composed of Orakzais, Afridis, Yeusafzais, Punjabi Musalmans, and Dogras.

Six days of peace were spent in England, and on 16th April I was back at my headquarters in Lestrem. Sir John French inspected two of our Brigades and Divisional troops on the 17th and 19th April, and spoke to the men in his usual chivalrous manner. I translated his speeches to all ranks, and the men were very pleased. After he had left an Indian officer said to me : " The *jangi* (war) Lord is an *asal* (real) bahadur. We cannot understand what he says, but we can tell what he means; and when you translate it we feel as if we had understood all his words as he spoke." Sir John certainly possesses the diction which appeals to Indian soldiers, and they always appreciated his visits.

Lieut.-Colonel Merewether, who was replacing Sir Frederick Smith as Recording Officer with the Indian Corps, joined us on the 21st April and we had a very enjoyable evening. It was sad losing F. E., who had always been a most cheery companion, and for whom I had established a high regard, but we were fortunate in having had him with us so long, for he is a man who will always bear witness to the tenacity of the Indian soldiers, and at his hands their reputation can never suffer.

After the battle of Neuve Chapelle the Indian Corps front was assigned to the Meerut Division. On 24th March we were moved farther north, having Neuve Chapelle on our extreme right, and took over the frontage of the 8th British Division ; and the Meerut was relieved at the end of the month by the Lahore Division.

Prior to this, once again, in order to make the most of our weak Indian battalions, the Brigades of both Divisions were readjusted as under :

MEERUT DIVISION

GARHWAL BRIGADE.—

    2nd Leicesters.
    3rd Londons.
    2/3rd Gurkhas.
    2/8th Gurkhas.
    The Garhwal Rifles (both battalions of the 39th having been
        amalgamated owing to shortage of men).

BAREILLY BRIGADE.—

    2nd Black Watch.
    4th Black Watch.
    41st Dogras.
    58th Rifles.
    125th Rifles.

DEHRA DUN BRIGADE.—

    1st Seaforths.
    4th Seaforths.
    2/2nd Gurkhas.
    1/9th Gurkhas.
    6th Jats.

DIVISIONAL TROOPS.—
>   4th Cavalry.
>   107th Pioneers.
>   Sappers and Miners as before.

LAHORE DIVISION

SIRHIND BRIGADE.—
>   1st Highland Light Infantry.
>   4th King's Liverpools.
>   1/1st Gurkhas.
>   1/4th Gurkhas.
>   15th Sikhs.

JALANDAR BRIGADE.—
>   1st Manchesters.
>   4th Suffolks.
>   40th Pathans.
>   47th Sikhs.
>   59th Rifles.

FEROZEPORE BRIGADE.—
>   Connaught Rangers (1st and 2nd battalions amalgamated).
>   4th Londons.
>   9th Bhopals.
>   57th Rifles.
>   129th Baluchis.

DIVISIONAL TROOPS.—
>   15th Lancers.
>   34th Sikh Pioneers.
>   Sappers and Miners as before.

On 28th April I was up in the aid posts of several units then in the trenches. The Boche, as was his usual custom, had selected one particular spot to shell, and was dropping them at regular intervals of time. Naturally I avoided this particular spot, but in passing a short distance from it I saw a sepoy carrying a load of trench props. He appeared quite oblivious of danger, as he deliberately walked into the ruined house that was chiefly receiving the attention of the German gunners. As he did so, a cloud of dust and smoke rose, timbers flew into the air, and I thought our sepoy had taken his *congé* from this world. I took out my glasses and watched till the atmosphere was clear, when I saw my gallant friend, apparently not in the least disconcerted, quietly picking up his props, which he presently shouldered again, and went on his way. I envied that man his cool contempt of danger.

The Highland Division, commanded by Major-General Bannatine-Allason, was posted to the Indian Corps and joined us on the 2nd May. This fine Division afterwards became the famous "Fifty-first Highland," commonly referred to as the "Fighting Fifty-first." My son in the Black Watch was with me the day I first inspected them, and two years later was sent to them as G.S.O., and shared in their glory at the battles near Rheims, where the Division was sent to assist the French during the big German push in 1918, and in the final phases of the war.

Allason had been one of my Brigade commanders in the Peshawar Division, and it was a great joy getting so fine a unit with us. This Division was transferred to the Fifth Army Corps on the 31st May, but once more rejoined us in June and remained as one of my Divisions till 24th July. Changes of Divisions were of course inevitable, but it was always a blow when just as we were getting to know them they were taken away.

In the same way the Eighth Division, which had fought so fiercely on our immediate left at Neuve Chapelle, joined the Corps on 1st June, and was again transferred, this time to the Third Corps, on the 26th. Major-General F. Davies was in command, and I was extremely sorry when he was transferred to Gallipoli, where, however, he got his chance and took it, as I knew he would do. Likewise the 49th West Riding Division (New Army) joined us on 31st May and left us again on 26th June.

The last Division to join the Corps was the Nineteenth (New Army), commanded by Major-General Fasken of the Indian Army. They arrived on the 24th July—strength, 13,400 bayonets, with their war proportion of officers, sabres, and guns. How Great Britain was awaking to realities! The Infantry of the entire Indian Army Corps in November 1914 did not number more than this one Division; and as for the equipment it was an education to look on it. The Nineteenth stayed on with the Corps and took part in the battle near Mauquissart in September 1915.

R

Amongst many notes and stories sent to me I extract a few giving some experiences of officers of the Indian Army. On one occasion a medical officer was extracting a tooth when a small mine exploded under the trench. He and his patient were both blown sky-high, and on his again alighting on mother earth he was so dazed that, holding his forceps, he ran round in circles and finally into a brother officer's dug-out. With the greatest indignation he demanded : " What do you call this ? War ? " " No," replied the officer, " a joke."—Laughter.

An officer, who had a great friend in a Gurkha regiment, could get no news of him. One day, whilst kicking a football it went over a low wall ; he jumped over to fetch it and landed on a grave, the cross on which showed it was that of his friend.

During my year in France I nearly always found that the French people were not only willing, but glad, to have officers of the Indian Army billeted on them. One Vicomte ——, who was at first quite annoyed when he was told that British officers of an Indian unit were to be quartered in his château, could not do enough for them after a few days' stay. With true French politeness he followed the fortunes of the unit after they had left, and frequently sent his card up to the trenches with enquiries as to their welfare. Later on he sent a formal request that all British officers who came to that neighbourhood might be sent to him.

For cool pluck a story I was told in France of Captain Wardell, 21st Punjabis (attached 58th Rifles), is hard to beat. He was one day in the trenches, which were being heavily shelled, and the men were getting somewhat jumpy under the ordeal. He was writing, when he suddenly discovered that his seat consisted of a bunch of fifty bombs. Some of the men knew this, but Wardell, in order to set a good example, pretended to make light of it and went on writing. Such examples are worth a lot in war.

I often recall the story of a sergeant in the Connaught Rangers, who was so determined to let the Huns know that that gallant Irish Corps had no respect for them, that he crawled up one night close to their trench and shouted : " Ye'll not lie there and die in peace of old age as long as I live." What waste of energy, but what a plucky fellow !

An officer who had been severely wounded in the head, and carried away unconscious, woke to find himself in a large hall with Germans, all talking. Hearing no English he concluded he was a prisoner and proceeded to try and crawl away, when he was relieved to hear in broad Cockney, " Where is that officer with the 'ole in 'is 'ed ? " The Boches were prisoners.

During the battle of Neuve Chapelle a batch of German prisoners, under escort of a few Gurkhas and Garhwalis, were suddenly caught by the German guns ; the prisoners all lay down flat, but the escort, determined to set them an example, stood strictly at attention. This is an authentic story and a very good sample of legitimate pride and good discipline.

An amusing incident occurred during the same battle. Lieut.-Colonel Sir F. E. Smith (now Lord Chancellor), our Recording Officer, had pulled up his horse by a roadside and was watching some German prisoners pass escorted by Indians. Suddenly one of the Boches rushed out of the ranks, and going up to F. E. said : " Mr. Smeeth, oh, Mr. Smeeth, I am so glad to see you again." F. E., not recognising him, asked who he was. " Oh, Mr. Smeeth, do you not remember you saved me in (naming the law case) in London. Well, a few days ago I was sleeping quietly in my house when I received the order to come to the war, and before I could realise where I was I found myself near this horrible place, and suddenly we were fighting, and I saw Indian soldiers right over our trench, and when I looked back more Indian soldiers behind us ; and I looked along our trench and saw all our soldiers throwing away their arms, and so, Mr. Smeeth, not wishing to be in any way peculiar, I also threw down my arms, and so, Mr. Smeeth, here I am. Oh ! save me again." Lucky fellow to have been taken prisoner so early in the war. Saved him a lot of trouble and discomfort.

The craze for souvenirs in the early days of the war

was remarkable.   After Neuve Chapelle, German helmets could be had for the asking, but shortly after ridiculous prices were being demanded for them.   An officer of an Indian unit relates how he saw a big British soldier with a horribly smashed leg come crawling round the end of the trench on threes, with a German helmet hanging from his mouth by its strap.   As he neared the officer the wounded man yapped at him, " Got my souvenir, sir."

The 39th Garhwal Rifles was a remarkably smart and clean regiment.   An officer of another Indian battalion told me that the most impressive sight he saw at Neuve Chapelle was a dying British officer being carried by four Garhwali soldiers through all the turmoil, confusion, and firing with a quietness and tenderness that astonished him.   He added, " and they looked so smart and clean."

The Indians at this battle were much impressed by the dash and bearing of the 3rd Londons.   One of them said to me : " What is this they are saying, that untrained regiments can fight as well as trained ones.   You always told us in India that without long and hard training we should be of no use in battle.   Why is it that this London *paltan* (regiment) can fight so well."   I said, trying to look wise : " They come from London and you from Lahore ;   there lies the difference.   Think it out, my friend."

I know no one who is more susceptible to good example than the Indian soldier.   At one time we were billeted in the same village with the Guards Brigade.   In my opinion there is no body of troops in the world to beat the Guards at anything.   One day I noticed a company of one of my Indian battalions being inspected. It was turned out as cleanly as in pre-war days, and I said to the Indian officers, " Your men look very smart to-day."   They replied, " Yes, but we have been quartered near the Guards Brigade, and although we have seen many of your best regiments we never saw men so well dressed and drilled, and we are following their example."

I wrote to Lord Cavan who was in command, adding my own testimony, and he told me he would let it be known to all ranks.

CHAPTER XVIII

ON the 22nd April 1915 I visited the town of Ypres, as a guest of General Alderson, commanding the Canadian Division. From his Headquarters I went on to Potijze, and from a tower close by scanned the country towards the German lines. From that same tower six days later the G.O.C. Lahore Division was (after a forced march northwards to help our imperilled line) directing the operations of his Division against the first German gas attack. I had long hoped that the Indian Corps might be moved north from the slimy dead level flats opposite Neuve Chapelle, and as this day I surveyed the rolling country north of Wieltje, and on my return journey about St. Eloi, I determined to make a request to Sir John French to give us a much-needed change. Had I succeeded I feel quite sure all ranks would have been delighted at the prospect, more especially the Gurkhas and Pathans. For here were real hills, valleys, and woods, and not only pestiferous bogs and almost treeless fields; but fate ordained otherwise. We were to remain on in our old hateful haunts to the end. At one time the Commander-in-Chief actually asked me if I would like a change up towards Nieuport, but it came to nothing for some reason.

And yet in a degree my wish was to be gratified, for even as I gazed on the German lines the Boche was preparing for an immediate attack, the first with his loathsome gas; and whilst I was motoring round this attack had begun, over the same ground I had looked across. Next day I received orders to hold the Lahore Division in readiness to move, and on the following morning General

245

Keary and his troops were *en route* to take part in the second bloody battle of Ypres.

As I look over my diary the names of numerous places, which had become as familiar to me as London streets, recur again and again, and when in 1918 the Huns made their great attack on the Lys and as far as the Nieppe forest, there was little need to refer to the map; I felt as if I was back in my old haunts, nor could any map have helped me to take in the situation, so clear did it all appear. But I was not there. Alack! I was home on a month's leave in 1919 and spent two days in going over all the old haunts—two happy, sad days.

Next day I applied to the First Army to be allowed to run north during the battle and see my absent Division, but permission was refused. My Corps was now entirely split up and I could easily have been spared for a few hours, but of course I could not go, and the remarks in my diary are not fit for publication.

After a very fatiguing march of thirty-one miles, the Lahore Division arrived at Ouderdom on the 25th April. It is as usual not my intention to describe the events which led up to this battle. The Germans trusted to the use of gas, a new feature in war, to break through our line and to capture Ypres. So unexpected was any such method of attack that the French Colonial Division, on which the brunt fell, was perforce obliged to abandon its front, and in so doing exposed the left flank of the Canadian Division on its right. The Canadians drew back their left, retiring on St. Julien with extraordinary steadiness and gallantry. The Huns meantime rushed over the vacated ground, killing and slaughtering the helpless victims of their devilish devices. After heavy fighting and attempts at counter-attack, by the evening of 24th April our advanced lines had retired to between St. Julien and Fortuin. Notwithstanding every effort on our part, the effect of the gas had done its work, but there was one thing the Germans had not as usual calculated on, as far as the Canadian Division was concerned, and that was that their foe consisted of men of the Anglo-Saxon race, and Canadian soldiers cannot be defeated by any enemy.

The Huns had had their turn, the day was not far distant when they would be hoist with their own petard.

By the 25th April the attack had been checked in some degree in the vicinity of St. Julien, and the following day brings us to the date on which the Lahore Division joined in to help stem the tide. Shortly the orders of the Second Army (under which the Division now found itself) were, that it was to be used in co-operation with the French, and on their right, in an attack in a north or north-east direction from about St. Jean. The actual time was to depend on that fixed by the French to deliver their attack.

The following extract from a letter from the Chief of Staff, Second Army, to Major-General Keary will explain the situation :

25th April. The Army Commander is determined not to commit your Division to the area east of Ypres until he is sure that the French plans have matured. . . . You will only be able to make an attack on a front of two Brigades with a Brigade in support. . . . Sir Horace (Smith-Dorrien) would not wish the Division to press forward unless the French on your left had already done so.

These directions were clear and left no room for doubt and uncertainty. The Ypres—Langemarck road was to be the dividing line between the French right and the Lahore Division's left; whilst the Lahore right would be in touch with the Fifth Corps to the east.

On the 26th April the Division marched as ordered : two batteries of Artillery and the Ferozepore and Sirhind Brigades by the road north of Ypres, and the Jalandar Brigade by the railway south of Ypres. A certain number of casualties occurred from shell-fire during the march, especially in the 40th Pathans, who lost 25 men from a single shell. It is on record that in this their first experience of shell-fire the Battalion showed no signs of uneasiness, but closed ranks and moved on steadily. The head of the Jalandar Brigade reached a position of readiness just south of Wieltje at 10.30 a.m. The Ferozepore Brigade, finding better cover at La Brique than south-east of St. Jean, went into a position of assembly there, arriving about 9.45 A.M. The Sirhind Brigade arrived north-west of Potijze about 11 A.M.

It had been arranged that the C.R.A., Fifth Corps, would support the advance with all the batteries west of the canal; and as the enemy's defensive line could only be conjectured, two Canadian 18-pounder and one howitzer battery, in addition to one howitzer and one 18-pounder battery of the Lahore Division, were assigned to the two attacking Brigades : a very useful support. The advance of the Lahore Division, which was echeloned a little in rear, was ordered for 2 P.M., in order to come level with the French, who were to move five minutes later.

On the march to La Brique of the Ferozepore Brigade (General Egerton), Captain Acworth, 55th Rifles (the same officer who had assisted the 1/39th Garhwalis in their night attack on 23rd November 1914), was wounded, as also was Lieut.-Colonel Murray, Connaught Rangers—a man who was justly proud of his regiment. In the 4th King's Liverpools 2nd Lieutenant Lydden was mortally wounded.

In order to reach a point from which the assault could be delivered the Brigades had to cross some 1500 yards of open shell-swept ground. They were therefore deployed on an east and west line through Wieltje, the right resting on a farm and the left on the Ypres—Langemarck road. The Division was to cover 1000 yards of front.

From the position of deployment the Brigades were to advance under cover of a bombardment by all the guns available. The order of advance was as under :

Right attack.—Jalandar Brigade. Frontage, 500 yards. 1st Manchesters, 40th Pathans, with 47th Sikhs on the left. Second line—59th Rifles, 4th Suffolks, following right and left battalions.

Left attack.—Ferozepore Brigade. 129th Baluchis, 57th Rifles with Connaught Rangers on the left and nearest the French. Behind the Connaughts the 4th Londons were in support, and the 9th Bhopals were in reserve.

The attack started punctually and moved forward

unchecked, but losing heavily from shell-fire. During the advance the Jalandar Brigade inclined to its left, and pressed the left of the Ferozepore Brigade across the Langemarck road. After crossing a crest north of the road the troops came under a very heavy rifle and machine-gun fire, and there was a tendency for units to bunch behind farm buildings or other cover. But the line held on, and the Manchesters on the right, together with portions of three battalions of the Ferozepore front line (Connaught Rangers, 129th Baluchis, 57th Rifles), all reached the close proximity of the German trenches about 2.15 P.M.; the 40th Pathans and the 47th Sikhs on the left of the Manchesters getting within fifty yards of the trenches also.

In the Manchesters Lieutenant G. B. Roberts was mortally wounded. In this battalion the casualties were heavy, as indeed was inevitable from the nature of the country and the fiery zeal with which they always advanced. Before midnight they included Lieut.-Colonel Hitchins, the gallant C.O., killed, of whom it may fairly be said, he lived for his regiment.

The Victoria Cross was awarded to Corporal Issy Smith for his conspicuous bravery in advancing towards the enemy in the face of heavy rifle and machine-gun fire to help a severely wounded comrade. He managed to carry and drag him in, a distance of 250 yards, under a hail of bullets. Not content with this he later assisted in bringing in several other wounded men. An Indian officer in telling the story said: "Issy Smith has a V.C. face." Their remarks are sometimes very apposite. Several Distinguished Conduct Medals were also won by N.C.O.'s and men.

The Manchesters at Ypres had just under 300 casualties. The casualties of the 59th Rifles, in support of the Manchesters, totalled 4 British officers and 60 others.

The 40th Pathans advanced rapidly. Lieut.-Colonel Rennick, the C.O., was mortally wounded and died the same evening. I had known him for many years; his military life was centred in his officers and men. How fast the old Indian " Contemptibles " were disappearing !

The story of the 40th Pathans is the story of the oft-repeated bravery of the various units composing the Army Corps. I would that I could find space to tell them all, it would be a joy to do so, but each battalion, battery, and other formation would need a pamphlet to itself. Through the leaden tornado officers and men ploughed their way, ever nearing the goal; whilst on the right, on the left, and centre were being performed deeds which will oft be told in far-off Hindustan. When the historian of future Russia describes what the Russian Medal of St. George was awarded for in the days of the now defunct Czar, he will have cause to feel that it was never better bestowed than on a heroic sepoy, by name Muktiara, who, scorning all danger, brought up his machine-gun over 250 yards, after all his comrades had been mown down.

Captain Christopher was killed, as also was Major Perkins, when almost in the German trenches. Captain Dalmahoy with six wounds fought to the very last, and brave Lieutenant Adams, in the attempt to save him, was himself badly wounded. Captain Waters was dangerously wounded. Twenty British and Indian officers in all were killed and wounded. Subadar Jahandad Khan (killed) and Jemadar Lehna Singh were awarded the I.O.M. The Pathans recorded a casualty list of 320 of all ranks.

The 47th Sikhs on the left of the 40th once again dyed red the banner of the Khalsa. Of 420 bayonets all told who started the fight but 92 unwounded remained when the carnage of second Ypres was over. Every British officer save one, Lieutenant A. E. Drysdale, was killed or wounded during the early stages of the battle. Major Talbot, Captains Scott and Cook, and Lieutenant Allardice were killed. Drysdale received the Military Cross.

The 4th Suffolks, who advanced in rear of the 47th Sikhs, suffered a loss during the battle of 3 killed, whilst 6 officers and 20 other ranks were wounded and missing.

And whilst the right Brigade was doing its part the Ferozepore Brigade on the left was grimly endeavouring to reach the same goal. The 129th Baluchis pushed up to within 300 yards of the Hun trenches, with a casualty list of 230 of all ranks.   Major Hannyngton, the C.O., was awarded the D.S.O. ; Sepoy Raji Khan gained the I.O.M., and Sepoy Ghulam Hussein of the 124th Baluchis (attached) won the I.D.S.M. for bringing Major Holbrooke, who was lying wounded, into safety through a heavy fire and gas fumes.

The 57th Rifles, under the cheery Major Willans, the centre battalion of the Brigade, with the dogged deter- mination of that distinguished Corps, reached to within ninety yards of the German defence.   Willans was wounded during the advance, together with two officers, whilst Major Duhan, Captain Mackie, Subadar Badawa Singh, and Jemadar Kirpa Singh were killed near the enemy trenches.

Here too fell Captain P. d'A. Banks of the Guides (attached 57th), an officer of particular and varied attain- ments, and one who was marked out for distinction.   His orderly, Bhan Singh, to whom I was talking four days previously, notwithstanding a severe wound he had received, carried Banks through a storm of bullets until he fell from overstrain, but some mark of his officer he must retain, and being unable to do more, he took off his accoutrements and brought them back.   Just like the Guides !

A glorious tale indeed to tell, their children sing to-day.
For each recruit the Guides e'er need, full ten are on the way,
To join the ranks, to don the drab, to bear the arms of pride,
To march behind the Surnai's wail, or listen to the battle tale,
To stand erect at tap of drum, and breathe the air the bagpipes hum,
         And say, " I am a Guide."

Bhan Singh received the I.D.S.M. and later the Russian medal of St. George.   Willans received a D.S.O., and Lieutenant Deedes (gassed) the M.C.   Naik Atma Singh gained the I.O.M.

Lieutenant Mein of the 55th Rifles (attached) received a Military Cross for his gallant work.   This officer through- out the year of my command rendered most valuable service. The 55th Coke's Rifles of the old Frontier Force added a still greater laurel to their records on this day.   A great friend of mine, Jemadar Mir Dast, who had won the I.O.M.

with me in the Mohmand expedition of 1908, and was now serving with the 57th Rifles, finding that his British officers were all killed or wounded, refused to leave his trench when the gas forced a retirement, and there he remained, rallying every one round him and encouraging them to hold on.   After dark, distinct orders reached him to retire, but he only did so slowly, collecting any stray men he could find.   In assisting to bring in a number of disabled officers he was himself wounded, but lived to wear the Victoria Cross.   The I.O.M. was conferred on Havildar Mangal Singh of the 57th Rifles.

The 57th at Ypres suffered a total of 270 casualties, including 3 British and 3 Indian officers killed.

The Connaught Rangers, who were on the extreme left, and hence next to the French Division (as they had been on the extreme right at Givenchy in December 1914), came under a fierce fire as they topped the ridge, but pushed on to within 120 yards of the German lines.   Corporal Flynn gained the Médaille Militaire.   Sergeant Coldwell, who had already won the D.C.M., was awarded the Russian Cross of St. George, whilst several N.C.O.'s and men were gazetted for the Medal of St. George.   Fifteen out of twenty officers present and 350 out of 900 other ranks were returned on the casualty roll ; three officers were killed.

I have a vivid recollection of my good friends the Connaught Rangers on many occasions during my year of command.   Not the least pleasant was one at Orleans on the way up to the Flanders front when I had occasion to speak to the battalion somewhat roughly regarding a certain matter.   Having exhausted my wrath, I was leaving the parade when I heard, " Three cheers for the ' Giniral,' " and then followed three such lusty cheers as I shall never forget.   The French liaison officer who had been waiting on his horse a short distance away said to my A.D.C., " I suppose the General has been telling them something they like."   Irish soldiers are the salt of the earth, and they never resent anything so long as it is fair and square.

The 4th Londons, who had followed the Rangers, lost two men killed and an officer and ten men wounded.

About this time the Huns turned on asphyxiating gas in great quantities. It was of a yellowish colour, and was distinctly seen in large jets coming over the German parapet. The gas struck the right of the French and the left of the Ferozepore Brigade attack, which gave way. The greater part of our line was affected by this retirement, but the Manchesters with about 100 Connaught Rangers and parties of other Infantry regiments, held on to their trenches. At 2.25 P.M. the Germans counter-attacked these detachments, which were forced back some eighty yards, where they succeeded in again entrenching themselves. The first news received at Divisional Headquarters was a telephone message from the Jalandar Brigade that the attack had failed, and that troops were falling back everywhere, together with the French. Shortly afterwards the Ferozepore Brigade reported that the attack was held up, that the centre of the Brigade was well up, but the French were retiring. At 2.35 P.M., in consequence of these reports, the Sirhind Brigade was ordered to move to La Brique to be ready for any emergency in that direction.

When the gas first caught our bewildered troops, totally unprepared for such devices, and forced them to retire rapidly, such was the confusion amongst units, British, Indian, and French, that an Indian havildar shouted out, "*Khabardar, Jehannam pahunche*" ("Look out, we've arrived in Hell").

But even so the gates of Hell can be held by brave men, and of such were Major Deacon of the Connaughts and Lieutenant Henderson of the Manchesters, with many of their own men and small parties of Indians, who held out for many hours, unconquerable! Major Deacon as well as Captain Ingham of the same regiment won the D.S.O., and Henderson received a Military Cross. They were eventually relieved by Captain Tarrant and a detachment of the Highland Light Infantry next day, and this detachment also held on until itself relieved on the 28th. An heroic episode! Tarrant's name always brings home to me the fact that, notwithstanding the earnest endeavour of the higher authorities to do justice to all, failure must sometimes occur. He had served with distinction at

Givenchy and Neuve Chapelle, and at Ypres he paid the supreme penalty, dying a glorious death. I had mentioned him in previous despatches, and always feel how well he (and many others) had deserved a reward.

About 3 P.M., 26th April, General Keary ordered the Sirhind Brigade to send up the Highland Light Infantry and 4th Gurkhas to the Jalandar Brigade, in order to carry that Brigade forward. Meanwhile the Ferozepore Brigade was ordered to hold on as best they could to support the movement and if possible to gain ground. At 3.30 P.M. the Ferozepore Brigade reported that the French line was restored. This was confirmed later by a message from the Second Army, which said that though the French attack had failed at first, it was now pressing forward. The Ferozepore Brigade was then ordered to push up reinforcements to assist the two companies Connaught Rangers who were near the German trenches.

The G.O.C. Jalandar Brigade reported that the shell and rifle fire, especially the former, was still so heavy that he considered it would be a useless loss of life to push forward the Highland Light Infantry and 4th Gurkhas, and the orders were cancelled.

News was received after 6 P.M. from the Canadian Division that the Northumberland Brigade had taken the trenches in front of St. Julien, and that the French had taken Lizerne. The 15th Sikhs and 4th Gurkhas were ordered up from the Sirhind Brigade to the Ferozepore Brigade to allow of a fresh attack being organised. At 7.45 P.M. these two battalions, supported by the 9th Bhopal Infantry, advanced under the orders of Lieut.-Colonel Hill, 15th Sikhs, their left resting on the Langemarck road. They reached a point about 300 yards in front of old British trenches, discovered Major Deacon and his gallant band, and established touch with the Manchesters on their right and the French on their left; but as the position of the German trenches was still uncertain, and as no other troops showed signs of advancing, they halted and entrenched themselves.

It is pleasant to record that amongst the D.C.M.'s earned during this battle was one given to Sergeant

F. Birley of the Madras Volunteer Rifles, attached Motor Cycle Corps, for sustained gallantry extending over several days.

At 12.30 A.M. on 27th April General Keary ordered the relief of the Jalandar Brigade by the Sirhind Brigade in the front line. On the completion of this by 3 A.M. the Ferozepore and Jalandar Brigades moved back to La Brique, whilst the Sirhind Brigade, assisted by the 34th Pioneers and 3rd Sappers and Miners, set to work to strengthen the position.

Major W. Maxwell, R.E., received a D.S.O. for his continued gallantry as C.O. of the Divisional Signal Company. He was spoken of in terms of the very highest praise by all who had observed his work. Four others, N.C.O.'s and men (two British and two Indian), received rewards for their gallant work with the same company.

On this day none of the exact locations of the German defences were known. The Divisional Artillery had not had time to register, nor to find good observation stations. In consequence, the artillery fire was not sufficiently accurate to subdue the musketry, to the degree necessary to enable a successful attack to be carried out over the very open ground which was the scene of the contest. The German position ran along a ridge at the top of a gentle slope, and the attack was fully exposed to a frontal and enfilade fire. In addition it was subjected to the unchecked fire of a numerous and powerful Artillery. Under the circumstances, and notwithstanding the utmost efforts of the gunners, the resistance could not be overcome.

Owing to the difficulty of gaining any information of the enemy trenches, it was imperative that reconnaissances should somehow be made by night, and whenever daring is necessary the British officer only needs the word. The corps of Royal Engineers keeps a large reserve of this indispensable article in hand ready for use, and in the persons of Captain Kisch and Nosworthy, young in years but by this time experienced campaigners, two volunteers were found to undertake this task. It was well carried out, under conditions of imminent danger, and a very satisfactory report and sketch of a large part of the German front trenches was obtained. Kisch was wounded during his reconnaissance, but got back safely, and for his services in France and later in Mesopotamia was awarded the D.S.O. Nosworthy, who was already suffering from gas poison, was severely wounded the following day and well earned the Military Cross he received. The information furnished by these two officers proved of great assistance in carrying out the operations on the following days.

CHAPTER XIX

AT 9.30 A.M., 27th April, a copy of the French Operation Orders was received from Second Army. From these it became apparent that the French were to continue the offensive both from the west and the south. From this latter direction the Moroccan Brigade of Colonel Savy was to attack, as before, along the west of the Langemarck road. Arrangements for co-operating with this Brigade were therefore put in hand. The Artillery bombardment was timed by the French to begin at 12.30 P.M. and the assault at 1.15 P.M.

At 11.20 a message was received from the Second Army, giving the intentions of the Army commander as regards the action to be taken by the Lahore Division. In this it was made clear that the Division was to be prepared to take advantage at once of any advance made by the French to gain ground ; but that it was not to be committed to the attack until the advance of the French had assured the safety of its left flank. The Artillery of the Fifth Corps and Lahore Division, which bore on the line of advance, were to co-operate. The Headquarters of the 27th and Canadian Divisional Artillery were in dug-outs close beside that occupied by Lahore Division Headquarters at Potijze. The following were the dispositions : Sirhind Brigade to attack with their right on an oblong farm, and the left along the Langemarck road. 1/4th Gurkhas on the right, 1/1st Gurkhas on the left. In support were a part of the Highland Light Infantry and the 15th Sikhs and 4th King's Liverpools. The Ferozepore Brigade was to prolong the Sirhind Brigade's right and to move forward under cover of the bombardment, so as to be up in line with

Sirhind Brigade at 1.15 P.M.   9th Bhopals on the right, 4th Londons on the left, in touch with Sirhind's right. The Connaught Rangers in support, with the 57th Rifles and 129th Baluchis in reserve.

As has already been stated, not only were many of these units very weak before the battle, but had after the previous day's losses dwindled to shadows of battalions.

At 12.20 P.M., 27th April, the Ferozepore Brigade started and their advance was systematically reported. The Sirhind Brigade advanced before the time fixed and by 1.15 P.M., when the bombardment ceased, the leading battalions of this Brigade had reached the edge of some enclosed ground on the slope towards the valley. The heavy enfilade fire caused the 1/1st Gurkhas to swing north-north-west to face it. The 4th Gurkhas maintained their direction but were held up. At 1.30 P.M. it was reported to the Divisional commander that the French were attacking to the north-west of an adjoining farm, and though losing heavily were continuing to form a firing-line. Our own front line was also reported as being checked and suffering heavy loss.

In its advance the Sirhind Brigade had to pass through heavy machine-gun and rifle fire, and casualties came fast. Before a party of the 4th Gurkhas had reached an old farm-house, which they tenaciously held, the C.O., Major Brodhurst, had been killed, and his Adjutant, Captain Hartwell, wounded. Two other officers, Captain E. C. Lentaigne and Lieut. C. F. Moore, were also hit. The Gurkhas, however, held on to the farm. A Gurkha officer, Jemadar Nain Singh Rana, was amongst the killed.

Meantime, the 1st Gurkhas rushed another farm 250 yards from the enemy trench, which was held by a company till dark. The greater part of the battalion, however, was held up at some hundred yards farther back. The Adjutant, Lieutenant St. George, was mortally wounded, and nearly all the other British officers present were wounded. Rifleman Ramkishan Thapa won the I.O.M. for a particularly plucky act.

A fire fight now ensued, which continued till 4 P.M., at which time the O.C. 4th King's, seeing that the 4th Gurkhas could make no progress, decided to reinforce them with part of his battalion. The King's advanced with great gallantry, and, although suffering severe losses, carried the line forward for some distance. A party under Major Beall got to within 200 yards of the German trenches.

The advance of the 4th King's was a very fine feat of arms. Straight from home they had joined in the tumult of Neuve Chapelle, and this day by their valour, which would take no denial, had already established themselves as a veteran battalion. Lieut.-Colonel Allen, the C.O., was awarded the C.M.G., and Major Beall the D.S.O. A few N.C.O.'s and men won the D.C.M. The casualties, as was to be expected, were very heavy, 380 of all ranks, including 2nd Lieut. Lloyd (killed), besides eight other officers wounded.

The Ferozepore Brigade as it advanced lost heavily from Artillery, and later from rifle fire. The attack of this Brigade was also eventually checked.

It was at this time that Major Jamieson, 9th Bhopals, of whom I had much to say in describing the fight before Neuve Chapelle in the autumn of 1914, was wounded. He was later killed in Mesopotamia. This battalion suffered 120 casualties, including Captain Etlinger, the Adjutant, killed. The 9th Bhopals had in India paid me a very special compliment by making me a life honorary member of their mess, and I hope I may one day again avail myself of the privilege.

The 4th Londons on the left of the Bhopals, keeping touch with the advance on both flanks, moved on until the general line of both Brigades was assimilated, when like the others they were brought to a halt. Captain Saunders was mortally wounded whilst engaged in reinforcing with his company. Lieut. Coates was also killed in the extreme front of the advance. Two N.C.O.'s who behaved most gallantly were awarded the D.C.M., and the M.C. was the reward of 2nd Lieut. Pyper.

The 1st Gurkhas of the Sirhind Brigade established their line beyond four heavy French guns, which had been abandoned, and which were thus enabled to be withdrawn at night.

An order from the Second Army directing the attack to be pressed vigorously was received by the G.O.C. Lahore Division at 2.40 P.M., and in order to give weight to this, the Composite Brigade, consisting of battalions of the Cornwall Light Infantry, York and Lancasters, West Ridings, and Royal Lancasters, but numbering less than 1300 all told, was placed at General Keary's disposal. This Brigade was commanded by Colonel Tuson, and left Potijze with orders to push forward and establish connection with the Sirhind Brigade. If the position permitted, a heavy bombardment was then to be carried out, prior to a fresh assault.

At 4.25 P.M., 27th April, a report was received from the Sirhind Brigade that their front lines were far enough from the enemy to permit of a fresh bombardment. This was accordingly arranged as soon as possible, and all guns opened fire. It began at 5.30 P.M., and under its cover the Highland Light Infantry (except a detachment who were facing north-north-west, 100 yards from the German trenches) and the 15th Sikhs pushed forward, but were temporarily checked, as there was nothing behind them to give the necessary support.

The Highland Light Infantry, however, moved on, and eventually in order to hold its ground, when the French Colonials on the left were once more forced back by renewed gas attacks, the battalion entrenched itself as best it could and held on to its position. Captain Tarrant, of whom I have already written, and his immortal detachment were found still occupying their isolated trench only 100 yards from the German line. Allied, British, and Indian soldiers had been driven before the terrible gas; shells and bullets had swept in tornadoes over them, but nothing could discourage that noble band. The brave commander paid for his valour with his life, but the Highlands will long re-echo his name and treasure the memory of those true sons of Scotland. If posthumous rewards cannot be given under present rules, the sooner such rules are changed to meet the exigencies of this great war the better. Is it too late ?

With Tarrant was his Company Sergeant-Major, R. Bell,

who, when a party of carriers coming up with ammunition were literally swept away by fire, went out with a few brave men and returned, to wear the Distinguished Conduct Medal he so well merited.

The 15th Sikhs, the other battalion in the front line of the Brigade, was met by severe shrapnel fire, whilst the incessant rain of bullets of course never varied.   Lieut.-Colonel C. A. Vivian was killed.   In the pages of *The Indian Corps in France* will be found a story of this officer's gallantry during the very early days of the war, which I can supplement by another instance of his keen courage.   One night in December 1914 he asked to see me and did not wish any one else to be present.   He then unfolded a plan to disguise himself and wander into the German lines.   His intention was to gain certain information which he knew was badly needed.   He felt sure of success and said it was well worth risking, and it was only because of the shortage of British officers with Indian battalions that he had come to ask permission instead of going off on his own. He begged me not to mention the matter to any one, which, of course, I only do now that he is no more.   I had to refuse his unselfish offer, but a few days later his restless spirit prompted him to go through the adventure related in the book above mentioned.

Sepoy Bakshi Singh during the advance repeatedly performed acts of signal bravery and was awarded the I.O.M.   Major Carden, the next senior officer to Vivian, was killed while endeavouring to save a brother officer, Captain A. H. Muir, who had been wounded.   The 15th Sikhs during the second battle of Ypres suffered a total of 100 casualties.

The commander of the Moroccan Brigade, who was in close touch with the G.O.C. Sirhind Brigade, now informed him that he would assault again at 7 P.M., 28th April.   The arrival of the Composite Brigade was expected before that time, and arrangements for a combined assault were carried out.

The French assault commenced punctually under cover of heavy Artillery fire and the Sirhind Brigade moved forward once more.   Shortly after, the Moroccans were observed streaming to the rear, but observation was difficult, owing to the clouds of smoke and asphyxiating gas. Suspecting a counter-attack on the left of the Brigade, the 15th Sikhs wheeled round to cover the left flank. Two battalions of the Composite Brigade were also deployed in the same direction, and the Brigade was then ordered to consolidate its position. The Highland Light Infantry and 15th Sikhs took over the front line, and the two Gurkha battalions and the 4th King's Liverpools were withdrawn to reorganise. The 34th Pioneers and Sappers and Miners were sent up to assist and the Composite Brigade was withdrawn into reserve. By 9 P.M. our Allies had gone forward again and touch had been re-established with the Moroccans. The deployment and advance of the Brigade had been carried out in full view of the enemy, and during the whole day the troops were subjected to a heavy enfilade and Artillery fire. They had behaved with the greatest firmness and done all that was possible to attain their object.

The Brigadier brought to special notice the dashing advance of the 4th King's, and the gallantry of the company 1st Highland Light Infantry under Captain Tarrant. At noon on 28th April the Division was placed under the orders of Plumer's Force, which had just been formed.

During the 28th and 29th April, various plans for an attack by the French were arranged and the rôle of our troops was laid down and communicated to Brigadiers, but the attacks did not take place. By this time it was known that the German position was a continuous line of trenches of great strength with strong points here and there at farms and other houses. During the night of 29th April, the Ferozepore and Jalandar Brigades were withdrawn to Ouderdom huts under orders from Plumer's Force. No attack took place on the 30th April, but a continuous bombardment was carried on, in which the co-operation of the Canadian Artillery was specially acknowledged by General Keary.

At 6 P.M. on 30th April Colonel Savy, commanding the Moroccan Brigade, was asked to state his intention, and informed the G.O.C. Division that his losses had been

very heavy and that he could not attack without reinforcements. During the early hours of the morning of
1st May a message was received from Plumer's Force
giving the substance of a communication sent to General
Plutz, commanding the French Army of Belgium, in which
it was explained to him that the Sirhind Brigade, the only
one available, could be utilised to support the French right
in an attack on the German trench line on Hill 29, and
orders for the Artillery were issued to suit the particular
form the attack was to take, and instructions allotting their
objectives were sent to the Artillery of the Canadian and
Twenty-seventh Divisions, which were to co-operate.

A message from Plumer's Force made it clear that
General Plutz understood that the Sirhind Brigade would
only advance to the attack in conjunction with the French,
and that their attack would not be converging. The
Brigadier reported that he would move off twenty minutes
before the French, so as to bring him level with the latter
when the assault began. The Artillery was ordered to
support this movement with a heavy fire, and at 2.50 p.m.
the Brigade advanced in the following formation:

> Right battalion—1/4th Gurkhas. In support 1st Highland
> Light Infantry.
>
> Left battalion—1/1st Gurkhas; with King's Liverpools
> in support. The 15th Sikhs to hold the advanced trenches.

It is on record that the Gurkhas were so overjoyed at
finding themselves for once out of a bog that they literally
tore over the rolling country until within 300 yards of the
German lines. An officer who was present, and who
afterwards went to Gallipoli, wrote to say that when his
men saw the barren hills there, they shouted, "Hurrah! at
last we shall be able to shoot on a hillside—no more snipe
jheels for us." Oh! if some one who knew what many
of our Indian battalions could do (outside of eternal mire)
had given us a chance in France, even for a short spell,
what an opportunity it would have been of proving once
for all that the hillmen of India with British officers
cannot be beaten in hilly country no matter who the foe.
But the depression caused by existence in the same fetid

morass for fourteen long and blood-stained months, without any change, was enough to turn sour the cheeriest mortal that ever shouldered a rifle.   I make bold to say that no other Corps, Division, Brigade, or unit in France was ever kept as long on such a narrow, cheerless front as was the Indian Corps, nor, had they been, would they have stuck it out any better.

The right battalion, 1/4th Gurkhas, in its rush arrived near the farm, the vicinity of which had been the scene of Captain Tarrant's exploit.   Here they were joined by their supporting battalion, the Highland Light Infantry. In this operation the rapidity of the Gurkha advance served them well, as only some fifty casualties were recorded. The Highlanders had eighty casualties, including 2nd Lieut. McIntosh of the Indian Army attached to the battalion, killed.

The 1st Gurkhas only finished their rush when but 200 yards severed them from the German trenches — that fateful " No Man's Land," so familiar to every soldier, so dreaded by every mother and wife, the Lethean zone which alone separated civilisation from modern barbarism ; that 200 yards which was more difficult to cross than the 600 leagues over which Xenophon retreated, or the vast expanses Marco Polo explored.   But in the ranks of the army of Great Britain's King the occasion always finds the man.

Close by the German front was a trench : Who was in it—friend or foe ?   Havildar Bhakat Sing Rana of the 2/4th Gurkhas, attached to the 1st battalion, offered to solve the riddle.   With a small chosen band he crept out and, cheating death, discovered it was held by our Allies. The Indian Order of Merit could not have been better won.

The 1st Gurkhas had about seventy casualties in this attack, and the supporting battalion, the 4th King's Liverpools, added forty-five, including Captain Lumsden killed, and Major Beall, who had led so well a few days previously, wounded.

I will quote from General Keary's report, which concisely explains the movements of the Brigade :

The leading battalions, moving rapidly forward, advanced without serious loss, and had passed before the enemy had formed a belt of Artillery fire on the crest of the ridge on our side of the valley, through which it subsequently became impossible to advance.   Owing to the German line being better known by this time, and owing to the more detailed instructions as to Artillery support, the hostile rifle fire was more effectively kept down on this day.

The troops advanced into the front French and British trenches.   The ground between them and the German trenches was a glacis slope, and by 5 P.M. it became apparent that the wire entanglement in front, some four yards deep, had not been cut.

At 7 P.M. the officer commanding 4th Moroccan Brigade sent a message to say that he had decided not to attack.

Accordingly orders were issued to the Sirhind Brigade to withdraw to the huts at Ouderdom.   Ends.

During the last four days of the operations the Lahore Divisional Artillery was chiefly employed in assisting the French.   It earned the thanks of the French Commander for the accuracy and effectiveness of its fire.   General Keary specially brought to notice the great assistance he had received from Brigadier-General Burstall and the Staff of the Canadian Divisional Artillery; throughout the operations they had co-operated with the utmost zeal and cordiality.   He also acknowledged the great help Brigadier-General Stokes and the Artillery of the Twenty-seventh Division had rendered.

Of 16,000 combatants of all arms detached from the Indian Army Corps to take part in the second battle of Ypres, over 24 per cent were returned as casualties.   General Keary, in forwarding his report on the battle, wrote :

In conclusion, I consider that the troops did all that it was humanly possible to do under most trying circumstances.   They had to pass along some miles of road and narrow streets under a hail of shell fire, advance to a position of assembly over open ground and from thence to a position of deployment under the same conditions.

The Germans had prepared a position which required the most accurate and intense gun fire to reduce it.   Owing to the hurried nature of the attack it was impossible to reconnoitre sufficiently to ensure such a fire ; nor were the guns registered. During the first two days the Infantry advanced against a position on an open glacis which was virtually unshaken. After the first two days only one Brigade was in action, and its action depended on that of the French, whose right was unable to advance to the attack.

In spite of all these disabilities the carrying of the position by the French and British was only prevented by the use of asphyxiating gases.

I think the following regiments deserve special mention for the gallantry shown by them :

> 1st Manchesters.
> Connaught Rangers.
> 1st Highland Light Infantry.
> 4th King's (Liverpool Regiment).
> 47th Sikhs.
> 57th Rifles.
> 40th Pathans.

The following letter was received from the Second Army :

SECOND ARMY.

G.O.C. LAHORE DIVISION—Having read the very complete and excellent report on the work of the Lahore Division in the heavy fighting near Ypres on the 26th and 27th April 1915, the Commander of the Second Army is confirmed in the views he formed at the time, that the Division had been handled with great skill and determination by Major-General Keary.

Sir Horace Smith-Dorrien fully realises the disadvantages under which the attack was made, insufficient Artillery preparation on our side and an open glacis-like slope to advance over in the face of overwhelming shell, rifle, and machine-gun fire, and the employment of poisonous gases on the enemy's side ; and that, in spite of these disadvantages, the troops, although only partially successful in wrenching ground from the enemy, effectually prevented his further advance and thus ensured the safety of the town of Ypres.

Sir Horace, whilst deploring the heavy casualties, wishes to thank the Divisional General, Brigadiers, and Commanding Officers and all ranks of the several Arms employed, for the great service they performed for the Second Army on those eventful two days.

I

GERMAN LINE

Fmé

Jullundur   Wieltje

Ferozepore

La Brique   Saint Jean   Sirhind Bde

Potijse   Div'l H.Q.

34ᵗʰ Pioneers   S & M

YPRES

LAHORE DIVISION
deployed for attack, April 26.15

GERMAN LINE

French
Fmé

La Brique   Saint Jea

Potijse

34ᵗʰ Pioneers

YPRES

LAHOR
after af

III

GERMAN LINE

French
Fmé

Sirhind Bde

Wieltje

ullundur Bde

ozepore   La Brique   Saint Jean
Bde

Potijse   Div'l H.Q.

34ᵗʰ Pioneers   S & M

YPRES

LAHORE DIVISION
morning of April 27. '15

GERMAN LINE

French

Sirhind Bde

Jullundur Bde

Ferozepore   La Brique   Saint Je
Bde   Potijse

34ᵗʰ Pioneers

YPRES

LAHO
a.m April 2

Yds.1000   500   0   1000   2000   3000 YDS   Contou

SCALE OF YARDS

In this respect he would specially mention the following regiments :

[The corps named by General Keary are then enumerated.]

(Sd.)   GEO. F. MILNE, Maj.-Gen., G.S., Second Army.
7th May 1915.

General Sir Herbert Plumer also wrote as follows :

G.O.C. Lahore Division—Will you please convey to the Brigadiers, Commanding Officers, and all Officers, Non-Commissioned Officers and Men of your Division my thanks for the assistance they have rendered in the recent severe fighting, and my appreciation of the way in which they have carried out the very arduous duties entrusted to them while under my command.

I deeply regret the very heavy casualties they have suffered.

By 5th May the Lahore Division had rejoined the Corps, and immediately proceeded to take its share in the severe fighting round Festubert.

I took the opportunity to see as many units as possible during the short interval, and it was a great pleasure to talk with Keary, and many others of all ranks, British and Indian. The universal note was satisfaction that they had tried to do their duty. General Keary again commanded his Division at the battles near Festubert and Mauquissart, in May and September 1915, but it was not till he had been in command of a Division in Mesopotamia, much later on, that he was given any reward for his distinguished services.

CHAPTER XX

On every occasion the Corps had so far been called on to take part in any definite operation, I had felt sure it would acquit itself well, and had cause for satisfaction. But by this time the numbers and composition of the Indian Infantry units had been so reduced that it became a question how to allocate the duties in any offensive movement which might be ordered. At the end of March my recommendation for reorganising the Army Corps had been approved, and the two Divisions had been practically reconstituted. Each of the six Infantry Brigades was now composed of one Regular, one Territorial, and three Indian battalions. In a later chapter I shall give some figures which will show that, notwithstanding a battalion having been added, the strength per Brigade was in most cases so far short of war establishment as to amount to a nominal figure. But still the orders came for a Division to do this and a Brigade something else.

Stern business was before us, and immediately the Lahore Division returned from Ypres it again took its place in the old trenches before Neuve Chapelle, whilst the Meerut Division got ready for the operations about to be undertaken for the capture of the Aubers Ridge and neighbouring villages and farms. The fighting for these lasted, as far as we were concerned, from the 9th to the 22nd of May, and during this period it was almost incessant. One attack succeeded another in monotonous sequence; if it was not on a farm it was on a strong point, or a distillery, or some position in a map square. Anyhow, it was the most unsatisfactory job that fell to our lot in France, and we were not alone in this respect, for the Fourth Corps on our left and the First on our right, as well as the Canadians, were to expend a great many lives and much effort with little gain to any of them.

The French were making an offensive between the right of the British line and Arras, and Sir John French, in pursuance of a promise to support the Allied Commander-in-Chief, directed the First Army to carry out an attack on the German trenches in the neighbourhood of Rouges Bancs by the Fourth Corps, and between Neuve Chapelle and Givenchy by the First and Indian Corps. A reason which we all thoroughly appreciated.

What, however, apparently was not appreciated was that we were unlikely to find the Germans napping again as we had at Neuve Chapelle in March, and that the defences of those days had probably been quadrupled in strength. This, in fact, we very soon learned to our cost, and the cheery optimism which named Don and other places we were likely to reach was about to receive a severe shock. But, after all, this is far better than being pessimistic, and even the modern Attila in the very early days of the war probably got more out of his Huns by telling them they would be in Paris before the autumn leaves had fallen, than he would have done by only naming, say, Verdun and Rheims.

The share of the Indian Corps in these operations was to attack between the First Corps on our right and the Fourth Corps on our left. Our immediate objective was the Ferme du Biez, after which we were to direct our advance on Ligny-le-Grand—La Cliqueterie Farm. The Fourth Corps, after carrying out its rôle on our left, was also to advance on Cliqueterie and effect a junction with the Indian Corps. I remember well, in imagination, picturing our Indian soldiers on the Aubers Ridge, the huge delight of the Gurkhas and Pathans at being actually high above a flat bog, and looking down on something instead of always looking up from a fetid trench. When I again visit India to see my friends, many will flatly maintain that the war was fought on a dead plain and the only mountain near it was the poor little Aubers Ridge.

However, to my story. The Meerut Division was detailed for the attack ; the Lahore Division to hold the line, and the guns of both Divisions, supplemented by others, were to support the attack. The assault was to be delivered by the Dehra Dun Brigade, the Bareilly Brigade being in support and three battalions of the Garhwal Brigade in reserve. The first attempt was carried out on 9th May on a front of 650 yards. The objectives were successively :

(a) Enemy's front and support trenches.

(b) La Tourelle and houses near three named points.

(c) The Distillery, Ferme du Biez, S.W. edge of the Bois du Biez.

(d) Ligny-le-Petit.

(e) Ligny-le-Grand—La Cliqueterie Ferme. The Bois du Biez was to be engaged simultaneously with the advance on Ligny-le-Petit by a special body of troops consisting of the Garhwal Rifles and 2/8th Gurkhas with two trench guns, under the command of Lieut.-Colonel Drake-Brockman, 39th Garhwalis.

General Anderson, commanding the Meerut Division, had made every preparation. He, his Staff, his Brigadiers, and his Commanding officers had each and all studied every possible situation that could be imagined, and at dawn I felt that if success did not attend their efforts, they certainly deserved it. As I read the Corps and Divisional Orders now, I do not believe any better could have been written at the time.

All troops were in position as ordered with but trifling casualties and the night of 8th–9th May passed quietly. Our own wire had been cut and bridges laid as directed. The bombardment commenced punctually at 5 A.M. and the enemy's wire was cut satisfactorily, but many of our rounds were reported as falling short.

At the appointed hour, the battalions of the Dehra Dun Brigade, the 2/2nd Gurkhas, 1/4th Seaforths, 1st Seaforths (6th Jats and 1/9th Gurkhas in support) went over the top preparatory to the assault. Even with the certainty of being met by an inferno of fire within a few seconds, one young officer was heard to ask another if he knew the Report Centre of his Brigade, and on his replying that he was not sure, a laugh was raised by the questioner saying, " Why, you have often been there, it is 96 Piccadilly "; and in fact it was so, but situated for the time being in the Rue du Bois.

The morning was bright, and from all appearances the Germans appeared quite unaware of our concentration and proposed attack.   However, immediately the Infantry crossed over the parapet to form up preparatory to the assault, heavy machine-gun fire was opened on them from guns sited almost on the ground level.   The enemy's Infantry also manned the trenches.

The 2nd Gurkhas as they started their rush met a terrific fire, and all the officers who had crossed the parapet were shot down.   Lieut. Collins and Captain C. M. Mullaly were killed at this time, and Captain Kenneth Park, a nephew of mine, who had insisted on joining in the battle although in very poor health, was mortally wounded.   The men from Nepal, notwithstanding every effort, were literally cut down and unable to advance beyond a ditch in their front.

The 4th Seaforths and 1st Seaforths advanced with their usual bravery but met with the same fate and lay for hours under a leaden sheet, getting back as best they could after dark.   In the 4th Seaforths, Lieutenants Tennant, Railton, and Bastian were killed.

Notwithstanding the most gallant efforts to cross the fire-swept ground, by 6 A.M. it was definitely known our attack had failed to reach its first objective.   One company 6th Jats, which had been directed between the left of First Corps and our right was practically annihilated, and Captain Dudley and Subadar Lekh Ram were killed.   The hostile guns, which up to now had not done much firing, opened a searching and heavy fire on our trenches and the Rue du Bois, in consequence of which the Dehra Dun and Bareilly Brigades suffered numerous casualties ; the 41st Dogras being particularly unfortunate in this respect.

Howitzer fire was accordingly turned on to the German trenches, and preparatory arrangements for a fresh assault were commenced.   At 6.35 A.M., the G.O.C. 1st Division on our right informed General Anderson that the first assault of that Division had also failed.   An hour later the 1st Seaforths made a second attempt to assault, but like the first this attempt also met with little success, and they too had to lie in the open with the other battalions unable to advance or retire. A special Howitzer bombardment of enemy trenches was arranged to commence at 7.45 A.M. and to last for twenty-five minutes, under cover of which it was hoped that the 2nd Gurkhas and 4th Seaforths would be able to advance.

The O.C. 4th Seaforths at this time reported that the enemy was being reinforced and was of opinion they would counter-attack. The G.O.C. Dehra Dun Brigade accordingly sent up two companies 9th Gurkhas to assist the 1st Seaforths, who had suffered very heavy losses, and ordered the O.C. 9th Gurkhas to support the 4th Seaforths with the remainder of his battalion, but owing to the congested state of the communication trenches only 200 men were able to move forward. At 8 A.M. the First British Division informed the G.O.C. Meerut Division that the attack of the 2nd and 3rd Brigades had failed, and that the 1st Brigade would hold the line while they were withdrawn.

At 8.20 A.M. I sent an order directing the further attempt at attack by the Dehra Dun Brigade fixed for 8.45 A.M. to be stayed, and that another assault should be organised to coincide with that of the First Division, which could not be ready for another two hours. The assault was consequently stopped.

As the attack by the 2nd and 3rd Brigades on our right had failed owing to the enemy's wire not being sufficiently cut, instructions were received from the Army commander to recommence operations at 12 noon after a further bombardment with H.E. 18-pr., by which it was hoped to break down the enemy's parapets and knock out his machine-guns.

On the urgent representation of the G.O.C. Dehra Dun Brigade, the hour for a fresh attack had been altered to 2.40 P.M. on this same date, 9th May. The Bareilly Brigade was also warned that it would have to relieve the Dehra Dun Brigade, and carry out the next assault. This assault was to be delivered by the 2nd Black Watch on the right, 58th Rifles in the centre, and 41st Dogras on the left, the 1/4th Black Watch and machine-guns of the 125th Rifles being in Brigade reserve. Meanwhile the Germans were

reported by G.O.C. 1st Group H.A.R. to be strongly reinforcing their second line, which appeared to be held in
strength.

At 10 A.M. the G.O.C. Seventh British Division reported
that the Eighth Division on our left was unable to make much
headway beyond the front line of German trenches owing
to fortified posts in rear, which were being bombarded
afresh. The Garhwal Brigade was placed in support of
the Bareilly Brigade. The 9th Gurkhas, which so far had
not been seriously engaged, was ordered to join the Garhwal
Brigade, which was short of Lieut.-Colonel Drake-
Brockman's detachment. The relief of the Dehra Dun
by the Bareilly Brigade was commenced and carried out
with considerable difficulty as the communication trenches
were full of dead and wounded, and the movement being
observed by the enemy, a heavy shell-fire was kept up by
them. Owing to the destruction of our trenches it was
found impossible to carry out the fresh attack, even at
the altered hour, and the First Army directed that both
the Meerut and First Divisions should assault at 4 P.M.

At 12 noon the G.O.C. Bareilly Brigade reported to
General Anderson that in the opinion of the G.O.C. Dehra
Dun Brigade (the morning attacking Brigade) the enemy's
position had been in no way weakened and that the machine-
gun fire which had caused the check of all efforts of the
Dehra Dun Brigade was as heavy as ever. He added that
the parapets were somewhat battered by our artillery,
but that this was compensated for by the German reinforcements which had since come up; that three of his
battalions had been exposed to heavy shell-fire, and that
he wished the above situation to be known before the
assault commenced.

On receipt of this report General Anderson considered
it advisable to inform me, but instructed the G.O.C.
Bareilly Brigade that meantime the attack would take
place as ordered. Whatever the circumstances, I considered it imperative to carry out this assault, and sent
instructions that it was to be pressed at all costs, and the
Divisional Commander added to this that it was to be
carried on into the night if necessary. The orders of the

T

First Army were distinct, and the movements of the First Division on my right depended on ours. I therefore felt bound to do all in my power to comply with the Army orders.

By 4 P.M. the 2nd Black Watch had relieved the 2/2nd Gurkhas on the right, the 41st Dogras the 1st Seaforths on the left, and the 58th Rifles had taken the place of the 1/4th Seaforths in the centre. The 1/4th Black Watch was in reserve.

The 1st Seaforths, on this 9th May 1915, had, if possible, beaten all their records for dogged valour. Nothing in war could exceed the determination to win through displayed by all ranks, and where they failed no other Corps could have succeeded. When I received their casualty roll I could have wept and felt no sense of weakness : seven officers and 130 other ranks killed or missing ; ten officers and 350 other ranks wounded, and mostly within a few short moments.

> Gashed with honourable scars,
>   Low in glory's lap they lie ;
> Though they fell, they fell like stars,
>   Streaming splendours through the sky.

The bombardment commenced punctually at 3.20 P.M., 9th May, and at 3.40 P.M. the assaulting troops crossed the parapet and formed up prior to the assault. Each battalion was formed in two lines, two companies in each line. The right battalion (2nd Black Watch) and right company of centre battalion (58th Rifles) were met by a heavy, well-directed machine-gun and rifle-fire from their front, left front, and left flank directly they showed over the parapets, and but few men succeeded in crossing the ditch to their front, the majority being disabled before reaching it. The left company of the 58th Rifles succeeded in advancing about 100 yards; but when our guns lifted they were at once exposed to a heavy fire and were unable to advance farther. The 41st Dogras on the left, in particular, had been exposed to an extremely heavy shelling from H.E. and shrapnel, both while getting forward and whilst waiting in the front line. In consequence, one company consisted of only twenty-eight men. The companies (what remained of them) crossed the parapet and aligned themselves with the 58th Rifles; but rifle and machine-gun fire brought them to a halt. Further attempts to advance by bringing up men from the rear companies did not help them, as in crossing the parapet most of them were shot down.

Our artillery bombardment at this stage was quite ineffective and short, and the Germans were not appreciably shaken by it. Their infantry was lining the parapets from the time we commenced to assemble in front of our own trenches, and the situation was for the time being entirely in their favour. About 4 P.M. orders were issued for battalions to reorganise, and be prepared for a fresh assault if ordered.

A good instance of the *camaraderie* between British and Indian soldiers was shown on this day. A Seaforth Highlander, who was badly wounded in the first attack in the morning, was lying out unable to be got in. A Dogra sepoy was wounded in the second assault during the afternoon and was lying near him. Hearing the Highlander groaning, he dragged himself up to him, patted his arm, and said he would stay by him and take him in later on. When darkness came on the Dogra dragged himself back and reported to his own battalion that he wanted some men to come and bring in the wounded Highlander. The officer commanding the company he went to said he would see about it and ordered him to get back to the dressing-station. He refused to go, as he said he had promised the *ghāgra* (kilted man) to save him, and intended to do that first and then go to hospital. The Highlander was rescued.

Then cease all ye who, in your pride, the creed of others would deride.
The Hindu idol ; crescent's sign ; the Shinto doctrine, laws divine
Confucius made and Christ decreed, all to one common substance lead,
No matter by what faith enthralled ; 'tis what men *do* not what
   they're called.

In the ranks of the 2nd Black Watch was a Lance-Corporal, David Finlay by name, a fine specimen of a fine Corps. As he topped the parapet a shell exploding near him knocked him flat, but quickly recovering himself he rushed on with his bombing party of a dozen men, defying death. Ten out of his twelve gallant comrades were killed or incapacitated before he cried a halt, but then only to add to his daring, for seeing a badly wounded man he carried him for 100 yards through a whirl of fire and brought him into our own trenches safely. David Finlay did not live long to wear the Victoria Cross he was awarded. Such brave souls never rest as ordinary men can. He lies 'neath the desert sands of Mesopotamia. And of the battalion whose fame he so much enhanced, three officers—Lieutenants W. Brownlow, the Hon. K. Stewart, and Sinclair—and seventy others gave their lives ; whilst the total casualties numbered 265, or fifty per cent of the strength which fought that day.

The 41st Dogras, who were engaged in their first offensive battle as a complete battalion, suffered very heavy losses. Lieut.-Colonel Hutchinson, whilst leading a double company, received three wounds, and his company officer, Lieutenant Vaughan, was totally disabled. At one time the only unwounded officer was a Dogra subadar, Jai Singh (attached from 37th Dogras). He behaved splendidly, but was himself twice wounded before the share of the battalion in this day of carnage had ended. The C.O., Colonel Tribe, received a shell-wound and Major Milne (82nd Punjabis), whom I had known well in the Peshawar Division, was severely wounded in the advance. In fact the Dogras were almost broken up as a unit. Five of the ten British officers present and seven of the Indian officers were rendered *hors de combat*; and the battalion suffered in all over 400 casualties out of a muster roll of 650. I well know the hills and vales from which most of these gallant soldiers came. I can hear ethereal voices, wafted on the warm summer breezes as they top the ridges of the sub-Himalayan hills, soughing, " Well done, loyal Dogras ! "

The 58th Rifles had a total of 250 killed, missing, and wounded, including Lieutenant Mackmillan, who died of wounds.

By 5 P.M., 9th May, it was clear from reports received from G.O.C. Bareilly Brigade, Artillery observation-officers, and the First British Division that all attacks, both of the

First and Meerut Divisions had failed.   After a telephonic
conversation with the G.O.C. Meerut Division the Garhwal
Brigade was ordered to take over the front line from
Bareilly, and this was finally effected by 1 A.M. midnight
of the 9th–10th May.   The failure of the attacks on this
day were due to the insufficient effect produced by the
Artillery bombardment and to the great volume of
extremely accurate machine-gun fire from front and flanks.
As regards the insufficient effect of the Artillery bombardment, it must be remembered that, after their experience
in front of Neuve Chapelle on 10th to 13th March, the
Germans realised that breastworks of exceptional strength
were required, and had accordingly devoted their energies
to the construction of improved parapets of great thick-
ness, especially on both sides of the Estaires—La Bassée
road, as to the safety of which they were anxious.   They
had also largely increased the number of machine-guns
employed in their front line, locating them in dug-outs
heavily strutted with timber, which admitted of the
machine-guns being fired just above ground level, and
ensured the safety of the detachments during the bombardment.   The light shell of our field-guns appeared to
produce but small results on these improved parapets,
and even high-explosive shell had only very local effects.
A very considerable proportion of our H.E. shell also
failed to detonate satisfactorily.   The fire of our 18-
pounder guns was accurate enough, as proved by the
manner in which the enemy's wire entanglements had
been cut, but owing to some defect in the construction of
the shell there were, and continued to be, a very unduly
large number of prematures.   As regards the fire of our
howitzers, both those of 4·5-inch and those of 6 0-inch
calibre, the extreme accuracy which we had become
accustomed to obtain with them had fallen off considerably as the guns became worn by the large number of
rounds fired.   In the various intensive bombardments,
too, it was reported by the Infantry that a large proportion of our shell had fallen short of the enemy's front line
parapets.   This was largely accounted for by the error
of the gun, which at the ranges fired at hardly ensured

more than twenty-five per cent of shell actually hitting the point aimed at.

The endeavour displayed by the Infantry in the various assaults left nothing to be desired. The successive attempts to reach the enemy trenches were brought to a standstill by the disablement of all but a small percentage of the assaulting columns, and by machine-gun and rifle-fire. This fire started from the moment the first of our men showed above our breastworks, and numbers were put out of action within a few yards of our own front line. Of those who succeeded, in spite of the heaviest losses, in getting out half-way between our lines and the Germans, the small number of unwounded men found themselves pinned to the ground, unable to advance or retire in face of the enemy's fire.

The casualties suffered on the 9th and 10th May were heavy, amounting to sixty-eight British officers, thirty Indian officers, and a total of all ranks, British and Indian, of over 2000, or about thirty-six per cent of strength.

On the 10th May General Anderson came to my Headquarters, and I communicated to him an order I had received, and which stated that it was vitally important not a round of gun ammunition should be wasted. At this interview I told him that no attack would take place on the 10th or night 10th–11th, but that one might take place on the night 11th–12th. That evening the Garhwal Brigade took over some 230 yards' extra front from the British Division on our right in anticipation of the attack. The Sirhind Brigade was ordered back from Croix Barbée, and again came under the orders of the Lahore Division, while the Dehra Dun Brigade was replaced at the disposal of the Meerut Division.

On the morning of 12th May the situation was as follows: the Garhwal Brigade held the line, the Bareilly Brigade was in support with Headquarters at Lansdowne Post, and the Dehra Dun Brigade in Divisional reserve at La Couture and Vieille Chapelle. I informed the G.O.C. Meerut Division that his Division, less the Dehra Dun Brigade and with the Sirhind Brigade added, would probably attack on a 300 yards' front on the night 13th–14th

May, in co-operation with the First Corps on its right, the front of attack being between two points designated V 5 and V 6, well known to us all.

I have since I first wrote this visited (1919) this bit of ground and located my friends V 5 and V 6, and I touched my hat not only to the brave men who died for us, but also to the German dead who held them so tenaciously and died like gentlemen.

At 4 P.M. this day, 12th May, the Meerut Division was ordered to be prepared to take over the Rue du Bois front, to Chocolat Menier Corner inclusive, during the night. At night I proceeded to Meerut Divisional Head-quarters and discussed the arrangements for the attack with Anderson; but next morning, 13th May, I was informed that the proposed night operations were post-poned for twenty-four hours, viz. till the night 14th–15th May. Orders were therefore issued directing the bombard-ment of the enemy's position which was to be attacked. It was to be deliberate and continuous till the assault was made. This bombardment commenced at 12 noon and was maintained till the attack was delivered, and it drew in reply a strong continuous fire on the trenches held by the Meerut Division.

The general outlines of the operations were as follows:

The First and Indian Corps were to renew the attack and to press forwards towards Violaines and Beau Puits, and to establish a defensive flank along the La Bassée road on the left, maintaining the right at Givenchy. The line to be established in the first instance was the general line of the road Festubert—La Quinque Rue—La Tourelle cross-roads—Port Arthur, which position was to be con-solidated. The First Corps was to assault with the Second Division on the right of the Meerut Division, and the assault of both Divisions was to be simultaneous. The subsequent advance was to be with the object of securing the Ferme d'Avoué and certain named roads.

The Seventh Division on our left was to deliver an assault in the early hours of the 15th May.

The Meerut Division, less Dehra Dun Brigade and one Brigade R.F.A., with the Sirhind Brigade added, was ordered to make the attack of the Indian Corps. The assault was to be made against named front-line trenches, all details being given. Should the first two objectives be attained, as the attack of the Second Division progressed our own was to push on and secure the road from Port Arthur to La Tourelle cross-roads inclusive, and consolidate itself thereon.

A deliberate Artillery bombardment was to precede the assault and was to be maintained for thirty-six hours. Owing, however, to the further postponement of the attack for twenty-four hours it was actually maintained for sixty hours.

No. 4 Trench howitzer battery was placed at the disposal of the Garhwal Brigade for the operations, and this Brigade was detailed to carry out the assault on the enemy's front-line trenches on a two-battalion front.

The Sirhind Brigade was in support of the Garhwal Brigade. The Bareilly Brigade was in Divisional reserve at Croix Barbée, and the Dehra Dun Brigade was in Corps reserve.

The 4th Indian Cavalry rendezvoused on 15th May in fields and orchards between Vieille Chapelle and La Couture. Nos. 3 and 4 Companies Sappers and Miners and the 107th Pioneers rendezvoused at St. Vaast on the evening of the 14th May. All assaulting troops wore masks soaked in solution. These were the early days of gas, and some of the devices to ward off this poisonous innovation were grotesque. Fond parents, wives, and relations had sent out every form of anti-gas invention. A Hindu sepoy best explained what the Indians thought of it all when he said : " I believe the British have been converted to our religion and are trying to imitate our many Gods. I have already seen many 'Hunumans,' and 'Ganesh' will shortly follow."

At 3.30 P.M. on the 14th May orders were received from First Army directing the assault to be delayed for another twenty-four hours, as the effect of the bombardment was not considered to have been sufficient ; the weather also was wet and the ground was soft and holding.

The night of the 14th–15th passed without any special

incident.   At 3.30 P.M. on the 15th May I sent the following instructions to the G.O.C. Meerut Division:

(*a*) If the night attack succeeds, hold on to V 6 at all costs, even if the Second Division on your right fails.

(*b*) If the night attack fails, you will not persist in it, unless the Second Division on the right has succeeded, when use every endeavour to connect with its left.

(*c*) If the attack of both the Meerut and Second Divisions fail, make a fresh attack at 3.15 A.M., to synchronise with that of the Seventh Division; this attack is to be preceded by a fresh bombardment, commencing at 2.45 A.M. and lasting till 3.15 A.M.

(*d*) If you fail again, re-form and prepare for another attack, which should be preceded by a further bombardment, probably six hours later, but further instructions will be issued as to the hour and class of this bombardment.

At 10.50 P.M., 15th May, all troops were in position. The 2nd Leicesters with six machine-guns were to assault with the right in the ditch passing through V 5, and were ordered to get into touch with the Second Division on their right.   The Garhwal Rifles, with six machine-guns, were on the left, with their right in touch with the left of the Leicesters.   The 3rd Londons and two companies 2/3rd Gurkha Rifles were in support of the Garhwal Rifles and 2nd Leicesters respectively.   The remainder of the 3rd Gurkha Rifles was in Brigade reserve.   The 2/8th Gurkha Rifles were holding the line in rear.   The units of the Sirhind Brigade were disposed as follows:

1st Highland Light Infantry, and 1/1st Gurkha Rifles in assembly trenches east of Garhwal Brigade Reserve.

15th Sikhs in trenches east of Lansdowne Post.

1/4th King's Liverpools in trenches about Lansdowne Post.

1/4th Gurkha Rifles in Lansdowne Post.

Immediately the bridges were in position the Leicesters and Garhwal Rifles commenced to move out, and by 11.25 P.M. were in position.

The assault started at 11.30 P.M., and at once the German machine-gun and rifle fire commenced, while their trenches appeared full of men.   The enemy front was lit, not only by the ordinary flares but also by bombs thrown over the parapet, which burned on the ground.   In spite of repeated efforts to reach the German trenches, the advance of both battalions was brought to a standstill, and each successive attempt was similarly stopped.

At 12.30 A.M., 16th May, the G.O.C. Garhwal Brigade reported that the Leicesters were held up and that the Garhwal Rifles had been unable to get forward more than thirty yards owing to heavy machine-gun fire.   At this time General Anderson became aware that, though the battalion of the British Division on his immediate right had also not succeeded in reaching the German trenches, others of the 5th and 6th Infantry Brigades had done so.   This proved that strong-point V 6 and its vicinity assigned to us were, as I had understood all along, one of the most formidable obstacles on our whole front.   The Leicesters and the Garhwal Rifles were accordingly withdrawn and replaced by the 3rd Gurkhas and 1/3rd Londons, and the G.O.C. Brigade was directed to make a further effort at 3.15 A.M.

In the meanwhile touch was maintained with the left of the Second Division, and the G.O.C. was informed that the Garhwal Brigade would again attack at 3.15 A.M. In reply, he stated that his left would simultaneously make another attack.   An intense bombardment commenced at 2.45 A.M., 16th May, and at 3 A.M. the battalions detailed to attack were in position with their leading platoons in the firing-trenches.   It was impossible, owing to the light, to launch the assault from the enemy's side of the ditch, as the troops could not reach that position unseen.

At 3.15 A.M. the assault was commenced, but the moment the men showed the enemy opened a heavy rifle, machine-gun, and artillery fire.   The majority of them were shot down as they crossed our parapet, and this assault also was entirely held up.

In both advances a certain number of officers and men arrived within a few yards of the German wire before they were shot, but none were able to reach the parapets. The battalions were now ordered to reorganise, and it was decided that no further attempts to break through on this front were to be made, but that troops should be pushed in through the opening already made on our right.

In these assaults the German machine-guns again succeeded, in spite of the previous heavy bombardment by Artillery and bomb-guns, in maintaining themselves in their covered positions and in coming into immediate action on our assault being launched. Both assaults were thus met by heavy fire from the front and from right and left flanks, and were brought to a standstill just as those on the 9th May had been.

The casualties, owing to the smaller front attacked, were not so numerous as those experienced on the 9th, but they were regrettably heavy, namely, twenty-one British officers, five Indian officers, 300 other British ranks, and 590 other ranks Indian, or about thirty per cent of the strength of the Brigade engaged.

In these difficult operations the Garhwal Rifles suffered 150 casualties, and the Leicesters lost in killed four subalterns, viz. Tayler, Brown, Gandy, and Crosse, besides twenty other ranks, and the wounded and missing, including five officers, numbered over 200. It is a sad tale to tell, this continuous long roll of dead and wounded, but it is necessary in order to explain the difficulties we had to encounter and the heroism of the troops, British and Indian, who, notwithstanding the hopelessness of the task, never hesitated to go manfully forward.

The 3rd Londons suffered over 100 casualties, and the 3rd Gurkhas over seventy, including two British officers killed. Lieutenant Nott-Bower was shot whilst bravely trying to save a wounded man of the Leicesters and a brother officer, Captain Grigg, was hit by a splinter of shell. Captain F. Hodgson of the 84th Punjabis, a personal friend, was another gallant soul who passed away in honour this day.

By 4.30 A.M., 16th May, the 6th British Brigade had taken the Orchard and the 5th Brigade had been able to continue its advance, but the battalion on our immediate right had again been unable to get on, as its flank was exposed. The G.O.C. Bareilly Brigade was now directed to be prepared to take over the front held by the Garhwal Brigade. The Army commander had meantime decided to form a flank where the left of the Second Division had got through, and I received orders to hold our trenches as a defensive front.

At 8.A.M., 16th May, the situation was as follows:

Garhwal Brigade was holding the line as a defensive front. The Meerut, Lahore, and Heavy Artillery were shelling the area V 6 and other re-entrant objectives. The Bareilly Brigade was *en route* to Lansdowne Post. The Sirhind Brigade and 107th Pioneers were under orders of the G.O.C. Second Division. Both companies Sappers and Miners and 125th Rifles were at St. Vaast and Croix Barbée. 4th Indian Cavalry was in its rendezvous at Vieille Chapelle; whilst the left battalion of the Second Division, which could not advance, was still holding its old front line in continuation of our right.

At 11.30 P.M. the Bareilly Brigade relieved the Garhwal Brigade on the front line, with Headquarters at Lansdowne Post.

Before dawn on 17th May I received First Army Operation orders, which directed the Indian Corps to remain in occupation of its line.

At 10 A.M. on 17th May, after a telephonic conversation with General Anderson, it was arranged that we should seize any opportunity of advancing into the enemy trenches. The Sirhind Brigade was again placed at my disposal, for the purpose of ensuring touch being kept with the left of Second Division in any advance which the latter might make.

At 11 A.M. the First Army directed that the duty of gradually establishing a defensive flank on the left as the attack proceeded, was assigned to the Indian Corps, and that as the attack of the Second Division progressed we were to gradually extend to the right and relieve troops of the Second Division as opportunity offered. The Bareilly and Sirhind Brigades were detailed for this duty.

At 3.30 A.M. on 18th May the Germans attempted an attack on one company of the 15th Sikhs, but were bombed and driven back. During the progress of reliefs of certain battalions of the British Brigade on our right the 1st Highland Light Infantry had five officers and seventy other ranks made casualties, including Lieutenant H. S. Davidson killed. It is interesting to note here that the 1st battalion which belonged to the Indian Corps actually relieved their own 2nd battalion which belonged to the British Brigade fighting by our side. A chance meeting under such conditions is rare, even under the varied circumstances in which the British Army serves.

This 18th day of May was to witness a deed of heroism which for sustained gallantry can surely not be surpassed. A British officer and ten men of the 15th Sikhs were those who added a brilliant page to the history of the Indian Army. Of the ten one Lance-Naik Mangal Singh and three sepoys belonged to the battalion, whilst four of the others were attached from the 19th Punjabis and two from the 45th Sikhs.

An isolated trench was held by a company of the 15th Sikhs, opposed to an ever-increasing number of the enemy, who showed signs of an immediate attack. Having expended all his bombs, the officer in command was in urgent need of more, and Lieutenant J. Smyth offered to make the attempt over the 250 yards which intervened. Ten Sikhs volunteered to accompany him, carrying a hundred bombs in boxes between them. Moving for sixty yards under cover, the party diverged, and at once came under heavy fire. Crawling over dead and wounded, through such cover as battered ditches and trenches could afford, they advanced under a galling and aimed fire. Man after man was shot down, and by the time Smyth had got to within thirty yards of his objective there were only three others besides himself unwounded, but the precious boxes were still intact. The Germans had seen and understood the object of this movement, and the ground here was swept by a tornado of bullets, and to carry the boxes any farther was absolutely impossible. Breaking them open, Smyth distributed as many bombs as possible between the survivors. One of the three gallant Sikhs was at the same time killed ; and this splendid young officer, with now but two others—a Naik and a sepoy—crawling on through mire and water, reached their goal. Smyth, who is one of the most modest, as he certainly is one of the bravest, of men, received the Victoria Cross, and the Naik the Indian Order of Merit, whilst the Indian Distinguished Service Medal was given to all who lived of that glorious band. The Gurus of the Khalsa could have wished for no greater proof of the right of the Sikh to style himself a Singh (lion).

On 18th May orders were received for the Indian Corps to attack the Ferme du Bois at the same time as attacks were delivered by the Seventh Division and the Guards Brigade more to the south.

The outlines of the operation were as follows : Meerut Division, reinforced by Sirhind Brigade, was to attack the Ferme du Bois at 4.30 P.M., in conjunction with an attack by the Guards Brigade on Cour d'Avoué, with the intention of obtaining possession of the Ferme du Bois and of three trenches up to the La Tourelle—Quinque Rue road. Touch was to be obtained with the Guards at a point marked Q 12.

The Artillery bombardment commenced at 2 P.M. The Sirhind Brigade was directed on the Ferme du Bois and certain other points, and after establishing itself at the Ferme, was to push forward in conjunction with the progress of the attack by the Guards Brigade. The Bareilly Brigade was to assist this attack by fire. The orders of the Sirhind Brigade directed the bombing parties to be supported by half a company 1st Highland Light Infantry ; and as the attack progressed the 4th King's had orders as to the part to be played by them.

At 4.20 P.M., 18th May, the Sirhind Brigade reported that, owing to the heavy German Artillery fire, the bombing parties and troops intended for the attack were being held up in their original trenches, and shortly after communication with the front became very difficult owing to all wires being cut.

By 5.40 P.M., 18th May, it was ascertained that the Guards Brigade were getting forward by short rushes, and the G.O.C. Sirhind Brigade was directed to use every possible endeavour to try and get his own attack forward also.

At 6 P.M. he reported that the bombing parties had

made three attempts to cross, but had so far failed. As the attack appeared quite unable to advance, I telephoned that if it could not attain its object by day it must do so by night, and further Artillery support was promised.

As the troops of the Second Division on our right were being relieved during the night 18th–19th May, I sent instructions that no attack should be made till this relief was completed, but added that it must then be made.

At 10 P.M. General Walker, V.C., in command of the Sirhind Brigade, represented that he considered the German position round the Ferme du Bois was such that the success of an attack was very doubtful, and that the probable loss of life would be great until our present position could be consolidated, and a front from which to advance was assured. While again reminding the Division that it was most desirable the attack should be made, I left it to the judgement of General Walker, an experienced officer, on the spot, to decide.

At 11.10 P.M. it was definitely decided that the attack should not be made. Throughout the night the Sirhind Brigade was in close touch with the Germans to its front.

The 15th Sikhs had been undergoing many vicissitudes during all the confused fighting of the past days, and as already related they had given a fine example of the stuff of which the Khalsa is made. Attached to the battalion was Captain F. C. Waterfield, 45th Sikhs, whom I had known for years. This promising officer was killed. His own regiment of Rattray's Sikhs was the one Corps of the Indian Army which in my young days I had most admired and had served alongside in Afghanistan. It was always a fine battalion, and has on the plains of Mesopotamia added still more to its reputation. As I said earlier in this book, if any Sikh battalions are to remain as Class Corps, none is more worthy of this honour than Rattray's Sikhs.

On the 19th May the 15th Sikhs lost the services of two officers, Captain Crozier and Lieutenant Thomson.

At dawn on 19th May I received orders to the effect that the Second and Seventh Divisions were consolidating their gains and that operations would continue on that day.   The Artillery of the Indian Corps was to assist by firing on the Ferme du Bois and certain named communication trenches.

At 10.5 A.M. the G.O.C. Sirhind Brigade reported that owing to rain the trenches were full of water and the parapets much damaged, and that in consequence of reliefs of Second Division his men had been on the move all night, and that his casualties during the past twenty-four hours had been severe.   He added that his battalions in the front line were somewhat shaken, and he considered it essential to relieve the 15th Sikhs by the 1st Gurkhas that night, as they were now reduced to about 250 men.   He also recommended that the King's should be relieved, and stated that he hardly thought an attack could be got out of his men that night.

At 6 P.M. the Germans made another attempt to bomb the left flank of Sirhind Brigade, but this attack was stopped. On the top of all this orders were received from the First Army that the Indian Corps was, at all costs, to capture certain named trenches and points by the morning of 22nd May.   During the night 19th – 20th the Garhwal Brigade relieved Bareilly Brigade, and certain inter-battalion reliefs desired by G.O.C. Sirhind Brigade were also carried out.   The situation remained normal during the night.

On the morning of the 20th May I visited General Anderson's Headquarters and discussed the operations for the capture of the Ferme du Bois which had been ordered by First Army.   This was to co-ordinate with the general plan, viz. that the Canadian and Highland Divisions should work southwards and secure the group of houses south of the Ferme Cour d'Avoué, and that the Indian Corps was to carry on active hostilities continuously, with a view to harassing the enemy and wearing down his resistance.

The orders issued by the Meerut Division were to the effect that the Sirhind Brigade as a first objective was to secure named localities about the Ferme du Bois before the morning of 22nd May, and that every endeavour was to be made to carry out this order.   The G.O.C. Sirhind

Brigade accordingly arranged that the 1st Gurkhas should
establish themselves in a named trench overnight, and that
patrols were to push on to the Ferme du Bois. Special
patrols were also to be sent out to ascertain the nature of
obstacles parallel to our front ; forming-up trenches were
to be dug for the assaulting battalions, and the 4th King's
were to be relieved.

During the night a thorough reconnaissance of the
position was carried out and a picquet was established by
the Sirhind Brigade 200 yards west of the Ferme du Bois.
Operation orders were telephoned to the Meerut Division.
The arrangements were as follows :

General Alderson's force (Canadians, etc.) was to co-operate
by carrying out an intensive bombardment on Cour d'Avoué
on 22nd May.

The Garhwal Brigade was to detail a bombing party,
supported by one company of infantry, and support the attack
by bombing along trench V 1 to V 2 with a view to establishing
themselves there. This party was not to commence operations
until ten minutes after the Sirhind Brigade attack had started,
unless the enemy opened fire on our attacking troops, in which
case it was to act at once.

A detailed artillery bombardment, which commenced at
1 P.M. on the 21st and was to continue till 5 A.M. on the
22nd, was arranged, on trenches and area in and near the
localities to be attacked, and to form barrages to prevent
arrival of reinforcements.

The Sirhind Brigade was to attack at 1 A.M. on 22nd May
in the following formation :

On the left the Highland Light Infantry had as objectives
two named trenches. In the centre were the 1st Gurkhas,
and on the right the 4th Gurkhas.

The 4th King's were in support, and 15th Sikhs in reserve.

All columns were in position correctly, and the attacks
were launched at 1 A.M. as arranged, and advanced
without at first being fired on. The right attack was
checked by a ditch about twenty yards from the enemy's
trenches, and here came under rifle and machine-gun fire
from the trenches in front, while the rear and right rear
were also heavily fired on ; the south-east corner of the

U

Ferme du Bois Orchard, in particular, was under a severe fire, presumably from Cour d'Avoué. This ditch was about six feet deep with three feet of water in it, and the ground between it and the enemy's trenches was wired. At this obstacle the leading company of the 4th Gurkhas was checked, but Major Moule and Captain Robinson with a detachment broke through the wire and were soon at the German trenches. They had nobly carried out their task and never returned to tell the tale. The battalion had 100 casualties.

Lieutenant Ballinger, 4th King's, commanding the two machine-guns of his battalion, had been detailed to follow the 4th Gurkhas. In his haste to join in the fight he moved on sooner than his instructions had allowed, and he and many of his men were killed close by the wire adjoining the German trench—another brave set of Englishmen who died as so many others did in the over-zealous discharge of duty.

The attack did not progress beyond this ditch, which perhaps seemed a greater obstacle in the night than it really was. The only remaining British officer with the attacking companies returned at 1.50 A.M. to take up reinforcements, but at 2.20 A.M., the senior officers with the three attacking columns having consulted, decided that as the attack was held up all along, it was inadvisable to send up more troops, and the attackers were ordered to withdraw.

The centre attack reached the Ferme du Bois with but little loss, owing to the protection afforded by the farm and ridge. A ditch was reached, and the assault at once came under heavy fire from the front and right flank. The leading company of the 1st Gurkhas, reinforced by a second, assaulted and captured a line of trench some thirty yards beyond the ditch. This trench had been covered by wire which had been cut by our artillery, whose support had been most effective. About fifteen Germans were killed here and the rest retired to a second trench twenty yards in rear. By this time all the British officers with the attacking companies had been killed or wounded, and Subadar Jit Sing Gurung, 1st Gurkhas, assumed command but was shortly afterwards ordered to retire, an order he carried out with coolness and judgement.

Lieutenant Heyland was killed while endeavouring to alter the configuration of a captured trench in which his men were being mown down. Three other British officers shared the same fate, Lieutenants Fry, Herbert, and Gamble all bravely seconding his efforts. This battalion paid dearly for its short but fierce fight, the total casualties amounting to 120. Subadar Jit Sing Gurung was awarded the Indian Order of Merit, and Captain Mellis earned the Military Cross.

The advance of the Highland Light Infantry on the left of the combined attacks was also held up by the ditch and by machine-gun fire taking the ditch in enfilade from the right and in the rear from the Cour d'Avoué. This battalion was faced by the impossible, but with its proven valour did all that could be done under the conditions, and in the attempt to carry out its task paid with a loss of over 120 of all ranks, including Lieut. J. Agnew killed, four officers wounded, and one wounded and missing, Lieut. B. Ivy.

Communication with the Sirhind Brigade Headquarters was interrupted till 3 A.M., when from all reports that he could receive, the G.O.C. decided that a second attack was impracticable. He directed the original dispositions to be resumed and the trenches to be held, up to where they had been barricaded, and this order was carried out.

In telling the story of incessant attacks or defensive actions in those days the infantry soldier naturally looms large, whilst the less conspicuous units sometimes escape notice. The corps of Indian Sappers and Miners has furnished unlimited material for tales of daring, and on this 22nd day of May 1915 a chivalrous gentleman, Captain Francis Douie of the Royal Engineers, and his equally gallant orderly, Jiwa Khan of No. 3 Company, 1st Sappers and Miners, did what one is proud to record. In broad daylight they noticed a wounded man lying only eighty yards from a German trench from which proceeded a heavy rifle-fire, whilst our own guns were shelling the self-same trench : but for such men death has no terrors.

They were soon over the parapet, and by sheer pluck and luck combined reached and brought in their helpless comrade. Jiwa Khan may well be proud of the Indian Order of Merit he wears, and Captain Douie of the D.S.O. he that day added to the Military Cross he had already won. I may add that it was only after very searching inquiry I was enabled to get full details of these acts of bravery, as apparently both actors appeared to be unconscious of having done anything beyond their ordinary duty.

The attack failed owing to excessive casualties in British officers of the attacking companies when these companies were held up. Of those with the assault all became casualties except two subalterns. Also the hindrance of a deep ditch in front of the objective under close rifle and machine-gun fire was a very serious obstacle at night, and broke the momentum of the advance. Issue from it would have involved facing frontal rifle-fire at very close range, while men in it were taken in enfilade and reverse by machine-guns from south-east of Ferme du Bois and from Cour d'Avoué. The fact that no simultaneous attack was being made on the Cour d'Avoué left the enemy in that direction at liberty to concentrate his fire on our assault at close ranges. Reconnaissance had been unable to ascertain with accuracy where the German trenches and machine-guns were located. Owing to the fact that the advance to the point of attack was carried out deliberately and in complete silence, no fire had opened on it until thirty-five minutes after the start, and the officer commanding the party which was to bomb along the trench in support of the attack, hearing nothing more than general heavy firing, was in doubt whether the attack had actually started. Inquiry from the nearest officer of the neighbouring battalion elicited the reply that it had not done so, and he accordingly delayed starting his operations so as to synchronise the two attacks.

It was now broad daylight and, of course, futile to order this attack to recommence. The officers commanding units on the spot decided that with the situation as it was known to them any further attempt, while the enemy was in undisturbed occupation of the vicinity of Cour d'Avoué, offered no chance of success, and would only have led to greatly enhanced losses, and that withdrawal before it became too late was the best course to pursue.   It would, perhaps, have been better to have ordered the attack at an earlier hour of the night, even though the Germans would probably have been found more on the alert than they were.   The casualties in this assault were heavy : nine companies were engaged, in which sixteen British officers, two Indian officers, 137 British other ranks, and 173 Indian other ranks were returned as casualties.

Although the British Division on our right had, like ourselves, been unable to make any advance during the early days of these prolonged attacks, there is no doubt that once they got a forward move on, they were severely handicapped by the inability of the Indian Corps to keep up with them, and the left battalion of that Division in consequence could not keep in touch with those farther to the right.   The situation, in fact, closely resembled that of our left Brigade at Neuve Chapelle, where we originally reached as far as the Bois du Biez but were obliged to again move back owing to the British Brigade of the Eighth Division on our immediate left finding it impossible to overcome the German defence to its front.

In the case now under review, we did all in our power to keep up with the advance, but the strong point V 6 baffled our efforts.   It might possibly have been better if the dividing line between the British and Indian Corps had not run just past this redoubt, but that is a matter of opinion only.   Be that as it may, it must be owned that notwithstanding many gallant attempts we could not get on at all, and thus hampered the later attacks of the British Division after it had captured its first objective.

CHAPTER XXI

IF for no other reason than for the sake of being alive to read the monumental history of Armageddon, I wish I were young again. How atomic appears one's own humble share in the great conflict. To Britishers who looked on manœuvres at Aldershot or Salisbury Plain as something to record, as Napoleonic military feats of arms which were an insurance against all aggression, how different do matters now appear. " The Contemptible Little Army " of those days is no more, but even so, it will ever remain the lodestar for the armies to come, and the historian of the five years' clash of the world's arms will have material to work on such as never fell to the lot of man. What an opportunity for still closer welding together the divers races and peoples that combine to make the Empire of Great Britain.

I will here cease for a while recording facts, and deal with matters which are of interest to those who look on the Indian Corps (minute as it was in comparison) as something else besides mere congeries of soldiers to feed the guns. There are some details which may not prove uninteresting to the student of psychology.

By the end of May it was plain that the Indians needed a complete rest and sorting out, if they were to continue as a Corps. The losses in France after the May fighting had totalled up to :

	Killed.	Wounded.	Missing.
British Officers	213	501	58
Indian Officers	88	260	53
Other Units, British	1,376	6,073	1,724
Other Units, Indian	1,943	10,650	2,504
	3,620	17,484	4,321

In addition, 450 Indians had died from various causes. (Taken from *The Indian Corps in France*.)

The above included the Territorial battalions forming part of the Corps, but not the losses of Divisions or Brigades temporarily attached.

In my opinion it was useless to retain two Divisions in name without the substance, and I recommended that one strong Division with Brigades averaging 4000 rifles each should be formed, the weakest and some other named Indian battalions being turned into a Reserve Brigade from which casualties could be replaced. Also, should reinforcements prove larger than I anticipated, complete battalions could replace others, and thus give all an opportunity of sharing in the fighting. The Highland Division had just been allotted to us also, and the two combined Divisions would have formed a fine Army Corps.

I explained that as matters then stood the British battalions were doing more than their share of work in the various fights. The quality of our Indian troops had deteriorated, as we received drafts of all sorts and kinds, and the old and tried British and Indian officers had been reduced to a minimum ; but with that spirit that animates the sons of Britain, the British units, without complaint, continued to give of their best (and it was of the very best). Not that I did not occasionally receive hints from the officers of both British and Indian regiments that this process could not be indefinitely continued, and they had good reason too ; and although I mostly kept my counsel I never failed to impress strongly on those in higher authority, that some drastic change was absolutely necessary.

I recommended three Indian battalions being transferred from France, and gave my reasons in full. The two Divisional Commanders were in complete accord with me in these suggestions, and as a proof that they were necessary I will give a few instances of the composition of units, which those who know the Indian Army will appreciate.

The 57th Rifles (one of the best Corps in India) was at this time made up from six different units—total strength 446; the 129th Baluchis, of seven different units—total strength 263 rifles. The 9th Bhopals consisted of men from eleven different units—strength 409. I recommended that the 57th and 59th Rifles should be combined, the total strength of the latter then being 271 rifles with seven officers all told.

The 15th Sikhs, with a total strength of only 250, was suggested for combination with the 47th Sikhs; the two battalions would then have numbered 701. Think of it, after over eight months of war. The 1st Gurkhas had only three Regular officers ; the 4th Gurkhas only four. In the 6th Jats only 160 of the original battalion remained.

The two battalions of the 39th Garhwal Rifles had already been amalgamated. They had both done most gallant service and proved themselves to be second to none in India. This combined corps was now short of ten Indian officers and 64 N.C.O.'s. The C.O. reported that he had " only four N.C.O.'s fit for promotion," and " hardly a single rifleman whose education would enable him to keep a company roll ! " What would some of our Solomons who came to judgement on the Indian Corps have said to this, if it had been possible to find similar conditions in two combined British battalions ?

On 26th May the First Army informed me that my recommendations had met with the approval both of the G.O.C. and the Commander-in-Chief. Some alterations regarding Staff officers and others had been made, but amongst them was one, that the appointment of Officer for Press Work (Lieut.-Colonel Merewether) might be abolished when the Indian element was reduced. Now if there was one person who should certainly not be got rid of, it was this officer. India had long enough been kept in the dark regarding the doings of her soldiers, and to have abolished him would not only have finally severed all connection with that country, as far as news was concerned, but would have made it impossible to compile any detailed history of the Corps for the benefit of future generations. I strongly protested against this on behalf of the Army and people of India, and pointed out that after the loyalty shown, that country would never forgive us if any such radical step was taken. India, in point of fact, during the war sent to France alone 86,300 combatants and 48,500 non-combatants ; whilst the numbers of both sent to all theatres of war totalled one million and forty thousand men.   Nothing came of it, as Lord Kitchener was then arranging to replace several of the battalions by others from Egypt and elsewhere, and had telegraphed to the Government of India regarding this.   Finally, before any great changes could be made, the Indian Army Corps had left France.

There is no need to string out many other modifications I proposed, and some I carried out, in the various Brigades. From this time till I left the Corps it was one continuous effort to keep things going.   It was necessary to carry out tasks with the best grace we could muster, and at the same time try and satisfy the powers that were.

I began this chapter with a remark that a student of psychology might find something of interest in it.   Put yourself in the place of a sepoy, say of the 9th Bhopal Infantry.   He had been brought up in a regiment composed of four classes of Indians : Sikhs, Rajputs, Brahmins, and Musalmans.   He had been bred to the idea that his regiment was his military home and that it was the best in the army.   He had understood that no man could be compulsorily transferred to another corps.   He had firmly believed that our Army was not only the best trained but best equipped in the world, and he trusted his British officers as only Indians can trust them, *i.e.* absolutely, implicitly.   Any recruit or trained soldier who joined his battalion he knew came there of his own free will, and he could not for a moment imagine that all sorts and conditions of men, out of all sorts of outlandish districts from Cape Comorin to Peshawar and from Quetta to Assam, talking different dialects and with entirely different ideals, might one fine morning arrive with shoulder badges denoting anything from police to Raj troops, and claim, not only acquaintance, but close comradeship with him as one of the 9th Bhopals.

And yet, dumped down in the heart of Europe mid ice and snow, shot, mangled, and torn day after day, many of these things, of which he was so sanguine, were suddenly directly reversed. His old battalion and his officers still stood to him in the same relation, but he awoke to the truth that ours was by no means the best equipped Army for war; far from it. The exigencies of the time had shattered his dream. All kinds of strangers entered the ranks almost daily ; all kinds of officers who did not understand him took command of his company. The promotion he had looked for in his battalion was going to outsiders ; his own officers were being wiped out week by week, and his periods of leave home were *nil*.

He was indeed a derelict ! but he still stood in his trench, his rifle ready and his loyalty unimpaired. Only one belief had not been shattered, and that was, that his family would regularly receive the small dole that was his due, and that if he died this would still continue. In this knowledge lay his contentment.

Is there not material here to ponder, for those who issued battle orders as if the whole Army was of Anglo-Saxon blood ?

Man is not cast in common mould ; as iron is to unwrought gold,
So is one man, ne'er mind his faith, distinct as love is far from hate,
From all his fellow-men.

It was Lord Kitchener who wisely made the appointment of " Recording Officer with the Indian Corps," and it must have been he who refused to consider his abolition under any circumstances.

On 2nd May, as on numerous other occasions, I had spent the whole day in the trenches. There alone could one understand the real life the men lived, and appreciate what they were doing. Besides, a big attack was pending, and a thorough survey of the ground to our front was necessary. The particular battalions I saw in the most advanced line this day were the 9th Gurkhas and 6th Jats. I chatted freely with the men and was struck by their eagerness to ask questions. One *jawan* of the Jats said : " We have been arguing as to whether there is a hill in this country : why, we had one even in my own village near Hissar (it was probably an old disused brick kiln), but although the troops who fought near Ypres in April

tell me that they saw hills and valleys, I can scarcely
believe it." I told him there were plenty of high mountains
on some parts of the Allied front. He said: " Then send
us for a motor bus trip, and if it turns out to be so, I will
give a banquet to my company when we again get a rest."
Another young Jat quickly added: " You are too generous,
You need not trouble about the banquet, for that time will
never arrive." This raised a general laugh, and as I
passed on I said: " You see we cannot spare the 6th Jats
because the Germans are afraid to attack as long as you
are up in the front trenches." " Well said, General
Sahib! now we understand," came from several men.

The G.O.C. First Army was a very frequent visitor to
our Corps Headquarters. I see in my diary over and over
again how often he came to see me and discussed operations
past or future. This was a great help in carrying them out,
and his intimate knowledge of the maps showing our
trenches, defensive posts, and situation generally, was
quite astonishing. It was only one of his many fronts,
but you had to be pretty quick with him, and I do
not doubt that he knew as much of the front he was
eventually responsible for as he did of our own short line.
He has since made a world-wide name as a soldier. I
wonder if he sometimes recalls the days when the Corps
yclept " Indian " was under his command.

In my diary of 10th May, the day after our severe
fighting at Festubert, there is an entry, " Nice letter from
Viceroy." As I have often said before in this book, Lord
Hardinge never failed to write fully regarding the Indian
Army. I have a big file of his letters, which as I re-read
them show plainly that no man could possibly have done
more to help the Corps in France.

On the 2nd June I inspected a company of the Hazaras
of the 106th Pioneers, who had just arrived as a reinforcement for the 107th Pioneers. It was worth a lot to see
these honest-looking men, for simple faith in the Government they served was written on their faces. A havildar
whom I asked what he thought of the country said, " Every
country to which the Government sends us is good." A
somewhat Oriental reply, but he looked as if he meant

what he said, though he was probably wondering where he really was.

On the 7th and 8th June I saw the 69th and 89th Punjabis, just arrived from the East to replace corps leaving France. The last time I had seen the 69th was on the Malakand Pass on the road to Chitral; it was a different scene now, although the ugly village they were billeted in bore the somewhat ridiculous name of "Paradise." They had justified their regimental motto, "By sea and land," and they rendered good service in Flanders. This battalion was originally raised in 1764 at Madura as the 10th Battalion of Coast Sepoys, and after undergoing many changes in name and constitution, received its present designation in 1903. Ill fortune attended their arrival, for the day following, both the Second in Command, Major Copeland, and the Adjutant, Lieut. J. R. Dill, who had gone up to visit the trenches, were killed by a shell. Dill was a brother of Captain R. F. Dill, 129th Baluchis, who had behaved with such distinguished gallantry at the first battle of Ypres, and received one of the first D.S.O.'s awarded to the Indian Army in this war. They were sons of the Very Reverend Dr. Marcus Dill of Alloway Manse, Ayr, who sent four sons to the war.

The 69th bears on its colours the battle honours, amongst others, of Mysore, Ava, and Pegu.

The 89th Punjabis was raised in 1798 as the 3rd Battalion of Madras Native Infantry, and like the 69th underwent many changes of constitution until 1903, when it received its present title. The battalion served in six different theatres of the Great War. One Naik Shahmad Khan won the Victoria Cross in Mesopotamia.

Another battalion which joined the Corps later on was the 33rd Punjabis. They were raised during the Indian Mutiny of 1857 as the "Allahabad Levy," and received various designations as Bengal Infantry. In 1903 it became the 33rd Punjabis. On its colours is shown "Burma, 1885–87."

On the 22nd June I visited the trenches and spent the night there with the 57th Rifles. How quickly one realises in the darkness the chances of being knocked out.

Even though nothing unusual occurred, so many bullets were flying about, ricochetting on every side, clattering on the tin roof of the dug-out, etc., that it was made plain at any moment any man might meet his end. And the men took it so much as a matter of fact and appeared so unconcerned. It was only the experience hundreds of thousands were going through every night, but it may be of some interest to write what I, as one humble individual of that great host, myself went through, for it just describes what occurred every day, more or less. Towards dusk it began to rain, and seeing a young officer who had to proceed to Divisional Headquarters on duty, starting without a waterproof, I offered him mine. The La Bassée—Estaires road was his shortest way, and although this was always kept under fire by the Germans, it was still a fairly possible bicycle route if you did not mind an occasional toss into a shell-hole, and was used by everybody who had urgent business. The officer returned before dawn, and in handing me back my coat said, " General, I am so sorry I have damaged it," and on examination I found two bullet-hole marks. Small thing, no doubt, but it showed the kind of life those lived who spent their nights on that God-forsaken road.

As the evening wore on a ration party assembled outside the C.O.'s dug-out, where I was then standing. Just as they were collected, a machine-gun, evidently fired on the signal of some watcher, pumped a shower of lead into them; no one was hit, but in an instant that ration party had disappeared. Evidently it was unsafe to show a head anywhere.

About midnight I lay down for an hour's sleep as I hoped, but hardly had I closed my eyes than a huge rat walked over my face. I jumped as if shot, with the result that I knocked my head against the supporting timber and remembered it for some days. I was fast appreciating the luxuries enjoyed by those millions of brave men who spent, not one, but hundreds of nights in this kind of inferno. But my experiences were by no means ended; the most interesting was to come.

After a night in which I saw much of my old comrades

of the 57th Rifles, I proceeded at dawn to return to my headquarters, and remembering my steel-bound leg, I took the La Bassée—Estaires road, instead of the longer route by a communication trench. Not being one of those who do not mind bullets whizzing about, I soon had cause to regret it, for the Germans had apparently chosen the self-same hour to search this road with a machine-gun. My orderly, Birbal, a Naik in the 69th Punjabis and a very old friend of mine, was with me, and as we moved along for over 1000 yards we were under a most unpleasant fire which swept past us in gusts. Birbal evidently thought " out of sight out of danger," for he insisted on opening his greatcoat wide and remaining on my weather side. I ordered him to cease his folly, but, brave fellow, he replied, " They will never see you as long as I keep this open." None of the party of four of us either had the time or inclination to argue, and our pace, to say the least of it, was exceedingly rapid, and Birbal had his way.

At last we reached the waiting motor car and were soon out of machine-gun range ; but as we spun along towards Headquarters, I could not but realise how strange must have been the feelings of thousands of Indians who underwent similar experiences daily and did it only because they had sworn loyalty to England's King. I also reflected for the hundredth time, how safe, ordinarily speaking, was the lot of a Corps Commander in comparison with those brave juniors who really won the war.

Sir John French, by his actions at different times during our year in France, proved his strong sympathy, even in trivial matters, with soldiers as a class. He could say a thing just in the right way to win the regard of all ranks. When he found that one of our few periods of rest behind the firing line coincided with the Mahomedan Ramazan, he immediately let me know that he was very pleased our men had this opportunity of observing a religious duty. In the same way, when I was gazetted G.C.M.G., the Commander-in-Chief did not fail to write and congratulate me. I hope, should the great Field-Marshal ever come across this book, he will believe that whatever I may have said in no way reduces the very high esteem in which I bear him. The Indian Corps owes him a debt of gratitude for his remarks in his book, " 1914."

Several French Generals also frequently sent their congratulations and best wishes to me and the Indian Corps. The *camaraderie* between the French and the Indians will ever remain a precious remembrance.

CHAPTER XXII

From the finish of the battle of Festubert until the Indian Corps took part in the subsidiary attack in front of Mauquissart on the opening day of the battle of Loos in September 1915, was for us what was called in France a quiet time. No big attack was undertaken and no special features marked this period. The troops, however, had plenty of hard work, and a few incidents are worth recording. Some of our old battalions left us, and a few others arrived from Egypt, etc. Among the departures were the 15th Sikhs, 6th Jats, 9th Bhopals, 41st Dogras, and 125th Rifles. I was sorry to miss the old numbers, but after being refitted, brought up to strength, and re-equipped, they again joined one or other of our numerous forces operating in the many theatres of war, and shared in the toils and triumphs of Great Britain's armies.

After the Indian Corps had left France, I wrote, as part of a story for a magazine, a tale of one Naik Ayub Khan of the 124th, attached to the 129th Baluchis. This was not allowed to be printed by the Censor, but all the same long before the war ended it appeared in full in *The Indian Corps in France*. I suppose if the Germans had found out that it was written by a former Commander of the Indian Corps it might have altered the whole course of events in Europe, so I presume it was that Solomonic Censor (and not Marshal Foch) who ended the war !

Here is the story, and I will give it in his own words :

At 10 P.M. on 21st June I started with one other man to patrol the ground in front of our own trenches. The grass for about 100 yards this side of the German trenches has been cut.

Their wire is about fifteen yards wide, and is composed of high wire entanglements (3 feet to 3 feet 6 inches high) outside, and *chevaux de frise* inside.   It commences about five yards outside the German trenches.

I arrived at the ditch on the left of the road close to the barricade on the road near Point 63 one hour before dawn.   I waited until it was light, and till the Germans stood to arms, and then stood up and held up my hands, saying, " Germany, I am an Indian Musalman."   The Germans immediately called an officer, who signalled to me to put down my rifle by the barricade.   I then gave up my bayonet and ammunition and climbed over the barricade.   The time was about 2 to 2.30 A.M.

There were many Germans in the trench, all wearing the number " 15 " on their shoulders.   They wore grey uniform and soft forage caps, with a stiff and black shining band, apparently made of the same material as the German helmet.   They had no pack on their backs, only a belt with several ammunition pouches and a bayonet.

The trench was very deep and strong, and is revetted entirely with boards held up with stakes.   The floor of the trench is boarded and is kept dry by means of pumps.

Traverses are frequent, I cannot say at what intervals, but about six to eight men between each traverse.   Dug-outs are well built and covered with sandbags.   Some have doors and windows; these probably belong to the officers.

The parapet is very strong.   There are a few loopholes in it for sentries and (perhaps) snipers, but in the case of attack the men would, I think, all fire over the top of the parapet (probably standing) on steps or sandbags.   The German trenches appear to be considerably stronger and better built than ours.

About five yards behind their front trench and parallel to it runs a communication trench, connected with the firing line in every traverse.   It is dry and in good condition and I was taken along part of it.

Until the sun rose I stayed with the officer who called me in, and then he took me along the trench to a senior officer about 500 yards towards the German right.

During my walk through the trenches I saw some iron loopholes, probably for day sentries, also some wooden loopholes which may be used at night.   There are more men in the

x

German front-line trenches than in ours, perhaps in the proportion of three to two.

The senior officer had a shoulder-strap covered with silver braid, and the number " 15 " : I could see no other marks. I was sent off in charge of one N.C.O. and two soldiers. I was treated well and the men in the trenches gave me cigarettes.

The support trench was about 100 yards behind the firing-line. There were no dug-outs, and the trench was absolutely unoccupied. I saw no third line of trenches.

The course I followed seems to have been *via* (here he described it in detail). I then entered a wood, and went through it by a *kacha* road. (He emerged at Point 72 or 73, and turned sharp to the left, going for about 200-300 yards with the wood on his left.) I was then taken to the second of two houses on the right, quite close to the turning. The first of these houses is half destroyed and is used as a telegraph and telephone office. A trolley line runs along behind the wood and turns to the right by these two bungalows.

I was taken into the second house and saw two officers. The younger had no coat on ; the senior, who saluted me (mark the salute) and gave me cigarettes, had silver braid on his shoulder and a brass crown and a number which I cannot remember. I think they must have been the C.O. and Adjutant. I stayed there only about five minutes.

I started off along the trolley line, which continued till it reached a main road, probably the Aubers road. (From here the description is vague. Apparently he went past the factory west of Illies church, on to the main La Bassée—Lille road, and thence to Wicres.)

After crossing a railway line, some five minutes afterwards we came to a small village, well built and with only a few houses damaged. There were French women and children in the village. I passed straight through the village, seeing on the right an unmetalled road on which were horse-drawn artillery wagons. I was taken to a house amidst trees in the fork of two main roads.

An officer who spoke a little Hindustani and had been in India came out with a senior officer (whom I took to be a General), white-haired and with a grey moustache, whose shoulder-strap carried thick silver braid as thick as my finger. The Interpreter brought a map and asked me what trenches I knew. I told him that I could not read.

He asked me why the —— Regiment had left. I said they had been engaged for a long time and had lost heavily. Other questions and answers were as follows :

Question.—Were you in the attack at Ypres ?

Answer.—Yes.

Q.—How many men did your Brigade lose ?

A.—About 300 killed and 200 wounded.

Q.—Is your Brigade very weak now ?

A.—No, a new battalion of 1100 rifles has just arrived.

Q.—What is this battalion ?

A.—The 89th Punjabis. (The Interpreter then produced a book and wrote this down.)

Q.—Have the 124th (Ayub Khan's proper battalion) come to this country ? It is not in my book. (He saw an old shoulder badge of the 124th in my pocket.)

A.—No. When the 129th had lost 300 men, 400 more came from the 124th to bring them up to strength. When we returned from Belgium drafts arrived from other regiments. We are now 100 under strength but there is a draft of 600 men waiting for us (a good lie) when we are relieved from the trenches. I told him that the present strength of our companies is about ninety men. (Indian battalions formerly had eight companies.)

Q.—Do you have plenty of rifle ammunition ?

A.—Each sentry is given a box and can fire what he likes.

Q.—Have the guns plenty of ammunition ?

A.—Each battery has a dug-out full of ammunition, and they can fire what they like. (Good lie!)

Q.—What rations do you get ?

A.—In the morning, tea, milk, and biscuits. In the evening, meat, bread, and vegetables.

Q.—Do you get pay ?

A.—We are fed and clothed and get soap from Government. We get ten francs monthly in the field, and the rest accumulates at the depot.

Q.—Why did you, a non-commissioned officer, desert ?

A.—My section is tired of the war, but dare not come over in case they get fired on. We discussed the matter and I decided to go alone and arrange for the others to come over. There are fifteen men in my section who want to desert, and I can find five more in the battalion.

The senior officer then said that, if I would come over to

the Germans, I should get very good pay, and that he would give me Rs. 300 if I brought over twenty men.

These questions were asked at about 12 noon on the 22nd.

I was then sent to sit in an orchard. They brought me milk and bread on three occasions. A number of soldiers came to look at me. I saw about eight men with the number " 55 " on their shoulder-strap, and about ten men with the number " 13."

I sat in the orchard until 9 P.M. with some German soldiers. They all had a crown on their shoulder-straps and another mark I could not understand. They wore an ordinary black German helmet, with a black board on the top, raised up a little. One man took the grey cover off and showed me his helmet. It had a big white badge in front. (N.B.—This appears to be the 16th Uhlans.)

At about 9 P.M. the Interpreter, one of the officers, and I returned to the trenches in a motor-car. The officers in the trenches did not want to let me go. However, it was arranged that at dawn I should bring over the twenty men and call out my own name. The men were to bring rifles with them but leave them in the grass. I then left the German trench and arrived back in our own trenches about midnight the 22nd–23rd instant.

I brought back my rifle, belt, and bandolier. They took my ammunition and bayonet.

As regards the distance of the place of interrogation from the German trenches I cannot remember, but was walking for about two hours on the morning of the 22nd. My motor-car ride the same evening was about five or six miles.'' Ends.

The story is a remarkable one and its general correctness was proved by subsequent events. Ayub Khan carried his life in his hand, for had his actions caused one doubt of any kind among his captors he would assuredly have been shot. One spot indicated by him as an ammunition dump was subjected to a heavy fire two days later and a very considerable explosion occurred which we at the time attributed solely to the information gained. The Hun was notified by unmistakable signs that the naik's treachery had been discovered and rewarded, as such conduct in war should be.

Meantime I had the pleasure of presenting Ayub Khan with a larger sum of money than he had been promised by the Germans, promoting him to a higher grade of N.C.O., and getting him the Indian Order of Merit. Promotion to the commissioned rank of jemadar soon followed his other rewards.

Towards the end of June 1915 I wrote to G.H.Q. through the First Army on the subject of the depots, convalescent camps, and drafts at Marseilles. I have before me reports of a Committee of experienced senior officers, also separate reports of other officers concerned. Those who only judge Army Corps by the number of rifles and guns available might receive a shock on reading these documents, and incidentally gather therefrom some of the difficulties that had to be faced by the Commander of the Indian Corps in France. The truth is that Marseilles proved to be the most unsuitable place that could have been selected as the Indian Base. When we first arrived it was intended to move it farther north, Havre or elsewhere, as soon as the main body of the Corps had reached the front; but once established, Marseilles remained our Base to the end. Its geographical position and the shortage of shipping, of course, had much to say to this.

The Committee did not shirk responsibility. On the contrary, its report is a document that should be valuable to those who may ever again be called on to select bases in Europe for Indian troops, and assist them to avoid the stupid blunders that were made and the chaotic conditions that prevailed. The Commandant, Colonel G. F. Tinley, did all a man could do. He worked all and every day, but he could not refashion a rotten system nor cleanse the Augean stable. Some of the reservists and drafts that were sent from India were a humiliation to our name. Some of the officers who passed them as fit should have been removed from the Army.

For what did it all mean? Merely this, that from reasons either of laziness or stupidity they did not hesitate to send men marked as fit for service in the field who were absolutely unfit, and who they must have known were unfit. They themselves were safe enough in India; if anything went wrong, well! their comrades in France and not they would suffer. As I look back on it all I cannot but hope that in most cases it was only ignorance, but of what use are such officers in the Indian Army?

It is difficult to write calmly on such a subject, for on 15th July I myself went down to Marseilles and remained there four days. I saw all that was being done, inspected every hospital, depot, and draft, and returned to Flanders, only realising fully for the first time that the authorities in India knew as much about the requirements of a European war as I did about a Zeppelin.

Talk of the mentality of the East: I truly learned more of it in those four days in Marseilles than I had in a life-time. The mind of India was laid bare. The ignorance of the West, when endeavouring to understand the view-point of the East, suddenly stood naked before me. I thought I knew something of Indians; I left Marseilles knowing a little more, but still very far from all.

A few details may amuse the reader; they certainly afford material for amusement, though little comfort was it at that time. I will quote from the official reports. One lot of reservists was classed as "utterly valueless." Of nineteen men of one regiment "three are fit for service." Another small draft was classed together as "particularly poor," of another out of thirty-five men sent "ten are plague convalescents who have not even yet recovered their full vigour." One boy was referred to as fourteen years of age, and another as a "mere child." Of a draft of sixty-seven reservists nine were of "indifferent physique" and fifty-eight "unfit." India appeared anxious to fill up sorely-needed shipping with trash of this sort. One draft of thirty Hindus was sent for the 129th Baluchis, a Class Mahomedan regiment that had not had a Hindu in it for thirty years, and of the thirty, twenty-two were pronounced unfit on arrival at Marseilles.

Finally this particular Committee closed its proceedings with the remark: "Of 212 men inspected only five or six —who (also) are temporarily unfit—are suitable for service in France."

G.H.Q. was shouting to us, "Promite vires," on the battle front, but we were fast reaching the Ultima Thule of our resources in the rear.

Attached to the Indian Corps was Captain P. J. G. Pipon of the Indian Civil Service. He had volunteered for active service and in addition to his military duties did much work of a political nature. His assistance in all matters connected with religion, interior economy, etc., always proved most valuable, and his inquiries at Marseilles unearthed many details which make strange reading. He received the Military Cross and C.I.E. for his services in the war. My Indian A.D.C., Risaldar Khwaja Mahomed Khan, I.D.S.M., accompanied him on one occasion, and then, as always, rendered invaluable service. Of course in the doing of this he made many enemies, and those who understand the East will know what this means. His loyalty and zeal deserve strong recognition, and I feel certain that should the Viceroy or Commander-in-Chief ever hear of these remarks they would not fail to inquire, and would assuredly see that this distinguished Indian officer was honoured by those who owe him a debt of gratitude. Captain E. B. Howell (I.C.S.), Censor with the Indian troops, rendered valuable service and received a C.I.E.

In March 1915 I had recommended to G.H.Q. that wounded Indians should not be sent back to the front, and the Adjutant-General had issued orders to this effect. They still continued, however, to be sent, and in May the G.O.C. First Army himself made similar recommendations, to which the A.G. replied that only those who volunteered would be returned. It was a great mistake keeping wounded men at Marseilles. They did little good and much harm, and they should either have been kept in England or returned to India. It was folly to mix them up with fresh drafts, who were not cheered on first arrival by meeting a lot of bandaged men. The Indian is not built that way.

However, it was eventually decided that all recovered wounded, as well as sick, should as soon as pronounced fit be sent back to the front. On this I made fresh recommendations for forming a working battalion behind our lines, which could be utilised, at any rate for military working parties. This project had taken shape before I left France. It was indeed the only way out of the difficulty, and served as a means of partially clearing that focus of discontent, Marseilles.

On 2nd July I attended the regimental sports of the 4th Cavalry. A big French crowd had gathered, and the proceedings recalled many happy days in India. The tent-pegging was quite good, and the jumping showed that the horses were in good fettle and well trained.

The 4th Cavalry, the Divisional Cavalry Regiment of the Meerut Division, was originally raised in 1838 as the " Cavalry Regiment of the Oudh Auxiliary Force," and received its present title in 1904. It was granted an honorary standard for service in Scinde in 1844, and served in Afghanistan (1879–80).

On 8th July Lord Kitchener visited us. He told me the Indians were to have a rest and also said very decidedly that he meant to keep them in France to the end of the war. He informed me that they would be formed into ONE Division, and not kept as two, which was the opposite of what he had sturdily maintained when I last saw him, so I presume the pressure brought to bear on him had been too much even for his determination. The G.O.C. First Army also informed me that the Indians were to have three weeks' rest, and that the British battalions were to be formed into two Brigades and have a third added whilst the Indians' rest lasted. By the 16th July this reorganisation had been completed, but was of short duration, as only a week later we were again ordered to change our front, and 3000 rifles of those in rest were sent to the Lahore Division, which had been detailed to hold the line whilst all the Indian units had been temporarily turned into the Meerut Division. Lord Kitchener on this visit was in peculiarly happy vein and made light of all his difficulties.

On 11th July the pipers of the 40th Pathans played in the square of the village where our Headquarters was located and a large crowd of French people gathered to listen. It was a very cheerful sight, and an old Frenchman who was bent double came up to me and said, " Your Indians are just like the British, you are a wonderful race of people."

My own old battalion, the 1st Leinsters, was at this time quartered at Armentières not far from us, and I went over to see them. Unfortunately I had selected the 14th July for my visit, not remembering that it was a great date in France, and that, in consequence, the Boches would certainly select it as a special day of hate. Before I reached the town this was forcibly brought home to me by the heavy shelling it was being subjected to. However, I had fixed an hour and I knew the battalion would be on parade waiting for me, shells or no shells. With some difficulty I wended my way in a motor-car by back streets full of debris, and arrived in time. I carried out a formal inspection while the big shells were falling in the Square quite close by; but the men were in high spirits, and I believe had a shell burst in our midst, not a Leinster would have budged even to pick up his comrade. I could not but compare it with the very last occasion on which I had met my old Corps in India and had the high honour of presenting it with new colours, a distinction that does not often fall to the lot of an ordinary officer.

We had lunch to the accompaniment of a chorus of projectiles, and I left after the Hun had poured out the vials of his wrath. The Irishmen looked grand. Would that we could enrol many Army Corps of such fine soldiers.

On 18th July Sir John Hewett, late Lieutenant-Governor of the United Provinces of Agra and Oudh, paid us a visit. He came on duty in connection with the " Indian Soldiers' Fund," for which he had done so much and which I have written of elsewhere. Sir John was one of the greatest of modern India's Proconsuls—a man full of saving common sense, strong in character, quick in decision, just in dealing, such an one, in fact, as Indians respect and love, and his visit was much appreciated by us.

Towards the end of July we received a very fine draft of 900 men from India. I saw them on parade and was very pleased with their physique and general appearance. They were nearly all highly trained and keen to see fighting, and I saw that the authorities had at last begun to realise that what we needed were soldiers and not useless reservists.

Hudson, by this time promoted Major-General, my

Chief of Staff, left us to command the Eighth British Division. I was truly sorry to lose so excellent a Staff officer and so good a friend. His knowledge and advice had been invaluable from the day we landed in France. Captain Langhorne, R.A., also rejoined his own Army, and I felt his loss much. Hudson was succeeded by Brigadier-General Charles, R.E., and Captain Forbes, 57th Rifles, relieved Langhorne.

It is of interest to record that at the beginning of July the casualties of the Indian Corps had reached a total of over 26,000, exclusive of nearly 500 other deaths among the Indians.

CHAPTER XXIII

DURING July very few interesting events had occurred in the Corps, and although there is nothing spectacular to record, it was just such incidents that kept up the spirits of the men and gave opportunities for individual distinction combined with very useful work. Of such was a reconnaissance made by Captain Roe, 4th Gurkhas. Starting by daylight, this gallant officer, accompanied by Lieut. C. C. Manson of the Indian Army Reserve of Officers attached to the battalion, and his acting Subadar Major, Senbir Gurung, spent five hours reconnoitring the enemy trenches from " No Man's Land." In the doing of this they all ran very considerable risks, but certain information was much needed and they did not hesitate to run every risk to gain it. I will not go into the details : suffice it to say they not only discovered and sketched many German traps, trenches fitted with armoured loopholes, dummy machine-guns, barricades, and other unpleasant accessories of trench warfare, but killed a German officer and another man, and returned with their information and a useful sketch.

Not content with this the same trio, accompanied now by eighteen N.C.O.'s and men, sallied out on 4th July and in three groups repeated the performance on a larger scale. Covering parties were told off and other necessary preparations made. Roe and his group were subjected to a sharp bombing which temporarily knocked them out, but quickly regaining their feet they outmatched the Huns in the bombing game, killing five of them. Senbir was very severely wounded, but refused to be moved and continued to exercise his command. Manson here got his chance, and with his

315

covering party just caught the Germans at the moment they were gaining a decided advantage. They were utterly surprised and as they very hurriedly retired a fortunate shell from one of our field batteries which was assisting the operation burst over them. This ended all opposition and the grand little Gurkhas returned full of themselves.

Roe received the D.S.O., Manson the Military Cross, and Senbir Gurung the Indian Order of Merit. Others who were awarded the I.D.S.M. will be found in the Appendix.

The Bishop of Nagpore visited us towards the end of July and accompanied me to several of our advanced posts and batteries. He gave us a very impressive service in the French schoolroom of the town, and we were glad indeed to have had one of our Indian Bishops in our midst. In this Corps we of course had less Christian chaplains than was naturally the case with others, but those we had have left a splendid record of devotion and will ever be remembered by all who served with them. Witness one name alone, Ronald Irwin, Indian Ecclesiastical Department, Chaplain of the Leicesters, who during the war won the D.S.O. and M.C. with bar.

I had a very pleasant duty to perform during July when on comparing statistics of all Brigades in the Corps I was able to report to First Army that for the two previous months the 1st and 2nd Battalions of the Connaught Rangers, who as I said before had been amalgamated into one unit, had not a single court-martial, and showed the lowest average of sick (1·37) amongst the British troops of the original Army Corps. All of these battalions could not be beaten in the Army, but it always rejoices me to see Irishmen setting the example, and they generally will set it if they are taken in the right way.

Sir John French, with that soldierly instinct he possesses in so high a degree, at once directed that an expression of his appreciation of the efforts of the C.O. and all other ranks of the Connaughts to raise the Corps to such a high state of discipline was to be conveyed to the battalion.

Major-General Lambton, the Military Secretary at

G.H.Q., had a difficult task. Considering the numerous details he had to deal with and the difficulty of following the ramifications of promotions and rewards in the Indian Corps, it was wonderful how successfully he managed. His fairness in apportioning them, and his desire to do justice to the Indians, were very apparent. In comparing the awards with those of other Indian Expeditionary forces, up to the time I left France, I think we perhaps suffered in proportion to our numbers and the conditions we lived in. There can be no question as to which force of Indians had the hardest task and the most trying conditions to contend with during the first months of the war, but the number of rewards for Indians were in some cases less than their more fortunate comrades received in other theatres. Writing of rewards I may add that Lieut. - General Sir Charles Anderson, who commanded the Meerut Division for eleven months and succeeded me in command of the Indian Corps, was perhaps the only Corps Commander who never received a French decoration. He later commanded a British Army Corps for many months, but he is still without anything to show that he served in France.

Lieut. - Colonel S. Barry of the Northamptonshire Regiment, A.D.C. to the Commander-in-Chief, was an officer who invariably exercised a tact that made visits to G.H.Q. a pleasure whenever he was on duty.

General Macready, Adjutant - General, G.H.Q., was always most anxious to help the Indian Corps, and we owe him a debt of gratitude for many actions taken by him to keep our house in order.

It will interest those who sympathise with the complications of this command to glance at the accompanying short extract from our "Summary of News," 1st to 5th June 1915. It was taken haphazard from many in my possession. In order to convey to the Indians some idea of what was going on in all theatres of war it was of course necessary to publish such news in their own language. This meant, first, translation of the ordinary summary issued to the Army into Hindustani, and then the local presentation of it in the Persian and the Hindi character. It was all done rapidly and regularly, with a result that the sepoy in the trenches was enabled to learn frequently what his comrades and the Allied Armies were doing. Without it he would have known nothing of either.

Summary of News, 1st June to 5th June 1915.

WESTERN THEATRE

British Front. — The British troops have captured the Château of Hooge, about 2½ miles from Ypres on the Menin road.

On the night of the 4th–5th June the British on the right of the Indian Corps captured forty-eight German prisoners of the 56th Regiment, Seventh Corps. These are mostly men between thirty-five and forty years of age, who have only recently been called up for service. From their statements it appears that in this neighbourhood the enemy has at present no apparatus for asphyxiating gas.

French Front.—The French continue to advance near Notre Dame de Lorette and Souchez, fifteen to twenty miles south of the Indian Corps. On the 31st May they captured the front German trenches of the large work known as the " Labyrinth," taking four officers and 146 men. The " Labyrinth " was composed of subterranean chambers believed by the enemy to be impregnable. The French also captured the Souchez Sugar Factory, a large and strongly defended building. During the night the Germans recaptured it, but were driven out again by our Allies at daybreak on the 1st June. During this battle the French captured over 800 prisoners, including nine officers, fifty N.C.O.'s and two machine-guns. They are now in firm possession of the building and of the trenches all round it.

The following particulars of the results of the fighting in this neighbourhood are issued officially by the French authorities :

" Between the 9th May and 1st June 3100 German prisoners, including sixty-four officers, were captured, and 2600 German corpses buried, all by one French Division." This probably represents a loss of at least 10,000 killed, wounded, and prisoners. " The losses of this French Division were about 3200 in all, of which two-thirds were only slightly wounded." Ends.

A month before I left France Lieutenant E. Bullard, of the Indian Postal Service, attached to the Corps, was

TRENCHES. INDIAN CORPS. 27 - 8 - 1915.

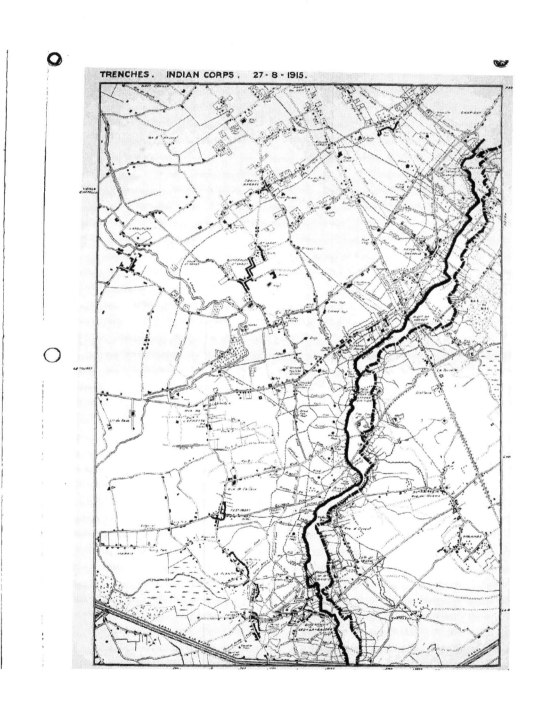

killed by a shell whilst in his motor-car on duty well behind the advanced posts. Poor lad, he had done excellent service, and this will readily be understood when it is remembered that he was responsible for the distribution of letters, packages, post cards, and a hundred forms of correspondence and gifts written in innumerable dialects or wrapped in the most impossible covers, and despatched in a manner that no Westerner can conceive. Notwithstanding this, like other exceptional matters, there was always an officer ready and capable of carrying them out. Indian training in this respect is difficult to beat.

During August a company of Bhutias from the Darjeeling district of Bengal joined us for ambulance work. Great Britain was indeed gathering her hosts from all parts of the world. I inspected them and never remember to have seen a more cheery detachment. They were accommodated in tents and plainly showed that they had come to enjoy the show, for they had no hesitation in calling the war a regular *tamasha* (sport, fun). They changed their mind as to the *tamasha* part of it, but were always in good spirits.

The 12th August was a proud day for me, for I had the honour of receiving from His Majesty's hands the G.C.M.G. he had been pleased to confer on me, and at the same time my son in the Black Watch was honoured by receiving the Military Cross. The King was kind enough to tell the boy that he was glad to see both father and son together, and after the Investiture I was summoned to an interview, when His Majesty told me he had heard good reports of the Corps and directed me to convey to the officers, N.C.O.'s, and men his good wishes. Of course this was speedily done, and little did I then realise that only three weeks later I was to leave my beloved Army Corps and field service for ever.

I again saw Lord Kitchener and he asked me if I had any objection to releasing a thousand Gurkhas from the Corps for service in Gallipoli. He wished four companies to be taken from four different battalions, but I suggested one whole battalion being sent and made up to a thousand rank and file. He agreed to this and I selected the 4th Gurkhas. It was a blow losing them, but necessity demanded it, I suppose.

Only a week later Lord Kitchener again visited us in France and saw all Corps Commanders of the First Army at St. Venant. On this occasion he informed me that it had been suggested to him to relieve the Indians, but he was determined they should stay on in France, and he said he was arranging reliefs of units.

For few perhaps in the British Forces in France has the 3rd September 1915 any special significance, but for me, without any kind of immediate warning, it was the last day of soldiering. For thirty-seven years the thought of suddenly ending my career had never entered my head, and I still hoped that if my Corps could be transferred to Egypt, Mesopotamia, or anywhere from France, I should have the satisfaction of seeing the war through. If we remained on in France, I knew it was only a matter of time when I should be forced myself to ask for a move. However, we were on the eve of the great attack at Loos ; the Indian Corps was in as good fettle as was then possible ; every kind of preparation was in process of completion for the attack ; and as far as I was concerned there was no immediate reason for any foreboding of evil. We had just received some excellent drafts from India and everything seemed to be going well.

But it is the unexpected that often happens in war, and in justice to myself and the Indians then in France, I say plainly that at a time of comparatively profound calm on the battle front, I was for very good reasons obliged to suggest to the G.O.C. First Army that as my services apparently no longer met with his approval I considered it best for the Army that I might be relieved of my command.

The war is over, I am only one humble individual, my staying or leaving could have no bearing on events, but justice is a thing we expect in our Army.

On the 2nd September 1915, with my old and valued friend, Colonel Sir Frederick Lugard, Governor-General of Nigeria, who was home on leave and paying a short visit to France, I went round almost the whole of our front trenches. It was a murky day and nothing beyond the usual shelling and firing was happening, but the Indians were glad to see me, as usual.

One section was held by Pathans, and some of them were singing to a *sitar* (guitar). My knowledge of Pashtu is limited, but I had years ago learned their favourite song, "Zakhmi Dil" (The Wounded Heart), so I joined in and gave them a verse. Men from other parts of the trenches came running over, and presently to dance and music we were having an improvised concert. I did not know it was to be my last with my brave comrades of many campaigns.

After a long day's tramp, and having personally inspected the various new trench positions for guns which were to be brought up to the very front, etc., we got home late, and for some reason I was in particularly good spirits. Loos was about to be fought, and the Indian Corps had been detailed to make a subsidiary attack from near Mauquissart and we had been preparing everything for many days.

Early on the 3rd September there was a conference of the First Army at Hinges Château; it was the first Headquarters I had been in when I took over our front in October 1914, and I found myself back in the old familiar room and seated at the same spot where we had begun our great adventure. How much had passed since those early days; how few of my old comrades of the Staff, or indeed of any kind, still remained with us!

My thoughts could interest nobody but myself, but to me as I look back they were the last I should ever reflect, as a fighting soldier; for within an hour I was no longer Commander of the Indian Corps. Discipline is the marrow of an army; silence, when it is imperative that one should uphold the authority which the King has placed over us, is sometimes hard to endure.

An hour later, on my way back to my Headquarters, I told my Staff officer that I had seen the Army Commander and my end had come. He was not surprised; who that was present could be? Only twenty days previously I

Y

had had the honour of receiving the G.C.M.G. at the hands of His Majesty, and had been summoned afterwards to his presence, as I have already told, when he graciously congratulated me and praised the work of the Indian Corps, and within three weeks I was forced to leave the Corps in which I had served with a loyalty that no man could exceed. *Nemo repente fit turpissimus.*

I had gone to the Conference in high spirits; I was leaving it, little caring whither I went. I should have to depart before even I could shake the hand of many brave Indians, officers and men, my lifelong friends. I felt I must perforce go without saying a word, lest any spark of ill-feeling should be revealed. The enemy was before us; individuals had to go under, rightly or wrongly, but, above all, no Indian soldier should know from me that his commander was leaving for such a reason. They would, of course, not understand it, and so I knew the bitter pill must be swallowed. I had long foreseen what must come; that it came with a greater suddenness than even I had imagined possible is another story.

In my Diary under 5th September I find :

This day last year I was appointed to command the Indian Corps and the selfsame day a year later I got my orders to go. The only order in fact I have received is, that I may proceed on leave, and that was given me verbally by the Military Secretary. It is war-time and so I must hold my peace for the foe is at the gates, but if this is justice then chivalry has indeed departed.

From that day to this I have never received any orders. ARGUMENTUM BACULINUM.

Even the India Office was not informed, and my own intimation some days later, that I had left, was the first they heard of the fact. Would this have been possible in any other Army Corps ?

Lord Kitchener saw me on 16th September, or ten days after my return, and informed me that he had heard verbally, but had no official report and had telegraphed for it.

I was the third senior officer in France; what must have been the fate of many junior to me ?

Had Lord Kitchener lived, I think I may safely say I should not have been cast on the scrap-heap; with his death vanished the last hope of re-employment in the war, and what other employment was worth having ?

I have a sufficient sense of discipline to refrain from further probing this story. I am still on the " Active List" of the Army and it is my duty to hold my peace; but I retain the right to tell my own tale when I am no longer employed, and I shall then do so. Even had I been totally deficient in " initiative and tactical skill," there are ways of doing things. I had during my thirty-seven years' soldiering served in fourteen campaigns; had received the Freedom of the City of London and a sword of honour, and the unique distinction of being mentioned by name in King Edward's first Speech from the Throne. Had I not the right to expect ordinary courtesy ? —but I belonged to the Indian Corps !—that explains much.

The story of my own share in the work of the Corps in France is finished. I have endeavoured faithfully to record, to the best of my ability, the brave doings of brave men, British and Indian. I have tried to repay in some small measure the heavy debt I owe to them, but especially to the soldiers of India, my faithful friends and comrades in many campaigns, through whose loyalty, courage, and devotion I have risen from Subaltern to General. The memories of the long years spent in India are, at least, a possession of which I cannot be deprived.

Ille terrarum mihi praeter omnes angulus ridet.

The following numbers of casualties, up to within a week of the date I left France, will give some idea of the part played by the Army Corps in the fighting and of the debt which England owes to her own sons and brothers from overseas; but still more to those chivalrous men, Mahomedans and Hindus, for they came from a sense of loyalty to their King-Emperor alone, although they had

no personal bias in the quarrel, except to uphold Great
Britain's righteous cause.

British officers	.	.	.	850
„ other ranks	.	.	.	10,300
Indian officers	.	.	.	420
„ other ranks	.	.	.	17,230
Total	.	.	.	28,800

CHAPTER XXIV

My own part in the Great War ended early in September 1915, and the share taken by the Indian Corps as part of the Army which attacked at and north of Loos (prior to its final departure from France) can only be told as I have gathered it from records and letters received by me ; but my information is derived from the most authentic sources and may be taken as absolutely correct. I should not consider this book complete without giving in some detail an account of the last, but by no means the least, of the fights waged by the Indians in Flanders. More especially do I deem it an honour to do this, as the command had devolved, on my own recommendation, on my friend, Lieut.-General Sir Charles Anderson, K.C.B., one of the most earnest fighting soldiers.

Moreover, certain Indian battalions took part in it which had joined just prior to, or immediately after, my departure. Like every other unit of the Corps, I had known and served with them in India, and it is a source of pleasure to record, as far as I can in a bald statement of facts, the part they played in the closing scenes of the drama of the soldiers of Hindustan. I had been partly instrumental in making the preliminary preparations for this battle, and therefore am in a position to understand thoroughly what occurred.

The events as they actually took place have convinced those who knew what was being done that the task assigned to the Indian Corps was, under the circumstances, a hopeless one, unless the wind and weather were both favourable for the use of gas, of which we understood but little at that time.

325

I had originally selected as the objective of the Corps the very same front it finally attacked, and had laid my plans before the Army Commander. A German deserter had, however, come in and stated that his own side was preparing a gas attack on the self-same front, and I had been ordered to select another portion of the German line on which to direct our assault. Later, a heavy fire had been kept up to detect if possible whether there was any collection of gas cylinders or apparatus in the vicinity; the deserter's report had been found to be untrue and I had been ordered to hold to my original plan again; but as the operation depended mainly on the successful use of gas, I had made certain suggestions in case of a failure of cylinders, or an ill turn of luck in wind and weather at the last moment.

Those who may read this story will at least see that my ideas were not only not groundless, but that, as I had deemed possible, the supply of gas was eventually merely a trifle of what had been planned—160 cylinders instead of the 1100 calculated—and of the 160 in the trenches only 30 could be discharged before the wind veered. The gas, moreover, had no effect on the enemy, as was proved after our first advance, whilst it very seriously hampered our own troops.

The end of a year of trench warfare, and the deterioration of Indian units as compared with our original battalions, was not the time to call on them to carry out such an attack, unless they were to be amply supported by guns, and of these I was very short. Given these and favourable conditions for the use of gas, much might have been done which the shortage of the former and handicap (as it turned out) of the latter made an impossible task. It is true that the push was only a subsidiary one, and designed to hold the enemy in its front and thus prevent him from sending assistance farther south; but distinct objectives had been assigned; and, even so, there is reason in all things, and in my opinion, as originally designed and as we were supposed to carry it out, there was not the slightest chance of our gaining our objective or retaining it if gained, whilst there was the certainty of very heavy losses amongst men who had already cheerfully made immense sacrifices for Great Britain.

I will not enter into the operations of the British Army as a whole; suffice it to say that the First Army assumed the offensive on September the 25th, and the orders for the attack of the Indian Corps, amongst others, were based on the following instructions :

The Army Corps south of the La Bassée Canal were to advance eastward to the line Pont-à-Vendin—Bauvin. The Corps north of the Canal were to engage the enemy vigorously and to prevent him from withdrawing troops for a counter-attack. Wherever the enemy gave ground he was to be followed up with the greatest energy.

The Second Division was to assault the enemy's trenches at Givenchy and to attack Canteleux; the Third Corps to assault the enemy's line near Bridoux with a view to eventually effecting a junction on the Aubers Ridge with the Indian Corps.

The Indian Corps was to capture the enemy's trenches in the vicinity of the Moulin du Piètre and to take advantage of any weakening of the enemy on its front, so as to secure the high ground about Haut Pommereau and La Cliqueterie Ferme. The attack was to be made by the Meerut Division, then commanded by Major-General Jacob, promoted from Brigadier Dehra Dun Brigade. The first objective was to secure and consolidate a line of a road which ran through Mauquissart to an enemy salient. Every opportunity was to be seized of pushing farther forward to gain the high ground about La Cliqueterie Ferme.

Detailed orders were also issued for the Lahore and Nineteenth Divisions.

In the event of the enemy showing signs of weakening, the Lahore Division was to attack and capture the Bois du Biez. Similarly, the Nineteenth Division was to be prepared to extend any success gained by the Second Division by advancing against the southern end of the Rue d'Ouvert. The Artillery bombardment was ordered to commence on September 21st, and continue day and night under instructions issued.

If the wind was favourable the attacks of the Second Division and of the Meerut Division were to be preceded by gas and smoke. The Lahore and Nineteenth Divisions were to assist with smoke barrages.

The Lahore Division was directed to put up a smoke barrage on the southern flank of the Meerut Division.

The Meerut Division was to arrange a similar barrage on its northern flank.

A mine was to be exploded under a designated enemy salient two minutes before gas was turned on.

The attack was to be preceded by a four days' deliberate bombardment by the Meerut Divisional Artillery, reinforced by No. 4 Group, H.A.R., one Brigade R.F.A., from Lahore Division, one 3-pr. Hotchkiss gun on trailer, and an armoured train. The assault was to be supported by the above Artillery, and was to be carried out by the Garhwal Brigade on the right, with the Bareilly Brigade on the left ; the Dehra Dun Brigade in Divisional reserve.

The troops were to be formed up by midnight 24th–25th September.

> *Garhwal Brigade.*—Three assaulting battalions (3rd Gurkha Rifles on the right, Leicesters in the centre, and 8th Gurkha Rifles on the left) from Sunken Street to sixty yards north of South Moated Grange Street.
>
> One battalion (1/3rd Londons) on the front line from Duck's Bill to Sunken Street.
>
> Garhwal Rifles in the Home Counties Trench.
>
> *Bareilly Brigade.*—Three assaulting battalions (1/4th Black Watch on the right, 69th Punjabis in the centre, and 2nd Black Watch on the left) from sixty yards north of South Moated Grange Street to Winchester Street.
>
> The 33rd Punjabis were in the Home Counties Trench, etc.
>
> The 58th Rifles were in Tilleloy trench.
>
> *Dehra Dun Brigade.*—In Divisional reserve.
>
> One battalion (2nd Gurkha Rifles) south of Moated Grange Street.
>
> The 1st Seaforths north of Moated Grange Street.
>
> 1/4th Seaforths in Rouge Croix East Post, etc.
>
> The 9th Gurkhas in Min and Rugby Posts and in Bacquerot Street.
>
> The 93rd Burma Infantry in Carter's Post.

Owing to the uncertainty whether atmospheric conditions would admit of gas being used, two programmes for the assault were drawn up.

Programme " A."—To be followed if gas and smoke were to be employed.

Programme " B."—To be followed if gas and smoke were not to be employed.

In both programmes the first objective of all assaulting battalions was the enemy's front and support lines.

As soon as the assault began, troops were to move up to replace those who had gone forward, the Divisional reserve going to Home Counties Trench, etc. This reserve was not to move farther forward without the orders of the Division.

Three companies 34th Pioneers and half of the 20th Company Sappers and Miners were placed at the disposal of Meerut Division for the first day of the operations.

Our wire entanglement was cleared by the assaulting Brigades during the days prior to the attack, the outer fringe being left till the night of the 24th–25th September.

Each man of the attacking Infantry carried two sandbags and two gas helmets.

The Lahore Division on the right and the Twentieth British Division on the left were to cover the flanks of our advance by fire, and after the front trenches were taken these Divisions were to send troops to hold the trenches opposite their respective fronts, and so protect our flanks in the advance beyond the German support line.

The deliberate Artillery bombardment commenced on the 21st September, and the results proved generally satisfactory. By the evening of the 24th the enemy's wire entanglements in front of their front line were reported to have been cut, with the exceptions where this could not be done owing to trees. This bombardment was accompanied by rifle, rifle-grenade, machine-gun, and trench-mortar fire from the front line, and by indirect machine-gun fire from points in rear of the front line. This fire was kept up day and night in order to prevent the enemy effecting any repairs. There was not much retaliation on the part of the Germans during the period of bombardment, and what there was did little damage and caused few casualties.

Special instructions were issued to the Dehra Dun Brigade, which was in Divisional reserve. The object aimed at was to ensure this Brigade being concentrated and ready to move quickly in any direction required.

From 6 P.M., 23rd September, when the Brigades commenced to move to their positions of assembly, the weather became wet and inclement. This made the trenches difficult, and by the evening of the 25th September a foot of water was standing in many of them.

Part of the Brigades got into position during the day of the 24th. The smoke and gas detachments were in their places by 6 P.M., and all troops were in their positions of assembly before midnight.

At 10.15 P.M. orders were received by the Meerut Division that Programme " A " was to be followed, *i.e.* the employment of gas and smoke.

During the night the wind was changeable, veering round from south to south-west.

About 4.40 A.M., 25th September, an enemy bomb burst in the Duck's Bill, smashing two gas cylinders, and the officer in charge of the operations there and several of his detachment were gassed. A considerable number of men of the 1/3rd Londons, who formed the garrison of the Duck's Bill, were also incapacitated.

The mine exploded to time, and it was ascertained later that the crater formed was 92 feet across. The charge was one ton of gun-cotton.

At 5.50 A.M. the gas should have commenced, but at that hour it was practically calm, and what wind there was made it unsafe to let it off in certain bays. In these bays the men of the detachments, on their own initiative, did not turn it on. Soon after the first cocks were turned on, a gust of wind from the south-east turned the gas into our own trenches. All gas was immediately turned off, the detachments doing this on their own initiative, but considerable quantities entered our own trenches and caused many casualties in the 2nd Black Watch on the leeward of our front.

The intensive bombardment commenced at 5.50 A.M. and was satisfactory, the field guns and the Hotchkiss gun in the front parapet participating.

The Infantry began to cross the parapet just before the assault, under cover of the smoke and of the Artillery bombardment, the Artillery lifting 100 yards and increasing their rate of fire, so as to conceal the increase of range and prevent the enemy realising that the assault was about to commence. This, combined with the smoke, had the desired effect, as the enemy was not expecting the assault at the moment it was delivered, and there was practically no hostile fire while the assaulting troops crossed the ground between the two front lines.

At 6 A.M. the assault commenced. Dense clouds of smoke, the result of the barrage on the right or south flank, travelling in a north-easterly direction made observation difficult, and caused some confusion and mistakes in direction. The Garhwal Brigade got up to the German wire, which was found to be impassable opposite the 3rd Gurkha Rifles and the right of the Leicesters. There the lanes cut by our Artillery had been filled up during the night with rolls of French wire. This stopped the assault sufficiently to give the enemy time to man his parapets and prevent these troops making good the attack. The left of the Leicesters and the 2/8th Gurkhas, however, found the wire destroyed and penetrated into the enemy's line.

In front of the Bareilly Brigade the wire had been destroyed by our Artillery and all three battalions got into the enemy's trenches with slight opposition. On the left, the Black Watch had to go through our own gas, which the wind had not been strong enough to disperse, and suffered more casualties. This battalion was not free from the vapour until it got into the enemy's lines. The smoke clouds, which the calmness and dampness of the day had turned into thick fog, prevented observation and hid guiding landmarks, and considerable intermingling of units occurred after the assault. Communication also was difficult, as the lines laid in advance of our front parapet by the assaulting Infantry and the R.A. officers accompanying them were continually being cut. This was especially the case with the Infantry communications, and the earliest information was obtained from Artillery Observation officers, which proved generally reliable.

Writing as I am for the first time of a battle when I was not in command of my Corps, I am tempted to describe from reports the gallantry of units and individuals well known to me, but I will refrain, and refer the reader to that interesting book, *The Indian Corps in France,* wherein he will find recorded the deeds of officers and men who on this day, although unsuccessful in completing the impossible task assigned to them, added brilliant pages to their regimental records.

The names of such officers as Colonel Brakspear, Lieutenants Bagot-Chester, Tyson, and Wood, of the 2/3rd Gurkhas, form a roll of honour not to be forgotten, and greatest of all in that fine battalion stands out Rifleman Kulbir Thapa, who on this day added the fifth and last Victoria Cross won in France by the men from Hindustan.

Palmam qui meruit ferat.

And what of the 8th Gurkhas who had begun the war on that bleak 30th day of October 1914 before Festubert ? The old battalion had practically disappeared, but although no longer the Corps that had suffered so terribly in those early days, it was determined to leave its mark deep cut on the soil of Flanders. Colonel Morris, the C.O., already severely wounded nearly a year previously, paid with his life. Add to his the names of Lieutenant Ryall of his own battalion and of the following attached officers : Lieutenants Taylor (1st Brahmins), Inglis, and Meldrum, of the Indian Army Reserve of officers, all of whom were killed, as well as four others wounded and eight Indian officers and 460 rank and file killed, wounded, and missing, and one may well pronounce that the 8th Gurkhas indeed did their duty and found their Valhalla.

I had left France ; I knew of the " mentions in despatches," but I searched in vain for any rewards given to the British officers of this and many other Indian battalions who fought round Mauquissart on that day.

The 2nd Leicesters, as they had ever done, fought with the stubborn pride of race they had so often displayed ; no need to say more. Over seventy were killed, including Captain Romilly, of whom I told at Neuve Chapelle, and Lieutenant Browne. Here, too, fell a good soldier, of that brave but merciful band the Royal Army Medical Corps, Captain Deane, attached for duty. He had already earned the Military Cross, and died as he had lived, " going about doing good." I hope I shall not be accused of aiding our next enemy when I give them my advice, viz. " Keep out of the way of the Leicesters."

Second Lieutenant Gedge of the 3rd Londons, one of the battalions in Brigade reserve, was killed. Another of these units, the Garhwal Rifles, had seventy casualties. The Garhwalis had established a grand reputation, but were by this time unrecognisable in their old form, and in finally passing out of this record I can say without fear of contradiction that they left a name which will be held in high esteem by all who ever knew them in France, and not least by the Germans. The last name mentioned to me after the Indians had left France was that of Lieutenant Rama Jodha Jang, who behaved right well on this day and was awarded the Military Cross.

By 6.30 A.M. our Infantry were reported to have penetrated into the enemy's position as far as the support line all along the front attacked; the Germans were reported to be surrendering freely, and there was little hostile Infantry or Artillery fire.

Shortly after, the Twentieth British Division informed Meerut Division that the Sixtieth Brigade had been ordered to advance at once to protect the left flank of the Indian attack.

From all indications it appeared now as if we had captured the German front and support trenches along the whole of the front attacked, and that the left of the Bareilly Brigade was pushing forward towards the German second line, but subsequently it was found that the situation was actually as follows :

On the right the Garhwal Brigade was held up by wire, but the 8th Gurkhas and one company Leicesters on the left had penetrated the German position.

Of the Bareilly Brigade, the 1/4th Black Watch had gone through the enemy's front system and had moved forward considerably beyond the line assigned to them as their first objective, and were digging themselves in opposite the enemy second line. The 69th Punjabis were pressing forward mixed up with the 58th Rifles and the 2nd Black Watch. One company, together with one from each of the 58th Rifles and 33rd Punjabis, were consolidating the position gained. The Black Watch, less two companies, which were blocking the trenches to the north, were advancing against the German second line of trenches, about the Moulin du Piètre. The 58th Rifles were pressing forward with the Black Watch and 69th Punjabis. The 33rd Punjabis were in our proper front line. The Garhwal Rifles had been delayed in their advance to our front line owing to congestion in the trenches, caused principally by the number of men suffering from the effects of our gas, and were still in their original position. Lastly, the Dehra Dun Brigade had commenced to concentrate forward.

The enemy's guns were active at this hour, and there was much intermixture of units, loss of direction, and confusion.

The consolidation of the captured trenches was not sufficiently considered, in the anxiety of all ranks to take advantage of the weakness of the opposition where we had penetrated the position. The Bareilly Brigade had passed over its first objective, and the flanks were dangerously exposed, especially as the attack of the Garhwal Brigade on its right had been held up. The natural anxiety to press our advantage led the 58th Rifles to advance on its own initiative, but I will later on more fully refer to this incident.

By 8 A.M. the Divisional Commander had learned that the Garhwal Brigade had been unable to enter the enemy's front trenches, and the following was the situation :

In this Brigade there was no correct information of the 3rd Gurkhas. The Leicesters were held up by wire, but one company had penetrated the German line and half of the 8th Gurkhas were in the German trenches. The other half had lost direction and were intermingled with the right of the Bareilly Brigade.

The Bareilly Brigade was making rapid progress. The 69th Punjabis and 4th Black Watch had taken the German first-line and support trenches. On the left of the attack the 2nd Black Watch had passed all the advanced trenches and were moving on the Moulin du Piètre. In support of this battalion the 58th Rifles were also moving forward. In fact, the entire Brigade had advanced so rapidly that their position was not fully realised. Unfortunately, the captured support line was not consolidated, owing to the companies detailed for this work having joined in the general advance and left the work uncompleted. Except in officers, however, the casualties so far had not been heavy.

Shortly after this hour it was reported that the enemy was massing in front of the Black Watch, and our guns were immediately turned on to the Moulin du Piètre. At the same time two companies of the 33rd Punjabis were moved forward to support the 69th Punjabis, and six machine-guns were sent to support the Black Watch and 58th Rifles in the mine salient.

At 8.15 A.M. this same day, 25th September, the Dehra Dun Brigade was ordered to move up one battalion in close support of the Garhwal Brigade. This battalion was to remain under the orders of the Dehra Dun Brigade.

About 9 A.M. the Corps Commander directed the Dehra Dun Brigade to be pushed through the gap made in the German line and attack towards the high ground between Haut Pommereau and La Cliqueterie Ferme. Half an hour later five field batteries from rearward positions commenced to move forward to the east of the Rue du Bacquerot, and at the same time the Bareilly Brigade confirmed the report that the Black Watch and the 58th Rifles had captured portions of the German second line but that the enemy still held the Moulin du Piètre. Casualties were reported as slight, and the O.C. 58th Rifles was of opinion that the Haut Pommereau Ridge could be won if fresh units were pushed through.

By 9 A.M. the Pioneers had commenced work on communication trenches under considerable machine-gun and rifle fire. Before this work had to be discontinued about 100 yards of fire trench had been completed. The party at work on No. 2 trench also suffered considerably from hostile fire and hand-grenades, but it had completed about 130 yards of traversed trench before it had to retire. No work was possible on two other communication trenches;

whilst the party on No. 4 trench continued work till 1.15 P.M. under constant fire.

The Garhwal Rifles could not carry out the fresh attack as planned for them, as they were unable to get forward out of the communication trenches, which had become very congested in their neighbourhood.

The general situation of the Bareilly Brigade remained as before. The few officers left were endeavouring to reorganise the units and to guard their flanks. On the right flank the 4th Black Watch were being echeloned back towards the left of the Garhwal Brigade in order to protect the right flank of the Bareilly Brigade.

Major Wauchope, commanding the 2nd Black Watch, made over to the 12th Rifle Brigade of the 60th British Brigade on our left the trenches which the two companies of the Black Watch had been consolidating, and arranged for the party to extend along a ditch to join up with the 58th Rifles. The remainder of the Bareilly Brigade gradually collected in the German second line, where there seem to have been great congestion and heavy losses, owing to the dense target offered to the enemy. It is impossible to establish the hour at which these various actions took place, as most of the officers responsible for them were killed or wounded.

Captain Hewett of the 41st Dogras, on the Staff of the Bareilly Brigade, was killed during the fighting. Like nearly every officer of the Indian Army who served on the Staff in France, he had won his own way by sheer merit.

But now a change came over the hitherto successful operations. After mid-day, Artillery Observation officers reported that a good many men were to be seen coming back, and being rallied in an old German trench ; and by 1 P.M. all our troops had fallen back to their original line.

The enemy's counter-attacks had developed at about 11.30 A.M. and were pressed home strongly and methodically against the front and both flanks. The front was able to hold its ground without difficulty, but on the flanks the enemy established a decided ascendancy in bombing. On our right flank the Germans outlasted our various parties with their grenade-throwing, and successively obtained the mastery of one point after another. The blocking of the trenches was ineffective after our supply of bombs was finished, and, although the men made a series of stands during the retirement, they were unable to maintain any position for long, as the Germans came bombing up from trenches on either flank.

On our left the Rifle Brigade (British Division) was unable to hold the " blocks " made by the 2nd Black Watch, as their supply of bombs also ran short very quickly.

With both flanks turned, the whole of the Bareilly Brigade had to fall back.

In the rapidity of their advance our troops had not systematically searched the enemy front-line dug-outs, and a considerable number of Germans remained in them and fired into the backs of our men, evidently singling out officers in particular, as the loss in officers was very heavy.

When it was established that the Bareilly Brigade had fallen back, the attack by the Dehra Dun Brigade, which was to have been directed against Haut Pommereau, was cancelled, and that Brigade was ordered to gain touch with the troops who were believed to be still holding out in the German trenches. Accordingly, the G.O.C. Bareilly and Dehra Dun Brigades proceeded to Winchester Road to discover whether the report was true, and to determine the best line on which the Dehra Dun Brigade should carry out its advance. One company of the 2nd Gurkhas and two companies of the Garhwal Rifles which attempted to cross to the German line were driven back by heavy fire from all parts of that line, and this showed that the German front line was held in strength, and that none of our troops were now holding any part of it.

At 4.45 P.M. the G.O.C. Indian Corps issued definite orders cancelling the attack being organised by the Dehra Dun Brigade. The fighting along our front practically ceased, and for the last time the Indian Corps had borne its share in one of the many fierce battles on the Western Front.

As I said before, I am writing this chapter from reports and letters in my possession, and hence it is not the same thing as describing events in which one has borne a part,

z

but in many instances the records of battalions and even individuals have become almost public property, and of such I feel I may justly give some account.

The 2nd Battalion of the Black Watch was well known to me and had served under my orders as a Brigadier, Divisional and Army Commander in India and for a year during the war.   I was well acquainted with the Commanding Officer, Colonel Harvey, who was now in command of the Dehra Dun Brigade.   The actual Commander on this day was Major Wauchope, D.S.O., who had served with them for years, and who afterwards commanded a Brigade in Mesopotamia.   Where Wauchope rules all is well, and on the 25th September he and his Highlanders well sustained the name of that famous corps before Mauquissart.

Many had been disabled at the very commencement of the attack by our own gas, but the spirit which never acknowledges difficulties permeated all ranks, and the Royal Highlanders, as they had done from Seringapatam to Waterloo, and from the Alma to Lucknow and Tel-el-Kebir, sweeping away all opposition, were almost into the Moulin du Piètre before they realised that they had not only gained their objective but were far (too far) beyond it.   Not finding the necessary support to enable them to advance, the Battalion held on to its gains, but eventually had to retire.   Bombed, mangled, and attacked on both flanks they moved back, but only over the bodies of their comrades did the Huns advance ; only after paying a heavy toll could the enemy regain his ground, and only after desperate fighting would the Scots quit each yard of trench. It had to be done, but the name Moulin du Piètre is worthy to be added to the other twenty-eight borne on the colours which commemorate gallant deeds performed from Guadaloupe, 1759, to Paardeberg 140 years later.   The losses suffered amounted to 360 killed, wounded, and missing, including sixteen officers out of the twenty with which the Battalion went into battle, and of these five were killed, viz. Captain Denison, a young officer of quite exceptional promise ; Lieutenants Sotheby, Henderson, Balfour-Melville, and MacLeod.

The halo of the 2nd Battalion had also encircled its

sister Battalion of the Brigade, viz. the 4th Black Watch—
Territorials to start with, but veterans in September 1915.
I can see the C.O., Lieut.-Colonel Walker, leading on his
men, for this he literally did. Major Tosh was near him
and fell; a sergeant quickly tried to save him, but in vain.
The bayonet avenged his and many other losses, and the
4th Black Watch, like the 2nd Battalion, looking only
forward, pushed on regardless of all but the Mill before
them. Dearly they paid, but the glory they won will
assuredly live when the Moulin du Piètre will remain only
a spot marked on old maps of the Great War. The Commander, Lieut.-Colonel Walker, his Second-in-Command,
and a young officer, 2nd Lieut. Anderson, were killed,
seventeen other officers were reported as wounded or
missing, or a total of twenty out of twenty-one officers
present that day; and 420 other ranks completed the
casualty roll.

Like the Highlanders, the 69th Punjabis never stayed
their rush till the prize, the Moulin, was almost within
their grasp, but they too were to earn renown alone. When
the fate of war overtook the others, the 69th also retired
fighting. The Commander, Major Stansfeld (attached
from the 74th Punjabis), was killed, and Captain Nelson,
Lieutenants Moberly and Fraser also gave their lives;
whilst three Indian officers and seventy others were killed
or missing. Amongst the wounded were four British and
six Indian officers and 260 others, or a total of over 50
per cent of strength present.

Captain Nelson was attached from the 3rd Brahmins.
We had spent three very good days together shooting and
fishing on the Ganges Canal eighteen months previously,
and I had been much struck by his keenness and zeal in
whatever he put his hand to. Major Bingham behaved
with great coolness throughout this day, but I could find
no record of rewards for the officers.

Of my good friend, Colonel Davidson-Houston, 58th
Rifles (Frontier Force), I have written elsewhere. His
battalion, in support of the Black Watch, cared for naught,
like its comrades, save the fatal Moulin. On that all eyes

were bent, and it must be won at any cost. The oft-repeated injunctions of the First Army to push on regardless of side issues had burnt into the souls of men who had for a whole year tasted the fruits of success and failure in varying degrees.

The 58th pushed on, and a part found themselves close up to the Mill; the remainder met with the same counter-attacks as the rest of the advance; they held on to their gains and consolidated as much as possible, but eventually were forced to retire to our own original line. Amongst the killed or missing were Colonel Davidson-Houston, Captains Flagg, Harcourt, McKenzie, and Lieutenants Nicolls, Deane-Spread (Indian Army Reserve of Officers, attached), and Milligan. Captain C. G. Wardell (21st Punjabis, attached) was severely wounded. Five Indian officers and 240 other ranks completed the roll of casualties.

As an example of the inferno through which the troops went on this day, I will instance the doings of Captain Wardell above mentioned. At the very start he was knocked over by the explosion of a shell close by; almost immediately a bullet smashed his water-bottle and a second one cut away the straps. In moving up to form a defensive flank in the second German line captured trenches he lost a good many men getting through uncut wire. Units in the front line were by this time indescribably mixed up; there were too many men, and very few officers left. An hour later a bullet cut the strap of his field-glasses and another smashed the glasses in his hand. A third passed through his lung, injuring several ribs and emerging through his coat pocket, but such was the situation that each and every British officer must perforce fight on, so a fresh pair of glasses was got, and whilst he was observing as best he could another bullet passed through his shoulder. Bleeding and sorely hurt as he was, I have been told on good authority that this brave officer remained with his command until sent back on a stretcher by his Colonel.

I looked for any rewards to British officers of this battalion, but I could find none.

The last of the Indian battalions to join the Corps in

France, and the last of which I shall write here, was the
33rd Punjabis. They had arrived the very day after I
left, and were not long before, in their reconstituted form,
they too had received their baptism of fire. The same
goal was theirs, the same vicinity of the Moulin was to be
the last resting-place of many of the men from the land
of the Five Rivers, and as their comrades had fought, so
now did they share in the glory and carnage of the strife.

As a Captain and Staff Officer at Delhi I had been present
when the old 33rd Regiment of " Bengal Infantry " was
mustered out, and the " 33rd Punjabi Mahomedans " took
their place. I had again seen them at Delhi, when
commanding the Northern Army, and I only missed them
by a day in Flanders. They may rest content in the
knowledge that although the last to join the Corps they
were not the least in the share they took on 25th September
1915, before Mauquissart, and to this fact their long list
of casualties attests. Killed and missing—Major Kelly,
Captains Price and MacCall, Lieutenant Grasett (attached
from 28th Punjabis). The Commanding Officer, Colonel
Ridgway, and Captain Vincent were wounded. Five Indian
officers were also killed or missing and three were wounded,
a total of fourteen officers all told. Of other ranks eighty-
seven were killed or missing and 160 wounded. The
senior Indian officer, Subadar-Major Bahadur Khan, and
the senior Jemadar, Akbar Ali, were among the killed.

General Jacob in his report on these operations made
the following remarks, which explain some of the reasons
for the failure of the Indian Corps to retain the ground it
had won. He says :

It was unfortunate that the wind, changing at the last
moment, blew the gas back on to our own trenches, . . . men
under the influence of gas seemed to lose all sense of direction,
and some are said to have charged down between the German
and our own front lines until stopped by the Duck's Bill.

After highly praising the keenness, spirit, *élan*, and dash
shown by all units, he adds :

The charge made by the 2/8th Gurkhas and the 2nd
Leicesters of the Garhwal Brigade and by the 2nd Black

Watch, 69th Punjabis, and 1/4th Black Watch of the Bareilly Brigade could not have been finer.

He explains how some of the attacking battalions in their eagerness to move on exceeded the limits of ordinary prudence and went too far, with the result that they were cut off and many valuable lives lost, and attributes the immediate success of the German counter-attack largely to their superiority in bombs and to our own supply entirely running out.

Regarding the action of the 58th Rifles; from the information now available, it would appear that the opinions formed by both the Divisional and Brigade Commanders at the time are quite open to explanation. These officers considered that the advance of the 58th was premature, but in *The Indian Corps in France*, on page 451 (second edition), is given Brigadier-General Wauchope's (then a Major in the 2nd Black Watch) opinion, and I have no doubt that both Generals Jacob and Norie agree with it.

In any case, it is to all of us who knew Colonel Davidson-Houston, the Commander of the 58th Vaughan's Rifles, a certainty, that in giving his orders for the battalion to advance, he acted either on some information which we shall never know, or because he considered it imperative he should do so, even if contrary to his instructions.   Such faults, if faults they be, are a credit to those who will take the responsibility, and I can well imagine my friend as he took it on this day.   He was a C.O. so devoted to the men he commanded and so absorbed in his regiment that more than once his actions were misunderstood whilst in France. On one occasion it was my good fortune to stand by him, when some very high personages differed from us both on a question of vital interest to the Indians.   We went to, and left the stormy meeting together, and somehow I felt we had " learned them " something they did not know before.   Davidson-Houston was indeed " a veray parfit gentil Knight."   His character partook of manly physical bravery, tempered with a fine discretion when he had to consider others.   He never asked any man to do what he was not ready to do himself if necessary.

Both the Corps and Divisional Commanders mentioned in terms of high praise the work and devotion to duty of the Technical troops, the Pioneers, and Sappers and Miners. The medical branch of the Corps received the credit which all ranks had well earned, as did the Staff, each and every one of whom was known to me.

It was pleasant to read in the report on this battle mention made for the first time in France, by the Army Commander, of the " Indian Corps " by name.

Shortly after this battle, rumours were rife, that the Corps would not remain another winter in France, and before the end of November the entire Indian personnel had left this theatre of war.

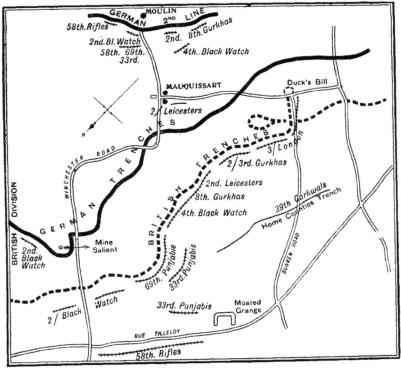

Mauquissart.

CONCLUSION

THUS ended for the sepoy the " Great Adventure " on the plains of Flanders. What memories it brings back ! what future possibilities it has in store ! Some of them may arise sooner than the most imaginative can foreshadow.

I have throughout this book endeavoured to do full justice to the Indian Army, both to its British officers and all Indian ranks, but I venture to offer one final word of advice to those in whose hands may lie the future destinies of that Army. This advice has at least one merit, it is based on a very wide and lifelong experience of India, its people, its Provinces, its Frontiers in every direction, and, above all, of its Army.

It is this. Whatever you do as regards the inhabitants of India, whatever form of Government they may eventually possess, so long as the Union Jack floats over Hindustan do not reduce the present status of the British officer. You will find Indians as brave, loyal gentlemen and splendid comrades, and hence you may find it difficult to refuse equality of command ; but you must make this a cardinal principle, for no argument decked in rhetoric will alter the fact, that you can NEVER replace the British officer in the Indian Army.

EPILOGUE

In 1919 I was home on short leave, and it happened that the Indian Contingent was in London for the Peace celebrations. I was a spectator when they marched to Buckingham Palace to be reviewed by their beloved King-Emperor, and as they passed on their return from the Palace, although I was in plain clothes, some of the Indian officers and men recognised me amongst the crowd. One of them shouted the Sikh war cry of " Fateh," and a number ran out of the marching ranks, saying, " Here is our General." It was a very short greeting, but it was none the less both moving and splendid.

A few days later I visited their Camp at Hampton Court. I will not attempt to describe what took place, but when I left in my motor car, this at least I clearly knew, that those faithful comrades would never forget their old Commander. It is my final and highest reward.

APPENDIX

PROMOTIONS AND REWARDS OF OFFICERS, NON-COMMISSIONED OFFICERS, AND MEN OF THE INDIAN ARMY AND DEPARTMENTS WHO SERVED WITH THE ARMY CORPS OR OTHER INDIAN TROOPS OR BRITISH UNITS IN FRANCE PRIOR TO 1916, AND WERE GAZETTED BEFORE 20TH FEBRUARY 1916.

Extracted from Official Lists, " London "
and " Indian " Gazettes, etc.

Victoria Cross

Sepoy KHUDADAD KHAN, 129th Baluchis (severely wounded).

Naik DARWAN SING NEGI, 1/39th Garhwal Rifles (severely wounded).

Lieutenant F. A. DE PASS, 34th Poona Horse (killed).

Lance-Corporal DAVID FINLAY, 2nd Black Watch (killed).

Rifleman GOBAR SING NEGI, 2/39th Garhwal Rifles (killed).

Private WILLIAM BUCKINGHAM, 2nd Leicestershire Regiment (killed).

Rifleman KULBIR THAPA, 2/3rd Gurkha Rifles.

Lieutenant J. G. SMYTH, 15th Sikhs.

Subadar MIR DAST, I.O.M., 55th Coke's Rifles (F.F.), attached 57th Rifles (F.F.) (wounded).

Corporal ISSY SMITH, 1st Manchester Regiment.

Lieutenant W. A. M'CRAE BRUCE, 59th Scinde Rifles (F.F.) (killed).

STAFF

Knight Commander of the Bath

Lieut.-General H. B. B. Watkis, C.B., Indian Army.

Companion of the Bath

Colonel (temporary Brigadier-General) F. W. G. Wadeson, Indian Army.

Colonel (temporary Brigadier-General) C. W. Jacob, Indian Army.

Colonel (temporary Brigadier-General) A. S. C. Cobbe, V.C., D.S.O., A.D.C., 32nd Pioneers.

Lieut.-Colonel (temporary Brigadier-General) G. de S. Barrow, 35th Horse.

Colonel R. H. Ewart, C.I.E., D.S.O., A.D.C., Supply and Transport Corps.

Lieut.-Colonel J. S. M. Shea, D.S.O., 35th Horse.

Major-General C. P. W. Pirie, I.A.

Colonel (temporary Brigadier-General) C. A. Fowler, D.S.O., I.A.

Colonel (temporary Brigadier-General) W. H. Fasken, I.A.

Companion of St. Michael and St. George

Lieut.-Colonel J. P. C. Hennessy, Supply and Transport Corps.

Lieut.-Colonel H. A. P. Lindsay, Supply and Transport Corps.

Lieut.-Colonel C. H. G. Moore, D.S.O., Supply and Transport Corps.

Major (temporary Lieut.-Colonel) H. E. Rhys Pryce, 18th Infantry.

Lieut.-Colonel (temporary Colonel) G. S. Sheppard, Military Accounts Department.

Major and Brevet Lieut.-Colonel H. C. Holman, D.S.O., 16th Cavalry.

Colonel F. C. Muspratt, I.A.

Distinguished Service Order

Major H. B. D. Baird, 12th Cavalry.

Major R. C. W. Lukin, 9th Horse.

Major J. H. K. Stewart, 39th Garhwalis.

Major A. Strong, 10th Lancers.

Major (temporary Lieut.-Colonel) L. R. Vaughan, 7th Gurkha Rifles.

Captain J. P. Villiers-Stuart, 55th Rifles.

Major G. D. Bruce, 61st K.G.O. Pioneers.

Major W. F. S. Casson, 27th Light Cavalry.

Major C. J. B. Hay, Q.V.O. Corps of Guides (F.F.).

Major F. S. Keen, 45th Rattray's Sikhs.

Captain D. G. Robinson, 46th Punjabis.

APPENDIX

349

Military Cross

Captain B. de L. Brock, 126th Baluchistan Infantry.
Captain M. A. Hamer, 129th Baluchis.
Captain H. L. Watkis, 31st Punjabis.
Captain R. G. Alexander, 11th K.E.O. Lancers.
Captain H. L. Dyce, 9th Hodson's Horse.
Captain E. St. C. Gray, 34th Poona Horse.
Captain E. D. Raymond, 30th Lancers.
Captain H. R. B. Reed, 39th Garhwal Rifles.
Captain H. L. Scott, 1/1st Gurkha Rifles.
Captain S. R. Shirley, 54th Sikhs (F.F.).
Captain W. L. O. Twiss, 9th Gurkha Rifles.
Lieutenant O. Gough, 12th Cavalry.

Order of British India, 1st Class, with title of " Sardar Bahadur "

Risaldar Khwaja Muhammad Khan, I.D.S.M., A.D.C., Queen's Own Corps of Guides.

French Order of the Legion of Honour, Croix de Commandeur

Lieut.-General Sir E. Locke Elliot, K.C.B., D.S.O. (retired). I.A.

Russian Order of St. Vladimir, 4th Class, with Swords

Colonel (temporary Brigadier-General) C. W. Jacob, C.B., Indian Army.

Major-General

Colonel (temporary Brigadier-General) H. Hudson, C.B., C.I.E., Indian Army.
Colonel (temporary Brigadier-General) C. W. Jacob, C.B., I.A.
Colonel (temporary Brigadier-General) W. G. Walker, V.C., C.B., I.A.

Brevet Colonel

Lieut.-Colonel (temporary Brigadier-General) W. B. James, C.I.E., M.V.O., 21st Cavalry.
Lieut.-Colonel (temporary Brigadier-General) H. J. M. Macandrew, D.S.O., 5th Cavalry.
Lieut.-Colonel (temporary Brigadier-General) W. M. Southey, C.M.G., 129th Baluchis.
Lieut.-Colonel R. E. Vaughan, D.S.O., Supply and Transport Corps.
Major and Brevet Lieut.-Colonel A. Skeen, 24th Punjabis.

Major and Brevet Lieut.-Colonel H. C. Holman, C.M.G., D.S.O., 16th Cavalry.

Lieut.-Colonel (temporary Brigadier-General) J. S. M. Shea, C.B., D.S.O., 35th Scinde Horse.

Brevet Lieutenant-Colonel

Major A. G. Stuart, 40th Pathans.

Major H. L. Tomkins, D.S.O., 28th Punjabis.

Major A. W. Peck, 25th Cavalry.

Major J. A. Longridge, 43rd Erinpura Regiment.

Major (temporary Lieut.-Colonel) C. A. C. Godwin, 23rd Cavalry (F.F.).

Major (temporary Lieut.-Colonel) C. C. Newnham, 6th K.E.O. Cavalry.

Brevet Major

Captain H. R. A. Hunt, 25th Punjabis.

CAVALRY

4TH CAVALRY

Companion of St. Michael and St. George

Lieut.-Colonel H. G. Stainforth.

Military Cross

Captain G. Howson.

Order of British India, 2nd Class, with title of " Bahadur "

Risaldar-Major Awal Khan.

Risaldar Saddha Singh.

Indian Distinguished Service Medal

Ressaidar Udmi Ram.

No. 333 Dafadar Karam Singh.

Russian Medal of St. George, 1st Class

No. 2210 Dafadar Amanatullah Khan.

Honorary Rank of Jemadar

No. 322 Dafadar and Head Salutri Lachman Singh.

9TH HODSON'S HORSE

Military Cross

Captain F. H. M. Moody (13th Lancers, attached).

Indian Order of Merit, 2nd Class

No. 2889 Lance-Dafadar Jit Singh (11th King Edward's Own Lancers, attached).

2614 Acting Lance-Dafadar Ganga Singh (11th K.E.O. Lancers attached).

11TH KING EDWARD'S OWN LANCERS
Military Cross

Lieutenant R. V. Sherston (attached 4th Queen's Own Hussars).

Lieutenant (temporary Captain) H. G. A. Fellowes (attached 1st Battalion Prince Albert's Somerset Light Infantry).

13TH DUKE OF CONNAUGHT'S LANCERS
Military Cross

Lieutenant D. Pott.

15TH LANCERS (CURETON'S MULTANIS)
Military Cross

Captain A. C. K. S. Clarke.

Indian Order of Merit, 2nd Class

Jemadar Malik Mihr Khan.

Indian Distinguished Service Medal

No. 346 Dafadar Ibrahim Khan.

No. 2176 Lance-Dafadar Alladad Khan.

20TH DECCAN HORSE
Distinguished Service Order

Captain A. C. Ross.

Military Cross

Lieutenant G. F. Tinley.

Indian Order of Merit, 2nd Class

No. 295 Dafadar Sardar Singh.

No. 255 Dafadar Shankar Rao.

Indian Distinguished Service Medal

No. 830 Sowar Gokul Singh.

25TH CAVALRY (FRONTIER FORCE)
Military Cross

Lieutenant J. Nethersole (attached 2nd Life Guards).

28th Light Cavalry
Distinguished Service Order
Captain A. Marshall (attached Royal Flying Corps).

29th Lancers (Deccan Horse)
Indian Order of Merit, 2nd Class
Jemadar Hayat Ali Beg.

31st Duke of Connaught's Own Lancers
Russian Order of St. Stanislas, 3rd Class, with Swords
Major A. F. C. Williams, D.S.O.

34th Prince Albert Victor's Own Poona Horse
Victoria Cross
Lieutenant F. A. de Pass (killed in action).

Indian Order of Merit, 2nd Class
No. 2743 Sowar Madhu.

Indian Distinguished Service Medal
Ressaidar Badan Singh.
No. 3027 Sowar Abdulla Khan.
No. 3250 Sowar Fateh Khan.
No. 3154 Sowar Firman Shah.

Russian Cross of the Order of St. George, 4th Class
No. 2085 Kot-Dafadar (now Jemadar) Abdul Ghafur Khan.

39th Central India Horse
Military Cross
Captain W. A. K. F. Fraser (attached 16th Lancers).

Royal Field Artillery
Indian Distinguished Conduct Medal
No. 4079 Naik Ilm Din, 5th Brigade, Ammunition Column.
No. 9483 Driver Fateh Khan, 18th Brigade, Ammunition Column.

Sappers and Miners
Distinguished Service Order
Captain A. J. G. Bird, R.E., No. 4 Company, 1st Sappers and Miners.

Captain F. M'C. Douie, R.E., No. 3 Company, 1st (K.G.O.) Sappers and Miners.
Captain F. H. Kisch, R.E., 3rd Sappers and Miners.
Captain J. C. Wickham, R.E., 2nd Sappers and Miners.

Distinguished Service Order and Military Cross

Lieutenant F. M'C. Douie, R.E., 3rd Company Sappers and Miners.

Military Cross

Captain E. H. Kelly, R.E., 1st Sappers and Miners.
Captain E. F. J. Hill, R.E., 1st Sappers and Miners.
Captain P. C. S. Hobart, R.E., 1st Sappers and Miners.
Captain F. P. Nosworthy, R.E., 3rd Sappers and Miners.
Captain E. K. Squires, R.E., No. 21 Company, 3rd Sappers and Miners.
Lieutenant F. E. Buller, R.E., 3rd Sappers and Miners.
Subadar Malla Singh, R.E., 3rd Sappers and Miners.
Subadar Gaurishankar Dube, 1st Sappers and Miners.
Lieutenant H. W. R. Hamilton, R.E., 3rd Sappers and Miners.
Lieutenant A. Mason, R.E., 3rd Sappers and Miners.
Second Lieutenant H. M. Hance (I.A.R.O.), 176th Mining Company, R.E.

Order of British India, 2nd Class, with title of "Bahadur"

Subadar Sundar Singh, 1st Sappers and Miners.
Subadar Gaurishankar Dube, 1st Sappers and Miners.
Subadar Ganpat Mahadeo, 3rd Sappers and Miners.
Subadar Ismail Khan, 3rd Sappers and Miners.
Jemadar Sada Singh, 1st Sappers and Miners.

Indian Order of Merit, 2nd Class

Subadar Malla Singh, 3rd Sappers and Miners.
Jemadar Ram Rup Singh, No. 3 Company, 1st Sappers and Miners.
No. 2479 Havildar Muhammad Khan, No. 20 Company, 3rd Sappers and Miners.
No. 3795 Sapper Dalip Singh, No. 20 Company, 3rd Sappers and Miners.
No. 2192 Sapper Shaikh Abdul Rahman, 1st Sappers and Miners.
No. 1694 Sapper Jiwa Khan, 1st Sappers and Miners.
Jemadar Uttam Singh, 20th Company, 3rd Sappers and Miners.
Jemadar Liyakat Ali, 21st Company, 3rd Sappers and Miners.

No. 3144 Driver Havildar Muhammad Baksh, 21st Company, 3rd Sappers and Miners.

No. 3108 Naik Gurmukh Singh, 21st Company, 3rd Sappers and Miners.

Indian Distinguished Service Medal

Subadar Sundar Singh, No. 4 Company, 1st Sappers and Miners.

Jemadar Abdul Aziz, 1st Sappers and Miners.

Jemadar Mehar Baksh, 1st Sappers and Miners.

Jemadar Niamutullah, No. 4 Company, 1st Sappers and Miners.

Jemadar Gangacharan Dikshit, 3rd Sappers and Miners (deceased).

Jemadar Ismail Khan, 3rd Sappers and Miners.

Jemadar Nur Alam, 20th Company, 3rd Sappers and Miners.

Colour-Havildar Chagatta, I.O.M., 1st Sappers and Miners.

No. 322 Havildar Sucha Singh, 1st Sappers and Miners.

No. 3144 Driver Havildar Mahamed Baksh, 21st Company, 3rd Sappers and Miners.

Sapper Suba Singh, 1st Sappers and Miners.

Jemadar Ali Bahadur, No. 20 Company, 3rd Sappers and Miners.

Jemadar Data Din Badhai, No. 21 Company, 3rd Sappers and Miners.

No. 4052 Sapper Indar Singh, 20th Company, 3rd Sappers and Miners.

No. 708 Sapper Basant Singh, No. 2 Field Squadron.

No. 312 Havildar Basant Singh, No. 4 Company, 1st (K.G.O.) Sappers and Miners.

No. 1910 Lance-Naik Hari Singh, No. 4 Company, 1st (K.G.O.) Sappers and Miners.

Subadar Fazl Shah, No. 3 Company, 1st Sappers and Miners.

No. 859 Naik Magh Singh, No. 4 Company, 1st Sappers and Miners.

No. 1029 Lance-Naik Bhawani Dutt, No. 3 Company, 1st Sappers and Miners.

No. 3348 Havildar Maraoti Jadhao, 21st Company, 3rd Sappers and Miners.

No. 2720 Naik Harnam Singh, 20th Company, 3rd Sappers and Miners.

No. 2869 Lance-Naik Shaikh Ramzan, 21st Company, 3rd Sappers and Miners.

No. 3450 Sapper Saleh Muhammad, 21st Company, 3rd Sappers and Miners.

Russian Cross of the Order of St. George, 4th Class

Jemadar Chagatta, I.O.M., 1st Sappers and Miners.
Subadar Ismail Khan, 3rd Sappers and Miners.
No. 3795 Naik Dalip Singh, 3rd Sappers and Miners.

Russian Medal of St. George, 2nd Class

No. 1007 Havildar Nowsher Khan, 1st Sappers and Miners.

Russian Medal of St. George, 3rd Class

No. 1773 Sapper Channan Singh, 1st Sappers and Miners.

SPECIAL PROMOTIONS IN THE FIELD

To be Havildar

No. 2779 Naik Liyakat Ali, 3rd Sappers and Miners.

To be Naik

No. 3056 Lance-Naik Fazl Din, 3rd Sappers and Miners.
No. 3132 Lance-Naik Narayan Ranowde, 3rd Sappers and Miners.
No. 3134 Lance-Naik Bhan Ranowde, 3rd Sappers and Miners.

SIGNAL COMPANIES

Distinguished Service Order

Major W. F. Maxwell, R.E., Lahore Divisional Signal Company.
Captain C. J. Torrie, 30th Punjabis, 35th Signal Company.
Major H. S. E. Franklin, 15th Sikhs, 31st Divisional Signal Company.

Military Cross

Lieutenant F. C. de Butts, 55th Rifles, 31st Divisional Signal Company.

Order of British India, 2nd Class, with title of " Bahadur "

Subadar Qasim Ali, 31st Divisional Signal Company.

Indian Order of Merit, 2nd Class

Jemadar Alah Rakkha Khan, Lahore Divisional Signal Company.

Indian Distinguished Service Medal

No. 91 Sapper Bawani Singh, Lahore Signal Company.
No. 13 Naik Bari Sher, 62nd Punjabis, Meerut Signal Company.
No. 44 Naik Khan Zaman, Lahore Signal Company.

No. 23 Lance-Naik Mushtak Husain, Lahore Signal Company.

No. 45 Sapper Ghulam Ayud Din, Lahore Signal Company.

No. 1209 Naik Imam Shah, 62nd Punjabis, Meerut Signal Company.

No. 2616 Sepoy Mihan Singh, 93rd Burma Infantry, Meerut Signal Company.

No. 42 Sapper Jai Singh, " A " Section, Indian Signal Company.

No. 4204 Sapper Changa, " C " Section, Lahore Divisional Signal Company.

No. 7 Sapper Gujar Singh, " C " Section, Lahore Divisional Signal Company.

Dafadar Mangal Singh, 33rd Light Cavalry (attached Meerut Signal Company).

No. 1776 Sepoy Bhagat Singh, 90th Punjabis (attached Meerut Signal Company).

No. 2636 Sepoy Sucha Singh, 92nd Punjabis (attached Meerut Signal Company).

No. 3475 Sepoy Jetta Singh, 107th Pioneers (attached Meerut Signal Company).

INFANTRY

6TH JAT LIGHT INFANTRY

Companion of the Bath

Lieut.-Colonel H. J. Roche.

Distinguished Service Order

Major P. H. Dundas.
Captain R. C. Ross.

Military Cross

Lieutenant C. J. Cockburn.
Captain J. de la H. Gordon.
Captain A. B. Macpherson.
Jemadar Incha Ram.
Jemadar Lakhi Ram.

Order of British India, 2nd Class, with title of " Bahadur "

Subadar Shib Lal.
Subadar Inchha Ram.

Indian Order of Merit, 2nd Class

No. 1821 Havildar Jai Lal.

Indian Distinguished Service Medal

Subadar Parshadi Singh (113th Infantry, attached).
Jemadar Lakhi Ram.
No. 1548 Havildar Badlu.
No. 3426 Sepoy Risal.
No. 1696 Havildar Harpul.
No. 2685 Lance-Naik Maru.
No. 1004 Sepoy Bagmal.
No. 1574 Havildar Mula.
No. 2960 Sepoy Rambhagat.
Subadar Ratna.
No. 1757 Havildar Har Lal.
No. 2822 Naik Hardwari.
No. 3106 Bugler Bhup Singh.
No. 3415 Sepoy Lehri.

Russian Cross of the Order of St. George, 4th Class

No. 2693 Havildar Debi Sahai.

9TH BHOPAL INFANTRY
Military Cross

Captain G. D. Martin.

Indian Distinguished Service Medal

Subadar-Major Bhure Singh.
No. 2206 Havildar Amar Singh.
No. 2069 Sepoy Abdul Latif.
No. 2867 Naik Angad Pande.

Russian Medal of St. George, 2nd Class

Subadar Nazir Khan.

Brevet Major

Captain C. H. Jardine (96th Berar Infantry, attached).

15TH LUDHIANA SIKHS
Victoria Cross

Lieutenant J. G. Smyth.

Distinguished Service Order

Captain J. A. S. Daniell (14th Sikhs, attached).
Major H. S. E. Franklin.

Military Cross

Lieutenant A. E. Barstow.
Captain R. J. MacBrayne.
Jemadar Bir Singh.

Indian Order of Merit, 2nd Class

No. 4011 Havildar Bishan Singh.
No. 698 Sepoy Bakshi Singh.
No. 529 Sepoy Tilok Singh.
No. 131 Lance-Naik Mangal Singh.
No. 4727 Havildar Mahan Singh.

Indian Distinguished Service Medal

Jemadar Wazir Singh (died of wounds).
Jemadar Bir Singh.
No. 4576 Naik Bishn Singh.
No. 702 Sepoy Lal Singh.
No. 638 Sepoy Sucha Singh.
No. 962 Sepoy Sapuran Singh.
No. 1255 Sepoy Sarain Singh (19th Punjabis, attached).
No. 1036 Sepoy Fateh Singh (45th Sikhs, attached).
No. 1001 Sepoy Ujagar Singh (45th Sikhs, attached).
No. 1249 Sepoy Sundar Singh (19th Punjabis, attached).
No. 1339 Sepoy Ganda Singh (19th Punjabis, attached).
No. 1360 Sepoy Harnam Singh (19th Punjabis, attached).
No. 4474 Lance-Naik Kesar Singh.
No. 53 Lance-Naik Bhagwan Singh.
No. 219 Sepoy Diwan Singh.
No. 435 Sepoy Dan Singh.
No. 4095 Sepoy Lal Singh.

Russian Order of St. George, 4th Class

Lieutenant J. G. Smyth, V.C.

Russian Medal of St. George, 1st Class

No. 4727 Havildar Mahan Singh.

Brevet Colonel

Lieut.-Colonel J. Hill, D.S.O.

Brevet Lieutenant-Colonel

Major C. A. Vivian (killed in action).

26TH PUNJABIS
Distinguished Service Order

Captain (temporary Major) G. O. Turnbull (attached 6th Service Battalion Royal Scots Fusiliers).

29TH PUNJABIS
Brevet Major

Captain (temporary Major) S. D. Massy (attached Royal Flying Corps).

30TH PUNJABIS
Order of British India, 2nd Class, with title of "Bahadur"

Subadar Diwan Singh.

34TH SIKH PIONEERS
Companion of St. Michael and St. George

Lieut.-Colonel E. H. S. Cullen, M.V.O., D.S.O.

Military Cross

Captain C. E. Hunt.
Captain G. F. J. Paterson.
Subadar Sant Singh.

Order of British India, 2nd Class, with title of "Bahadur"

Subadar Natha Singh (II.), I.O.M.

Indian Order of Merit, 2nd Class

Subadar Natha Singh (II.).
No. 1871 Havildar Nikka Singh.
No. 1148 Havildar Pala Singh.
No. 4563 Sepoy Mastan Singh.
No. 2775 Lance-Naik Tota Singh.
No. 2071 Naik Bir Singh.
Subadar-Major Jwala Singh, "Sardar Bahadur."
No. 1907 Naik Guja Singh.
Jemadar Kharak Singh (32nd Sikh Pioneers, attached).
No. 3623 Havildar Mangal Singh (32nd Sikh Pioneers, attached).
Jemadar Maingha Singh (12th Pioneers, attached).

Indian Distinguished Service Medal

Subadar Sher Singh.
Subadar Wasawa Singh (32nd Pioneers, attached).

No. 1452 Havildar Narayan Singh.
No. 2578 Sepoy Ishar Singh.
No. 3063 Sepoy Sant Singh.
No. 3013 Sepoy Gopal Singh.
No. 2398 Sepoy Katha Singh.
No. 1576 Havildar Prem Singh.

Russian Medal of St. George, 3rd Class
No. 4563 Sepoy Mastan Singh (32nd Pioneers, attached).

Russian Medal of St. George, 4th Class
No. 1804 Lance-Naik Teja Singh (12th Pioneers, attached).

Brevet Lieutenant-Colonel
Major E. N. Heale (121st Pioneers, attached).

1ST BATTALION 39TH GARHWAL RIFLES
Victoria Cross
No. 1909 Naik Darwan Sing Negi.

Military Cross
Captain F. G. E. Lumb.
Captain J. T. H. Lane.
Lieutenant A. H. Mankelow (killed in action).
Second Lieutenant Rama Jodha Jang Bahadur (Indian Native
    Land Forces, attached).
Subadar Dhan Sing Negi.
Subadar Bishan Sing Rawat.

Order of British India, 2nd Class, with title of " Bahadur "
Subadar Jagat Sing Rawat, I.O.M.
Subadar Baij Sing Rawat.
Subadar Bije Sing Kandari.

Indian Order of Merit, 2nd Class
Jemadar Prem Sing Negi (killed in action).
No. 1810 Havildar Alam Sing Negi.
No. 2408 Lance-Naik Sankaru Gusain.
No. 2605 Lance-Naik Kiyali Gusain.
No. 1674 Rifleman Kalamu Bisht.
No. 2172 Rifleman Ghantu Rawat.
No. 1715 Rifleman Dhan Sing Negi.

No. 2417 Rifleman Partab Rana.
No. 2480 Rifleman Banchu Negi.
No. 2285 Rifleman Jawarihu Negi.
No. 4423 Sepoy Beli Ram (30th Punjabis, attached).

Indian Distinguished Service Medal

Subadar Kedar Sing Rawat.
Subadar Dan Sing Negi.
Jemadar Goman Sing Negi.
No. 1321 Lance-Naik Dangwa Ramola.
No. 1085 Rifleman Raichand Negi.
No. 1760 Rifleman Kutalu Bisht.
No. 2854 Rifleman Keshi Bisht.
No. 2697 Bugler Bhola Bisht.

Russian Cross of the Order of St. George, 4th Class

No. 1729 Havildar Padam Sing Rawat.

Russian Medal of St. George, 4th Class

No. 2103 Lance-Naik Jit Sing Negi.

Brevet Colonel

Lieut.-Colonel E. R. Swiney.

2ND BATTALION 39TH GARHWAL RIFLES

Victoria Cross

No. 1685 Rifleman Gobar Sing Negi (deceased).

Companion of St. Michael and St. George

Lieut.-Colonel D. H. Drake-Brockman.

Distinguished Service Order

Captain G. W. Burton (killed in action).

Military Cross

Subadar Nain Sing Chinwarh.
Jemadar Pancham Sing Mahar.
Jemadar Sangram Sing Negi.

Order of British India, 2nd Class, with title of " Bahadur "

Subadar Nain Sing Chinwar.
Subadar Makhar Sing Kawar.

Indian Order of Merit, 2nd Class

No. 762 Havildar Butha Sing Negi.
No. 463 Naik Baktwar Sing Bisht.
No. 1283 Naik Jaman Sing Bisht.
No. 541 Rifleman Madan Sing Rawat.
No. 1342 Rifleman Ganesh Sing Sajwan.

Indian Distinguished Service Medal

Jemadar Lachman Sing Rawat.
No. 617 Havildar Bir Sing Danu.
No. —— Havildar Ranjir Sing Pandir.
No. —— Havildar Diwan Sing Padhujar.
No. 1480 Naik Kedar Sing Mahar.
No. 289 Rifleman Kesar Sing Rana.
No. 870 Rifleman Nain Sing Rawat.
No. 1598 Rifleman Chandar Sing Negi.
No. 1465 Rifleman Gopal Sing Pharswan.

Russian Medal of St. George, 3rd Class

No. 1211 Rifleman Man Sing Bisht.

Russian Medal of St. George, 4th Class

No. 1448 Rifleman Karam Sing Rithal.

40TH PATHANS

Military Cross

Lieutenant F. C. G. Campbell.
Lieutenant F. L. R. Munn (46th Punjabis, attached).

Indian Order of Merit, 2nd Class

Jemadar Lehna Singh.
Subadar Jahandad Khan, " Bahadur."
No. 4551 Havildar Abas Khan.

Indian Distinguished Service Medal

No. 3435 Sepoy Haidar Ali.
No. 3362 Colour-Havildar Shiraz.

Russian Medal of St. George, 4th Class

No. 3893 Sepoy Muktiara.

41st Dogras

Companion of St. Michael and St. George

Lieut.-Colonel C. W. Tribe.

Distinguished Service Order

Lieut.-Colonel II. W. Cruddas.
Major and Brevet Lieut.-Colonel C. A. R. Hutchinson.

Military Cross

Captain W. E. Fleming.
Lieutenant E. L. E. Lindop.
Captain R. M. F. Patrick (42nd Deoli Regiment, attached).
Captain R. M. Brind (37th Dogras, attached).

Order of British India, 2nd Class, with title of " Bahadur "

Subadar Mehar Singh.
Subadar Sundar Singh.

Indian Order of Merit, 2nd Class

No. 1011 Havildar Gujar Singh (38th Dogras, attached).

Indian Distinguished Service Medal

No. 409 Havildar Saudagar Singh.
No. 1090 Lance-Naik Jamit Singh.
No. 306 Sepoy Sidhu.
Subadar Mehar Singh, " Bahadur."
Jemadar Gujar Singh, I.O.M.
No. 547 Naik Surjan Singh.
No. 1389 Lance-Naik Dhiyan Singh.
No. 4902 Sepoy Albel Singh (29th Punjabis, attached).
No. 2061 Sepoy Thakur Diyal.

Russian Cross of the Order of St. George, 3rd Class

Subadar Jai Singh.

Russian Medal of St. George, 4th Class

No. 1033 Lance-Naik Devi Singh.

47th Sikhs

Companion of St. Michael and St. George

Lieut.-Colonel O. G. Gunning (35th Sikhs, attached).

Military Cross

Captain A. M. Brown (killed in action).

Lieutenant G. S. Brunskill.
Lieutenant A. E. Drysdale.
Captain S. B. Combe.
Captain R. F. Francis.
Captain W. H. Ralston.
Subadar Thakur Singh.

Order of British India, 2nd Class, with title of " Bahadur "
Subadar Saudagar Singh.

Indian Order of Merit, 2nd Class
Subadar Bakshi Singh.
Subadar Harnam Singh (killed in action).
Jemadar Sucha Singh.
No. 231 Havildar (now Jemadar) Narain Singh.
No. 337 Havildar Lachman Singh.
No. 514 Havildar Gajjan Singh.
No. 2270 Sepoy Rur Singh.
No. 2277 Sepoy Bhagwan Singh (36th Sikhs, attached).
No. 2103 Havildar Bir Singh (35th Sikhs, attached).
No. 2479 Lance-Havildar Lal Singh (35th Sikhs, attached).
Subadar Mota Singh (killed in action).

Indian Distinguished Service Medal
No. 355 Naik Jagat Singh.
No. 1336 Naik Mota Singh.
No. 1189 Naik Mit Singh.
No. 1791 Sepoy Waryam Singh.
No. 3201 Sepoy Asa Singh (35th Sikhs, attached).
No. 228 Havildar Bhola Singh.
No. 1410 Sepoy Kesar Singh.
No. 2266 Sepoy Buta Singh.
No. 482 Havildar Bhagat Singh.
No. 1308 Sepoy Kehr Singh.
No. 337 Havildar Lachman Singh.
No. 2116 Naik Kishen Singh.
No. 2882 Havildar Mula Singh (35th Sikhs, attached).

Russian Cross of the Order of St. George, 3rd Class
No. 337 Havildar Lachman Singh.

Russian Cross of the Order of St. George, 4th Class
Jemadar Mota Singh.

Brevet Colonel

Lieut.-Colonel H. L. Richardson.

Brevet Lieutenant-Colonel

Major S. R. Davidson.

SPECIAL PROMOTION IN THE FIELD
To be Havildar

Naik Bhagat Singh.

57TH (WILDE'S) RIFLES (FRONTIER FORCE)
Victoria Cross

Jemadar Mir Dast, I.O.M. (55th Coke's Rifles, F.F., attached).

Companion of St. Michael and St. George

Lieut.-Colonel F. W. B. Gray, D.S.O.

Distinguished Service Order

Major T. J. Willans.

Military Cross

Captain D. H. Acworth (55th Rifles, attached).
Lieutenant E. K. Fowler.
Lieutenant D. B. Mein (55th Rifles, attached).
Lieutenant D. Bainbridge.
Lieutenant R. B. Deedes (31st Punjabis, attached).
Subadar Arsla Khan, I.O.M.

Order of British India, 2nd Class, with title of " Bahadur "

Subadar Arsla Khan, I.O.M.
Subadar Imam Ali.

Indian Order of Merit, 2nd Class

Jemadar Mangal Singh.
No. 2584 Havildar Yakub Khan.
No. 2630 Havildar Gagna.
No. 2718 Lance-Naik Said Akbar.
No. 2554 Lance-Naik Lalak.
No. 3576 Sepoy Daulat Khan.
No. 1695 Sepoy Usman Khan (55th Rifles, attached).
No. 2609 Naik Atma Singh.
No. 2632 Sepoy Palla Ram.

Indian Distinguished Service Medal

Subadar Fatch Jang (died of wounds).
No. 1991 Havildar (now Jemadar) Bur Singh.
No. 2595 Havildar Karim Khan.
No. 2583 Naik Narayan.
No. 2760 Naik Sahib Sher.
No. 2063 Naik Sohan Singh.
No. 2589 Sepoy Bahadur Khan.
No. 2702 Sepoy Ram Saran.
No. 3484 Sepoy Alvas Khan.
No. 2108 Sepoy Mir Badshah.
No. 3119 Sepoy Mir Badshah.
No. 3223 Sepoy Mir Baz.
No. 2625 Sepoy Mehr Khan (55th Rifles, attached).
No. 2540 Havildar Sar Mast.
No. 5510 Sepoy Bhan Singh (Q.O. Corps of Guides, attached).

Russian Cross of the Order of St. George, 3rd Class

Subadar Mir Dast, V.C., I.O.M. (55th Rifles, attached).

Russian Cross of the Order of St. George, 4th Class

No. 2630 Havildar Gagna.

Russian Medal of St. George, 3rd Class

No. 5510 Sepoy Bhan Singh (Q.O. Corps of Guides, attached).

Russian Medal of St. George, 4th Class

No. 3361 Sepoy Sahib Jan.

SPECIAL PROMOTION
To be Naik

No. 3028 Lance-Naik Gul Hasham.

58TH (VAUGHAN'S) RIFLES (FRONTIER FORCE)
Distinguished Service Order

Major C. E. D. Davidson-Houston (killed in action).
Major A. G. Thomson.

Military Cross

Captain G. S. Bull.
Jemadar Indar Singh.
Jemadar Hawinda.

Order of British India, 2nd Class, with title of "Bahadur"

Subadar Abdul Ali.
Subadar Raj Talab.

Indian Order of Merit, 1st Class

Subadar Suhel Singh.

Indian Order of Merit, 2nd Class

Jemadar Harchand Singh.
Jemadar Suhel Singh.
Jemadar Muhammad Arabi.
No. 1811 Havildar Karam Singh.
No. 1848 Havildar Roshan Khan.
No. 3572 Havildar Saidak.
No. 3032 Lance-Naik Lal Badshah.
No. 2834 Lance-Naik Sher Khan.
No. 2742 Sepoy Isar Singh.
No. 1925 Havildar Santa Singh.
No. 2830 Naik Kashmir Singh.
No. 3131 Lance-Naik Phangan Singh.

Indian Distinguished Service Medal

Subadar Raj Talab.
Subadar Phuman Singh (died of wounds).
Jemadar Hamid.
Jemadar Indar Singh.
No. 2008 Havildar (now Jemadar) Hawinda.
No. 2763 Havildar Arjun.
No. 3136 Havildar Sarfaraz.
No. 2164 Havildar Sundar Singh.
No. 3212 Havildar Lashkar.
No. 2198 Havildar Fazl Dad.
No. 2758 Naik Dewa Singh.
No. 2634 Naik Zargun Shah.
No. 3404 Naik Baidullah.
No. 3066 Naik Sardar.
No. 3080 Naik Zar Baz.
No. 3567 Lance-Naik Said Asghar.
No. 3374 Sepoy Dewa Singh.
No. 3133 Sepoy Maluk Singh.

Russian Cross of the Order of St. George, 4th Class

No. 3080 Naik Zar Baz.

Russian Medal of St. George, 3rd Class

No. 3457 Naik Safirullah.

Russian Medal of St. George, 4th Class

No. 3156 Sepoy Banta Singh.

59TH SCINDE RIFLES (FRONTIER FORCE)

Military Cross

Lieutenant J. A. M. Scobie.
Captain R. D. Inskip.
Subadar Parbat Chand.

Order of British India, 1st Class, with title of " Sardar Bahadur "

Subadar-Major Nasir Khan.

Indian Order of Merit, 1st Class

No. 27 Sepoy Zarif Khan.

Indian Order of Merit, 2nd Class

No. 3063 Havildar Abdul Wahab.
No. 3191 Havildar Dost Muhammad.
No. 3638 Havildar Muhammad Jan.
No. 3663 Havildar Muzaffar Khan.
No. 3705 Lance-Naik Buta Singh.
No. 3902 Lance-Naik Biaz Gul.
No. 27 Sepoy Zarif Khan.
Subadar-Major Nasir Khan, " Sardar Bahadur."

Indian Distinguished Service Medal

Subadar-Major Muhammad Khan.
Jemadar Zaman Ali.
No. 4264 Havildar Niaz Gul.
No. 3529 Naik Amir Ali.
No. 3581 Naik Ghammai Khan.
No. 2520¼ Lance-Naik Chur Khan (52nd Sikhs, F.F., attached).
No. 4845 Sepoy Akbar Khan.
No. 4731 Sepoy Lal Khan.
Subadar Bishan Singh.
Jemadar Mangal Singh (52nd Sikhs, F.F., attached).

Russian Medal of St. George, 1st Class

Subadar-Major Nasir Khan.

Russian Medal of St. George, 2nd Class

No. 3063 Havildar Abdul Wahab, I.O.M.

Russian Medal of St. George, 4th Class

No. 3890 Sepoy (Ward Orderly) Sadardin (attached 112th Indian Field Ambulance).

Brevet Lieutenant-Colonel

Major (temporary Lieut.-Colonel) T. L. Leeds.

Brevet Major

Captain B. E. Anderson.

89TH PUNJABIS

Military Cross

Captain R. F. D. Burnett (42nd Deoli Regiment, attached).

Indian Order of Merit, 2nd Class

No. 2316 Sepoy Indar Singh.
No. 3275 Sepoy Suleiman.
No. 1088 Colour-Havildar Hira Tiwari.

Indian Distinguished Service Medal

No. 1528 Havildar Harnam Singh.
No. 2352 Naik Muhammad Sadik.
No. 2029 Naik Ramji Misr.
No. 1485 Naik Karam Dad.
No. 2102 Sepoy Muhammad Khan.

107TH PIONEERS

Companion of St. Michael and St. George

Lieut.-Colonel N. M. C. Stevens.

Distinguished Service Order

Captain A. T. Sheringham (121st Pioneers, attached).

Military Cross

Captain E. B. Mangin.
Lieutenant F. H. F. Hornor.
Lieutenant B. H. Wallis.

2 B

Order of British India, 2nd Class, with title of "Bahadur "
Subadar-Major Labh Singh.
Subadar Hashmat Dad Khan.

Indian Order of Merit, 2nd Class
Subadar Khan Zaman.
No. 4050 Bugler Nathu Singh.

Indian Distinguished Service Medal
Subadar Labh Singh.
Subadar Hashmat Dad Khan.
No. 3417 Havildar Bhagat Singh.
No. 2980 Naik Achar Singh.
No. 3991 Sepoy Phaga Singh.
Subadar Fateh Muhammad Khan.
No. 1027 Havildar Dal Khan (121st Pioneers, attached).

Russian Cross of the Order of St. George, 4th Class
No. 2762 Sepoy Sundar Singh.

125TH (NAPIER'S) RIFLES
Military Cross
Captain W. F. Odell (123rd Rifles, attached).

Order of British India, 2nd Class, with title of "Bahadur "
Subadar-Major Umar Din.

Indian Distinguished Service Medal
No. 2602 Sepoy Gul Sher.

129TH (DUKE OF CONNAUGHT'S OWN) BALUCHIS
𝔙ictoria 𝔠ross
No. 4050 Sepoy Khudadad.

Companion of St. Michael and St. George
Lieut.-Colonel W. M. Southey.

Distinguished Service Order
Major J. A. Hannyngton, C.M.G.
Captain R. F. Dill (killed in action).
Major H. Hulseberg (127th Baluch Light Infantry, attached).

Military Cross

Lieutenant F. M. Griffith-Griffin.
Lieutenant H. V. Lewis.
Captain C. M. Thornhill (24th Punjabis, attached).
Subadar Zaman Khan.

Order of British India, 2nd Class, with title of " Bahadur "

Subadar Zaman Khan.
Subadar Makmad Azam, I.O.M.

Indian Order of Merit, 2nd Class

Subadar Makmad Azam.
Jemadar Mir Badshah.
Jemadar Ayub Khan (124th Baluchis, attached).
No. 4280 Naik Sar Nir.
No. 118 Lance-Naik Nek Amal.
No. 3814 Lance-Naik Hobab Gul.
No. 453 Sepoy Sahib Jan.
No. 250 Sepoy Saiday Khan.
No. 4333 Sepoy Redi Gul.
No. 2524 Colour-Havildar Ghulam Muhammad.
No. 471 Sepoy Raji Khan.
No. 3836 Havildar Fatch Haidar.

Indian Distinguished Service Medal

No. 2268 Havildar Nur Khan.
No. 105 Sepoy Kassib.
No. 2813 Sepoy Lal Sher.
No. 3600 Sepoy Lafar Khan.
No. 4182 Sepoy Said Ahmad.
No. 2102 Sepoy Aulia Khan.
No. 4267 Sepoy Mehrab Gul.
No. 4231 Sepoy Ghulam Hussein (124th Baluchistan Infantry, attached).
No. 4305 Sepoy Mistakin.
No. 246 Sepoy Dad Khan (127th Baluchis, attached).

Russian Cross of the Order of St. George, 4th Class

No. 118 Sepoy Nek Amal, I.O.M.

Russian Medal of St. George, 1st Class

No. 4355 Havildar Wasim Khan.

Russian Medal of St. George, 4th Class

No. 3836 Sepoy Fateh Haidar.

SPECIAL PROMOTION IN THE FIELD

To be Naik

No. 3640 Lance-Naik Ayub Khan (124th Baluchis, attached).

1ST BATTALION 1ST KING GEORGE'S OWN GURKHA RIFLES

Companion of St. Michael and St. George

Lieut.-Colonel W. C. Anderson.

Military Cross

Captain A. R. Mellis (Indian Army Reserve of Officers, attached).

Indian Order of Merit, 2nd Class

Jemadar Sasidhar Thapa.
No. 1843 Naik Ramkishan Thapa.
No. 2205 Rifleman Balbir Thapa.
No. 2719 Rifleman Jitman Thapa.
Subadar Jit Sing Gurung (2nd Battalion 3rd Gurkha Rifles, attached).
Subadar Autbir Thapa (2nd Battalion 4th Gurkha Rifles, attached).
Jemadar Kharakbir Thapa (2nd Battalion 4th Gurkha Rifles, attached).

Indian Distinguished Service Medal

No. 2814 Rifleman Bahram Thapa.
No. 2515 Rifleman Kansi Gurung.
No. 2734 Rifleman Khamba Sing Gurung.
No. 2397 Rifleman Phalman Gurung.
No. 1946 Rifleman Lalbir Thapa.
No. 2650 Rifleman Chitabir Thapa.

Russian Cross of the Order of St. George, 4th Class

Subadar Puran Sing Gurung.
No. 2719 Rifleman Jitman Thapa, I.O.M.

Russian Medal of St. George, 3rd Class

No. 2205 Rifleman Balbir Thapa.

2ND BATTALION 2ND KING EDWARD'S OWN GURKHA RIFLES

Distinguished Service Order

Major D. M. Watt.
Major F. H. Noric (Indian Army retired, attached).

Military Cross

Captain A. D. Smith (1st Battalion 2nd Gurkha Rifles, attached).
Lieutenant E. J. Corse-Scott.
Lieutenant G. A. P. Scoones.
Subadar Kharak Sing Rana.

Order of British India, 2nd Class, with title of "Bahadur"

Subadar-Major Fateh Sing Newar.
Subadar Sarabjit Gurung, I.O.M. (1st Battalion, attached).

Indian Order of Merit, 2nd Class

Subadar Dan Sing Lama.
Jemadar Arjun Rana.
No. 1618 Naik Padamdhoj Gurung.
No. 1959 Rifleman Bhagat Bahadur Gurung.
No. 2265 Rifleman Tula Gurung.
No. 2515 Rifleman Hastobir Roka.
No. 3266 Rifleman Jagtea Pun.
No. 4024 Rifleman Manjit Gurung.
No. 2447 Rifleman Partiman Gurung.
No. 1599 Rifleman Ujir Sing Gurung.
No. 1597 Naik Bum Bahadur Gurung.
No. 2693 Rifleman Anarupe Rana.

Indian Distinguished Service Medal

No. 1222 Havildar Ran Patti Gurung.
No. 1280 Havildar Judhia Sarki.
No. 1432 Havildar Janglai Gurung.
No. 1628 Havildar Bag Sing Thapa.
No. 1473 Naik Ramparshad Thapa.
No. 1517 Naik Bhimbahadur Thapa.
No. 1679 Naik Gamer Sing Bura.
No. 1593 Naik Patiram Thapa.
No. 2153 Lance-Naik Sher Sing Ghale.
No. 2392 Lance-Naik Amar Sing Pun.
No. 2618 Rifleman Kalu Grung.

Russian Cross of the Order of St. George, 4th Class

No. 3184 Havildar Sarabjit Gurung.

Brevet Colonel

Lieut.-Colonel C. E. de M. Norie, D.S.O.

Brevet Lieutenant-Colonel

Major S. B. Boileau (1st Battalion 2nd Gurkha Rifles, attached).

2ND BATTALION 3RD QUEEN ALEXANDRA'S OWN GURKHA RIFLES

𝔙𝔦𝔠𝔱𝔬𝔯𝔦𝔞 𝔠𝔯𝔬𝔰𝔰

No. 2129 Rifleman Kulbir Thapa.

Companion of the Bath

Lieut.-Colonel V. A. Ormsby.

Distinguished Service Order

Captain J. T. Lodwick.

Military Cross

Lieutenant H. C. F. McSwiney.

Order of British India, 2nd Class, with title of "Bahadur"

Subadar-Major Gambhir Sing Gurung.
Subadar Kharak Bahadur Thapa.

Indian Order of Merit, 2nd Class

Subadar-Major Gambhir Sing Gurung.
Subadar Bhim Sing Thapa.
Jemadar Harak Bahadur Thapa (deceased).
No. 1569 Havildar Bahadur Thapa.
No. 1805 Lance-Naik Hark Sing Gharti.
No. 1757 Lance-Naik Jhaman Sing Thapa.
No. 1749 Rifleman Gane Gurung.
No. 2252 Bugler Kharak Bahadur Ale.

Indian Distinguished Service Medal

Subadar Baru Sing Thapa.
Jemadar Puran Sing Thapa.
No. 1313 Havildar Motilal Gurung.
No. 2118 Rifleman Ganpati Thapa.

Russian Cross of the Order of St. George, 4th Class

Subadar Dalkesar Gurung.

Russian Medal of St. George, 2nd Class

No. 1760 Naik Rupdan Pun.

Russian Medal of St. George, 3rd Class

No. 3530 Rifleman Kharkbir Pun.

1ST BATTALION 4TH GURKHA RIFLES
Distinguished Service Order
Captain L. P. Collins.
Captain A. T. Cramer-Roberts.
Captain C. D. Roe.

Military Cross
Lieutenant C. F. F. Moore (123rd Outram's Rifles, attached).
Second Lieutenant C. C. E. Manson (I.A.R.O., attached).

Order of British India, 2nd Class, with title of " Bahadur "
Subadar Senbir Gurung (2nd Battalion, attached).

Indian Order of Merit, 2nd Class
Subadar Senbir Gurung.
Jemadar Gangabir Gurung.
No. 4252 Naik Diwan Sing Gurung.
No. 4015 Rifleman Khamba Sing Gurung.
No. 4509 Rifleman Parbir Gurung.
No. 4578 Rifleman Wazir Singh Burathoki.
No. 1840 Havildar Bhakat Sing Rana (2nd Battalion 4th Gurkha Rifles, attached).
No. 2417 Rifleman Bhandoj Rai.

Indian Distinguished Service Medal
No. 4203 Rifleman Deotinarain Newar.
No. 3994 Rifleman Patiram Kunwar.
No. 798 Lance-Naik Asbir Rana.
No. 4945 Lance-Naik Lachman Gurung.
No. 1074 Rifleman Garbha Sing Gurung.

Russian Medal of St. George, 3rd Class
No. 4578 Rifleman Wazir Sing Burathoki.

2ND BATTALION 8TH GURKHA RIFLES
Distinguished Service Order
Captain G. C. Buckland.

Order of British India, 2nd Class, with title of " Bahadur "
Subadar Shamsher Gurung.

Indian Order of Merit, 2nd Class
No. 3110 Havildar Hari Parshad Thapa.
Subadar Sarabjit Gurung.

No. 1632 Rifleman Narbahadur Gurung (Naga Hills Military Police Battalion, attached).

No. 1348 Rifleman Budhiman Thapa (Chin Hills Military Police Battalion, attached).

Russian Medal of St. George, 4th Class

No. 4078 Rifleman Dhamraj Thapa.

1ST BATTALION 9TH GURKHA RIFLES

Companion of the Bath

Lieut.-Colonel G. T. Widdicombe.

Military Cross

Captain J. R. L. Heyland (killed in action).

Captain G. D. Pike.

Lieutenant L. C. C. Rogers (1st Battalion 7th Gurkha Rifles, attached; died of wounds).

Lieutenant R. G. H. Murray.

Subadar Haridhoj Khattri.

Subadar Bakht Bahadur Adhikari.

Order of British India, 2nd Class, with title of " Bahadur "

Subadar Balbahadar Khattri.

Subadar Chandrabir Thapa.

Indian Order of Merit, 2nd Class

Subadar Mehar Sing Khattri.

Jemadar Shibdhoj Mal.

No. 2016 Lance-Naik Jhaman Sing Khattri (2nd Battalion, attached).

No. 2721 Rifleman Panchbir Mal (2nd Battalion, attached).

No. 2589 Rifleman Tika Ram Kunwar.

Indian Distinguished Service Medal

Subadar Chandrabir Thapa.

Subadar Haridhoj Khattri.

Jemadar Damodhar Khattri.

No. 1922 Havildar Gambhir Sing Bohra.

No. 1515 Havildar Lalit Bahadur Mal.

No. 2017 Naik Kharak Bahadur Basnet.

No. 2027 Naik Kulman Khattri.

No. 2096 Lance-Naik Jowar Sing Khattri.

No. 2118 Lance-Naik Samar Bahadur Mal.

No. 2314 Lance-Naik Sirikisan Khattri.
No. 2772 Rifleman Manbahadur Sahi.
No. 2799 Rifleman Kharak Bahadur Bhandari.
No. 2588 Rifleman Dhan Bahadur.
No. 2492 Rifleman Gajbir Bisht.
No. 2885 Rifleman Balbahadur Khattri.
No. 3055 Rifleman Ranbahadur Sahi.
No. 3075 Rifleman Dinbahadur Kunwar.

Russian Cross of the Order of St. George, 4th Class
Subadar Bakht Bahadur Adhikari.

Russian Medal of St. George, 3rd Class
No. 2589 Rifleman Tika Ram Kunwar.

SPECIAL PROMOTION IN THE FIELD
To be Havildar
No. 2721 Rifleman Panchbir Mal, 2nd Battalion 9th Gurkha Rifles (attached to 1st Battalion).

UNATTACHED LIST, INDIAN ARMY
Military Cross

Second Lieutenant A. C. Curtis (attached 1st Bedfordshire Regiment).
Second Lieutenant C. S. Searle (attached 1st Royal Berkshire Regiment).
Second Lieutenant (temporary Lieutenant) A. F. Logan (attached 2nd Battalion Bedfordshire Regiment).
Lieutenant (temporary Captain) T. Layng (attached Durham Light Infantry).
Second Lieutenant (temporary Lieutenant) C. H. H. Eales (attached 2nd Battalion Royal Irish Rifles).
Second Lieutenant (temporary Lieutenant) F. Powell (attached Bedfordshire Regiment).

MEDICAL SERVICES
Companion of the Bath
Colonel B. B. Grayfoot, M.D., I.M.S.

Companion of St. Michael and St. George
Lieut.-Colonel C. H. Bowle-Evans, M.B., I.M.S. (attached 8th Gurkha Rifles).

Lieut.-Colonel F. Wall, I.M.S. (attached 3rd Gurkha Rifles).
Major H. M. Cruddas, I.M.S.
Lieut.-Colonel J. A. Hamilton, M.B., F.R.C.S.
Major W. W. Jeudwine, M.D.

Distinguished Service Order

Captain J. Taylor (attached 1st Battalion 39th Garhwal Rifles).
Major G. C. L. Kerans, I.M.S.
Major R. A. Needham, M.B.

Military Cross

Captain Kunwar Indarjit Singh (attached 57th Rifles; killed in action).
Captain J. S. O'Neill, M.B., I.M.S.
Third Class Assistant Surgeon F. B. A. Braganza, Indian Subordinate Medical Department.
Assistant Surgeon E. B. Messinier, Indian Subordinate Medical Department.
No. 298 Second Class Sub-Assistant Surgeon Ram Krishna Ganpat Shinde (attached 1st Battalion 39th Garhwal Rifles).
Captain H. S. C. Cormack, M.B., F.R.C.S., I.M.S.
Captain C. A. Wood, M.B., I.M.S.
First Class Assistant Surgeon W. J. S. Maine, I.S.M.D.
Third Class Assistant Surgeon E. H. Boilard, I.S.M.D.

Distinguished Conduct Medal

Third Class Assistant Surgeon K. P. Elloy, Indian Subordinate Medical Department, No. 7 British Field Ambulance.

Royal Red Cross Decoration, 1st Class

Miss H. A. M. Rait, Queen Alexandra's Military Nursing Service for India.
Miss P. F. Watt, Queen Alexandra's Military Nursing Service for India.

Royal Red Cross Decoration, 2nd Class

Miss M. D. Knapp, Queen Alexandra's Military Nursing Service for India.

Indian Order of Merit, 2nd Class

No. 1116 First Class Sub-Assistant Surgeon Nagindar Singh, Indian Subordinate Medical Department.

No. 128 Field Ambulance, No. 1124 First Class Sub-Assistant Surgeon Maula Baksh.

No. 111 Field Ambulance, No. 988 First Class Sub-Assistant Surgeon Tek Chand.

Third Class Sub-Assistant Surgeon G. K. R. Rane (attached 21st Company 3rd Sappers and Miners).

Sub-Assistant Surgeon Harnam Singh (attached 34th Sikh Pioneers).

Senior Sub-Assistant Surgeon Pandit Shankar Das (attached 47th Sikhs).

No. 111 Field Ambulance, No. 2421 Stretcher-bearer Jaganaut.

No. 8 Company Army Bearer Corps, No. 8001 Havildar Bihari.

No. 862 First Class Sub-Assistant Surgeon Ram Singh, I.S.M.D. (attached 1/4th Gurkha Rifles).

No. 1230 Second Class Sub-Assistant Surgeon Pargan Singh, I.S.M.D. (attached 6th Jat Light Infantry).

Indian Distinguished Service Medal

No. 7 Company Army Bearer Corps, No. 7032 Lance-Naik Surjoo.

No. 8 Company Army Bearer Corps, No. 8316 Bearer Ram Sabatu.

No. 8 Company Army Bearer Corps, No. 937 First Class Sub-Assistant Surgeon Muhammad Umar.

No. 8 Company Army Bearer Corps, No. 3039 Naik Achroo.

112th Indian Field Ambulance, First Class Senior Sub-Assistant Surgeon Gaure Shankar.

129th Indian Field Ambulance, No. 1171 2nd Class Sub-Assistant Surgeon Zafar Husain.

112th Indian Field Ambulance, No. 4009 Naik Wadhawa.

19th British Field Ambulance Army Bearer Corps, No. 7017 Naik Khushali.

20th British Field Ambulance Army Bearer Corps, No. 11018 Lance-Naik Surjoo.

1st Class Sub-Assistant Surgeon Narayan Parshad Sukal, 112th Field Ambulance.

2nd Class Senior Sub-Assistant Surgeon Mahadeo Parshad, attached 1st Battalion 1st Gurkha Rifles.

No. 8037 Lance-Naik Mangli, No. 8 Company, 113th Field Ambulance.

No. 772, 1st Class Sub-Assistant Surgeon Pohlo Ram, I.S.M.D. (attached 1/9th Gurkha Rifles).

No. 1246, 2nd Class Sub-Assistant Surgeon Kishan Singh, I.S.M.D. (attached 113th Indian Field Ambulance).

No. 1360, 3rd Class Sub-Assistant Surgeon Mathura Parshad Sarswıt, I.S.M.D. (attached 57th Wilde's Rifles (F.F.)).

No. 3000 Havildar Nıkka, No. 7 British Field Ambulance (Army Bearer Corps).

No. 7034 Lance-Naık Kundan, No. 19 British Field Ambulance (Army Bearer Corps).

No. 7052 Bearer Bhujjoo, No. 19 British Field Ambulance (Army Bearer Corps).

No. 7455 Bearer Mulloo, No. 19 British Field Ambulance (Army Bearer Corps).

No. 7339 Bearer Naıian, No. 19 British Field Ambulance (Army Bearer Corps).

No. 4349 Bearer Madan Sıngh, No. 112 Indian Field Ambulance (Army Bearer Corps).

No. 4397 Bearer Mastan Singh, No. 112 Indian Field Ambulance (Army Bearer Corps).

No. 7074 Lance-Naik Ram Charan, No. 128 Indian Field Ambulance (Army Bearer Corps).

No. 7204 Bearer Benı, No. 128 Indian Field Ambulance (Army Bearer Corps).

No. 7259 Bearer Chabi, No. 128 Indian Field Ambulance (Army Bearer Corps).

Russian Cross of the Order of St. George, 4th Class

3rd Class Assistant Surgeon K. P. Elloy, I.S.M.D., No. 7 British Field Ambulance.

Russian Medal of St. George, 2nd Class

3rd Class Sub-Assistant Surgeon Gopınath Agarwal, 128th Indian Field Ambulance.

Brevet Colonel

Lieut.-Colonel W. W. White, M.D., I.M.S.
Lieut.-Colonel A. H. Moorhead, M.B., I.M.S.

Brevet Lieut.-Colonel

Major H. Boulton, M.B., I.M.S.
Major G. Browse, M.B., I.M.S.

Senior Assistant Surgeon with Honorary Rank of Lieutenant

1st Class Assistant Surgeon W. J. S. Maine, I.S.M.D.

3rd Class Assistant Surgeon

4th Class Assistant-Surgeon E. R. Hill, I.S.M.D.

French Croix de Guerre

7204 Bearer Beni, 128th Field Ambulance.

SUPPLY AND TRANSPORT CORPS
Distinguished Service Order

Major A. K. Heyland.

Order of British India, 2nd Class, with title of "Bahadur"

Ressaidar Amir Khan, 2nd Mule Corps.

Indian Order of Merit, 2nd Class

31st Mule Corps, No. 1357 Driver Sayad Abdulla.

Indian Distinguished Service Medal

11th Mule Corps, No. 904 Naik Miram Baksh.
11th Mule Corps, No. 831 Naik Painda Khan.
11th Mule Corps, No. 1526 Lance-Naik Rafiuddin.
11th Mule Corps, No. 605 Driver Chedu Beg.
11th Mule Corps, No. 1315 Driver Fakir Muhammad.
11th Mule Corps, No. 986 Driver Shubrati.
No. 1406 Driver Abdullah Shah, 2nd Mule Corps.
No. 182 Kot-Dafadar Feteh Khan, 9th Mule Corps.
No. 82 Kot-Dafadar Bahawal Din, 9th Mule Corps.
No. 694 Naik Khan Gul, 9th Mule Corps.
No. 343 Naik Mahomed Khan, 9th Mule Corps.
No. 862 Driver Rup Singh, 27th Mule Corps.
No. 319 Lance-Naik Sundar Singh, 38th Mule Corps.

Brevet Lieut.-Colonel

Major W. F. Smith, Meerut Divisional Train.
Major W. N. Lushington.

Honorary Major

Commissary and Honorary Captain E. J. Goodhall.

INDIAN ORDNANCE DEPARTMENT
Military Cross

Sub-Conductor J. L. N. M'Dougall.

Distinguished Conduct Medal

Sub-Conductor E. V. Johnson.

REMOUNT DEPARTMENT
Companion of St. Michael and St. George
Lieut.-Colonel C. F. Templer, I.A.

INDIAN MISCELLANEOUS LIST
Assistant Commissary with Honorary Rank of Lieutenant
Sub-Conductor W. Forsyth.
Sub-Conductor F. C. Marks.
Sub-Conductor C. G. Jackson.

INDIAN VOLUNTEER CORPS
Distinguished Conduct Medal
Corporal W. Gurdon, Calcutta Volunteer Rifles.
Sergeant F. Birley, Madras Volunteer Rifles.

MILITARY WORKS SERVICES
Distinguished Conduct Medal
Sub-Conductor P. J. Fitzpatrick.

ROYAL INDIAN MARINE
Companion of St. Michael and St. George
Commander (retired) G. E. Holland, C.I.E., D.S.O. (temporary Colonel R.E.).

SPECIAL LIST
Companion of the Indian Empire
Temporary Captain P. J. G. Pipon, I.C.S.
Temporary Captain E. B. Howell (Indian Civil Service), Censor of Indian Mails with the Indian Expeditionary Force in France.

Military Cross
Rev. R. J. B. Irwin, M.A., Indian Ecclesiastical Department.
Temporary Captain P. J. G. Pipon, I.C.S.
Temporary Lieutenant A. H. Parker (Indian Civil Service), Punjab Volunteer Rifles (attached Royal Flying Corps).

INDEX[1]

[1] In Indexing the many Indian names the indexer has followed the method used in the India Office *English* catalogues.

2 c

2 D

Printed in Great Britain by R. & R. CLARK, LIMITED, Edinburgh

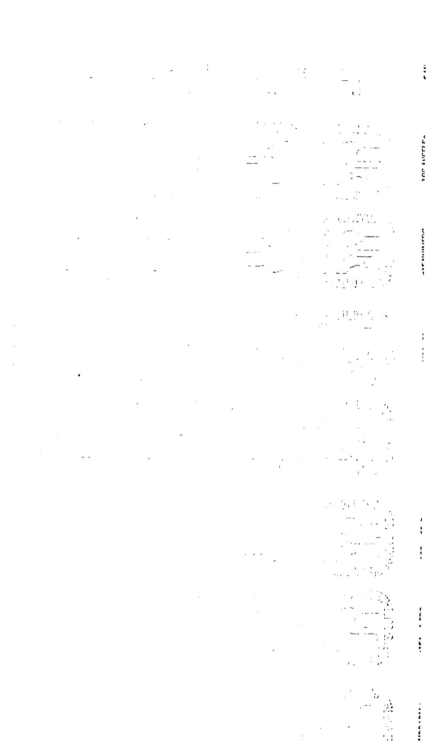

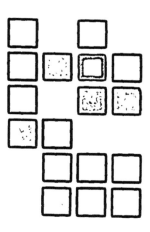